TAKEDOWN

RICK COWAN

———

DOUGLAS CENTURY

G. P. Putnam's Sons   New York

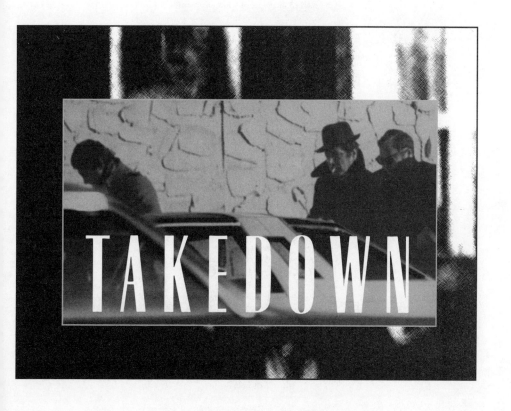

The Fall of the Last
Mafia Empire

The views expressed in this book are those of the
public servant alone, and are not necessarily
the views of his agency, or the city.

G. P. Putnam's Sons
Publishers Since 1838
a member of
Penguin Putnam Inc.
375 Hudson Street
New York, NY 10014

Photographs on title page and page 107 courtesy private collection;
all other chapter opener photographs © Olegna Productions, Inc.

Map on page xi: Arthur S. Tuttle, *Borough of Manhattan*.
New York, Board of Estimate and Apportionment, 1938 (detail).
Legend added with permission. Reprinted by courtesy of
Map Division, The New York Public Library,
Astor, Lenox and Tilden Foundations.

Map on page x: J. H. Muirhead, *The City of New York
Five Borough Map*. New York, 1930 (detail). Legend added
with permission. Reprinted by courtesy of Map Division,
The New York Public Library, Astor, Lenox
and Tilden Foundations.

Library of Congress Cataloging-in-Publication Data

Cowan, Rick.
Takedown : the fall of the last Mafia empire /
Rick Cowan and Douglas Century.
p.   cm.
Includes bibliographical references.
ISBN 0-399-14875-2 (alk. paper)
1. Organized crime investigation—New York (State)—New York.
2. Undercover operations—New York (State)—New York.
3. Mafia—New York (State)—New York.   I. Century, Douglas.
II. Title.
HV8079.O73C69   2002   2002069754
364.1'06'097471—dc21

Printed in the United States of America
1   3   5   7   9   10   8   6   4   2

This book is printed on acid-free paper. ∞

BOOK DESIGN BY MEIGHAN CAVANAUGH

Dedicated to the memory of

JAMES E. COWAN

brother and friend

1958–2002

and in memory of

ABE LEVY

1910–2002

CONTENTS

AUTHORS' NOTE

The seven-year investigation recounted in this book is one of the most thoroughly documented in the history of the New York Police Department. In the course of Operation Wasteland, thousands of hours of covertly recorded conversations and thousands of pages of official police documents were generated. The dialogue involving criminal conduct has been verified against tape recordings and transcripts introduced at trial. Those conversations of a more casual nature, involving family and friends, have been reconstructed from the best recollections of the participants.

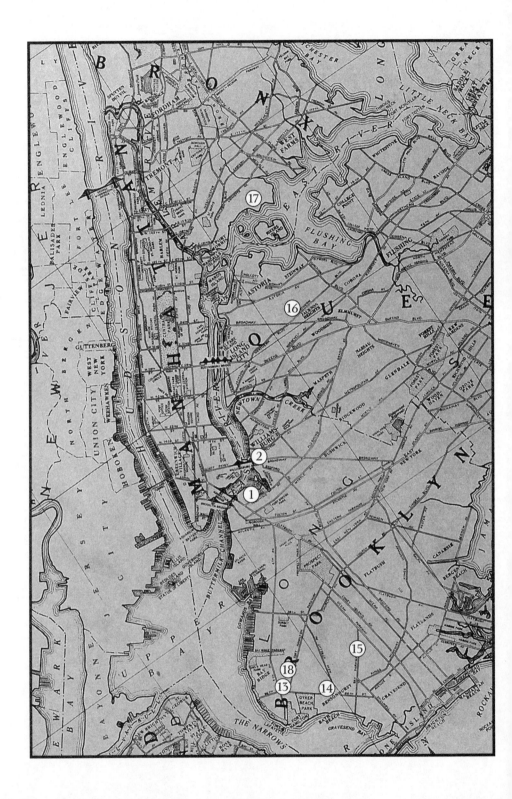

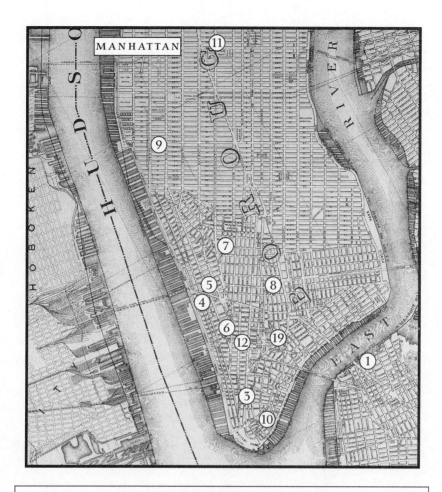

NEW YORK CITY

1. *Chambers Paper Fibres Corp.*
2. *Giando Ristorante*
3. *One Wall Street*
4. *Ponte's Steakhouse*
5. *Greater New York Waste Paper Association (controlled by Genovese Crime Family)*
6. *Association of Trade Waste Removers of Greater New York (controlled by Gambino Crime Family)*
7. *Triangle Social Club (headquarters for Vincent "Chin" Gigante)*
8. *Ravenite Social Club (headquarters for John Gotti)*
9. *Duffy Waste Removers (owned by Joseph "Joey Cigars" Francolino)*
10. *55 Water Street*
11. *HBO headquarters*
12. *Pierino's Restaurant*
13. *Pastels Disco (headquarters of Alphonso "Allie Shades" Malangone)*
14. *Veterans and Friends Social Club (headquarters of James "Jimmy Brown" Failla)*
15. *Kings County Trade Waste Association (controlled by Genovese Crime Family)*
16. *Queens County Trade Waste Association (controlled by Gambino Crime Family)*
17. *Charles Green Company*
18. *Americana Diner*
19. *One Police Plaza*

For the Trojans themselves had drawn the horse into their fortress, and it stood there while they sat in council around it, and were in three minds as to what they should do. Some were for breaking it up then and there; others would have it dragged to the top of the rock on which the fortress stood, and then thrown down the precipice; while yet others were for letting it remain as an offering and propitiation for the gods. And this was how they settled it in the end, for the city was doomed when it took in that horse, within which were all the bravest of the Argives waiting to bring death and destruction on the Trojans.

—*Homer*, THE ODYSSEY, *Book VIII*

TAKEDOWN

PROLOGUE

PLYMOUTH STREET

I'd love to tell you that I came down to the Brooklyn waterfront that morning ready to kick start the biggest organized-crime investigation in the history of the New York Police Department. I'd love to say that I had it all mapped out in my mind, that I knew I'd be going deep undercover inside the Mob cartel. But the truth is, the only thing on my mind that day was finding Plymouth Street. I got lost, had my Hagstrom *Five Borough Pocket Atlas* in my lap, and had been driving in circles all along the Brooklyn side of the East River. Somehow, I ended up around the Brooklyn Navy Yard, then managed to wander into that industrial no-man's-land called DUMBO—Down Under the Manhattan Bridge Overpass. Finally, under the Manhattan Bridge, I spotted the Chambers

Paper Fibres warehouse and noticed that the firebombed garbage truck
had already been towed away by the Fire Department.

I'm driving my unmarked department Buick, and I know any wiseguy in town is going to make me instantly in this thing. Don't do the
lazy cop routine, I tell myself. I park two blocks farther up and walk. On
my way back down Plymouth, I run into Kevin Dunleavy, another detective, who's accompanying me for the interview. Chambers Paper Fibres is a large transfer station—tons of garbage coming through there
every day—and it smells like it. The warehouse is six stories high, a red-
brick factory that stretches a full city block, built around the time of the
Civil War.

I thought I was going to be sitting down for an interview with a guy
named Salvatore Benedetto, president of Chambers. A little over a week
earlier, on May 4, 1992, in the shadows under the foot of the Manhattan Bridge, one of Sal Benedetto's new packer trucks had exploded in
flames, and the arsonists were seen speeding away down Plymouth Street
in a 1981 Oldsmobile. The heat of the fire was so intense that the
green-painted metal and plastic of the truck cab liquefied, melting in a
molten soup. The New York City fire marshals were never able to determine the precise accelerant used in the crime.

In many ways the Organized Crime Investigations Division (OCID)
of the New York Police Department—the unit to which I'd been assigned for three years—is more like an intelligence agency than a conventional police unit. As an OCID detective, you conduct yourself in
a covert manner, even during routine interviews. You don't flash your
shield. You don't announce to the world that you're a cop. Stepping
inside the Chambers building, I wanted to be as inconspicuous as possible. Even though the job demands that you use a holster, I prefer keeping my Glock tucked into my waistband, with my polo shirt untucked
and covering the gun butt.

At first, I just felt Sal Benedetto out, because I didn't know him and
I'd never heard of his company. In my few years working organized
crime, I'd learned to be suspicious about anybody associated with the

garbage-hauling business, an industry that's been mobbed-up for generations, long before I was born.

First appearances can be misleading, of course, but when we came into the front office, I immediately sensed that this guy was no gangster. Sal was in his mid fifties, stood about five foot four. Big smile, big voice, big belly. A jovial, Lou Costello type. I later learned that he had polio as a kid, which explained why he was shuffling around his office with a little limp.

He started telling us his story, how last week this goon was seen monkeying around in the cab of the truck and then a few minutes later it blew up, doing some $21,000 in damage. The two guys had been in the transfer station earlier that day, pretending to be union officials, hassling Sal's employees about their union cards. Sal was smiling, almost laughing, the whole time he was talking. And I was trying to get a read on this guy's body language; he was either exceptionally brave, or he had some kind of strange defense mechanism. He was an old-timer, and he had to know the deal: Screwing around with these garbage gangsters could get you killed in a heartbeat.

But as I learned in the months ahead, Sal was a complicated character. You could easily mistake him for a street guy—the way he talked with a "*deese* and *dose*" Brooklyn accent—but I learned that he was actually college-educated, held a degree in engineering from Lowell University. There was a lot I had to learn about Sal: That the gangsters always called him Fat Sal—sometimes worse. That his own family called him Sally Skates because he had an uncanny ability to talk his way out of trouble, glide his way out of any jam. For such a heavyset guy, I learned, Sal was very light on his feet.

We took our seats in Sal Benedetto's hot, windowless office, glancing around at the paper-industry trade journals stacked two feet high. I watched Sal's face carefully, waiting for just the right moment to ask a loaded question: Whether or not Chambers belonged to one of the four Mob-controlled trade-waste associations, the Mafia's so-called garbage clubs, being run by top-echelon mobsters like James "Jimmy Brown" Failla and Alphonso "Allie Shades" Malangone. We knew that the trade-waste associations formed the foundation of a vast criminal monopoly that had skimmed hundreds of millions of dollars over the years to benefit members of all five of the New York crime families: Genovese, Gambino, Lucchese, Colombo, Bonanno. But the Genovese and Gambino factions, being the country's two largest and most powerful Mafia *borgata,* had the loudest voices, really called all the shots.

Each year, untraceable cash fortunes filled the pockets of the two big bosses: the boastful, hand-tailored suit–wearing Gambino kingpin, John Gotti, and his archenemy—and polar opposite—the tight-lipped, shadow-loving, bathrobe-sporting Genovese boss, Vincent "Chin" Gigante.

"Garbage clubs?" Sal said, laughing. "The boys? Jimmy Brown and them? You're kidding, right? Look, you gotta understand one thing: We're an independent paper-packing company. My grandfather Dominic started in this business down on Cherry Street in 1896."

He got up from his desk and hobbled out to the hallway, showing us the framed black-and-white photograph of one of his grandfather's early paper trucks, a flatbed with wooden spokes, parked beneath the tenements of the Lower East Side in the 1910s. "We're a clean company. We've always been a clean company. We've got several subsidiaries, one up in Canada. We've got another transfer station up in the Bronx. Why the hell would we want to be around them racketeers? My whole life we never dealt with them. My dad warned me about them when I was a kid down on Cherry Street; told me all about their 'property rights,' and the way they enforce that racket. Yeah, sure. With the business end of a baseball bat.

"But look, we had to get into the garbage business lately, because the boys"—this was the second time Sal had referred to "the boys," a taste of vintage Brooklynese that had me picturing snap-brim fedoras on thick-necked guys named Lefty and Louie—"they been gettin' into our business. It's caused us nothing but problems. I figure if I don't talk to the cops, I might as well padlock my doors, 'cause sooner or later they're gonna put me out of business."

The new recycling laws of 1991, Sal explained, had thrown the paper world into turmoil. Turf wars were breaking out all over town. For almost a century the two industries had functioned separately: There were guys who made their livings hauling trash, and there were guys who made their livings recycling paper. Sure, Sal said, there'd always been mobsters in the paper-packing trade. But recycling, with its constantly fluctuating rates and numerous grades of paper, was too complicated an industry for the boys, who preferred to use their often impressive mathematical skills calculating the odds at Aqueduct Racetrack or totaling up the columns on their illegal gambling packages, rather than sitting around some freezing, rat-infested factory warehouse, trying to give their customers a fair rate on high-grade ledger stock.

But with the passing of the nation's most ambitious recycling laws, every business in New York was suddenly mandated to "source-separate" the paper, glass, and plastic from the putrescible—or "wet"—waste, and the Mafia men who controlled all the commercial garbage pickups in the city were now realizing it made sense for them to pick up that valuable paper and cardboard too.

It was highway robbery what these gangsters were up to, Sal told us. The boys were giving the honest, independent paper man a bad name. Look at it this way: If a business is source-separating all the recyclables, they're reducing the garbageman's total trash volume. Logically, the garbageman should start lowering his rates for the customer. But the mobsters weren't lowering a goddamn thing. Instead, led by a powerful multimillionaire named Angelo Ponte—a politically connected carter who owned the largest fleet of garbage trucks in the city and a paper-recycling mill in New Jersey, as well as a popular, celebrity-packed Italian eatery on the lower West Side of Manhattan—the boys started jacking *up* the prices, adding on charges for picking up the recyclable paper, which they were then going to turn around and sell at a sweet little profit.

The Mob carters started to take paper accounts from Chambers—

accounts that the Benedetto family had been servicing without inter-
ruption since the 1930s. In retaliation, Sal said, he picked up the garbage
account at One Wall Street from the Barretti Carting Company, the
city's second-largest hauler.

Barretti? I shot a quick glance at Kevin Dunleavy when I heard Sal
mutter that name. Phil Barretti was a Mob figure that I knew a bit
about. He was not only one of the *richest* but also one of the most feared
garbage gangsters in New York. Although Phil wasn't a wiseguy—
wasn't officially "made"—he was a major earner with powerful connections to both the Gambino and Genovese families. I knew that he
reported directly to Jimmy Brown and Joe Francolino at the Association
of Trade Waste Removers of Greater New York—the Gambino club,
down in TriBeCa. He owned a large transfer station on North Fifth
Street in Greenpoint, about a ten-minute drive up the Brooklyn waterfront from Sal's office in Chambers.

I know when you hear the word *garbageman* you probably get the image of some poor slob in banged-up steel-toe boots and filthy work
pants hanging off the side of a reeking truck at six in the morning.
That's *not* Philip Barretti. With guys like Phil, you have to picture hand-
tailored Italian suits and diamond pinky rings, mansions and yachts in
Florida, fleets of Jaguars and Mercedes sedans. Guys like Barretti were
living like kings—trash kings. It was nothing for Phil to drop thousands
in a poker game. These guys made tens of millions annually carting
away the city's garbage. Barretti's trucks picked up the trash from some
of the biggest businesses in the city: American Express, IBM, Citicorp,
Merrill Lynch, Chase Manhattan. He even had the accounts for the
Federal Reserve Bank and the U.S. Customs House.

Phil's bread and butter was his string of connected waste-management
companies—Barretti Carting, Nekboh Recycling, and Bay Sanitation—
but he also owned legitimate restaurants, bowling alleys, a piece of a
golf course. He divided his time between a Tudor mansion in Essex Fells,
New Jersey, a waterfront home on the South Jersey shore—where he
docked his forty-two-foot yacht—and a third, million-dollar vacation

home down in Boca Raton, sitting right on the back nine of a golf course.

Phil was a distinguished guy in his mid-fifties, about six foot two, always dapper. He had a full head of hair and a neatly trimmed gray mustache. Some people said he looked like movie star Cesar Romero, the Cisco Kid. But to me, Phil always was more of an Edward G. Robinson or a Jimmy Cagney. Most guys in the industry in the tristate area were afraid of Barretti—petrified. And for good reason: He was a slick-dressed organized crime associate who wouldn't hesitate to send a guy out with a gun or a bomb to put you out of business for good.

"Look, I took a stop off Barretti," Sal tells us. "We *coexisted* for a while. I had the paper, he had the garbage. I've always had the paper at One Wall Street—it's the Bank of New York. My family's had the paper there since they built the place, in 1930, since it was the Irving Trust. Couple months ago, Barretti starts picking up the paper at One Chase Manhattan Plaza—knocks me right out of the building. And that was my biggest account. So, tit for tat, I took the garbage account from him at One Wall Street. Since then, my drivers have been followed out in the street and threatened. Now my brand-new packer blows up, burns down to a cinder. . . ."

I jot all this down on my clipboard as fast as I can and then, about fifteen minutes into the interview, Sal's door flies open and in rushes the foreman for the Chambers transfer station. His name is John Glenn, a tall black guy with graying hair who's been working at Chambers for many years. "Sorry to interrupt, Sal"—John looks shaken, visibly scared—"they're back!"

"Who?"

"The guys who burned the truck just drove by again!"

I look at Kevin Dunleavy and neither one of us can believe it.

I jump up and run out of Sal's office. It's just a short distance to the warehouse door, and I'm planning to rush down the street and try to get a license plate. There's a steel fire door to the street, and as I'm coming out with force—*boom*—the first thing I see is these two guys on their way in. One is about five foot seven, thin build, black hair, wearing a black leather jacket. His hand is in his pocket, clearly holding a gun. I freeze in the doorway and start to back up. Everybody else is following me—John, Kevin, Sal—but they're still stuck inside the building.

Now I'm blindsided by the second guy, this big menacing-looking thug with swept-back hair and Italian-looking features. We later learned that he's actually Puerto Rican, a hood named Raymond Ramos. Ramos was six foot two, two hundred fifty pounds, built, like a heavy-weight fighter, a lot bigger than me or Kevin Dunleavy, and he's waving his big fist in my face. We didn't know his rap sheet at the time, of course, but when we checked him out, we learned we had a badguy on our hands, a career criminal, always in and out of prison for assaults and drug-related crime.

The first words out of his mouth are a crazy howl: "Get the *fuck* outta One Wall! What the fuck youse doin' in that stop? Youse got greedy and now there's gonna be a sit-down! Then what the fuck youse gonna do?"

Sal's still three deep behind me, and I'm thinking, *I'm either going to get shot here, or this thug and me are going to go at it in the street.* For a split second my instinct was to charge Ramos, but that would've been a stupid thing to do. Any one of us could have been shot.

These thugs had the drop on us: We never expected them to come back to the shop. It was just a bizarre coincidence. Here we were, taking a statement from Sal Benedetto on the very day that he could get his head blown off.

Right away I knew I had to defuse the situation, and the best way to do that was to start talking fast. Fortunately, they couldn't see my gun or shield, so they had no way of knowing Kevin and I are detectives.

"Take it easy!" I said. "We're all businessmen. Whaddaya talkin' about? Whaddaya doin'?" I'm not really sure what I'm saying, but I do know that I'm trying to get him to use Phil Barretti's name. "Calm down," I said. "Who sent you anyway? Phil? We know Phil had One Wall—"

This got Ramos more pissed off, and I thought he was going to actually throw the first punch. "Never mind who sent me! Who the fuck are you?"

Before I can even open my mouth, I hear Sal behind me saying, "Oh, that's just Cousin Danny—he works here."

Cousin *Danny?*

There was no planning, no scheme behind it.

That's why they call him Sally Skates: He's so quick to see the angles and talk his way out of a jam. Now my adrenaline's pumping and my face is red hot, and if this thug Ramos would've asked me, "What's your name again?" I wouldn't've been able to remember it. He jabs a finger in my face, and the other guy, named Roblis, is still holding that gun in his jacket pocket. Finally, Ramos calms down a bit and hands me a business card that says: R&R RUBBISH REMOVAL. We later checked it out and no such company existed. It was a dummy card, a complete sham. "One Wall is my stop," Ramos says.

"Your stop?" I didn't believe him for a second.

"Youse fucked up and now there's gonna be a sit-down over this. I want a call by two o'clock today."

"Listen, we're businessmen and we don't want any trouble. Let's talk. I give you my word as a man that I'll call you."

"Okay, fine."

I knew that when I called this guy, I was going to have a tape recorder hooked up to the phone.

Ramos and his partner disappeared around the corner, got into a light-green Oldsmobile, with a third guy who we couldn't see too clearly at the wheel. Kevin Dunleavy and I waited about thirty seconds. Kevin's car was parked closer than mine, so we jumped in, hoping we could still tail them and catch a plate number. We caught up to the Olds near the Gowanus overpass, just as it was about to hit the entrance ramp to the Brooklyn-Queens Expressway. Now I jotted down the plate: L4V-824. But then they turned right around, circled the block, and pulled up again in front of Chambers. We made it back just in time to see Ramos jumping out in front of the bay door, running up to John Glenn, screaming like a maniac. Evidently he didn't feel he'd made his point clearly enough.

"Listen, if you don't straighten this thing out, I'll be back and I'll burn the whole fuckin' *place* down!"

Then they drove off for good. I ran inside and called my boss, Sergeant Tony Mazziotti, and Tony immediately got Assistant District Attorney Marybeth Richroath in the Manhattan DA's office on the line.

"We came down to interview Sal Benedetto and these two thugs showed up, jumped right in my face. We thought we were going to get shot. I couldn't even collar 'em. I had to just play along, try and calm 'em down."

Within a few minutes we have the DMV running the plate on the Oldsmobile: Sure enough, it comes back as registered to the Barretti Carting Corporation, Two North Fifth Street in Brooklyn.

"Ricky," Tony Maz says, "they actually *threatened* you?"

"Yeah. Looks like we're making a case."

1 | THE CANDY STORE

What did I do that J. P. Morgan didn't do? It's all a racket. Isn't Wall Street a racket where the strong take advantage of the weak? Every industry needs a strongman. After you put us in jail, another strong man will come up to keep the industry from becoming a jungle.

—JOHN "JOHNNY DIO" DIOGUARDI

To understand what we were up against to make a case against the cartel, you have to flash back a few decades—back to 1956. President Eisenhower signed the Federal Aid–Highway Act, creating the interstate highway system and ushering in the golden age of the automobile in America. The first transatlantic telephone cable was completed, and halfway around the world, over the remote Pacific island chain called Bikini Atoll, a B-52 bomber dropped the first airborne hydrogen bomb.

And in New York City, in the summer of '56, the Mafia made its own bold move into the modern age. Long before the coining of the term *disposable society,* organized-crime figures had seen their future in garbage. The mastermind of the new racket was a minuscule mobster in horn-rimmed spectacles named Vincent "Jimmy" Squillante. Newspapers liked to describe him as "jockey-sized"—he stood five foot one and weighed 122 pounds—but Jimmy Squillante was nobody's featherweight. At forty, he was one of the most influential *caporegimes* in the family headed by Albert Anastasia, the brutal Brooklyn boss whose crazed temper and fondness for homicide had earned him the nicknames the Mad Hatter and the Lord High Executioner.

Even as the mushroom cloud was rising over the idyllic islands of the western Pacific, Squillante and his cohorts, sitting high in their elegant skyscraper office on Park Avenue, had cracked the secret of organized crime in the consumer age. Control the flow of garbage, and just as surely as if you owned the supply of fresh water or electricity, you had an entire sprawling metropolis by the jugular.

Garbage: It would become the Mob's most lucrative empire since Prohibition, and the City of New York could thank itself for laying the foundation. From the early years of the twentieth century, New York's businesses were required to pay private carting companies (many owned by Italian immigrants) to haul their waste, while the residential trash was collected by the Department of Sanitation. On July 1, 1956, the City closed a longstanding loophole that allowed businesses operating in residential blocks to have their garbage hauled for free by the Department of Sanitation. Overnight, more than fifty thousand businesses were up for grabs. With the zeal of rats tearing into leaking sacks of rubbish, enterprising gangsters like Squillante (who owned the New York Carting Company) pounced on the chance to shake down the business world. Members of the five Cosa Nostra families—known to us today as Genovese, Gambino, Lucchese, Bonanno, and Colombo—divided up territories within the five boroughs, suburban New York, New Jersey, and Connecticut, forming highly secretive trade associations and clubs.

The Mafia cartel formed in '56 would, in many ways, mirror the national crime syndicate established by Luciano, Capone, Costello, Johnny Torrio, and Meyer Lansky in the days of bootlegging: There would be peace and criminal prosperity, no price-cutting, no open warfare, and all territorial disputes resolved by the bosses.

As mobsters like to say, it was the start of a *beautiful* thing. At night the truck fleets could command the city, stinking of waste and clogging side streets with impunity. Generations of New Yorkers would watch the army-green trucks with operatic-sounding names painted on their sides in banana yellow and candy-apple red—V. Ponte & Sons, Vigliotti & Sons, Mongelli Catering—and think, *Everyone knows who picks up the trash in this town.*

So thorough was the Mob's control of the carting industry that by 1995, most organized-crime experts ranked garbage as the Mafia's number one "legitimate" money-earner: a $1.5-billion-a-year business. The so-called Mob tax—the amount that gangsters were overcharging customers—was estimated at forty percent, a staggering $600 million annually. The ripple effect on the business climate in New York was inestimable.[1]

John Gotti, the Gambino crime family boss who'd patterned his staccato speech and thuggish swagger on his childhood hero Albert Anastasia and who became the nation's most media-mythologized gangster since Capone, was more flippant in his private conversations. "A candy store," was how Gotti liked to refer to the Gambino stake in the Mafia's dirty empire. In a secretly recorded conversation, referring to James "Jimmy Brown" Failla, the *caporegime* who'd been running the Gambino interests in garbage since the unsolved disappearance of Jimmy Squillante, in 1960, Gotti marveled to Frank Locascio, his underboss: "Jimmy Brown took garbage and turned it into a candy store."

To organized-crime investigators and to the general public, it was an open secret that the Mob had an iron-fisted cartel in place. "New York City's commercial garbage disposal industry occupies a special place in

---

[1] Rudolph Giuliani, an up-and-coming federal prosecutor with his gaze set on a future in politics, explained in 1990: "What it means is that the cost is passed along to the customer. It's a large part of the reason that the cost of living in New York is so high and so disproportional to many other places in this country. It also contributes to the lack of having the kind of resources available to deal with our social problems—rebuilding and modernizing the infrastructure of New York."

the imagination of the American people," a report by the New York State Assembly's Environmental Conservation Committee said. "Its reputation for being racketeer-infested, given to violence and murder, is the stuff of which legends are made." But the inner workings of this massive criminal monopoly were understood only in the abstract: No detective or federal agent could get close enough to describe the details and live to tell the tale. In 1997 the United States Court of Appeals for the Second Circuit compared the Mob cartel to "a 'black hole' in New York's economic life."

> Like those dense stars found in the firmament, the cartel cannot be seen and its existence can only be shown by its effect on the conduct of those falling within its ambit. Because of its strong gravitational field, no light escapes very far from a "black hole" before it is dragged back. . . . [F]rom the cartel's domination of the carting industry, no carter escapes.[2]

Enforcing an illegal "property rights" system—in which Mob-controlled carters were granted permanent "ownership" of their customers and locations—the Mafia had turned one of the most basic precepts of the American republic on its ear: There was no free enterprise in their universe. No carter could compete for a customer "owned" by another without bringing down the wrath of the cartel. With no competition to get in the way, the Mob's profit-margin remained exponential.

They were equal-opportunity extortionists: Everyone doing business in New York had to pay—a mom-and-pop bodega in the Bronx, a Brooklyn subway-sandwich shop, a Queens florist, or the Fortune 500 companies of Manhattan's gleaming glass-and-steel canyons. Even the journalists working on hard-hitting pieces about the Mafia for *The New York Times*, *The New Yorker*, and *The Wall Street Journal* could glance out

---

[2] See *Sanitation and Recycling Industry, Inc. v. City of New York*. United States Court of Appeals for the Second District. Docket No. 96-7788. Decided February 28, 1997.

their office windows and watch mobbed-up carters wheeling away the mountains of curbside trash.

It was, as even John D. Rockefeller might have acknowledged, the most "perfect" monopoly in American history. The Cosa Nostra bosses were like corrupt chess masters, playing both sides of the board: They owned the carting companies, they controlled the unions, they placed wiseguys in the leadership of the trade associations that arbitrated any disputes. British journalist Tim Shawcross, in his book *The War Against the Mafia,* wrote of the Mob's stranglehold:

> *If Mafia strategists had studied* Das Kapital *by Karl Marx and synthesized the essence of economic power into an organized system which allowed them to reap profits by exploiting the strengths and weaknesses of both sides of the labor and capital equation, it is unlikely that they would have come up with a better industry upon which they could practice their philosophy.*

Of course, law enforcement did not turn a blind eye to the Cosa Nostra candy store. Since the 1950s there had been nearly forty investigations into the carting industry, involving every level of government—local, state, and federal—without any lasting success. In November 1957 the Select Committee on Improper Activities in the Labor or Management Field, chaired by Arkansas senator John L. McClellan, spent considerable time probing the monopolistic practices of New York's private sanitation industry.

The committee's boyish chief counsel, Robert F. Kennedy, flanked by his older brother John, had hoped to speak to Albert Anastasia and Jimmy Squillante about their criminal rubbish ring. But in October 1957, a scant three weeks before he was due to appear before the committee, Anastasia, the Lord High Executioner, was himself executed as he awaited a shave in the Park-Sheraton Hotel. And Squillante, who'd managed to slither away from the adjacent barber chair, took his seat alone in front of the Senate Committee, staring down the Kennedy brothers, wagging a contemptuous finger—clearly itching to speak his mind, but, at the advice of counsel, pleading the Fifth Amendment more than a hundred times.

Squillante would never talk publicly about his control of the garbage rackets. Nor would he discuss one of the underworld's great rumors: that he'd personally gunned down Frank "Don Cheech" Scalise, Anastasia's underboss, in front of a Bronx fruit stand (a setting some believe later inspired novelist Mario Puzo); that he'd killed Scalise's vengeance-vowing brother Joe, chopped up the corpse, and hauled away the pieces in one of his own garbage trucks. Over the years Squillante's method for untraceable body disposal would become a Mafia favorite, so commonplace that you could almost refer to those hissing ten-wheel packer trucks as Mob hearses. In the '70s and '80s, the Gambino *capo* Roy DeMeo ran a Brooklyn-based crew that killed an estimated 200 people, dismembering the corpses and leaving them, neatly bagged curbside, for friendly carters to haul away to the nearest landfill. Veteran hit men knew that any corpse dumped in a landfill would be stripped clean by rats and seagulls—down to a skeleton—within days.

But more than committing homicide with impunity, the Mob's greatest power to terrorize lay in the very nature of garbage itself. With a snap of the fingers, a silk-shirted mafioso could buckle the knees of any mayor and bring the entire city to a stop. In the able hands of Jimmy Squillante, "Jimmy Brown" Failla, and their trade-unionist co-conspirators, garbage had become the ultimate Mob racket.

Controlling the movement of garbage in a metropolis as densely populated as New York is to have a short-delay timer on a form of biological weapon. Within a few short days of any strike action, the world's financial capital is transformed into a Third World slum: Over one hundred thousand tons of trash buries the city—rotting mountains overflowing in front of the New York Stock Exchange, the United Nations, Madison Square Garden, and Bloomingdale's. And the town comes *alive* with vermin: millions of cockroaches and flies; hordes of rats carrying fleas and the risk of cholera, yellow fever, and even more deadly airborne diseases like the bubonic plague. Now the mayor is faced with a devil's bargain: Settle the strike—on the Mob's terms—or declare a citywide health emergency.

By the early '90s, the garbage-hauling cartel had been in place nearly four decades, four times as long as the Mob's last license to print money—since the reign of Luciano and Capone and Dutch Schultz, since the heyday of rum-running and speakeasies. In the eyes of many veteran investigators, this was one criminal empire that would never be broken up. If anything, the cartel kingpins now seemed to be thumbing their noses: sending *caporegimes* of the two largest families—Gambino and Genovese—to personally engage in a collective bargaining session with the mayor. Perhaps worse, the Mob had begun to export its putrid brand of gangsterism beyond the confines of the five boroughs, targeting America's heartland—rural communities in the Midwest and Appalachia—for illegal dumping of hazardous materials, including asbestos, medical waste, even radioactive materials.

But for all their power, the cartel bosses were about to fall prey to a scheme straight out of the Trojan War—a plan to wheel a white-horse company inside the criminal club. To take down this massive enterprise, I was going to have to pull off the scam of a lifetime: Convince these cagey old-time Italian gangsters that a thirty-four-year-old Irish detective was actually one of the boys.

2 | SINISTER SHADOWS

Under New York state law, a telephone call can be recorded without a court order if one of the two parties consents to the taping. I was the consenting party to the conversation, and Sal Benedetto agreed to let us use his office phones. Just a few hours after my freakish "Cousin Danny" encounter with those goons in front of the Chambers warehouse, Sergeant Tony Mazziotti arrived on Plymouth Street to supervise our first undercover phone call of the case.

Tony was a sharp boss, born and raised in Queens, athletically built, with curly black hair and a thick black mustache. We'd only known each other for a few months; we'd met in January of '92 at a surveillance plant out in Staten Island when Tony became the boss of Headquarters One, back when we were still in the conventional stage of the case, do-

ing surveillance on Alphonso Malangone, the big-time Genovese skipper. Tony'd been on the force since 1973, working his way up from a
patrolman's beat in the Three O—the Thirtieth Precinct—in Harlem to
working undercover Narcotics in Brooklyn to becoming a major case
supervisor in the Organized Crime Control Bureau at One Police Plaza.

But even Tony, with all his years with undercover investigations,
couldn't have imagined the direction we were taking today; none of us
had any idea that the phone call we were about to place would be the
beginning of my five-year undercover trip to gangland. Sal *certainly* had
no clue what he was getting himself into. While Tony and I tried to get
our professional recording device hooked up to the office phone, Sal
stood there jingling the change in his pockets—his signature move—
smirking at us, his belly shaking as he laughed. For some reason none
of our Tech Services equipment—top-of-the-line NYPD surveillance
gear—would work on Sal's business phone.

"What is this *junk*?" Sal said finally. Then he opened his closet and
lent us his personal Panasonic tape recorder and a gadget for recording
calls he got from Radio Shack for about ten bucks. And Sal's stuff
worked—recorded a cleaner call than all of our heavy-duty NYPD
equipment.

But we didn't have much time to be monkeying around with equipment. I was supposed to place the call to Ray Ramos by two P.M. and it
was already after three-thirty. It was a pretty straightforward call, but I
was getting nervous. All my previous undercover training was in Narcotics, making heroin buys on the streets of the Lower East Side and
Washington Heights, where I'd play the role of some bad guy, an addict,
a street tough, a biker. I never had to demonstrate any particular business knowledge, besides being a believable junkie looking to score. But
now, after only minutes talking with Sal, I had to try to master the weird
jargon of the garbage industry—be able to talk about "pulls" and "yards"
and "DCA maximums"—and sound plausible doing it, or else they could
smell me a hundred miles away.

I sat at Sal's desk, shuffling Sal's paperwork and invoices, getting myself psyched up, staring at the Brooklyn telephone number printed at a crooked angle on the bogus R&R Rubbish business card. I watched Tony Maz, a pack-a-day Marlboro man, polishing off another smoke.

In the NYPD, every time you record a phone call or wear a concealed wire, you have to carefully prepare the tape with the date, time, and other identifying information so that it can be used as evidence. We call that "heading" the tape.

"I'm Detective Richard Cowan, shield number number 1143 of OCID, the New York City police department," I said. "Today is May 11, 1992. I'm about to make a call to Raymond Ramos at R&R Rubbish Removal at 555-8582. The time is 0340 hours." I drew a deep breath, picked up the phone, and dialed—then immediately hung up again and hit the Stop button on the Panasonic.

"What the hell's my name again?"

"Danny." Sal laughed. "You're Danny Benedetto."

Dan. Danny. Daniel. Danny Benedetto. Dan Benedetto. I rolled my new Italian name around on my tongue a half-dozen times before I felt comfortable saying it out loud.

I dialed again and the phone rang three times before I heard the gruff voice on the other end.

"Hello. Can I speak to Raymond?"

"Yeah, this is Raymond."

"Hey, this is Danny at Chambers Paper. I spoke to you—I saw you today with Sal—"

"Right. Then youse guys started getting stupid and started following me."

"No, we were leaving, we saw you backing up down the street—"

"I'm not no stupid."

"Listen, I'm not stupid either. Listen, Sal and I were talking, we'd like to sit down and get together."

"That's great. When do you wanna meet?"

"Sal's going on vacation, he won't be back until the Tuesday after Memorial Day."

I told Ray that we'd sit down like gentlemen, but I needed some assurances that nothing violent was going to happen. I needed him to meet me halfway.

"I'll meet you halfway," he said. "The only thing I want is for us to sit down and discuss this like men."

"Sal's gonna be away for a week, but in that time, you gotta assure me that nothing else happens."

"I give you my word as a man, hope to die right now. Let my mother and father rest in peace, I give you my word, as long as we got this sit-down by next week, everything'll be fine."

"I don't want any of the drivers to get followed around, or trucks on fire, or someone get beat up or nothing."

"Nothing will happen up to that day of us sitting down, until we got something worked out."

Ray insisted that he wasn't "no stupid," but I guess he thought I was. At first he wanted me to meet him outside, on the waterfront, at the end of Old Fulton Street, down by the piers. I said no and Tony Maz agreed—it was too desolate. I could easily get shot down there. We decided the meeting had to be inside Chambers, right in Sal's office, where at least we could control everything.

By stalling for a week while Sal was supposedly out of town, we had time to strategize, to set up properly. We applied to the court to get eavesdropping devices, both audio and video, installed in Sal's office. As soon as the court order was granted, we had Tech Services come in and put a tiny camera and listening device in the drop ceiling and into the wall. There were a bunch of nail holes in the wall, so you could never detect the bugs. It took us several days to wire Sal's office, and we were up in the ceiling, covered in soot from head to toe. It was disgusting up there, filthy. Over the next few months I was up there constantly—those little hearing-aid batteries in the surveillance cameras go dead pretty fast—and I always came out looking like a goddamn chimney sweep. Never failed to give Sal a great laugh.

We knew that what we were trying was pretty crazy, but we also knew we better grab this chance: We were never going to get another shot like this again. All our previous years of work looking into the carting industry, the long investigative hours we'd spent conducting surveillances, preparing affidavits and warrants for phone taps—I'd personally broken in, under the court order, to install bugs right under the nose of Allie Shades Malangone in Pastels Disco, his Bay Ridge nightclub—that all paled in comparison to the evidentiary opportunity we'd stumbled onto with this freak encounter.

Of course, we never imagined the scope that the investigation was going to take—never imagined it would stretch on for years, swell into the largest organized-crime investigation in the history of the NYPD and the Manhattan DA's office. We thought that at best I would go undercover short-term and collar Philip Barretti for extortion and possibly conspiracy to commit arson.

It would have been insane to think we were going to try to tackle the entire Mafia cartel, go after the leadership structure, powerful wiseguys like Allie Shades and Jimmy Brown and Joe Francolino. This didn't start as a well-plotted undercover operation with years of advance planning, like the Feds pulled off back in the '70s with agent Joe Pistone posing as jewel thief Donnie Brasco. Our case was more of a fluke, a fumbled kickoff. But I was ready to pick up the ball and run with it.

We agreed: By the middle of May, I'm no longer just Rick Cowan, Detective Third-Grade. Now I'm going to start juggling a double life— as Sal's cousin, Danny Benedetto, an executive in a hundred-year-old family-run paper-recycling business that's feeling the fire of Mob intimidation.

By beginning my undercover role, I knew I'd be putting my life on the line—but as a cop, I'm paid to do that. Without a doubt, the person in greatest danger here was Sal Benedetto. He told us that he was ready to go forward, even though he knew full well what had happened just two years ago out on Long Island. In August 1989 two carters named Robert Kubecka and his brother-in-law Donald Barstow were murdered execution-style right in Kubecka's office on the orders of a Lucchese *capo* named Sal Avellino. Kubecka and Barstow had done the same thing Sal Benedetto had done: They'd violated a Mob carter's "property rights." And worse, they'd been cooperating with the authorities, scheduled to testify in a civil suit about organized crime's control of the garbage rackets on Long Island.

The Mob never needs too much of an excuse to murder a guy. Especially if they think he might be cooperating with the law.

Almost immediately, we caught another break. A week later, on May 15, 1992, we learned that a plot against Sal was already in the works. A veteran investigator in the Manhattan district attorney's office, a former NYPD detective named Frank DeMarco, had received a routine inquiry from an old friend on Long Island, Detective Frank Morro of the Suffolk County Police Department.

Both DeMarco and Morro were very experienced detectives: If you got a lead off them, you could take it to the bank. Morro told DeMarco that in the course of an unrelated organized-crime investigation, he'd intercepted and recorded a chilling cell-phone conversation that referred to the Brooklyn firebombing of some company called Chambers.

"Did you guys hear of anything like that?" Frank Morro asked. "Got anything on this place Chambers?"

Frank DeMarco began making inquiries around the Manhattan DA's office and one of the young assistant district attorneys, Marybeth Richroath, spoke up. "Yes," she said. "They're a legitimate company. What did you guys hear?"

"We caught a threat on a wire. You want to hear it?"

The next afternoon, Tony, Marybeth, and I drove out together to the Suffolk County district attorney's office. There, in a confidential meeting held in the Suffolk County DA's Rackets Unit, we were briefed about a long-term investigation targeting Tommy Masotto, a Gambino crime family associate based in Freeport, Long Island. Detective Morro explained that just two days earlier, on May 13, shortly before eleven

A.M., he'd intercepted Tommy Masotto on his cell phone talking with Philip Barretti about the situation with a certain "Sal at Chambers."

We all immediately recognized the seriousness of this intelligence. We all knew that Philip Barretti was a wolf in sheep's clothing—a gangster posing as a respectable businessman. There was very little pose to Tommy Masotto: He was a mobster. The FBI had been investigating Masotto since the summer of 1990, looking at him as the leader of a violent crew, engaged in hijackings, armed robberies, and burglaries on Long Island. For over a year Masotto's gunmen had been stealing truckloads of cigarettes, fabric supplies, telephones, and electronics equipment.

Tommy Masotto wasn't a made guy, but his father—also named Thomas Masotto—had been a soldier in the Gambino crime family. Within underworld circles, the Masottos' claim to fame was that they were related to Mob royalty, cousins to two bosses, Carlo Gambino and Paul Castellano. In 1968 the elder Masotto had been observed by Pennsylvania law enforcement driving the hawk-nosed, Machiavelli-quoting Don Carlo to a secret meeting with the Philadelphia crime kingpin Angelo Bruno.

Out on Long Island in the late '80s and early '90s, the younger Tommy Masotto drew the attention of the FBI as a cowboy and hothead—so hotheaded, in fact, that he had recently decided to turn his firebombing tactics on the FBI itself.

The FBI had established a surveillance post in a building located on Woodcleft Avenue in Freeport, the same block as Michael's Ristorante, an Italian eatery owned and operated by Tommy Masotto. In early 1991, when Masotto discovered that the FBI had a plant right on his block, he lost his temper and gave orders to two of his crew members, Frank Scerbo and Joseph Lucas, to firebomb the building. On February 22, 1991, Scerbo and Lucas did just that. The FBI considered it a minor miracle that none of its agents were killed in the blaze.

Tommy Masotto is crazy enough to commit an act of arson against the Feds, and now we're listening to him conspire with Phil Barretti to go after Sal. The irony is, Sal and Tommy Masotto grew up together. Their fathers knew each other and Tommy and Sal had gone to high school together at the LaSalle Military Academy out in Oakdale, Long Island.

It was a respectable Christian Brothers military school, Sal told me, founded in 1883, with a number of prominent alumni, like former White House chief of staff John Sununu. But there was also a pretty good smattering of wiseguys mixed in too. Later on in the case, Sal showed me his old LaSalle yearbook. *The Long Gray Line,* it said. All these young, fresh-faced kids in gray West Point–style uniforms. Sal keeps pointing out his school chums who grew up to achieve great things in politics, the media, and the business world. I keep pointing out his school chums who grew up to achieve not-so-great things in the underworld. Some pages in the yearbook are like a gangland Who's Who. I saw Tommy and Joe Gambino—sons of Carlo himself. I saw Sal Avellino, the Lucchese *capo* running the garbage rackets in Long Island in partnership with the Gambino family. Turns out Sal Benedetto's cousin was even Sal Avellino's roommate. There's Tommy Milo, who owned Suburban Carting, whose father had been a big Mob enforcer in the Bronx back in the '50s. And then, just a year ahead of Sal in the yearbook, I spot young Tommy Masotto.

"You gotta understand, we were all kids," Sal tells me. "These guys didn't act like no gangsters—didn't seem like such badguys back then."

So even though they're childhood friends, this doesn't stop Tommy Masotto from plotting to clip Sal. I'm sitting there in the Suffolk DA's office with Tony Maz and Marybeth Richroath listening to the tape from the intercept. Masotto's on his cell phone plotting with Barretti, in blunt, ugly language, about setting up Sal.

"But you gotta change those two kids," Masotto says. "Then you can always deny things . . . use another vehicle . . . if you got the same faces, then they can prove it."

"Right," Barretti agrees.

"You gotta get a nigger," Masotto says. "You gotta get a fuckin' drug addict. A guy with a bottle o' whiskey, y'understand? Where it looks like it was a holdup."

"Yeah."

"You don't want it to look like the same MO."

They were going to either shoot or stab Sal—no doubt about it. They weren't going to stop at sending the Benedettos that message of a blown-up truck. Masotto counseled Phil to be careful about threatening Sal's cousins, the other, straight-laced Benedettos, because those "assholes" would go running straight to the cops.

At one point Phil and Tommy had a pretty good laugh at Sal's expense. "And he works for fuckin' nothing," Masotto says. "He works like a fuckin' jerk. He's still charging by the ton—eleven dollars a ton."

What he means, of course, is that Sal's a sap for charging his customers a fair market price for their paper, not gouging them like all the crooks in the cartel.

"He's a jerk, then," Barretti says.

"He's too fuckin' stupid," Masotto says. "And this guy, he's got almost as much money as *you*."

"He's got *more* than me."

And just like that, they switch gears:

"So, did ya go out for macaroni?" Masotto says.

"Yeah."

"I was up at six o'clock. I just left our friend, you know, with the cigar? I had some bagels and lox with him at 9:30. . . ."

Tommy Masotto was making a coded reference to Jimmy Brown Failla—"our friend, you know, with the cigar"—the Gambino *caporegime* who was the industry's longtime kingpin.

And as the tape played, Tony, Marybeth, and I are sitting there stunned. It's one of the scariest conversations we've ever heard—real hoods, real cold-blooded badguys, caught on tape casually plotting a murder between their chitchat about macaroni and bagels.

Fortunately for Sal, our timing couldn't have been better, because Tommy Masotto couldn't hang around to supervise the rough stuff personally. He was going down to North Carolina for a few weeks, heading off to Duke University to check himself into an obesity clinic. Wiseguys are always heading off to Durham, the weight-loss capital of

America, to try to drop the thirty or forty pounds that their doctors tell them are going to kill them any day.

Little did Tommy realize that when he got back to New York, newly slimmed down, he and his whole little regime were going to get locked up. Suffolk County was very close to collaring Masotto for the string of hijackings and for firebombing their surveillance post out there in Freeport. You set fire to the FBI plant and it tends to piss them off. It wasn't just the Feds in the building either: There had been innocent civilians in there, and if they hadn't gotten out in time, Tommy's little attention-getting stunt could easily have turned into a flaming multiple homicide.

Only a few weeks after our meeting in the Suffolk County DA's Rackets Unit, the FBI locked up four members of Masotto's hijacking crew and flipped them, got them to agree to testify against Tommy.

If Tommy Masotto had stayed on the street, our case would never have gone anywhere. Tommy had known Sal and all the other Benedettos for too many years. No way in hell he was going to buy me as the new cousin who just showed up working one day at Chambers. He would sniff me out as a cop the first time he saw me.

One day in May, Barretti even had Tommy Masotto call down to Chambers, asking Sal a bunch of pointed questions about the truck fire. Tommy asked Sal if he's been speaking to any cops, because some suspicious people—no doubt Kevin Dunleavy and I—were seen poking around the Chambers building. Sal tells Tommy yeah, he filed a police report, but only for insurance purposes, so he can collect on the $21,000 in damages done to his new packer truck. He assures Tommy that he didn't tell the cops anything and that none of his employees saw the guys who started the fire. Sal's been around the block and he knows what he's supposed to say to keep breathing: Nobody saw nothin'. We all caught a case of amnesia.

The FBI and Suffolk County DA's investigation was a godsend to us, because six months later, by the end of '92, Tommy Masotto's on trial in a major RICO case, charged with leading the hijacking crew and firebombing the FBI surveillance post. The jury ended up convicting him on fourteen out of fifteen RICO counts, and Tommy got shipped off on a twenty-one-year stretch in the federal penitentiary in Atlanta.

It was just lucky for us that Sal's old boarding-school buddy was crazy enough to commit an act of arson against the FBI. Now it meant we only had to worry about Phil Barretti and his violent crew. Or at least that's what we assumed.

The murder plot intercepted by the Suffolk County district attorney's investigators hinged on the concept of "property rights," a violently enforced antitrust crime that was the glue holding the Mob's monopoly together.

Property rights had been in place in the metropolitan New York area since the mid-1950s. By 1957, when the Senate convened its Select Committee on Improper Activities in the Labor or Management Field, the chief council for the committee, thirty-one-year-old Robert F. Kennedy, sat grilling a parade of flashily attired gangsters about New York City's then $50-million-a-year garbage rackets.

Most prominent of the committee's remaining witnesses was the tiny bespectacled Bronx mobster Vincent "Jimmy" Squillante—Albert Anastasia's personal empire-builder—who proceeded to take the Fifth Amendment one hundred and eleven times, biting his tongue throughout the proceedings, barely able to restrain himself from lecturing the committee members. More voluble than Squillante at the hearings were two Long Island carters, John and Tony Montesano, partners in the East Meadow Sanitation Service, who'd previously run afoul of Squillante. In 1954 the Montesano brothers had been summoned to Jimmy's elegant office in the Greater New York Cartman's Association offices on Park Avenue. *The New York Daily News* reported on their Senate testimony—GARBAGE BOSS LINKED TO MAFIA, DOPE RACKET—on November 14, 1957:

> *The Montesano brothers testified that Squillante told them about "property rights." Under this code, if a customer moves from a "stop," the garbage collector who had him claims that "stop" as his "cousin" and no one can*

take it from him. If someone "jumped" a "stop"—took over a "property right"—he could be fined $100 for every $10 the "stop" brought in.

Having tried to buck the property rights system—and been labeled "outlaws"—the Montesano brothers received a grim warning: Play by Mob rules or die by them. Arkansas senator John L. McClellan, chairman of the select committee, vividly recalled the Montesanos' account in his 1962 book, *Crime Without Punishment:*

> *There were sinister shadows behind Squillante. John Montesano, during an altercation with Squillante, received a phone call from a relative who was a very prominent figure in the Brooklyn underworld. Mr. Montesano resented the interference from this racketeering relative, but he listened to the telephonic advice. "Don't you realize that they could put you out of business and they can hurt your family?" Mr. Montesano replied heatedly: "If they can hurt me, let them hurt me." The relative cautioned him again, obviously with full knowledge of the men he was talking about: "Don't forget, you have kids . . . Sometimes they won't hurt you but they will hurt the kids."*

Decades later, the mob would exact its revenge on John Montesano. On April 13, 1981, the fifty-year-old executive was shot and killed on the lawn of his Sayville, Long Island, home. In May 1978, in an interview with *Newsday*, Montesano had eerily predicted his own murder: "You know there's a contract on me. Because I testified, I was the heavy. I did the right thing. . . . Now I hear they're going to whack me out . . . leave my brains on the street."

As early as 1957, when the cartel was still in its infancy, Bobby Kennedy and the McClellan Committee heard testimony of fourteen homicides connected to Jimmy Squillante and his trash-hauling associates. And, as Senator McClellan noted, "that figure of fourteen slayings includes none of those with which Albert Anastasia and his henchmen in Murder, Inc., might have been charged."

Four decades had passed since the Montesano brothers' brave testimony, but nothing had changed in New York City: In the spring of 1992, Sal Benedetto was similarly branded an outlaw—a man haunted by "sinister shadows." An outlaw carter could easily lose his life by violating the property rights to a small-scale stop in some desolate stretch of the Bronx, Brooklyn, Staten Island, or Queens. But Sal's beef with Barretti involved a much more lucrative account—a high-profile stop in "New York," as the mobsters always referred to Manhattan's corporate skyline. New York was the cartel's easy cash: Millions were at stake in those glass canyons, and the gangsters acknowledged as much in the slang they bandied about. "Creampuff accounts," they called their skyscraper stops, "14-karat-gold buildings."

By now Sal had fully briefed me about the various ploys that the boys were using to rip off their corporate clients, their brazen scams for overcharging. They rigged up bogus meters to give an innacurate volume. They monkeyed around with the garbage compaction so that, even if the building manager looked carefully at his astronomical monthly bills, everything appeared legitimate. They figured out exactly how much they should be charging per month, Sal said, and then they doubled it. Tripled it. Quadrupled it. Just depended how much balls a guy had, how much he was willing to try to steal. If a guy had big enough balls, he might try to get ten times the amount he should be charging legally. What difference did it make? There was no free enterprise in this racket. Ask any New York businessman who ever complained about his carting rates. The carter on the other end of the phone begins laughing in his ear: *Fuck you. Where you gonna go?*

Sal Benedetto had broken the sacred property-rights code by underbidding Philip Barretti and winning the account to One Wall Street on January 1, 1992. Sal had sent his salesmen to survey The Bank of New York, calculated the fair rate for the garbage collection based on the guidelines set by the Department of Consumer Affairs. The maximum rate allowable for One Wall Street was $3,400 a month. Now, this made Phil Barretti look pretty bad, since he'd been charging The Bank of New York nearly three times that much: $9,400 a month—more than $112,000 a year.

Built in 1930, One Wall is the cousin of the more famous uptown art deco skyscrapers: the Empire State and the Chrysler buildings. As the bronze plaque affixed to mirrored limestone attests, One Wall Street sits on the precise site on which Peter Stuyvesant, in 1653, built a six-foot-high wooden wall stretching between the East and Hudson rivers to protect the citizens of New Amsterdam from Indian attacks—the very wall which gives the narrow street at the world's economic epicenter its name. The building itself, formerly the Irving Trust Building, today houses the headquarters of The Bank of New York, Alexander Hamilton's brainchild, one of the oldest banking institutions in the world.

In late May, just as I was beginning my role as Danny Benedetto, I took a drive down to New York's Financial District to inspect the actual property in dispute. Sal told me his drivers had been harrassed at One Wall Street; he said that the tires of his packer trucks had been shot out one day, so I had to be wary poking around One Wall. I approached Wall Street on foot. I didn't dare pull up in a police department vehicle.

The building was down in the oldest section of New York City. I've always been something of a history buff, especially interested in the battles of the Revolutionary period and the Civil War. I have family members who fought for our country in every war since the War of 1812. My dad was in the Naval Reserve for eight years; he was given the middle name Lawrence—it's my middle name also—in honor of our family's most famous forebear, Captain James Lawrence, a hero of the War of 1812. Wounded during a sea battle off Boston while commanding the USS *Chesapeake,* Captain Lawrence uttered the words "Don't give up the ship!" before dying. He is buried in the graveyard of Trinity Church, with his last words—one of the Navy's most famous rallying cries—engraved on his black tombstone.

So on that May afternoon I stood right across the street from Captain Lawrence's resting place, the eastern fence of the Trinity churchyard, looking up at the fifty stories of gray limestone rising at One Wall. Playing the part of a curious tourist, I strolled through the bank's revolving doors and saw some nine thousand square feet of glittering gold, red, and orange tiles called the Red Room, considered one of the little-known architectural wonders of lower Manhattan. It was a pretty stark contrast to the back of the building, behind several large bay doors, where I found One Wall's trash, some sixty yards of compacted garbage. This was where Phil Barretti's thugs came to surround and threaten Sal's drivers—here in this narrow alleyway, just a stone's throw from the back of the New York Stock Exchange. Here, beside the bales of cardboard and the yards of black plastic–encased trash, dozens of NYSE floor traders, in their blazers of royal blue and sky blue and emerald green, hustled down the sidewalk, grabbing quick cigarette puffs before re-turning to the crush of the exchange floor.

These were the property rights—the right to pick up rubbish from an art deco skyscraper towering over the buzzing stock market—that nearly got Sally killed.

A few days later, I'm sitting in Sal's office at Chambers in my role as Cousin Danny when we get our second visit from Raymond Ramos. Of course, at this point, he's never told us his full name. He's simply been calling himself Ray from R&R Rubbish Removal. But we had his phone traced by now, and I knew he was Raymond Ramos.

By now we've got the video and audio surveillance going, and we're capturing everything Ramos says and does in living color. He's making some beautiful threats. "I'm only gonna give you a little more time," he says. "Something's gonna happen if I don't get One Wall back."

Over the course of several days, we had several meetings there. Each time, Ramos came in looking more enraged. "Youse guys ain't well liked," he tells me. "Youse are takin' your chances." He says it shouldn't take this long to work something out, and it's a miracle that Sal "is still fuckin' walking around."

But now I've done my homework and I'm ready to play a little hard-ball with this guy. Sal's prepped me a bit on the industry lingo and I know I can trip Ramos up. I'm honing my undercover personality too.

I'm supposed to be Sal's streetwise cousin who's stepping into the family business, now that it's getting heavy. I'm supposed to be a tough guy—not exactly half-a-hood, but a guy who won't back down from a fight. All the other Benedettos are real white-collar people, college educated: They show up to work each day in tassel-loafers and oxford shirts. Sal and his younger brother Joe are the only ones in the family who even had the remotest whiff of the streets on them.

At one point, I actually insulted Ray on the phone. "Look, Ray," I said, "I checked into a few things. You told us that the yardage over there was two. We know that it's really ten to twelve yards. A big difference there. I don't know why you're bullshittin' us with that, but it's a *big* difference." He couldn't say anything in response: If he'd really had the account to One Wall Street, he'd know precisely how many cubic yards of trash the building was generating every day; garbage guys are supposed to bill their customers based on that cubic yardage. What's more, I told Ray that I'd had a talk with the manager at One Wall and he said he'd never even heard of a company called R&R Rubbish Removal. Ray hemmed and hawed and made excuses about how his name wasn't on his truck when he made the pickups. "I don't know why you're lying to us," I said, "but you're wrong with the yardage, they never heard of you at the stop. Basically, nothing you're telling us makes any sense. Let's face it, you're not in a position to give us a guarantee about anything. We just don't want to negotiate with you anymore."

"So which way do you want to go with this?" Ray says threateningly.

"Now Sal can talk to your *boss,* Phil Barretti. We're still willing to work something out, but not with you. That's the way it's gonna be, between Phil Barretti and us, all right?"

Ramos is pissed off, but what's he going to do? I called his bluff. He knows he doesn't have the stop and he knows he can't get over on me. A week later we hook up the recorder and ask Sal to place a call to Phil at his office, saying he wants to set up a meeting to settle the dispute. Barretti tells Sal that he wants to meet him alone in the parking lot of Giando Ristorante (sometimes called Giando on the Water) on Kent

Avenue in Williamsburg. We agree to it. Giando is a big Italian restaurant, very popular with wiseguys—a huge shoebox-shaped building sitting right on the waterfront, a few blocks from Barretti's transfer station.

It's not an ideal spot for a meet. We can't control the situation like we could in Sal's office, but I can tell Phil's not about to come down to Plymouth Street. The meeting's going to take place in broad daylight, and we figure we can have a dozen detectives from the field team surrounding the place, ready to jump in.

The trick was to convince Sal to wear a wire. This was a big hurdle. We had to do a lot of sweet-talking to get him to strap on a Nagra. Over the years of the investigation, our Tech Services people kept improving the technology. The recording equipment kept getting smaller and easier to conceal. But in those days the best we had was the Nagra, a thick metal box the size of a paperback book that you've got to wear taped to your abdomen or lower back.

I can see Sal's scared shitless, so I try a little levity. "It's one of the nice things about being a big guy," I tell him. "We can hide five or six Nagras on your body and no one will ever find them."

Sal and I had spent a lot of time driving around together, grabbing cups of coffee in downtown Brooklyn and Bensonhurst, talking about the industry and its characters. Sal let me drive his car, a decrepit old Mercedes that made a racket like a buzzsaw and I felt like Lieutenant Columbo driving his old clunker of a Peugeot. The more time I spent with him, the more I admired Sally Skates. It's very rare in law enforcement that you get a civilian who agrees to gather evidence against the Mafia. Ninety-nine times out of a hundred, it's because we've got something on them, evidence they're jammed up in some criminal activity, and they're desperately trying to cut themselves a deal. But here was this guy Sal, completely clean, completely upstanding—we had absolutely nothing on him. Sure, he wanted to keep his business viable and had a profit motive not to lose more accounts to this gangster Barretti. But even so, what's One Wall Street—what's $3,400 a month to him? He's actually putting his life on the line just to do the right thing.

A couple of days before the big meeting, we're driving on Seventeenth Avenue on the borderline of Bensonhurst and Sunset Park when I get beeped by headquarters at One Police Plaza. It was some sensitive information about Barretti I'd been expecting, so I pull Sal's Mercedes over at a pay phone. As I jump out of the car to use the phone, I see a heavyset black lady coming down the sidewalk, slowly, almost waddling. She sees me heading for the phone, too, and I pick up the pace. She picks up the pace and makes it to the phone just before I do. She and I look at each other, but she takes the phone. When I return to the car, Sal shakes his head.

"Big tough cop! Got a badge and a gun—and the old lady pushes you off of the phone!" Soon as she hangs up, I go back to the phone, grab the receiver, but realize I don't even have a pen. I hustle back across to the passenger's side window of Sal's Benz.

"What happened?"

"Got a pen, Sally?"

"What kind of cop are you? How can you not have a pen? I never saw a cop who didn't have a pen to write tickets with."

"I don't write tickets, Sal. I'm a *detective*. Just gimme a pen, before someone else gets on the phone."

He reached into the glove compartment and handed me one of his Chambers Paper Fibres ballpoints. I jog across the street, back to the pay phone, and find I don't have any coins in my pockets either. Jesus, I did not want to have to walk back to that grinning guy in the Mercedes.

"What now?"

"I don't have any change, Sal. Lemme borrow a quarter?"

He reaches into his pants for some change and I see that the Mercedes has started to visibly shake. Big as he is, you have to realize, when Sal laughs—really laughs from the gut—he could rock the whole car. And now I can't keep a straight face either.

"Jesus, I'm gonna get myself *killed*," Sal mutters. "First all your wiretap equipment is shit . . . now you don't got no pen, don't got no quarter. What the hell am I doin' here? I put my life in the hands of the fuckin' Keystone Cops. . . ."

On June 11, the day of the face-to-face with Phil Barretti, Sal was done with his joking. Everyone on the field team was extremely tense. I secured the Nagra under Sal's gut, ran the wire carefully up his dress shirt. During the drive over to Giando Ristorante, I kept repeating, "Sal, if this thing gets ugly and I gotta jump in to help you, I'm jumping in as your Cousin Danny. Don't forget that. I'm *not* coming in as a cop. Got it?"

"Sure. Cousin Danny. Not a cop."

Then, just as we drove by Giando, my beeper went off like crazy. It was the crisis code from the field team. I jumped out to use the pay phone, and Detective Joe Lentini tells me that Raymond Ramos and another goon were spotted in the area, right across the street from the parking lot. It was supposed to be just Sal and Phil, one on one, but I can see that this treacherous bastard Barretti is escalating this meeting into something worse.

"Look, Sal," I said. "Stay in my presence at all times. Do not leave my sight, y'understand?"

Barretti was late for the meeting, so Sal and I sat in the Mercedes, making small talk, trying to stay loose. Sal said he couldn't believe that during my years of working organized-crime investigations, I'd never been to Giando, this waterfront joint that he said was a favorite with "the racketeers."

"No, never been here," I said. I was trying to keep Sal's eye on the ball. "Remember, we wanna try to link the fire and all that bullshit to Barretti," I whispered.

He nodded. "Yeah. I'll walk out towards the street—you think that'll be good for photographing? Now where the hell are *your* guys?"

Of course, the last thing in the world you want is for an informant or cooperating witness to know where your field team is set up. If something does get ugly, just on reflex Sal might start looking for help in the direction of the team and blow the surveillance on the case. But I tried to reassure him. I pointed to a bunch of parked cars across the street—a position directly opposite the one where our detectives were actually watching with cameras and zoom lenses. "There's some good observation posts right there," I said. "Over there too. . . ."

It was hot as hell in Sal's Mercedes. He drove one of those diesel sedans imported straight from Germany and the air-conditioning was nonexistent, barely a cool whisper. Both of us kept wiping the sweat from our foreheads. "Yeah, these European cars got the worst air-conditioning in the world," Sal said. "Over there they're not used to this weather. Only American cars got good air-conditioning." (Years later I was asked on the stand about the precise year and make of Sal's Mercedes. "All I know is that it's so old it belongs in the Smithsonian," I testified.)

Finally, we spotted Phil Barretti pulling up in his own mint-condition Mercedes.

"Okay, here we go."

But as many times as I'd warned Sal to stay in my line of sight, what happens? As soon as Barretti shows up, he puts his arm around Sal and waltzes him straight out of the parking lot, behind a big concrete wall. They're completely out of my sight. I'm sitting there blinded and sweating in the sun.

Tony Maz and the team had a perfect surveillance mapped out. Ten cops set up in positions. This is one of the most important parts of the meeting: documenting and photographing the surveillance with zoom lenses. But now, with Sal and Barretti walking off the set, we were in crisis mode.

I'm fuming. I had repeated it until I was blue in the face: "Sal, do not *ever* leave my sight." But now I couldn't see him anywhere. And I didn't know if our field team could, either. Our whole playbook was out the window. Later the field team gave me their account of the botched surveillance; Tony Maz put it over the radio: "If you can't see Sal, move in close. Someone get an eyeball on him! Ramos is in the area. Sal could be gettin' beaten like a baby seal right now!"

My thoughts were racing: *Should I jump out of the car and check on Sal? But if I do make a move, will it raise Barretti up and make things worse? Phil has been specific about Sal coming alone. Maybe it's better that I sit tight, let Sal try to talk his way out of the jam, let him try to pull the Sally Skates routine.*

Finally, for Sal's safety, I jump out, go through the lot, and around the concrete wall to check them out.

"What's doin', Sally?"

Sal looks a little frightened but he shrugs it off. "It's all right, Dan. Go back to the car."

As I'm walking back to the car it happens: Ramos jumps out. The field team scrambles to get Sal in sight, but all they see is a violent flash: Sal reeling backward. They don't know if he was punched or stabbed or what. And just at that moment a passing bus blocks the surveillance completely. Tony Maz gave the order to move in for the takedown. But then Detective Dunleavy saw that Sal was on his feet, still talking normally, and Tony changed the order: "Hold back from making the collar."

I couldn't see what was happening, either. Later, I heard the conversation clearly on the Nagra.

"Hey, Ray, how you doin'?" Sal says as Ramos walks up. Then Sal turns nervously to Phil. "That's your buddy?"

"No, that's not *my* buddy," Barretti says, trying to act like this big goon striding up is just a coincidence.

"Don't you worry about Phil," Ramos says, grabbing Sal. "Listen, I want my fuckin' stop. I want my stop."

He starts punching and slapping him, then moves on to choking Sal.

"Whattaya doin'?" Sal says falling back, losing his footing.

"I want my fuckin' stop!"

Sal is flailing, waving his arms, trying to run away. Then Ramos rips Sal's shirt, nearly exposing our wire.

"Hey, come on," Sal says. "I'll make a deal with *him*. Come on! I got a bad leg here!"

I'll say one thing for Sal: Even though he gets roughed up, he has a lot of balls. He keeps his cool, remembers my instructions to get the evidence, try to link the truck fire to Phil Barretti.

"You two work together?" he mumbles, even as he was getting choked.

"I don't work for him—remember that?" Ramos shouts.

"Oh, come on. How'd he know I got a meeting over here with you? You tell him or what? My truck burns up and all that shit . . ."

"Yeah, I did it," Ramos says.

"You did it?"

"Yeah, I did it! Don't fuck with me again. I don't care what *he* says. It's what *I* say, boss."

But as terrified as Sal is, as soon as Ramos pulls back, he stands toe-to-toe with Phil Barretti and continues arguing. I guess knowing that there were ten armed detectives in the vicinity gave him more courage. "Let's cut out the bullshit," Sal says.

"You're the kind of guy that don't wanna know nothin'—don't talk to nobody," Barretti says.

They get down to haggling over the garbage and paper rights to One Wall Street and One Chase Manhattan Plaza.

"I was getting eight thousand dollars a month from the bank," Phil says.[1]

"Yeah, but you were overcharging them!"

"That's none of your business. Do I tell *you* what to charge the bank?"

"I went in at $14.70 a yard, and that's all I can charge," Sal says. "I don't wanna go to jail. That's the maximum amount." It's the truth: $14.70 per yard was the maximum ceiling set by the Department of Consumer Affairs.

"I don't need you to educate my fuckin' customers, Sal. I don't need you to cut my fuckin' prices! . . . I was chargin' them eight thousand dollars a month. You made me look like a fuckin' jerk."

They go at it like that for ten minutes, tit for tat; who went to war with who first; who had the high-grade paper first at which location. They can't agree on their facts and finally Sal throws up his hands. "What's the sense of talkin'?"

---

[1] Actually, it was later shown that Barretti was charging The Bank of New York at One Wall Street $9,400 a month.

You can hear on the tape recording how this drives Barretti crazy. Nobody has ever stood up to him this way; nobody has ever showed this kind of moxie. Here is Sal, this funny-looking, reclusive paper guy who suddenly, crazily, has the heart to compete with the tough-as-nails garbage gangsters.

"Why are you in the garbage business anyway?" Phil shouts.

"Because you fuckin' guys are takin' all the paper!" Sal comes back. "I stayed out of it for thirty fuckin' years until you guys went into it. Now all of a sudden you think you own *all* the paper in New York City!"

"We gotta work out this problem, otherwise we're gonna have more problems down the road."

As they walk away Sal says, sarcastically, "Whattaya gonna send your guy Ramos around—this guy who don't work for you?"

This was the second *major* screw-up on Sal's part: Raymond Ramos had never once told us his full name. Most hardened criminals—even not-too-bright ones—are very careful about that. We only knew him as Ray. We'd run our departmental checks and found out his last name was Ramos, but I had never told Sal. How the hell would a citizen like Sal have known that?

This might seem like just a little slip, but with the Mob it's the tiny mistakes that can get you killed. Sal had overheard a couple of detectives on the field team using the name Ramos in conversation. I got annoyed. "Don't use that fuckin' name around the C.W.!" I didn't want Sal to know more than he absolutely needed to. And look what it led to: In the heat of the moment, after getting slapped and punched, he blurted out Ramos's name.

Luckily, Barretti wasn't sharp enough to pick up on it now. If we'd been dealing with a smarter, cagier gangster—a Jimmy Brown, Joey Francolino, Allie Shades—it would have been game over. Those guys would have been raised up, figured Sal for a rat, found the Nagra on him, and he'd be lying dead in Giando's parking lot.

But Sal stumbled back toward the Mercedes with his skin intact. They ended the meeting with nothing at all resolved. They agreed that they were going to get all the paperwork together, fax each other later that afternoon, prove whose stop it really was, how much garbage One Wall Street was generating each month, and how much the bales of high-grade paper were worth.

Ramos and the other goon got in their car, then Sal came back to the Mercedes, soaked in sweat, and collapsed in the passenger seat next to me. Barretti got into his Mercedes—mind you, his is the 500 SE, jet black, tinted windows, brand new, or at least thirty years newer than Sal's rattling relic.

"Who's that?" Barretti asked Sal, pointing at me.

"That's Danny Benedetto, my cousin. I had him drive me over."

"Hey, I wasn't worried," Phil said with a tough-guy shrug. "I came over by myself. I don't give a fuck."

We drove a few blocks down the waterfront; I reached into Sal's shirt and turned the Nagra off so I could debrief him. Sal told me what happened with Ramos and was still so traumatized that he couldn't catch his breath.

Phil's a real class act. Cesar Romero, my ass. Here he had his thug Ramos jumping in to choke and smack around a short, overweight fifty-four-year-old man with a bum leg and a heart condition. I sat there fuming as Sal told me about it.

And months later I was still so steamed, I couldn't even sit across the table from Phil in the Waste Paper Club on Canal Street or the Americana Diner in Bensonhurst, without wanting to kick the shit out of him for what he did to Sal in the parking lot of Giando's.

As I debriefed him, Sal was hyperventilating and his sweat was cold. I really thought he was going to have a heart attack. And given what happened to him later, it was amazing that Sally didn't die on me that day.

3 | ALLIE SHADES

After that assault in Giando's parking lot, I met with Tony Mazziotti at a secret OCID plant in Staten Island and asked to be allowed to take on the role of Dan Benedetto full-time. Sal was terrified now, hiding out in his office, afraid to turn the ignition key in his car—and who could blame him? After experiencing Phil Barretti's treachery firsthand, Sal and his cousins didn't want to see any of these hoods face-to-face. From this point forward in the investigation, I'd have to be the point man in any future negotiations and confrontations.

Tony knew that initiating a full-time undercover assignment would be no small undertaking: It would require a lot of delicate maneuvering with the NYPD brass. And as the boss on the case, Tony would be responsible for navigating the complex bureaucracy of the NYPD, the

world's biggest police department. Down the road the department would
have to agree to rent an apartment for me; in fact, over the course of the
investigation, my Danny alias would come to "live" in three separate
apartments: one on Plymouth Street, above the Chambers warehouse;
one on Cropsey Avenue, in Bensonhurst; and one in the Clove Lake
section of Staten Island.

Sending a detective to work deep undercover inside a Mafia-controlled
industry required a stream of internal memoranda. First thing: Tony had
to fire off a UF-49 memo to the Confidential Identification Unit of the
Investigative Support Division of the Organized Crime Control Bureau,
requesting a "real" New York State driver's license, Social Security, and
working credit cards in the name of his new operative Dan Benedetto.

Of course, on the simplest level, I had to pass for a scrappy Italian kid
named Benedetto. Luckily, I have dark hair and dark eyes; the first time
I met Tony, in fact, even with my Irish-sounding name, he'd thought I
was a fellow Italian-American.

"Sure you're really an Irishman, Ricky? Irish-Catholic?"

"Protestant, Scotch-Irish. We're Presbyterian on my father's side,
Episcopalian on my mother's."

"Well, you had me fooled at least. You could pass for a *paisan*. . . ."

We spent days and nights driving around—Tony with his Yankees
cap pulled down over his curly black hair, always puffing Marlboros—
strategizing about Danny's past life. We had a starting point, at least; we
had a safe father—a deceased dad. Sal had given us the name of an old
lawyer in the family, John Benedetto, part of what Sal called "the Staten
Island crowd," who'd been dead since 1964. Okay, so I would be John's
son, the kid who was only seven when his father died. John had been
active in Democratic party politics and had several sons; one, named
Robert Benedetto, had become a well-known priest. I was supposed to
be John Benedetto's youngest, the black sheep of the family. This meant
there had to be something mysterious, something a little off-center
about my character.

Maybe Danny had some school problems as a kid, got in too many
fights, been a juvenile delinquent, had been sent to live with his grand-

mother. Maybe he'd been a bit too wild for the rest of the Benedettos—
that's why they kept him away from the family business. Actually, I have
the face of a guy who's seen a few fistfights, the bridge of my nose broken so many times that it never set completely straight. I knew Staten
Island well—lived there all the years I'd been on the job—and so I
was able to pick the neighborhood, the very address, where Danny had
grown up with his grandparents. I figured out exactly which junior high
and high school Danny would have been kicked out of.

In a lot of ways, Danny's blue-collar background wasn't that different
from mine. I was born and raised in Essex County, New Jersey—and
growing up, I learned to handle myself in rough situations. After high
school I worked for a couple years doing welding and construction jobs,
then started off my law enforcement career as a corrections officer in
Essex County before getting onto a couple of smaller Jersey police forces.
But I'd always dreamed that someday I'd get to the big city and wear
that famous NYPD shield.

I was hired by New York City in 1983, and, like every young cop, I
started out walking the beat—all over Brooklyn, put in a lot of shoe-
leather tours in the Seven Eight, Seven One, and Six Seven precincts.
It was while walking a beat out of the Six Seven precincthouse in
Flatbush that I got my first taste of undercover work. I'd been doing
footposts in the Six Seven, the most boring assignment you could get:
stuck in the middle of nowhere, nowhere to eat, seeing little action. An
RMP—radio motor patrol—always beats you to the good stuff. Every
day I would watch all these charged-up plainclothes guys coming in and
out of the station house, and they told me about this sixty-day program
for temporary undercovers in the Organized Crime Control Bureau—
not a permanent assignment, just a tryout to see if you were suited for
that kind of work.

I submitted my name and then forgot about it. Months went by without my hearing a word. I moved up from walking footposts and landed
myself a seat in a radio car. I had a great partner, Billy Aronstam, affec-

tionately known in the precinct as Crazy Horse, strong as a bull at six foot
five and two hundred forty pounds, with a knack for breaking down
doors—even when they were locked and bolted. Crazy Horse and I were
patrolling our sector of East Flatbush, answering jobs from Central, and I
loved it. It was a busy house in an extremely high-crime area—the drug
"posses" had taken over East Flatbush in the mid-'80s—and the whole
precinct was like a family, just a tremendous, tight-knit group of cops.

One day I got a telephone message telling me that my temporary undercover assignment had come through and I'd been transferred to
Manhattan South Narcotics. The irony was, now I didn't want to go,
because now I was chasing down badguys in a sector car with Crazy
Horse Aronstam, making collars and in the action—what I'd dreamed
of coming to the NYPD to do. I was about to say no to the undercover
training opportunity, but one of the lieutenants in the Six Seven, a red-
headed Irish guy, took me aside and gave me a piece of advice I've never
forgotten.

"Look, Rick," he said, "you don't have a rabbi. You don't have a
hook. You shouldn't turn this chance down. If you don't like the undercover work, what the hell, it's just a temporary assignment. But don't
ever close any doors in this job."

The NYPD is like a massive civilian army, a complex force of some
forty thousand troops, and one of the traditions, established by generations of officers before me, is that to get ahead you need a "rabbi,"
"hook," or "contract"—a well-placed politician or friend, a cop with
connections, who can get you an assignment in a good unit. Without a
rabbi, a lot of guys feel like they're just going to waste their careers, wal-
lowing in obscurity, walking beats in Flatbush into their forties.

Moving to Manhattan South Narcotics, I found myself doing a new
kind of police work. I was learning from an older undercover named
Woody Drury, who was a master of disguises, always wearing creative
getups. Woody broke me in, and just like him, I started dressing in different outfits, even experimenting with theatrical makeup to give my
face scars and bruises and bumps. We worked on the Lower East Side,
primarily in the confines of the Ninth Precinct, which covers Alphabet

City, from Houston Street up to Fourteenth Street, and from the East River over to Second Avenue. It's a tough, downtrodden neighborhood, and the dealers would brazenly line up to sell their heroin and coke. I started to make a lot of buys. I had this '64 Chevy Impala, and sometimes I'd "put it on"—the slang we use for taking your personal vehicle, entering it in the logbook, and getting it authorized by your sergeant. In the Spanish neighborhoods like Alphabet City, they *loved* my old Impala. They'd gather around and talk to me about it, because it was in mint condition, and they knew that no undercover cop was driving around in an outdated twenty-year-old muscle car like that. I grew a beard, wore a leather jacket like an outlaw biker, and—with my fake bruises and busted nose—I looked fucked up. Soon I was buying heroin all over the Ninth Precinct. Sometimes I'd go on the same set twice on the same afternoon, just change my getup and go right back in. I was lucky to be schooled by street-savvy veterans like Sergeant Dan Mac-Sweeney and Lieutenant Jimmy Wood—real legends in the Narcotics division.

When my bosses saw that I was capable of buying a lot of heroin, they asked if I wanted to stay with undercover work when my sixty-day training period was up. I could work toward my gold shield. Again, without a hook, I saw another door suddenly opening up for me.

After a few months back in a radio car in the Six Seven, I got into Narcotics permanently, continued buying heroin, nothing huge, mostly eightballs—packages of an eighth of an ounce. The biggest buy I made was five ounces up in Washington Heights. But I was steady. All told, I had six hundred buys in thirty-three months as an undercover. One day I was asked to give a presentation to Police Commissioner Ben Ward. The PC had asked each captain in every borough's narcotics unit to pick one undercover and bring him in to One Police Plaza. He wanted to hear the truth about what was happening in the street. I'd been keeping a detailed notebook on all the brands of heroin and coke I'd bought; I went in and told the commissioner what I'd seen firsthand, rattled off a shitload of different brand names. Crack had come onto the scene by then and it was all anyone in the media was talking about. But I told

Commissioner Ward that heroin was actually making a big-time come-back because all the crack-smokers were short-circuiting their cardio-vascular systems, suffering strokes and heart attacks. I found that these streetwalking pharmaceutical freaks would smoke crack, get all wound up, and then shoot some heroin to level off the high and not keel over from a stroke or heart attack. To know that information you'd have to be right out there with these addicts every day. And I was, let me tell you. I found myself huddling in shooting galleries, even held the spoon when they cooked. I had a couple of close calls but never had to shoot it myself. But time and again, I was in these scary, burned-out places where it was pitch black and the only light in the room was the lighters cooking up the heroin.

The commander for the NYPD/DEA Task Force was in the room during the presentation and he complimented me and asked me if I had a desire to come to the DEA. Frankly, I was tired of the drugs; I wanted to get into a kind of investigation where I could use my mind more, rather than just buying bags and bundles, *dame dos*–ing[1] on the street corner. I'd always had some interest in the Mob: Growing up in my area of New Jersey, you couldn't help but hear the stories of crime bosses like Willie Moretti, Simone "Sam the Plumber" DeCavalcante, and Ruggiero "Richie the Boot" Boiardo.

Leaving One Police Plaza, my captain, Steven Nasta, invited me to lunch and said that since I was one of the senior undercovers, with thirty-three months in, I would be getting transferred soon. "Do you have any idea where you want to go?" he asked.

"I hear they do all kinds of diverse investigations in OCID," I said.

Captain Nasta reached out to Inspector Donald Faherty, my former commander in Manhattan South Narcotics, who was now the com-manding officer of the Organized Crime Investigations Division. That got me a grueling hour-and-fifteen-minute interview. If you're a cop with a rabbi, those interviews can be a formality, lasting just ten min-

---

[1] Spanish for "Gimme two." Common New York drug vernacular used when buying two "decks," or bags, of heroin.

utes. Without a hook, I was sweating it out. It was a tough interview. A lieutenant from Field Control, an internal-affairs unit of the Narcotics Division, looked at me skeptically. "You made so many buys?" he said. "You appear to be a little heavyset to be out there playing the part of a drug addict." I stared right back at the lieutenant, who was a little chubby himself. "Even with this suit and tie," I said, "I'll take you out to a streetcorner in Alphabet City and *dame dos* 'em right now." That got all the bosses laughing.

In June 1989 they took me on and I came into the organized-crime unit as a "white shield"—a regular patrolman who works in plainclothes but doesn't have his detective's gold shield yet. My first job was as part of a team working a labor racketeering case involving Painters Union District Council 9, located on Fourteenth Street in Manhattan. I had no experience with organized crime at this point, but I quickly saw that there was a mystique about Mob work. Not the glamour that they depict in the movies, but there certainly are some vivid characters—wiseguys like Peter "Fat Pete" Chiodo, a five-hundred-pound Lucchese *caporegime* who I personally arrested during our Painters investigation.

A couple months into the Painters case, I got promoted to third-grade detective. That's the biggest day of your whole career. Some guys chase that gold carrot around for years. It seems like the job is always dangling it out in front of you and you never quite reach it. When you do get the shield, the department gives you this major ceremony with the police commissioner and all the high-ranking chiefs. Your whole family is called in—your wife, parents, brothers and sisters, and in-laws. You snap pictures with all the top brass in the police department, smiling and showing off that gold shield. It's a proud day, and one of the few times your family gets to be a part of your police work.

I may not have had a hook in the police department, but a year into my stint with OCID, a heavyweight gangster in sunglasses became my guide through the world of organized crime. His name was Alphonso "Allie Shades" Malangone and he was the best education an organized-crime detective could ever have. Two years of watching Allie Shades taught me more about the Mafia than I could have learned in a lifetime of expert seminars down in the FBI academy in Quantico.

Alphonso "Allie Shades" Malangone was a huge earner for the Genovese family. Within Mob circles he was widely liked and respected, on close terms with bosses and *capos* in all the five families. Skippers from the Bonanno family like Anthony Spero used to come to Allie for advice. Even though there was often tension between the Gambinos and the Genovese family, even though Allie's own boss, Vincent "Chin" Gigante, couldn't stand John Gotti, Allie was on close terms with the Gambino boss and used to meet John at the Ravenite on Mulberry Street.

They called him Allie Shades because he always wore these aviator-style tinted glasses. Even in the dead of the night, coming out of Pastels or the Ravenite, you'd see Allie in those shades. Over the years I got to know his personality very well, and I have to admit, for a hood, he had some likable qualities. He had more of a sense of humor about himself than most Mob guys. He wasn't book-educated, of course, but he wasn't a fool, either.

Just to glance at him, Allie was a scary son of a bitch. He's about six foot three, powerful build, sandy-haired, hands like catcher's mitts. For years he had had those giant mitts of his in every Mob racket: He ran a huge illegal gambling book, had shylock money on the street, controlled a good chunk of the Genovese interests in the Fulton Fish Market, dabbled in pump-and-dump stock swindles on Wall Street. (In a Mob-fronted pump-and-dump, a team of crooked stockbrokers cold-called all kinds of unsuspecting victims, got them to "pump" up the price of their stock, then bailed out and "dumped" their own shares at a tremendous profit, crashing the price of the stock and leaving the average Joes with a bunch of worthless paper.) We also knew—but couldn't yet prove—that Allie's real power was in garbage, that he ran Brooklyn for Vincent "Chin" Gigante. And the Chin—although he might be seen wandering around the West Village, drooling in his bathrobe and tweed cap—was the biggest wiseguy in America.

We never would have got near Allie Shades if we hadn't first stumbled onto Alan Longo, one of the soldiers in Allie's crew. Everyone on the street calls him Baldie. He's even taller than Allie, about six foot five, shiny dome, paunchy, bad posture, nearsighted. Baldie's a big bookmaker, but he's also a degenerate gambler. He'd bet on two cockroaches running up the shithouse wall. At one point Alan Longo was so in hock, he owed over a million dollars to various loan sharks in the Genovese, Gambino, and Colombo crime families. That's a lot of money to owe shylocks. If Allie Shades wasn't his skipper, Baldie would probably have been clipped long ago.

We started looking at Alan Longo for a penny-stock manipulation case back in 1990. It was a good case and we ended up collaring thirteen guys, all associates of Longo's. But they were stockbrokers, white-collar guys, not thugs. They did not want the cops breaking down the doors in their nice suburban neighborhoods. It was a fairly straightforward pump-and-dump operation; all these suspender-wearing stockbrokers jumped at the chance to plead guilty.

We knew that Alan Longo was the main organized-crime figure behind them, but we couldn't nail him for it. But at least we now had probable cause to start watching his whole operation. Longo lived in Staten Island with his girlfriend, and he had a good-sized gambling package going.[2] But he was really big into the numbers, the old policy game that's been virtually unchanged since the days of Dutch Schultz. In all the black sections of Brooklyn, in all these little bodegas and storefronts, Alan had his numbers people raking in the dough.

We surveilled Longo around the clock and things started to get interesting. We had our plant in Staten Island in an apartment right near Alan's place. You have to understand: In general, surveillance work is extremely tedious, and draining on a detective's morale. Monitoring intercepted telephone calls is about as mind-numbing as it gets. Some nights you practically need an intravenous caffeine bag just to keep yourself alert. Most cops prefer the adrenaline rush of hitting the streets,

---

[2] *Gambling package* refers to a bookmaking operation that has the blessing of an organized-crime figure to operate in a given area.

actively trying to lock up badguys, and sitting in some shitty little apartment day and night listening to boring hoods making boring phone calls can drive you insane.

It happened one time when we were watching Longo's gambling operation. There was an old detective on the team who was disgruntled and really hated being there. His job was to be on the wire, to log every phone call that Alan Longo made throughout the night. Here's what kind of weird bird Alan Longo is: If he dialed a number and got a busy signal, he would not wait even fifteen seconds between calls. He would immediately hang up and dial again, and if you're the detective monitoring it, that means you're trying to keep the line sheets and the counter and the time, you're doing your damnedest to keep the record neat and accurate. With Baldie making twenty-five calls a minute, forget about it, the line sheets are shot to shit.

This old hairbag detective suddenly blows his stack, picks up the phone, dials Longo's number, and somehow—big miracle—between all that rapid-fire redialing, Alan's phone rings. "You better knock it off, you fat bald fuck!" the detective shouts. Then he hangs up. We all looked at each other in disbelief.

Two minutes later Alan calls his cousin who's in his crew. He's fuming. "Somebody just called me a fat bald fuck—and I know *exactly* who it is!" He thought it was some other jerk out in the streets. Can you imagine? Some poor bastard caught a beating from Baldie for something he didn't even do.

Next we tried to put a bug in Alan Longo's car. Turns out to be a big fiasco. Alan drives this big fat-ass maroon Lincoln Town Car and we had been trying to get a listening device in it for weeks. Now our time was just about up. The warrants you get for these things go stale in thirty days. It was our last possible moment, a hot summer day in 1990, around 3:30 or 4 in the afternoon, and I saw this big dummy Alan Longo double-parking in front of Pastels like he owns the place. If you or I did it, we'd get summonsed or towed in two minutes. He does it all the time, and it's like he's immune. It was Baldie's luck. Badguy luck.

I had a key for Baldie's Lincoln and the Tech Service support team waiting in the wings, and I decided, *This is it, I've got to go boost the Lincoln right now.* Members of the field team in the vicinity were detectives Frank DiGregorio, Matty Higgins, Cathy Hart, and this good buddy of mine from Narcotics, Dave Grinage. I knew that they would all watch my back no matter what happened.

It was such a perfect summer day and all the boys were out there, Allie Shades and his whole crew smoking cigars, suntanning on the sidewalk in their chaise longues. "Fat Gerry" Guadagno, Johnny "Geech" Giangrandi, and a whole bunch of other Pastels characters—real toughguys in this crew. If they ever caught you messing around with one of their cars, you better believe they'd beat you to a pulp.

I had a special key provided by Tech Services. But just as I was about to try the key, the manager of Pastels, Mikey Rosenbaum, walked out the door and almost caught me in the act. I got scared and I knew I had to get myself off the set, get recomposed, and wait for another opportunity. I called Dave Grinage on the radio. "Dave, the next red light, take the intersection—I don't care what happens, just pull right out and block all the fuckin' traffic!"

Rosenbaum kept on walking. I tried the key in the door—it's the fourth one we've had made; all the others were duds—and lo and behold, the Town Car opens. I threw myself inside, and before my ass even hits the leather seat, I had the ignition going. One problem: Baldie's six foot five, I'm five foot nine, and I had no time to adjust the seat. It felt like I was driving from the backseat. Plus he had this tape of Pavarotti turned up to the max and I couldn't even find where to turn the music down. All I could hear was Luciano screaming at me like a lunatic while I floored the Lincoln.

Dave Grinage took the intersection like a pro and tied up all the traffic at Fifth Avenue and Eighty-seventh Street in his Caprice. I raced through the red light, everybody wailing on horns, Pavarotti bellowing. I got on the Gowanus Expressway, drove toward Manhattan, and I still couldn't find the volume switch till I'm all the way to the Battery Tunnel—at the toll booth. All that way I couldn't talk to the field team over the deafening opera.

I drove to an empty building in Chelsea, Tech Services gets to work on this bug, and then we drop the Lincoln off a half a block from this garbage company owned by Frank Allocca, a close associate of Allie Shades. It was uncanny. Longo got his car back within the day. I put a bunch of Budweiser cans and empty White Castle hamburger boxes all over the car so he'd think it was just kids joyriding. But the bug was useless in the end. The thing worked for two blocks, then shorted out.

So we tried it again. This time we sent him tickets to a Yankees game. Told him he was the proud winner of four tickets to see the Bronx Bombers, mailed them to his girlfriend's house. "Look at this, I got four tickets to the Yankees game," he said. "I won 'em from some organization." His girlfriend was in the background: "I don't know about that, Alan. Sounds pretty suspicious to me." She was a lot sharper than he was. But then, Baldie Longo was no Rhodes scholar.

He drove to Yankee stadium and I tailed him into the parking lot. I was wearing a full Con Edison workman's uniform. Baldie went in to watch the Yankees, and within seconds we had the whole Lincoln ripped apart, installing the bug. But three quarters of the way through the installation, the cops inside the stadium radioed that he was on the way out. We barely had time to get his seats put back in place. As it turned out, Longo was only on a bathroom run.

The bug worked for exactly two blocks and then crapped out a second time. Manufacturer's defect. It was draining his battery. He took his Lincoln to the shop but the mechanic couldn't figure out what was going on with his battery. Later, Longo left his car double-parked right in front of a fire hydrant on Mulberry Street in Little Italy. We towed the Lincoln and ripped our bug right back out. All that work for nothing. What was the point of trying again? We realized that we were no match for Baldie's badguy luck.

But by now Alan Longo had served his purpose. He'd led us straight to a much bigger fish: Allie Shades Malangone. That's the way it works in real-life police investigations. Forget the simple A-leads-to-B-leads-to-C stuff you see in those cop shows. It's rarely that straightforward. There are a lot more stumbles and false starts. A lot more screwups and manufacturers' defects. You've got to be prepared to make ten wrong turns before finding your way to the open road.

Alan Longo made a promising target for us, but he was a small fry in relation to a *caporegime* like Alphonso Malangone. Watching Allie Shades hold court outside Pastels Discotheque in Bay Ridge, we started seeing much higher-caliber gangsters coming and going each day. We observed heavyweights like Michele Generosa, underboss of the Genovese family, dropping in to visit with Allie.

The years of the Pastels surveillance coincided with the so-called Colombo War. The Colombos have always been known as an unstable *borgata:* That was the family of "Crazy Joe" Gallo, who started a shooting war by trying to murder his boss, Joe Profaci; and of Joe Colombo, who was gunned down in broad daylight in Columbus Circle, after embarrassing Carlo Gambino and the other shadow-loving bosses by pulling his bizarre publicity stunt of an Italian-American Civil Rights League.

By June 1991 there was a new war tearing open the Colombos, pitting two factions—one loyal to imprisoned boss Carmine "the Snake" Persico and his son "Allie Boy," and another to hot-tempered would-be boss Vic Orena—against each other in bloody gun battles not seen in Brooklyn since Crazy Joe's generation. There were countless shootouts in South Brooklyn, and innocent civilians were sometimes caught in the crossfire. In all, the NYPD tallied some twelve homicides in those bloody months of Colombo strife.

A lot of the shootouts took place right near Allie's club. I was on surveillance at Pastels when this young kid named Matty, who was just working as the counter boy in a bagel shop, got murdered just down the block. It finally got so hot in the streets that we started seeing a few Colombo soldiers coming around Pastels with Allie and his crew, clearly seeking Allie's protection. Smart move on their part. The Colombos were a bunch of crazy cowboys, but nobody was so crazy that they'd shoot up the nightclub of a Genovese skipper like Allie Shades.

One day while tailing Allie we got our big break: We discovered that he had a wire room—the headquarters of his gambling operation—at 86 Church Avenue in Brooklyn, just off Ocean Parkway. At night, when the wire room was closed, a couple of Allie's guys would get in a car, drive over to Bay Ridge, and pull up in front of Pastels Disco, which was also completely dark at the time. They'd go in the service door, pop into Pastels, and be right back out in thirty seconds.

We were now documenting probable cause: What we suspected was the dropping off of gambling action. Because of this, and other information, we could apply to the court for a warrant to get surveillance bugs inside Allie's club. I was the case officer on the investigations and went into Pastels myself to get the lay of the land for our Tech Services team.

I had a warrant and a duplicate key to the nightclub's service door. (For obvious reasons, we can never reveal precisely how we go about defeating security systems.) About three o'clock one morning, I busted into Pastels. This is how you do it: You make it look like a regular burglary job, dress in jeans and sweatshirt like a burglar would. But if you're caught in the act, you'll be taken for a *real* burglar, and they might shoot you or bash your head in.

All I wanted this time was the name of alarm companies and any numbers I could see on the boxes. I had just gotten inside when, suddenly, I heard the field team shouting over my radio:

"Six Eight rollin' on the block! Rick, you set the alarm off!"

The field team had spotted an RMP from the Six Eight Precinct arriving to check on a burglary in progress.

The Organized Crime Investigations Division is an extremely compartmentalized division of the Police Department. We're almost like a spy-ring cell, self-contained, and we don't work in coordination with the local precinct cops. So if these guys from the Six Eight catch me in the act, depending on their experience level, they might panic and start shooting.

I turned my radio off. I could hear the two patrolmen outside the door talking to each other. Thinking quickly, I decided to hold on to the door handle as tight as I can. The latch seemed secure, but I couldn't be sure. I had goose bumps all over: Here I was on the inside, in street clothes, and another cop was on the outside, in uniform, and we were both pulling in opposite directions with all our strength.

It was pitch-black inside this gangsters' nightclub. Those tiny red lights on the alarm boxes were the only lights I had. I held my breath, pulling back on the handle with all my weight, hoping the door didn't give way.

And then I was alone again. I could hear the cops getting back in their RMP.

The guys from the Six Eight assumed that there'd been an alarm malfunction inside Pastels. Having been on patrol just like them, I know that it happens a hundred times a night in Brooklyn. You just double-check that there's no burglary in progress, call the alarm company, and go about your tour.

It gave Tech Services enough time to get the audio bug in place. We didn't have enough time to get our video camera finished, but we came back again a few weeks later and got the video up in the ceiling of Allie's back office.

Now, this was beautiful: Every day and night it was like we've got our own private wiseguy network back at the plant in Staten Island. All Allie Shades, all the time. Allie had shit going on inside Pastels Disco that was unbelievable. Talk about bookmaking, loan-sharking, roughing guys up. He had soldiers and connected guys coming in giving him fat envelopes of cash, kissing him on the cheek—even kissing his ring like he's Don Corleone. And he talked like Don Corleone sometimes. One day Allie's landlord made the mistake of trying to raise the rent on Allie's parking lot. Allie went ballistic. He called the landlord up in a rage, started quoting lines right from the movie:

ALLIE SHADES: I heard you wanna raise the rent over there in the lot.
  Go fuck yourself. I'm not payin' *nothin'*. The rent—you see *The
  Godfather*? In the movies? "Da rent it staysa da same. . . ."
LANDLORD: That was in the movie?
ALLIE SHADES: Yeah, in *real life* too.

Born in Brooklyn in 1936, Allie Shades had first came to the attention of law enforcement in the mid-1970s as a fast-rising gambler, bookmaker, and all-purpose gangster. A soldier in the crew of Genovese *capo* Tommy Contaldo, Allie also came under the tutelage of a renowned old-timer named Toddo Marino; by the 1980s, he had risen to take over the Genovese family's interests in the carting industry, which had previously been run by Joseph "Joe-by-the-Bay" Schipani (who got his nickname because he lived in a large home in Brooklyn's Sheepshead Bay section).

Early on during the Pastels Discotheque surveillance, we observed Allie talking about an informal high school reunion he attended at Garguilo's restaurant on Coney Island. Allie was excited about seeing the old crowd, a motley crew that he described as a blend of criminals, civil servants, and various law enforcement types:

"No wives—detectives there, crooks, robbers, postmen, gangsters . . . fuckin' cops, bodyguards, the FBI, Ruggerio—from the Secret Service—what a fuckin' crew—all kinds of mixed fuckin' people. . . ."

The handful of Genovese associates gathered around the file cabinets in his darkened office got a big kick out of the story—and so did the handful of OCID detectives watching with me in the surveillance post in Staten Island. Allie even got up and reenacted the speech of introduction to the old Brooklyn boys:

"Hey, I'm Allie. You all know me—I'm a hoodlum and a gangster. I've been a bookmaker. . . . Yeah, I never changed. I'm wanted. . . ."

Sure, Allie Shades could often be humorous and entertaining; but he could also be cold-blooded. Though Allie didn't have a big street reputation as a killer, he was more than ready to use violence whenever it served his purposes. Like most wiseguys, he saw murder as a simple occupational necessity; he was completely unemotional when talking about the ideal technique for killing.

On May 30, 1991, at approximately 2:30 P.M., we overheard an

unidentified male coming to Allie Shades for advice about a "problem."
Allie launched into a tirade that was equal parts pep talk and primer on
committing a Cosa Nostra hit:

ALLIE SHADES: Then you should go kill the fuckin' guy if you feel that
    way. Just don't let nobody know. And when they come, say, "I didn't
    do it—what do I know?"
UNIDENTIFIED MALE: "What do I know?"
ALLIE SHADES: So if you're so fuckin' hot and heavy the way you
    are . . . then go do it, don't talk about it. Go fuckin' do it. Kill him
    [and dump him] in the fuckin' river. Whatever you say you're gonna
    do. Go kill him, don't fuckin' say—
UNIDENTIFIED MALE: Wait.
ALLIE SHADES: And don't brag about it. Truckin' fuckin' junkie cock-
    sucker. I said, don't brag about it. You kill him. 'Cause then you'll
    get caught.
UNIDENTIFIED MALE: Botch it up . . .
ALLIE SHADES: If that's the way the way you feel about it, if it eats
    your stomach that much, that's what you're supposed to do. If you
    wanna be so fuckin' smart. And then when they come back and say,
    "What'd ya do, kill that guy?" "Hey, you fucks, maybe I'm in a
    bar"—tell 'em, "I was with my cousin—I was in the movies with
    my girl." Just don't talk about it.
UNIDENTIFIED MALE: What a pity, though.
ALLIE SHADES: Buddy, you see—that's the way you do it.

They were too well schooled to use any names, but from the context of
the call, we thought we knew who Allie and this other hood were conspiring to kill. This is one of those moral dilemmas you find yourself in
doing surveillance work. On the one hand, you're gathering solid evidence for a major racketeering case down the road, and the last thing in
the world you want to do is blow your cover. On the other hand, you've
just intercepted direct evidence of conspiracy to commit murder in the
second degree.

As an NYPD detective, you've only got one course of action: Your first obligation is always to protect life and property. If somebody's going to be murdered, to hell with the wiretap, we have to try to notify this guy.

That's just what we did. We believed that the guy who was about to get whacked was a Genovese associate. I got in touch with two excellent OCID detectives, Joe Moore and Brian Dunigan, and we went to the hood's house. His wife was home and she immediately lawyered up. We had to give the lawyer all these assurances that we weren't going to arrest his client, that it was just very important that we meet immediately with him. I mean, he was being a real ball-buster. All we were trying to do was save this clown's life and he really jerked us around. All his stalling might have presented the killers with the opportunity to do the hit. He agreed to meet us, in public, in front of the University of Staten Island Hospital. When he finally showed up, he was scowling and strutting like a real tough guy. I was hanging in the background, trying to preserve my anonymity so I could continue the surveillance, because this guy had frequented Pastels. I let Joe Moore and Brian Dunigan do all the talking. Joe was so pissed off, he didn't even sugarcoat it:

"Look, do you know anyone who might want to kill you? We have very good information that you're about to be murdered. That's it. Have a nice day."

And they walked away. Didn't give him any names, dates, or other information about who was plotting to whack him. Just the fact that he was this close to getting his brains blown out. He knew they weren't bullshitting him. The moment Joe Moore said it, this big tough guy went completely white, shrunk about two feet, and melted like a marshmallow on the bumper of his Cadillac.

In the summer of 1991, Allie Shades and four members of his crew talked about taking a trip to Las Vegas. By now I understood Allie's patterns of movement pretty well, and this seemed like it could be a

promising lead. There was a chance the trip was related to ongoing de-
velopments in the carting industry. I contacted my boss, requesting authorization to follow the Brooklyn gangsters on their desert junket on
July 17, 1991.

But before I left New York, I called Las Vegas Metro police to see if
they could provide some assistance. I was just going out there with one
investigator, Tommy Freeman, from the Manhattan DA's office; we had
no guns, no cars, no cameras. Las Vegas said sure, they would help us.
They told us Allie had checked into the Mirage under the name Mc-
Coy. We wanted to keep this low-scale, but when I got out there and
checked into the Mirage myself, I realized that there'd been a leak and
it was a huge law enforcement operation now: The FBI, the Gaming
Commission, Las Vegas Metro—everybody was watching Allie.

All weekend, I hung out right behind Allie's poolside cabana. I saw
Allie meeting with Charlie Meyerson, this seventy-five-year-old,
white-haired Jewish gambler from Brooklyn. Now Meyerson was the
casino host at the Mirage, walking around all day comping high rollers
like Allie Shades and his crew. At one point, Allie and an unknown man
met in the middle of the pool, and Allie's crew in their bathing trunks
formed a circle around them like a splashing, water-treading buffer. But
that was the extent of it. That was the only suspicious moment the
whole weekend. The rest of the time Allie was just gambling and drinking and having a good time.

But just as we were checking out of the hotel, this Las Vegas Metro
cop came up to me and said, "Two of the guys with Allie are known
felons." He was talking about a couple of guys in Allie's crew: Carmine
Russo and Elio Albanese. Okay, by law felons are supposed to report to
the authorities in Las Vegas: It's an arrestable offense if they fail to do so.
I begged the guy not to lock them up. I even went to see his lieutenant.
He had on fancy cowboy boots and a silver belt buckle the size of a
New York City manhole cover and the Hoss Cartright ten-gallon hat
hanging on his coatrack. I'm from the city, and I'm trying to talk sense
to *this* guy? I told him, "You might expose some very sensitive inves-

tigative work that we have going on back in New York. Please don't do this. You're gonna raise 'em up."

The lieutenant didn't want to hear a word I was saying. "We helped you fellas out with manpower: I had a whole team of guys on Malangone twenty-four hours a day," he said. And then they went ahead and locked up Russo and Albanese for their nonsense misdemeanor. For failing to check in with the locals. As Allie and his crew arrived at the airport in their limo, Metro cops surrounded them and collared Russo and Albanese, making all kinds of derogatory anti-Italian remarks as they cuffed them: "You no-good guinea greaseballs—stay the hell in New York where you belong." One cop tried to ask "Mr. Malangone" for his cooperation, but Allie started screaming: "Hey, whaddaya mean, *cooperation*? I don't like that word! Don't use it with me again! If you have somethin' to say, *say* it!"

What's worse, these Metro cops had even called in the press to capture it all. As Allie and his boys were getting harassed and collared, an investigative reporter named George Knapp was there with his television cameras rolling. The next day it was the big headline in the Las Vegas papers:

MOBSTERS INVADE FROM NEW YORK
"DARK GLASSES" NEEDED AT MIRAGE POOL

It was insane. The articles referred to Allie Shades as the "number three" man in the Genovese crime family under Chin Gigante—and we all knew how the Chin *hated* to have his family dragged into the spotlight. The reporters speculated that Allie had come out to Las Vegas to mastermind some racket involving the disposal of Nevada's toxic waste.

Of course, when Allie got back to Brooklyn, he was livid, in a rip-roaring state. For several days on the Pastels bug, we could hear him reading aloud from the articles that were being faxed to him from Las Vegas. One of them referred to his crew as Murder Incorporated.

"I can't fuckin' believe what I'm readin' here," Allie barked. "Alphonso 'Allie Shades.' Fuckin' rat motherfuckers, can you believe this? 'Meetings at the pool.' You know this whole thing is, it's all bad on me. It's no fuckin' good."

He even picked up the telephone to call Charlie Meyerson at the Mirage Hotel.

"Charlie," he said, "sorry for your troubles. I just read these articles in the papers—I can't believe what they did to you and me. First of all, they said we had six rooms registered under McCoy. Whattaya talkin' about? Now they're bringing in all about the guys that you know—they got a whole half a page on *you*! I mean, they're fuckin' crazy. I swear to Christ. . . . It's heartbreaking. But you know what it is, Charlie? What you said: They saw nothin', they know we didn't do nothin'. So why are they puttin' them lies in the paper? What meetings did we have in the pool? Tell us what meeting! We had a meeting with you. If *you're* a fuckin' hot potato, then that's the meeting we had. Oh, I'm an *expert* on toxic waste!"

Listening to Allie rant, I was in stitches with all the other OCID detectives in our plant in Staten Island.

"Oh, I'm the 'Third Man,' I'm this, I'm that. They know they got nothin', they're just writing whatever they wanna write. Fuckin' meetings at the pool. You gotta see what they did to us on TV—they had it again today on TV. They got nothin' to do in that town but jerk off and fuck each other in the ass, and they wanna bother us?"

Now one of Allie's soldiers, Johnny "Geech" Giangrandi, pipes up with his creative suggestion. "But I wouldn't worry about going back," Johnny Geech said. "Fuck 'em. I'd go back with four or five guys. Check in with the cops and the news media and say: 'We're here. You wanna leave a reporter with us? He can come around with us. Teach you how to do the mambo like in that movie.' Remember that movie, when the FBI was doing the mambo? Unbelievable."

Luckily, Allie was blaming the whole mess on the FBI and the Vegas Metro cops; he had no clue that the NYPD might be involved.

"They're the worst motherfuckin' treacherous scum," he said. "The Feds and the Metro. *They* put us in the paper. Even the fuckin' headlines. 'Dark glasses are needed at the Mirage pool.' Oh, I'm 'Murder

Incorporated.' 'Visit by reputed mobsters probed.' Whattaya nuts? We went there to have a fuckin' good time! Motherfuckin' cocksuckers!"

As it turned out, the routine tipoff I'd made to Las Vegas Metro had far-reaching repercussions throughout Nevada and even beyond. Shortly after the arrests of Russo and Albanese, the *Las Vegas Review-Journal* named Charlie Meyerson as the Mirage employee who'd been socializing with Genovese crime family members, and the Nevada Gaming Control Board used that as a pretext to begin hearings into Meyerson's alleged ties to such organized-crime figures as former Genovese boss Anthony "Fat Tony" Salerno.

The hearings generated a lot of negative publicity for the Mirage Casino, but Meyerson was ultimately granted his "key employee" license on April 15, 1993—in effect, cleared by the board of any wrongdoing. The Mirage's owner, Steve Wynn, immediately launched his counterassault. He filed a $10-million lawsuit against Las Vegas Sheriff John Moran, the Las Vegas Metro Police Department, and individual officers of the Intelligence Bureau for "malicious, vindictive and retaliatory harassment." In the end, the civil suit was settled when Sheriff Moran offered a written apology, and Wynn dropped his request for damages.

The biggest loser in the messy affair was poor Allie Shades. Although he was never sanctioned by the Nevada authorities, New Jersey gaming regulators saw fit to add the name Alphonso Malangone to their socalled Black Book of undesirable characters. As a known gangster with a taste for games of chance, Allie Shades was banned forever from setting foot in Atlantic City casinos.

During the nearly two years on the Pastels Disco surveillance, we amassed plenty of evidence to collar Allie Shades on illegal bookmaking charges. But to most organized-crime investigators, and to wiseguys themselves, gambling cases are seen as little more than a nuisance. (Allie was previously convicted on gambling charges, but he'd been sentenced to serve his jail time on the weekends.) The real evidentiary breakthrough of the investigation, revealed on the Pastels bugs and the wiretaps of Malangone's cell phone, was the window into Allie Shades' powerful role as puppet master in the private sanitation industry. We overheard Allie explaining the property-rights code, laying out the rules of the massive—but invisible—criminal cartel. We surveilled Allie as he met with other key figures in the New York garbage rackets: with Brooklyn carting company owners; with Frank Allocca, a gray-haired World War II veteran and the president of the Genovese-controlled Kings County Trade Waste Association. On several occasions, Allie went on walk-and-talk meetings in front of the Bensonhurst social club of the Gambino family's garbage kingpin, the gruff, cigar-chomping *capo,* James "Jimmy Brown" Failla, who'd been the undisputed powerbroker in the carting industry since the downfall of Jimmy Squillante in the late 1950s.

Jimmy Brown and Allie Shades formed a perfect criminal partnership: They were extortionists extraordinaire. As the representatives of the two strongest Mob families in America, Allie Shades and Jimmy Brown (along with Jimmy's heir apparent, Joe Francolino) wielded a formidable economic whip over the New York metropolitan area. Rarely did they need to resort to something as crude as threats of violence. Simply by shutting down the orderly collection of garbage, they could cripple the densely populated metropolis in a matter of days.

Jimmy Brown and Allie Shades demonstrated this power, with stunning audacity, in December 1990, when the twenty-one hundred unionized drivers in the private sanitation industry began to grumble about going out on strike.

Local 813 of the International Brotherhood of Teamsters had been controlled by Bernard Adelstein—variously identified over the years as the union's president, secretary-treasurer, and business manager—since the early 1950s. Bernie Adelstein stood only five foot two and hobbled around on a prosthetic limb—his right leg was ripped off in the spokes of a wagon wheel in 1917, when Bernie was six years old—but he had a reputation for being pugnacious and bad-tempered. During the Mc-Clellan Committee hearings in 1957, Bernie Adelstein had taken such offense at being called a liar by Robert F. Kennedy that he lunged across the table at the startled young lawyer and had to be held down by another Senate staff member. Now well into his eighties, Bernie was one notorious, pint-sized Jewish labor boss. His roots in the rackets went back so far that he was connected to the Gambino family when it wasn't yet known as the Gambino family. Originally, under the regimes of bosses Vincent Mangano and Albert Anastasia, Adelstein had answered to garbage czar Jimmy Squillante. But following Squillante's mysterious disappearance—and presumed murder—in 1960, Adelstein's loyalty passed like a baton from one Jimmy to another, to the young frog-faced soldier Jimmy Brown Failla, trusted bodyguard and chauffeur of the family's new boss, Carlo Gambino. Failla and Adelstein would be co-conspirators for more than thirty years.

"Bernie Adelstein answers directly to Jimmy Brown," said Sammy "the Bull" Gravano, the highest-ranking mobster ever to flip, during his testimony in the federal murder trial of his former friend and boss John Gotti in 1991.

Under Adelstein's leadership, Teamsters Local 813 had frequently wreaked labor havoc on the city throughout the '50s, '60s, '70s, and '80s, calling strikes that often resulted in assaults, truck explosions, and gunfire, bringing normal life in the city to a halt. In 1981 the striking Teamsters had stopped all commercial trash collection for seventeen days, forcing then-mayor Ed Koch to declare a citywide health emergency.[3]

---

[3] Organized-crime experts now see these frequent strike actions as little more than a carefully orchestrated Mafia shell game. "They were all a ruse," says J. Bruce Mouw, former FBI supervisor of the Gambino Squad in New York and the man who led the team that took down Gotti. "When both the employees and employers are controlled by organized-crime families, how can it be a valid strike? The Teamsters walk out, the garbage piles up. They settle the strike and the union guys get more money. Then the carting company owners can go crying to the city, saying, 'We need higher rates so we can pay our union guys.' The city raises the rates the companies charge, and everybody gets screwed." [Interview with Douglas Century]

In December 1990, with the winter chill hanging in the air, Bernie Adelstein's Teamsters started grumbling again with various wage and benefit complaints. On December 10, unable to reach a settlement with management, the Teamsters' drivers stopped picking up the trash from the more than two hundred fifty thousand commercial establishments of New York City. Once again city officials faced a ticking time bomb: Each day the strike continued, an additional ten thousand tons of trash would accumulate, piling six feet high in places, blocking sidewalks, clogging restaurant entrances, burying fire hydrants. As with most carting industry strikes, the newspapers were soon filled with reports of citywide violence—firebombings, shootings, and assaults on any businessman reckless enough to enlist nonunionized men to remove the trash from his premises.

The December 12 edition of *The New York Times* warned that conditions in the city had changed drastically in the past decade: Unlike the 1981 strike, there were now increased numbers of homeless people tearing open the rubbish, scrounging for bottles and anything else of value. "In normal times, their pursuit can lead to a mess," *The Times* wrote. "During a strike, when torn garbage bags may sit indefinitely in the street, unsightliness gives way to health concerns." The pressure was clearly on David Dinkins, the first African-American mayor in the city's history, to negotiate a prompt settlement to the strike.

It was the third night of labor unrest, and I was in a car tailing Allie Shades as he and several crew members rode in Malangone's late-model Lexus from Bay Ridge, across the Brooklyn Bridge, into Lower Manhattan. Detectives in the plant were monitoring the intercept of Malangone's car phone conversations, as Allie's chauffeur, Rocky Cimato, circled around looking for an address on Church Street, near City Hall. Allie's Lexus stopped in front of 110 Church Street, the building that housed the Office of Municipal Labor Relations and the Office of Collective Bargaining. At approximately 8:30 P.M., preparing to enter 110

Church, Allie had the following conversation with an individual who was in close proximity to the mayor of New York:

> *Yes sir, ya need me, I'll come right up. Huh? Ya need me, I come right up. Who's that, Mayor Dinkins? Ask if he knows Jimmy Higgins. . . . All right, did you call that other guy? Yeah, he's with us. I'm right in front of Rocky. Yeah, I'm on the street. Does Dinkins—did ya ask if he knows Jimmy Higgins? Dinkins? Yeah, ask him.*[4]

Allie did go upstairs and the negotiation session was brief, lasting barely forty-five minutes. At 9:10 P.M., Detective Cathy Hart and I watched Allie and Jimmy Brown exiting 110 Church Street. Carmine Russo and Elio Albanese—later convicted as part of a violent Genovese bank-robbery team—stepped out of Allie's car to greet them. They showed Jimmy Brown the appropriate respect, kissing his fleshy cheeks.

We tailed Allie around Manhattan for the rest of the night. He and his crew went out for dinner, drove down to Il Molino restaurant on West Third Street—the heart of the Genovese territory in the West Village—then back uptown for a nightcap at the Columbus Café on Sixty-ninth Street, a joint frequented by movie stars like Robert De Niro. We were intercepting Allie's car phone, of course. First he called his wife, told her, "Yeah, we just caucused. We're going out to eat—we're very close to settling. They don't want nobody to go home until we settle." He said it was the mayor himself who didn't want anybody to go home yet.

Then Allie called up his associate Frank Allocca, his front man in the

---

[4] Malangone was boasting of his friendship with one of the most prominent police union officials in the city. Jimmy Higgins was at the time the Patrolmen's Benevolent Association's recording secretary and a member of its executive board. The relationship would be the subject of a January 27, 1997, *Daily News* investigative story ("PBA Secretary Is Probed in Series of Meetings: Cop Union Big & Mob Link Eyed") detailing allegations that Higgins met with Malangone at Pastels nightclub in Brooklyn at various times beginning in 1990. Higgins emerged from the controversy unscathed: In June 1999, he ran unsuccessfully for the presidency of the PBA, and continued his role as the union's recording secretary until his retirement.

garbage association. "Frank, get the men to go up and vote and accept this thing," he says. "Tell 'em, that's what they accept." We've got the pen registers[5] for Frank Allocca's phones, so we know that he called a couple of other company owners, Ray Polidori and Danny Todisco, spreading the word from Allie Shades and Jimmy Brown: Tell your men to accept the new terms.

Early the next morning, while Allie and the guys in his crew were still sweating off their hangovers, Local 813 meets at the Sheraton Hotel. The rank-and-file Teamsters voted overwhelmingly to accept the new terms. Simple as that: Contract ratified. Forty thousand tons of stinking trash gets hauled off the streets. And New York City is back in business: The sidewalks in front of Macy's and Bloomingdale's are swept clean just in time for the Christmas shopping rush.

Watching Allie and Jimmy Brown coming out of that meeting exchanging kisses, lighting up their cigars, that's when I fully realized how brazen these gangsters were. Later on in the case, when I was deep undercover in my role as Danny, this understanding would prove to be very helpful, when I needed some perspective on what I was up against—the overwhelming scope and power of the Mafia conspiracy. I'd been there to see it with my own eyes that cold night on Church Street.

Historically, in other areas and industries that the Mob controlled, they'd always try keep the illusion with a front man who was somewhat clean: Even out in Vegas in the freewheeling days of the Chicago Outfit, the Mob had professional-looking guys running the casinos for them. It didn't look right to have made guys standing front-and-center doing the talking. But New York's billion-dollar-a-year garbage racket was so corrupt—everybody knew it had been corrupt for generations—why should they even bother with appearances? They could send their top-notch wiseguys—guys with *nicknames*—to sit down and do their collective bargaining right in the shadow of City Hall.

Allie was in such high spirits when he left the meeting with Jimmy

---

[5] A pen register is a court-authorized electronic device that records all numbers dialed from a particular phone line.

Brown. He was smiling ear to ear. And why wouldn't he be? It was a pretty good night's work for a guy who hadn't changed since high school—a guy who was still "a hoodlum and a gangster." This was no small-time Brooklyn extortion game. Allie Shades and Jimmy Brown had just pulled off one of the slickest shakedowns in American history. They'd just dragged the mayor of the greatest city in the world to the bargaining table by his balls.

4 | THE BOYS

Becoming Danny: That became my mission. Beginning in the summer of 1992, I devoted nearly all my tour—and plenty of off-duty hours—to getting inside the skin of a young paper-packing executive from a large Italian-American family named Benedetto. Each morning I left the condominium in Staten Island where I lived with my wife, Claire, crossed the Verrazano Narrows Bridge into Brooklyn, passed through Bay Ridge—Allie Shades country—until I came to the concrete anchorage of the Manhattan Bridge.

The first morning I reported to work, Sal led me around the transfer station, introduced me to the union guys as Cousin Danny—one of the Staten Island crowd. I nodded, making the rounds, shaking all those work-gloved hands.

"How you doin'? Yeah, I was with Dom Ben, but now I'm gonna be working down here."

Dom Ben Realty, named for Sal's grandfather Dominic Benedetto, was the family's real estate and property-management company; owner of several prominent Manhattan skyscrapers. Though the recycling and real-estate concerns were technically under one corporate umbrella, the Dom Ben and Chambers employees had no daily contact with one another.

"Danny's gonna be with us, helping out more," Sal said. "He's gonna be straightening out some beefs. I'm getting too old: My heart can't take this crazy shit no more. . . ."

Sal decided that, of all the Chambers working men, only two guys should be in on our secret: John Glenn and Johnny Tuzzio. John Glenn was in on it from the start: He'd been there that morning when Ramos came down and threatened us. Over the course of our investigation, I got to know John Glenn really well. We worked together on a daily basis. He was as trustworthy a man as I've ever met. His daughter was a police officer up in the Bronx. All the Chambers employees were real hardworking union guys, getting up before dawn, putting in long hours in the freezing cold of winter, and in the transfer station there's always these giant mangy water rats, running all over the place. I mean, it's not a glamorous business.

Johnny Tuzzio was one of the great old-timers of the industry. He'd been with Chambers since the 1930s, gone off to fight in "the Big One" (as he put it) at Anzio and throughout Europe, came back to the Plymouth Street warehouse, and only recently retired at the age of seventy. Johnny Tuzzio looked like a typical Italian grandfather from Bensonhurst, wore his baggy pants cinched high over his belly and his plaid workshirt buttoned to the top button. He'd known all the younger generation Benedettos since they were toddlers. He was also well known to a lot of the key players in the paper business; down the road, powerful executives like Angelo Ponte could be counted on to start asking casual-sounding questions of Johnny Tuzzio: *How long have you known this*

Cousin Dan? Sal realized there was no point even trying to bullshit old Johnny—it was much safer to tell him that I was an NYPD detective who was coming into the business undercover, and swear Johnny to secrecy.

The first night I ventured out to an industry function in my undercover role, Sal brought me along with Johnny Tuzzio to a meeting at Ponte's Steakhouse in TriBeCa. That's when he tipped Johnny about the investigation. He said, "Johnny, Dan Benedetto's going to be attending the meeting at Ponte's with us tonight."

"Dan *who?* There's no Dan Benedetto."

"Johnny," Sal said, "tonight there's a Dan Benedetto, okay?"

On my first day at work, touring that cavernous warehouse, I got a bizarre but reassuring vote of confidence from one of the workmen. Gene Fulp, the gray-haired forklift driver and foreman, came over and slapped me hard on shoulder.

"Shit, I remember you when you were *this* high," Gene said, holding his hand at mid-thigh. "I remember you as a kid, Danny. You know something? You still look the *same.* You ain't changed one bit. I used to chase your ass—remember when you and your brother used to run around the warehouse, playing in the bales?"

"Sure, Gene," I said. "How could I forget?"

When we were alone in his office, Sal warned me that if I was going to try to meet and haggle with these garbage gangsters on their own turf, I'd have to start doing some serious homework. Bullshitting was only going to take me so far.

Thinking on my feet with a guy pointing a gun at me, that wasn't the hard part. I'd been in that situation before and I was confident I could talk my way out—or do whatever had to be done. Doing buy-and-bust work in Narcotics for three years teaches you to get yourself out of jams. Sure, a couple of times I had to come to blows with the other guy. But this was different. I wasn't going to be some Harley-riding outlaw biker trying to buy heroin on the Lower East Side. I was now supposed to be an executive in a thirty-person company that was part of a complex billion-dollar industry—an industry that affected every segment of business life in New York City. The garbage aspect alone was complicated enough, but the paper-recycling end had me buried.

All that first summer and into the fall, I tried to learn the nuts and bolts of the business, because I knew Sal was right: Sooner or later, I was going to have to fend for myself in conversations with corrupt carters and wiseguys who were born and raised in garbage, who'd lapped up these details with their mother's milk. I started reading *The Trade Waste News* and *The Paper Stock Report,* trying to educate myself about the jargon and trends of the industry.

He might not have been the most articulate of teachers, but Sal was certainly an expert in the paper-and-pulp trade. He liked to show off the family's collection of black-and-white photos of the horse-drawn D. Benedetto, Inc. carts down on Cherry Street, telling stories about the rag- and paper-pickers on the crowded Lower East Side.

"Sure, we was all down there together—the rag and the paper and the scrap-metal guys. Rags—that was all Jews. Same with scrap metal. Paper was pretty much all Italians. All the *paisans* wrote home and said, 'Cousin, come to New York, I'm in the paper business now.' "

Before the Italian immigrants like Sal's grandfather got into paper-packing, the post–Civil War industry had been dominated by the Irish. But recycling went way back before that, Sal told me, back to the Colonial era. Even before the signing of the Declaration of Independence, the patriots had been recycling their rags and scraps.

Over the weeks and months, I started soaking up Sal's rapid-fire paper talk: "Yeah, y'know—ya got mixed-office waste, ya got newsprint, ya got corrugated cardboard, ya got computer printout, ya got white ledger." Pristine envelope-cuttings still fetched the top dollar, but nobody saw those too much anymore.

Much of the paper used in America today, Sal called PC—meaning "post-consumer"—newspapers and magazines, tissue paper, pizza cartons, breakfast-cereal boxes, take-out coffee cups. Chambers had fleets of tractor-trailers rumbling down Plymouth Street every day, leaving for paper mills in Canada, heading out across the continental United States, shipping out to far-flung ports in Europe and Asia. "Japan buys a lot of our paper," Sal said. "They don't have any forests over there—they need a cardboard box to put the VCR in, don't they?" The freighters sailed into New York laden with brand-new VCRs, and sailed back to Japan with their containers jammed with secondhand cardboard.

Now I'm supposed to be a manager in the company, and that means I have to keep abreast of the changing price per ton for all these different types of paper: If a product gets hot suddenly, the price the Benedettos pay at the door can fluctuate wildly. I have to know what to offer other carters for their paper—whether to pay a customer $8 or $20 or $140 a ton, depending on what kind of paper they're bringing in and what condition it's in. Sal always told me that we came from a proud clan, that the Benedettos had always been known across the United States as fair businessmen.

"So if the stuff's comin' in clean, Danny, we gotta pay 'em top dollar."

"This is fuckin' complicated, Sal."

"Sure it is. Now you understand why the boys stayed out!" Sally let out one of his patented belly laughs.

Your typical garbage guy, he told me, gets up early in the morning, but not *too* early—just early enough to get his trucks rolling along the collection routes. Around noon he meets with the other boys, bullshits for an hour or so, grabs some pasta fagiolo and espresso, then it's out to the track. After the ponies, they go back to the club, play some poker, bet a few thousand bucks, bullshit some more, eat some cannoli and sip some more espresso, call it a day. Three hours of work and six hours of play—not a bad racket, right?

Now, the paper business—that's a different story. You have to get up *earlier* in the morning—4 A.M., maybe 4:30. You pick up your paper, sort it, and bale it. And *then* you try to sell it. The real trick is, even though you've agreed to pay a fixed price for your customers' old paper, you never know what you're getting for that same paper until it's sold. It's no different than a farmer going to market: At the end of the day you don't know what you're getting until you've got it.

This was far too much work for "the boys," as Sal called the Mob-connected carters. That's why they stuck to the collection end of it. With collection there's nothing to understand except trucks. And the boys understood trucks real good.

There was one other area of research I had to nail down: the Benedetto family history. I had a notepad with a full diagram of the family tree, spent hours practicing, getting Sal to quiz me about how I was related to this or that cousin and uncle. It was going to be a tricky bluff, because not only had cagey gangsters like Tommy Masotto and Sal Avellino gone to boarding school with Sal in Long Island, but there were other big-time players in the industry who'd known the family from its days on the Lower East Side.

The Benedettos had come over from a tiny village in Southern Italy called Craco, southeast of Naples, in Basilicata, a poor desert region right on the sole of the Italian boot. I found photographs of Basilicata in the library: It looked like the scenes in *The Godfather* when Michael Corleone is on the lam in Sicily, a barren landscape with sunburnt peasants and wine barrels and donkeys. The families of several powerful carters, the Pontes, Vitales, and Gioves, also came from this obscure little town of Craco, and if I crossed paths with them—which I surely would—I'd be grilled by *paisans* about "the old country" and the trivia of Benedetto family history.

After a few intense weeks of study, it got to a point where I really did know all the Benedettos by heart—knew all my first and second cousins.

But I still felt pretty unsettled about the guy Sal had chosen for Danny's father. It didn't make sense—this deceased John Benedetto was much too old to be my dad. John would've had to be nearly sixty years old when I was born in 1957.

I don't know how many times I complained about it. "Sal, come on, let's think this through a bit better—let's figure out a different dad." But Sal kept brushing it off. This was the best damn story he could come up with. And anyway, what difference did it make whose kid Danny was supposed to be?

Sal and I settled into a routine: Every morning around ten, we'd head out for coffee in Brooklyn Heights, have a general paper-industry-lesson, girl-watching, all-around-bullshit session. One of those summer mornings we came strolling back along cobbled Plymouth Street, sipping from cups of steaming deli coffee, and I said, "This place looks like something out of an old movie, Sally. The way the light hits—the whole block's got that look like Old Gotham."

He grinned at me. "Aw, c'mon. You know how many movies we shot here? You ever see *Once Upon a Time in America*? Sergio Leone?"

For his gangland epic, the Italian filmmaker had changed every streetlight along Plymouth Street, turning the clock back to the 1920s. Leone shot a scene of a fat bootlegger pulling into the Chambers loading dock in an old Model T Ford, walking right through those towering paper bales. Johnny Tuzzio, in his buttoned-up workshirt and suspenders, even made small talk with Leone and his all-Italian film crew. None of the visitors spoke English and Johnny was the only guy in Chambers who knew fluent Italian.

Sal rattled off the list of actors who'd used the family premises as a stage set since the late 1940s: Jimmy Cagney. Lee Van Cleef. Peter Falk. Al Pacino.

"We shot a bunch of *Naked City* too—remember *Naked City*?"

"Kinda before my time, Sal."

"Oh, sure. Eight million stories in the naked city."

It sometimes seemed like we had eight million stories just inside that massive warehouse. Chambers had over a hundred tenants in the building; upstairs were huge loft apartments, mostly rented out to artists. By now I'd set up shop in a little dive of an apartment on the third floor, just a little windowless studio without any phone service. But it was

pretty quiet and I could sit at my police department Selectric in seclu-
sion and type up my daily DD5s.[1]

The artist tenants had turned the upper floors into free gallery space,
their murals and brightly painted doors and fifty-foot-long canvases left
on display in different hallways. I had to laugh when Sal told me that
some of those bizarre-looking canvases with bits of thrown-away fabric
and broken glass stuck to them were selling in Manhattan art galleries
for big money—tens of thousands each. Downstairs there was tons of
rubbish heading out for Pennsylvania landfill, and upstairs there was art-
work bound for the apartments of Manhattan millionaires.

It took some getting used to, but after a while I loved coming to
Chambers every morning. As the case went forward I really did work
there full-time as the manager for more than two years. I'd tally up scale-
house loads, issue dump tickets, send tractor trailers out on the highway,
see that stops were picked up.

And I formed close friendships with the working guys, John Glenn,
Gene Fulp, Johnny Forklift. A bunch of great guys. The only part of the
job I never got used to was the rats. I was always leery of walking in certain parts of the warehouse. They were swarming all over the place—at
face level, too. Picture this: You're walking down a dark corridor of paper bales, corrugated cardboard, white office paper, all stacked twenty
feet high—a giant maze of paper bales, with no end in sight—and
there, at face level, you see these large, well-fed, filthy rats, burrowing
in, making homes, looking for a scrap of pizza cheese or an Oh Henry!
wrapper stuck to paper. It was unnerving.

One morning, I find myself deep in the maze, midway down the
main corridor, when I confront a mangy river rat on the floor. The
thing has bald spots all over him—he's either shedding or dying—and
he's the size of a small cat. He's staring up at me, so I stomp my foot.

---

[1] The Complaint Follow-up Informational—originally known as Detective Division
form number 5—is the primary document in any continuing NYPD investigation. In a
complex investigation DD5s are generated in foot-high stacks. In cop jargon, they're
also known as Fives.

But the rat doesn't run: He actually makes a move to come at me. I jump right over the rat and keep running—my best forty-yard dash—and when I turn around I see that the rat's hauling ass right after me. I let out this wild yell and keep sprinting, and then at the next turn, I run into Gene Fulp on the forklift. Big Gene—who swears he's known me since I was a kid—almost flattens me. He's been there so long—all the working guys have—that these giant water rats don't faze them one bit. But how does this look? Here I'm supposed to be half a tough guy, ready to fearlessly negotiate with gangsters, and a goddamn rat is chasing me around the warehouse and making me scream like a little girl. Gene Fulp nearly pisses himself laughing.

"Danny, you ain't never changed—you was always a jumpy kid!"

As the shop manager, rats were not my only concern. I had constant brushfires to put out. The worst were the film crews that were always taking over Plymouth Street. In the course of the undercover investigation, we must have had a dozen different movie productions in the street or in the warehouse.

These crews have to get a permit from City Hall, and since they're paying New York City handsomely, they assume they have free rein. They think they can take over whole neighborhoods and shut down traffic for blocks. They'd start shooting before sunup and go until the early afternoon. Sal had his own strategy for dealing with them. If they blocked the bay doors so our trucks couldn't dump, Sal used to threaten to pick up their equipment with the forklift and move it off the block. This was against the law, of course, but it usually did the trick.

It's so tight down there, on Anchorage and Plymouth, right under the Manhattan Bridge, that if you block one street, no one can get around: The old narrow streets become gridlocked and you shut our whole business down. If it goes on for a few hours, it's costing us a fortune.

One morning, first thing when I get to Chambers, I saw that we had garbage trucks and tractor-trailers snarled for blocks. The whole neighborhood was gridlocked. All these out-of-town truckers were stuck on the little cobbled side streets, wailing on their horns. To a long-haul trucker, making good time is everything; these guys are trying to make it up to paper mills in Canada today, they're ready to hit the highway, but the arrogant film yuppies are blocking our bay doors.

John Glenn rushed right out to the film crew—all these snot-nosed kids holding metal clipboards and sipping cappuccino in take-out cups. "Hey, you're blocking our bay! I got long-haul trucks—don't you see all these guys complaining?" These yuppies blew John off.

"Sal's gonna be here any minute—let's just wait for Sal," I told John.

"Yeah, Sal's gonna show 'em what's what."

By now the whole neighborhood was shut down. When Sal got to work, he was furious and went out there to complain to one of these yuppies. I watched them arguing for about ten minutes, the director waving his official permit in Sal's face.

But for some reason Sal wasn't on top of his game that morning. He'd lost his edge. He walked away, exasperated and defeated.

I was standing there, steaming, thinking, *The nerve of this guy—he sees what he's doing to our business. Would it kill him to move his truck up a bit?* I looked at John Glenn. "Just follow my lead. Follow everything I say. If this guy doesn't listen to me, I'm gonna tell you to get the forklift. Pull it around and put the fork under his pickup. You know the routine."

"Yeah, Dan."

We walked over to raise hell, but this one flunky was blocking our path. The kid was about twenty-nine, artsy-looking, wearing a long overcoat with some ridiculous little beanie on his head. I told him I want to see the man in charge.

"He's busy right now—he can't talk to you."

"He'd better come out or there's gonna be a problem here. I'll tell you what, if you don't get him out here, you're gonna be responsible for what happens."

That got his attention. The flunky huffed and puffed and then went inside this white trailer, a ministudio on wheels, to get the Grand Pooh-Bah. What a pompous ass.

"Who *are* you?"

"Who am I? I'm Dan Benedetto. I *own* this company," I told him. "I

heard all about your permit and all that fuckin' bullshit. It don't give you
the right to hurt *my* business. You got two minutes to move this truck
or you'll be fishing it outta the East River! John, go get the forklift!
Now!" John Glenn marches off. The big-shot director threatened to call
the cops on me. I stared right back at him. "You got two minutes. You
think I'm fuckin' around, asshole?"

Before long, John pulled around the corner on the forklift, and he
was just about to lift the pickup filled with expensive cameras and
equipment and take it the hundred feet to the edge of the East River
when the director caved. He not only moved the pickup truck up fifteen feet, he moved it clear off our block.

This hump had no idea how *lucky* he was. He had to be from someplace where they didn't know about the garbage industry in New York.
It just so happened that all those long-haul truckers we had backed up
around the block were legit companies from Canada and upstate New
York. If they'd been Brooklyn truckers, mobbed-up carting companies,
they would not have been yelling and honking their horns. In a heartbeat, the director would've got his clock cleaned.

A few months later it got even worse. We actually had all these California types commandeering our office. Sal had agreed to rent out the
Chambers warehouse to a TV show called *New York Undercover*. The rest
of the Benedettos were accustomed to having film crews take over the
offices for a few days' shooting. To me it was a royal pain in the ass. The
actors and cameramen were decent enough, but all these low-level
helpers had no respect at all. They'd get on the Chambers phones, calling out to California for hours. They'd leave their knapsacks all over the
office, piles of clothes on every chair, plates of smelly Chinese food and
cold coffee. It was one thing to disrupt the Benedettos' recycling business, but it was *another* to disrupt a secret NYPD organized-crime investigation. Every day I was trying to record conversations with other
mobbed-up carters, and these kids are tying up every telephone, talking
nonsense.

Sal told me to calm down, to try to be cooperative. We went up to the third floor to gorge ourselves at the on-site caterers' table. Sal had given them a room for a whole big spread. But when I came back down I blew my stack. I heard this one ponytailed kid gabbing on my phone, leaning back in his chair with his feet on my cousin's desk, using expressions like *totally awesome, dude*—all that lingo that I can't stand.

Something snapped: I went back to my days as a Brooklyn beat cop. "That's it, pal. Get off the fuckin' phone, get your fuckin' feet off my cousin's desk—and while you're at it, get the fuck outta my office! That's it—off limits!" I hung up his phone, grabbed all his belongings and tossed them on the floor. "Take your knapsacks and your shit with you. You're *through!*"

I nearly choked when Sal told me what these guys were shooting. He'd got a glance at one of the scripts lying around. The *New York Undercover* episode was about an NYPD detective trying to infiltrate the Mob through the garbage unions.

Even as I was putting long tours in at the Chambers warehouse, trying to perfect my undercover identity, I was still the case officer on the investigation, which made me responsible for overseeing ongoing wiretap and cell-phone interceptions. Sal's beef with Phil Barretti over One Wall Street was still simmering, ready to explode again at any time, and I'd worked with ADA Marybeth Richroath to receive authorization from a judge for us to wiretap Barretti's business and personal phones. The DA could already have indicted Barretti on charges of assault and arson, and they had a strong racketeering case that Barretti was trying to exercise his property rights, an antitrust charge under the Organized Crime Control Act—New York State's version of the federal RICO statutes. With the court-ordered wiretaps on Barretti's phones, we hoped to cast an even wider investigative net.

From June until November 1992, I was running myself ragged, splitting my time between Chambers Paper Fibres in Brooklyn and our Staten Island plant—a nondescript apartment rented out by the NYPD and converted into a confidential eavesdropping post—where, night and

day, we had a team of detectives up on Phil Barretti's phones. Gradu-
ally we were gathering solid evidence that Barretti Carting Corporation
was engaged in an assortment of crimes: Illegal dumping of hazardous
waste, coercion, threatening its customers with violence. We'd hear various Barretti executives—sometimes Phil himself—screaming into the
receiver: "Where you gonna go? Who you gonna get? No one's gonna
service you!" We heard Barretti's son chuckling, talking about sending
one of his goons to deal with a difficult customer.

"Hey, why send a poodle when you can send a *pit bull*?"

The Barrettis weren't muscling street characters, either. They'd be on
the phone with high-placed executives of major corporations, Citibank,
Chase Manhattan, American Express: big shots with Ivy League degrees
and Brooks Brothers suits, Fortune 500 executives who were being
gouged for their garbage rates. And they had no choice but to take this
abuse from pinky ring–wearing, cigar-chomping garbage gangsters.
Every single executive was too intimidated to talk back to Barretti or
call the cops. Every single one of them was well aware that, going back
nearly a half-century, the garbage business in New York City had been
run by these crooks. The garbage gangsters could threaten with complete confidence: *Cocksucker, where you gonna go, huh?* Because there was
nowhere to go. Everyone was trapped.

It was during the Barretti eavesdropping that we noticed Phil getting
regular calls from the Greater New York Waste Paper Association, or
WPA, on Canal Street in Manhattan—Vincent "Chin" Gigante's paper
club. In fact, it was the Chin's driver and trusted aide, Vito "Bruce"
Palmeri, who did most of the calling. Palmeri was under the Chin for
many years. We surveilled him walking the Chin around the Village,
when the Don was pulling his crazy act and Vito Palmeri was right
there with him, opening doors and holding umbrellas. Formally, Vito
Palmeri was listed as the business agent of the WPA, but really he was a
bagman for the Chin, getting off-the-books cash payments to bring
straight to Gigante. He'd call up Phil every month around the same

time, using veiled language: "Phil, I need to get that, uh, thing, y'know, so I'll be swinging by."

"Okay, I'll leave it in the drawer," Phil would say. We learned that Barretti was leaving two or three grand in envelopes for Vito Palmeri to pick up.

Then something unusual happened: We started overhearing these calls from a guy named Frank at the Waste Paper Association. His voice sounded young, but he talked with a lot of authority. He was very confident. A routine beef had arisen involving this discount department store called Conway in Manhattan, and three different carters were putting in bids for the garbage account. Their method this time was their usual Mob–style collusion: Put the account out for bids, try to make the bids look competitive, but the guy who "owned" the stop would always come in a little bit lower than the other bids and keep his customer.

This Conway bid process got all screwed up—there was a bump in the road, and somehow Barretti lost his stop. Barretti wasted no time in calling the "winning" carter up and threatening him, ranting and raving. This new carter took the beef to young Frank at the Waste Paper Association. Now, with young Frank on the line, suddenly the Phil Barretti Express came screeching to a halt.

"*Wait a fuckin' minute,*" Frank tells him, "Did *I* say that, Phil? Who the fuck are you talkin' to? Did Lenny say that I said that, Phil?" Barretti's a big multimillionaire thug that everybody in the industry is petrified of, and here's some young kid who's got Phil stammering, coughing, sounding like he's shitting his pants. "Listen, Phil, don't *ever* put words in my mouth again."

"Okay, okay," Phil says. "Take it easy, *champeen.*"

We were sitting there in the Staten Island plant, monitoring this conversation. It was Tony Maz, Kevin Dunleavy, Joe Lentini, and myself, all saying, *What the hell just happened here?* Nobody could believe it. Who was this kid Frankie from the Association? This was an industry dominated by old men, a bunch of crusty old World War II–generation guys like Jimmy Brown and Angelo Ponte; where the hell did this kid come from? We didn't even have his last name. He was always just "Frank from the Association."

But we put two and two together, started to draw some conclusions about Frank. Obviously he wasn't just some up-and-coming street thug. This guy had clout—he'd been put in a trusted position, cracking the discipline on a billion-dollar industry. We could tell that he was sharp and extremely careful, said next to nothing over the phone. We didn't have a last name or face, but we knew one thing for sure: We had a very well-schooled young gangster on our hands.

We weren't able to put a face to the young gangster until December 1992, when Chambers Paper Fibres, through its Bronx-based subsidiary, Paper Fibres Corporation, began servicing a Weber's department store located on West Thirty-second Street in Manhattan. Almost immediately Peter Porri, president of Porri Waste Removers, Inc.—the previous carter at the Weber's store—called up the Paper Fibres manager, Ralph Coppola, demanding his stop back.

On December 12, 1992, the middle-aged, trench-coat–clad Porri appeared in person, unannounced, at the Paper Fibres transfer station in the Bronx, accompanied by a muscular, swarthy young man, approximately twenty-nine years old, who identified himself only as Frank from the Waste Paper Association. Frank's manner was surly and aggressive; he stood extremely close to Ralph Coppola and poked his finger at his chest.

"What local do youse guys have here?"

"Local 970."

"Whatta youse think you're doing robbin' one of my members? Youse are outlaws—you can't just go in and rob one of my members. I want this straightened out right away. Here's two numbers where you can reach me."

We had teams of OCID detectives now surveilling the Waste Paper Association on Canal Street; we'd see the Chin's driver, Vito Palmeri, and the Chin's son, Vinnie Esposito, showing up regularly. (Vincent Gigante kept two residences, one in the West Village and one on the Upper East Side, one for his wife and one for his mistress. Both women, coincidentally, were named Olympia. Vinnie Esposito was the son of Olympia Esposito on East Seventy-seventh Street). Our team observed the comings and goings of Angelo Ponte, the pint-sized mogul and man-about-Manhattan, whose family real estate company, Ponte Equities, owned the building that housed the Waste Paper Association. One of Ponte's cluster of garbage and recycling companies was headquartered there too. And then, sure enough, the team spotted and photographed a young man who matched the description Ralph Coppola had given. *Olive-complected, mid-twenties, five eight, muscular build, thick black hair swept back.* He left the Association in a blue Buick, a car registered to Laborers' Local 958. One evening we put two organized-crime detectives in patrolman's uniforms and they performed a routine traffic stop. The impatient driver handed them a New York State license that said FRANK GIOVINCO.

Now it made sense. Frank Giovinco turned out to be the nephew of a Genovese associate named Joe "Joey Carpets" Giovinco, owner of an auto-body shop in Queens and a member in the crew of Frederico "Fritzie" Giovanelli—a notorious sixty-eight-year-old Genovese *caporegime* who'd been tried, and acquitted, three times of murdering thirty-four-year-old OCID detective Anthony J. Venditti.[2]

Young Frank had grown up on Long Island near the Queens border,

---

[2] On January 21, 1986, Detective Venditti and his partner, Detective Kathleen Burke, were on surveillance duty at Castillo's Restaurant in Ridgewood, Queens, when Venditti was shot four times in the parking lot and killed. Fritzie Giovanelli and two other Genovese gangsters pleaded self-defense in the murder, claiming they thought Venditti was a criminal who'd been sent to kill them. Giovanelli's two previous trials for the murder ended in deadlocked juries. Prosecuting a sweeping RICO case, U.S. Attorney Rudolph Giuliani won a homicide conviction against Giovanelli, but the murder portion of the charges was overturned on appeal. In 1994, Giovanelli was finally acquitted in his fourth trial for the same murder. No one has ever been convicted in the homicide of Detective Venditti.

where he'd been an all-state high school football player. He didn't have anything major on his rap sheet—in his early twenties he'd been hooked up with an organized-crime crew on Long Island and had taken a routine collar for possessing stolen property. He'd risen quickly, becoming an organizer for the Genovese-controlled laborers' union, LIUNA.

LIUNA Local 958 was run by Greg McCarthy, son of Jack McCarthy, described by a U.S. Senate panel in 1967 as one of New York's leading racketeers. The older McCarthy had been jailed four times for union corruption. Although officially Greg McCarthy was the boss, Local 958 was firmly in the pocket of Vincent "Chin" Gigante. Just as the Gambino crime family had long controlled Teamsters Local 813 through Bernie Adelstein, the Chin owned LIUNA Local 958 through the McCarthys. Of course, the wily Gigante would not entrust some young hothead with a position as labor organizer: Young Frankie Giovinco was definitely on the fast track to power.

One night shortly after Ralph Coppola was threatened in the Bronx, Sal Benedetto attended a business meeting at Ponte's Steakhouse and was approached at the bar by Frank Giovinco. "Sal, remember me from 958?" Giovinco said. "I'm with the West Side now. It'd be really beneficial for you to join." Sal hemmed and hawed, his noncommittal Sally Skates routine, telling Frank: "I'm late for a meeting . . . I'll think about it . . . I gotta go . . ."

Sal understood very well the message Frank Giovinco was sending. By using the code words *West Side,* Giovinco was referring to the Genovese crime family. Rarely do New York wiseguys—from any of the five families—utter the name Genovese. They generally refer to America's most powerful crime family as the West Side. Since the days of Vito Genovese and Anthony "Tony Bender" Strollo right through to Vincent Gigante, the West Village has belonged to the Genovese crime family. For decades the nondescript, black-painted Triangle Social Club, located on Sullivan Street, was the family's power base, and many nights, the Chin himself could be seen stumbling along Bleecker Street in his slippers and bathrobe after a long night playing cards with *capo*s and soldiers in the Triangle.

It's only a short walk farther down the West Side to Canal Street, where the Chin kept another club, his "paper club"—the Greater New York Waste Paper Association—where he'd placed his handpicked representatives, his son Vincent Esposito, driver Vito Palmeri, young Frankie Giovinco, and that little multimillionaire named Ponte.

Angelo Ponte was the Great Gatsby of garbage—an enigma in jeweled cuff links and hand-tailored suits. For twenty-five years Ponte had walked the delicate tightrope of his double life: As a philanthropic business executive and popular restaurateur, and as a secret power of the underworld, described in 1984 eyewitness testimony before the Senate Select Committee on Crime as a well-shadowed New York mobster.[3]

Born on the Lower East Side in 1925, Ponte was paunchy and squat, no taller than five foot five, sporting black wire-rimmed spectacles and a well-groomed goatee—its whiskers a blend of snow white, iron gray and jet black—that gave his face the thoughtful appearance of a university professor. But there was no moth-eaten cardigan and pipe; Angelo favored Italian double-breasted suits, French-cuff shirts, and fine cigars.

Ponte operated the largest carting company in New York, V. Ponte and Sons, started by his father, Vincent—by all accounts, an honest, hardworking Italian immigrant—with a single wooden-wheeled pushcart on the Lower East Side in 1909. Eighty years later Angelo had built an impressive clientele: He picked up the trash from the Empire State Building, General Motors, Saks Fifth Avenue, *Forbes* magazine, the United Nations, Giants Stadium, the Waldorf-Astoria, Chemical Bank, and the United States Postal Service. Ponte owned a paper mill in New Jersey. He divided his time between a palatial estate in Alpine, New Jersey, and another multimillion-dollar home in an exclusive Fort Lauderdale community, where he often jetted away to sail around the Caribbean in his yacht, the *Maria Antonia*.

Ponte Equities, his family's real estate company, had the foresight to ac-

---

[3] See *Newsday*, February 20, 1986, "The Group Linked to the Deal"

quire nearly forty properties near the Hudson River north of the Financial District, when the neighborhood was still gritty, unfashionable, and nameless—did anyone actually use the term lower West Side?—before some clever realtor dreamt up the acronym TriBeCa (Triangle Below Canal), before the arrival of famous residents like Robert De Niro and John F. Kennedy, Jr. Ponte's presence in the neighborhood was so dominant that a *Daily News* story once dubbed him "the Baron of TriBeCa." Decades before De Niro launched his star-studded restaurants, TriBeCa Grill and Nobu, Angelo and his restaurateur brother, Joe, were luring crooners, shortstops, middleweight champs, and diverse politicians down to the jewel in the family crown: Ponte's Steakhouse on Debrosses Street.

Ponte's was a sprawling, two-story, candlelit eatery inside the historic Longshoreman's Hotel building, done in red velvet and dark-stained wood, where the veal scaloppini was accompanied by a mandolin serenade and a peppermill the size of a Louisville Slugger. On the wood paneling hung Ponte's personal hall of fame, autographed photos of Frank Sinatra and Tony Bennett, Jackie Robinson and Joe DiMaggio. One particularly striking shot captured Angelo and his clean-shaven brother, Joe, mugging it up in the arms of Muhammad Ali: "The Greatest" glancing down, smiling, as Angelo and Joe showed him their fists adorned with pinky rings.

There were also plaques and framed certificates that trumpeted Angelo Ponte's many honors and connections to the New York political establishment. Mayor Abe Beame had named him an Honorary Sanitation Commissioner back in the '70s. He was a prominent member of Cardinal O'Connor's Committee of the Laity, which led to the Vatican naming Ponte a Knight of Malta, the highest honor a layman can receive within the Roman Catholic Church; membership in the secret society, which dates back to the time of the Crusades, put Ponte in the company of men like former CIA director William Casey, Senator Pete Dominici, General Alexander Haig, William F. Buckley, and Lee Iacocca.

Angelo had been one of the founders of CopShot, a program offering cash rewards to citizens who phone in tips in unsolved police shootings. He'd donated one hundred thousand dollars to the New York Public

Library system; and in 1991, the U.S. military had formally thanked Angelo for donating the trucks that cleaned up the ticker-tape parade when the Gulf War veterans rode through the Canyon of Heroes.

But sitting there enjoying the Chianti and Neapolitan love songs, a casual visitor to Ponte's might never suspect that, according to organized-crime investigators—both FBI and NYPD, whose intelligence on such matters did not always agree—Angelo had long-standing connections to the country's most powerful Mafia family.[4]

A lot of times people get caught up in those Mafia myths about "made guys" and "button men" that Hollywood has sold them. Of course, it's always been true that Italian crime families have a hierarchy. That all goes back to the days of Maranzano, who was obsessed with Roman history, who took a loose gang structure and modeled it after the Roman army, with a pyramid of ranks and a chain of command. At the top is the boss, then his underboss, *consiglieri,* and the *capodecini,* or captains of ten. Under the skippers, you have the crew of soldiers—also known as button men, wiseguys, goodfellas, *amici nostri*—"friends of ours." And below them come the associates, or connected guys—on the street you'll use the phrase *half-a-hood* or *half-assed wiseguy.*

In recent years the Gambino and Genovese families have hovered between 20 and 25 skippers with a total family size of 260 to 300 soldiers, and then there are as many as 2,000 associates. Most of the associates are subordinates of wiseguys, but not always. Some guys who aren't officially made are just as powerful—more powerful, even—than guys who are straightened out, because of their particular area of business or criminal expertise. Guys who are major earners throw around a lot of weight on the street.

---

[4] "Ponte was on our charts as a Genovese associate," says Brian F. Taylor, retired FBI Special Agent and the former coordinating supervisor for the FBI's New York Organized Crime division. [Interview with Douglas Century]

Take Angelo: Technically he's a Genovese family associate—a connected guy. In Mob terms he's not "straightened out," meaning he isn't formally inducted by blood oath. But I can tell you that on the street, in real life, Angelo wielded a lot more power than many made men. He had *much* more juice than that degenerate gambler Alan Longo.

Angelo has a shrewd business mind. He's clever as a fox and he's a huge earner. Within the industry, guys call him Little Caesar—but always in a whisper.

Just look at the caliber of people he attracts to his restaurant. On our drive to Ponte's the first time, Sal told me about the grand opening of the steakhouse back in 1967 and all the movie stars and boxing champs he saw. Rocky Graziano stood in one corner, and when Sal looked across the room he noticed Johnny Dio, the old Lucchese *capo*, one of the most notorious labor racketeers in American history. Johnny Dio, the guy who blinded journalist Victor Riesel with acid, was right there mingling and sampling the smoked mozzarella.

We poked around Ponte's a few times in the fall of '92. We weren't really looking at Angelo as a target. Honestly, we didn't think we could ever get *near* Ponte. We were just hoping to be approached by Frank Giovinco. Giovinco was initially the target of the investigation—that's how modest our goals were at the time.

Frank was there briefly one night, but he just flashed by us going into the back room with a girl and disappeared. Then, on December 8, Sal and I went down there for a big Christmas party and who did we see? Allie Shades and Joe Francolino going into the back room for a card game. We also observed Gene Santora, son of the former underboss of the Genovese family. And then when I turned around I spotted Angelo Ponte sitting at a dining table with a couple of distinguished gentlemen. With one of them there appeared to be two state troopers as bodyguards. For a second, I didn't really believe my eyes. "Sal, is that who I *think* it is?" I said. He nodded. It was Senator Alphonse D'Amato. Angelo was sitting there with Senator D'Amato and this guy Marty Bernstein, president of a major paper and pulp company called Ponderosa.

"Bernstein's a completely legit guy," Sal told me. "D'Amato went to college with him."[5]

Sure, Angelo could hobnob with senators and congressmen: Back in 1990, there was a photograph in the Jersey papers of Senator Bill Bradley touring Ponte's new paper mill.[6] You can rest assured that Bill Bradley's going to think twice before having his photo snapped with wiseguys like Jimmy Brown Failla or Allie Shades Malangone. But with a "legit-imate" multimillionaire like Angelo, that's more of a gray zone. To the upperworld, Angelo's clean. He's never been convicted of a crime. The FBI and NYPD have been surveilling his restaurant for years as a known Mob hangout, but he's still got an air of respectability.

You have to think about it from the Mob's perspective: How would it have benefitted Gigante if Angelo was straightened out? Once a guy is formally made, to the law enforcement community he's got a target on his head. By being on the outside and the inside at the same time, cultivating that air of respectability while still getting down and dirty with wiseguys like Jimmy Brown, Joey Francolino, and Allie Shades, Angelo was having it all—the best of both worlds.

For the big holiday party at Ponte's Steakhouse on December 8, I showed up wired for sound. It was my first foray into a mobbed-up restaurant in my undercover role as Danny Benedetto, so I was tense. That night at Ponte's was the beginning of several years in which I used my body to gather evidence against the Mafia. But I never could have imagined that in the course of our investigation—later dubbed Opera-

---

[5] The senator's association with Angelo Ponte was previously a matter of public embar-rassment. In 1986, during a heated senatorial campaign, D'Amato had been accused by Democratic challenger Mark Green of accepting contributions from four men with organized-crime ties: Emedio Fazzini, Thomas Ronga, Nicholas Ferrante, and Angelo Ponte. D'Amato promptly returned checks totaling $5,450 in October 1986.

[6] Ponte's Recycled Paperboard Company mill opened in July 1990, helped by a $10-million loan from the New Jersey Economic Development Authority and a $700,000 urban development grant from HUD.

tion Wasteland—I would secretly record hundreds of conversations with mobsters and their associates, more than three thousand hours of conspiratorial talk.

Over the years of the investigation, the technology of our covert surveillance devices kept evolving, but they always fell into two camps. We had body recorders like the Nagra (and later the digital J-Bird) that I wore with a tiny microphone and wire taped to my chest; and we had radio transmitters known as Kel devices. Each has its pros and cons. With a body recorder you'll get cleaner-sounding recording, but I hated having to strap such a bulky box to the small of my back. A taped-down Nagra could easily be detected by a savvy wiseguy who just happened to run his hand down your shirtback while saying hello.

To an undercover, the advantage of using a Kel transmitter is that it's much easier to conceal. The early Kels had to be taped to your body, but later Tech Services could hide the mike inside standard cell phones and beepers. The Kel isn't a tape recorder: It sends a short-range radio transmission that needs to be picked up by another detective in the vicinity with an aid receiver and recorded.

The Kel gives you peace of mind, because you know that your field team can monitor your conversations and, should a situation get ugly, move in. But in terms of quality, the Kel transmissions leave a lot to be desired. Like any radio waves, they can be broken up by concrete walls, passing vehicles, electronic interference. And, being radio transmissions, they present the very real risk of exposure. Some mobsters today are sophisticated enough to purchase antitransmission equipment, mail-order spy gadgets that alert them if somebody in their presence is strapped with a transmitter.

The minuscule covert surveillance devices used by CIA operatives are not an option for an NYPD detective who ultimately will be expected to testify as his recordings are played in a court of law. During the pre-trial discovery process, the prosecution has to tell the defense precisely how those recordings were obtained—and, in effect, expose the police department's latest technology.

I knew that the mobsters whose incriminating conversations I'd be trying to capture were highly surveillance-conscious—all too savvy about law enforcement's tricks of the trade. It was up to an undercover detective to be just a bit savvier, use all his wits and street instincts to avoid detection. There are simple rules to the game, and both sides know them. Within Mob circles, getting caught wearing a wire is an instant death sentence.

I decided to strap on both a Nagra and a Kel that night at Ponte's. No matter how carefully you prepare, there are *always* technical problems, you lose parts of conversations, get squawks and static and dead spots. And I was so keyed up going to Ponte's, I didn't want to lose *anything*. We were going to a combination Christmas party and meeting of the New York Association of Paper Mills, Dealers, and Supplies. Sal was on the board of directors. It was the only association that the Benedettos belonged to, a legitimate group that met every few months to exchange new information about the industry and gave real paper dealers a chance to network. Not like these other *fugazy* associations run by the Mob, which were just part of the giant citywide scheme.

It was at Ponte's that night that I first saw the whole landscape. It was a perfect night to observe Angelo and his double life. There were the legitimate paper people meeting in one room, and then in the back room, playing poker, there were all the wiseguys like Joe Francolino and Allie Shades. The hoods would come out from their card game to troll around the bar, puffing cigars, looking to put the arm on legit guys. Sal threw a little chum in the water. Standing at the bar, within earshot of a couple of his friends, he muttered that I was his cousin Danny, just coming into the paper business from Dom Ben Realty. And I was introduced to several key industry figures.

Old Johnny Tuzzio was standing there with us, too, which gave us even more legitimacy. Johnny knew *everybody*. Johnny knew everybody's *father*. We were having a drink, laughing, and Johnny grinned at me. "Dan," he said, "you ain't like the rest of them Benedettos—you wasn't born with a silver spoon in your mouth." He's got a wink in his eye: I know he means Danny, but he also means *me,* Rick Cowan. From the way I speak, he can tell I never went to college, that I'm not from some rich family. He knows I'm just a blue-collar guy who worked all kinds of hard-hat and welding jobs before becoming a cop. I guess that's why I got along so well with Johnny Tuzzio and all the Chambers union guys. They weren't too different from my dad or most of the men in my family.

The paper mill association had booked a whole room filled with round tables. We had to go around in turn and introduce ourselves. That was the first time I had to stand up in public and say, "Hi, my name is Dan Benedetto. I'm the manager at Chamber Paper Fibres in Brooklyn."

Man, was I in over my head. Some expert was up there giving a big lecture about the economics of overseas shipping, complicated financial stuff, and I turned to one of the guys next to me. "I don't understand what the *hell* he's talking about. I'm down in the transfer station. I'm dealing with trucks and customers." He was an older guy from the Midwest. He shrugged at me, whispering, "You know something, my friend? I don't understand it either. I'm not in that end of the business." Which made me feel like less of an idiot.

About halfway through the meeting, I noticed I was having a problem in my pants. I'd wrapped the transmitter in medical gauze and then surgical-taped it to my crotch inside my shorts. Later on in the case I got more sophisticated with this stuff. I'd shave first and use a cutoff tube sock to wrap the Kel. But that first night in Ponte's it was so hot, and my nerves were making me so sweaty that I suddenly felt the Kel transmitter starting to shift and slide out of position. It had come loose from the tape and was now pressing directly against my skin.

There's a three-watt transmitter in there, and after a while it started to get hot, really burning me. I had to be careful getting up, because I was afraid it was going to fall clear out of my pants, slide right down my pant leg as I passed all the wiseguys smoking stogies at the bar. I had to get up very gingerly and start limping toward the bathroom.

The coast looked clear, but as I ducked into the men's room I got that feeling of someone coming close behind me. And when I glanced back I almost shit myself. It was Joe Francolino.

If there was one guy in the world I didn't want catching me with my pants down it was Francolino. *Joey Cigars.* John Gotti's handpicked guy. Actually, at that unpleasant moment in Ponte's, I really didn't know much about him, besides the fact that he was a fast-rising wiseguy in the Gambino family. We knew he was the number two guy in the Gambino garbage club, being groomed by Gotti to take over from old Jimmy Brown. We knew he owned a big company on Nineteenth Street called Duffy Waste Removal. I'd been checking with our NYPD Intelligence Desk, Gambino Section, but they didn't have much else. He'd never been arrested in his life, not even for something minor, which was unusual for a gangster who'd been on the scene for quite a while. Even the FBI didn't have much on Joe. The one thing the Feds did know: From their secret tapes made in the apartment above the Ravenite social club, was that Gotti talked about him quite a bit. They had Gotti on tape saying he personally inducted Joey into the *borgata*.[7]

We knew that Francolino was a cousin to Eddie Lino, a Gambino soldier—later a *capodecina*—who, according to Sammy the Bull's testimony, was one of the team of shooters who'd murdered boss Paul Castellano in front of Sparks Steak House in 1985. (Lino was himself murdered in 1990.)

After the Castellano hit, there were many guys in the Gambino family still faithful to Big Paul; Jimmy Brown was one of them. But Joe Francolino was considered a true-blue Gotti loyalist. He dressed flashy, walked with a strut just like John coming down Mulberry Street. That night at Ponte's, he had on the three-thousand-dollar Italian suit, gold cuff links, silk tie. There was a fat diamond pinky ring flashing on one hand, and a freshly lit cigar between his teeth. Joe was in his mid-fifties

---

[7] John Gotti to underboss Frank Locascio, December 12, 1989: "I grabbed Joe Francolino. I told Joe Francolino, 'Listen, Joey, you're a nice fella. You're a *friend of ours*—I made you a *friend of ours* . . .'"

and wore his thinning hair in these short, curly bangs, a little like Julius Caesar.

He was a very intimidating presence to be alone with—not the tallest guy in the world, maybe a shade under six feet, but he had the most intense stare in his blue-gray eyes. And the broken boxer's nose that let you know he was no fake tough guy.

Tonight we were alone in the men's room together and Joe started unzipping. I made a beeline for the stalls. The pain in my crotch was excruciating. I couldn't wait to pry the burning Kel device off my skin.

But the whole time Francolino was taking his time, lurking right outside the stall, and I didn't dare start stripping the surgical tape off the Kel. I don't know what Tony Maz and the rest of the field team actually heard—some rustling, maybe some breathing. It's really not something they can prepare you for in the Police Academy: how to sit on the crapper, remove a Kel transmitter from your package without making a sound, while a gangster is standing three feet away from you, taking a leak.

At last I heard Joe leaving the bathroom, and I started tearing off the surgical tape. With a little adjustment I got the Kel back into position and made it out of the bathroom. It was a small miracle that I never raised anybody up. I came back into the paper mill association meeting, took my seat next to Sal and Johnny Tuzzio, still struggled to understand the lecture in progress. But after my encounter with Joe Francolino, I found myself even more distracted. For the rest of the night I kept glancing back at the bar, where Joe and Allie Shades and the other flashy Mob guys were laughing and bellowing over their martinis and cigars.

I hoped that someday, with a little luck, I'd be standing there in those clouds of cigar smoke, laughing it up with them.

5 | THE WEST SIDE

On January 20, 1993, two grim-faced men entered the Chambers offices, demanding to speak with Sal. The older of the two men was Frank Allocca, a stoop-shouldered, gray-haired, sixty-five-year-old ex-paratrooper who wore a brown snap-brim fedora and heavy-framed spectacles, spoke in raspy tones, and smoked heavily. Allocca drove a blue Ford LTD and was officially the president of the Kings County Trade Waste Association—the so-called Brooklyn garbage club—and a well-to-do carting executive, the owner of V.A. Sanitation, Inc. Unofficially he was known as the mouthpiece and front man for Genovese *capo* Allie Shades Malangone.

With Allocca that morning was Dominick Vulpis, a powerfully built fifty-two-year-old with a deeply suntanned face and a thick head of brushed-back steel-gray hair. Vulpis was an aggrieved carter who claimed that the Benedettos had "robbed" him, taking one of his most lucrative garbage accounts.

What Vulpis called "robbery" most businessmen would call standard practice under the free-enterprise system. The company Vulpis was representing, Rosedale Carting, had recently been convicted in federal court on charges of illegal dumping on Staten Island. Anthony Vulpis, Dominick's brother, was now serving a twelve-year federal sentence for the crime, and their company, still owing some $11 million in fines, had been confiscated by the government. (In just four months of operation, the illegal dump site on Staten Island had become a $15-million cleanup operation.)

The United States Justice Department had tried to sell off Rosedale's lucrative garbage routes—along with those belonging to codefendant Angelo Paccione, also convicted of illegal dumping and fined an additional $11 million—but so far they could find no takers. None of the publicly traded, national garbage conglomerates (also known as "majors"), such as Waste Management, Inc., Browning-Ferris Industries, Inc., and Allied Waste Industries, Inc., would touch the seized routes. The majors—mostly headquartered in western states like Arizona and Texas—had long wanted to crack the billion-dollar New York marketplace, but fear of the Mafia's terror tactics had kept them at bay. No CEO of a major was willing to run the risk of having his drivers beaten or shot, his trucks firebombed or hijacked at gunpoint.

Even though a court-appointed federal trustee had oversight of his brother's company, Dominick Vulpis was still playing the part of the tough guy. "Look, we want this stop back," he snarled at Sal before they could even exchange handshakes. "That's why we're here, okay?"

Now I stepped up, trying to take some of the heat off Sal. Dominick Vulpis was the real McCoy, a stocky, violent, fierce Brooklyn carter. He was accusing us of robbing him of the Ferdinand Guttman stop. Guttman had a large textile business on Fourteenth Avenue in Bensonhurst. Vulpis was strangling Guttman, charging a ridiculous rate, over ten thousand dollars a month for service that was spotty at best. In December 1992, the Guttman manager reached out to Chambers, said he heard that Sal and the Benedettos were honest and fair guys. Just like he did with One Wall Street, Sal surveyed the Guttman place, made an accurate calculation, and quoted them a rate that would save them about thirty-five thousand dollars a year. Of course, Ferdinand Guttman was thrilled. Dominick Vulpis was not. He went to Frank Allocca at the Brooklyn club and together they stormed into Sal's office, trying to put a taste of fear in us. I was sitting there with Sal, and we had the video and the hidden mike going, capturing all of it on tape. Frank Allocca was a crusty old guy who'd been in the garbage rackets since the beginning of time—or at least since the '50s. He was wearing a suit and tie, chomping on a cigar that he never lit, and talking in a sandpaper whisper—his natural voice, but it made him sound like he was doing Marlon Brando doing Don Vito.

I was cagey with them, batting around some numbers. I told Vulpis I was concerned that if we tried to work something out, the FBI and the Department of Consumer Affairs were going to start poking around. Sal said he wished we could find another way to settle this problem. He started asking a few too many direct questions for Dominick's liking. *Shit,* I was saying to myself, *slow it down, Sal. They're gonna get raised up.*

And they did. Without warning, Vulpis jumped to his feet, his face turned maroon, the veins in his neck popping out.

"Frank, let's get the fuck outta here!" he said, pointing at Sal. "It's like talking to a *wire!*"

Vulpis was so hot that Allocca had to walk him out of the office—he looked like he was ready to start breaking heads right there.

A few weeks later Frank Allocca was back again. This time he didn't bring Vulpis. He brought Ray Polidori, owner of Crest Carting, a board member in the Brooklyn club. They were still beefing about the Guttman textile account, but now they were also complaining that we "robbed" a bunch of Fayva shoe stores—a very big account with fifty outlets around the city. Frank was chewing Sal out, telling him it's not "morally right" to go around robbing other garbage guys by offering lower rates.

"In the end," he said, "who wins? The *customer* wins."

"But that's competition," Sal said, trying to play dumb.

"That's right," Ray Polidori said. "Is that what you want?"

I asked if we were talking about the stops that Frank and Ray had lost personally. "No, we're speaking for the *whole* industry in Brooklyn," Ray said. So this was getting heavier and heavier. We still had our One Wall Street beef simmering with Phil Barretti—and even with Tommy Masotto out of the picture on federal charges, Phil was capable of pulling something treacherous. We had the beef brewing with Pete Porri over the Weber's department store, and Porri had taken it to young Frankie Giovinco in the Chin's paper club.

"Frank," I said, "I'm getting beefs with the guys in Manhattan. I'm getting beefs with you guys in Brooklyn. Guys up in the Bronx. I'm fighting on three fronts here."

"No, Dan," he said. "It's not three fronts. It's all the *same* front."

Meaning it's all one massive, Mob-run cartel—that's what he's telling me. This was something we'd been trying to prove forever. We spent two years on the Allie Shades surveillance trying to get evidence that all these Mob-run associations were acting in concert. Not to mention that law enforcement, going back to 1957, had launched dozens of investigations into this cartel and had never been able to make a good case. Suddenly we were getting it all on audio and video right in Sal's dingy little office.

Ray Polidori demanded that we surrender the Fayva Shoes account, and then he made a clear threat of violence. "Look," he said, "this has been going on for a long time. There ain't gonna be no more *conversations.* For every action there's a *reaction,* Sal. And we're at the reaction point. Think about it." He looked at me hard. "Dan, listen to me. Sal is from the old *school.* You're the young generation just coming into this business. You should think about doing things the right way."

"Maybe you guys should think about renting a room," Frank added.

"Whattaya mean, renting a room?"

I didn't know what he was talking about, but I had a hunch he meant joining the cartel, playing by the Mob rules. Still, I wanted to coax Frank into saying something more explicit for our tapes. As an undercover you always have to play a little dumber than you really are, get guys to spell everything out for you. Whenever you're having a conversation in the here and now, you're also imagining how it's going to sound played years later in court.

"So you would have a place," Frank said. "You would come down to our place."

I asked him if we had anything to worry about with Dominick Vulpis, considering how insane and red in the face he got the other day. Frank shook his head, said he couldn't help us with Vulpis. With crazy Dominick Vulpis, that "loose cannon," we're on our own.

"Thanks for the reassurance," I said.

"There's no reassurance!" Polidori shouted, and then he stared at Sal, who was being Sallie Skates again, grinning in the face of danger. "Sal," he said, "there's nothing to smile about."

Chambers was, as I've said, a big family-run business, with numerous cousins and relations working closely together every day. Aside from Sal, who'd agreed to be part of our police investigation, all the other Benedettos were just regular working people, trying to go about their daily business without any hassles. (For reasons of their own safety and privacy, I don't want to mention any of the other family members by name.) In general, the other Benedettos were completely different from Sal. Where Sal had some rough-edges, cursed, and mumbled, the other Benedettos were very proper and well spoken. They almost always came to work in neatly ironed khakis, button-down oxford shirts, and tassled loafers.

It was a pretty small office, and Sal's family couldn't avoid hearing the threats. First, there'd been the firebombing on the premises, and Ramos and his partner poking around, scaring people. Now they see Dominick Vulpis going purple with rage. They knew something was going to blow—something was going to go down soon. Everyone in the carting industry remembered how Robert Kubecka and Donald Barstow had been gunned down by Lucchese hit men right in their offices for coop-

erating with law enforcement. Kubecka had even managed to call 911
to tell the world he was dying.

This was the last straw: The other Benedettos told Sal that he could
no longer bring these gangsters into the Chambers office. Who could
possibly conduct business under these conditions?

Now we realized our whole case was going to change. Sal was too
vulnerable. And he was just a civilian. We couldn't use the surveillance
cameras and bugs in his office anymore. I was going to have to start
meeting the carters on their own turf, going into their clubs, companies
and restaurants by myself.

The first carter I arranged to meet on my own was Pete Porri. We
agreed to have a drink at noon at the Nile Restaurant at 371 Seventh
Avenue in Manhattan. It was too risky to wear a Nagra recorder so I
opted for the Kel, taping the transmitter to my crotch—this time making sure it was insulated inside a cutoff cotton sock. When I got to the
bar I saw this gray-haired guy in a tan-colored trench coat, looking like
Humphrey Bogart in *Casablanca*. "You Dan?" he whispered.

We went to a dark corner of the restaurant to talk in private. Pete
kept asking why I couldn't simply walk away from the Weber's department store on Thirty-second Street, why I couldn't do the right thing
and "respect" his work.

"I know you guys in the Association have a theory that certain guys
own certain areas," I said. "But that's between you guys. I'm an independent paper-packing guy. I don't belong to the Association. Us independent guys don't work like that."

"We should all be united," Pete said. "We should work together and
then we wouldn't need to go to the Association."

Pete gave me the classic three alternatives. One: I can give Pete back
the stop. Two: I can give Pete a stop of a comparable value. Three: I can
agree to compensate Pete based upon the monthly collection rate, applied to a multiple between 35-to-1 and 60-to-1. That was the "restitution" he expected to be paid on a monthly basis.

"Hey, Pete," I said, "I'll have to get back to you on this."

I offered Pete a lift back downtown. I had a J-Bird eavesdropping device hooked up inside the dashboard of my vehicle, and it captured the rest of our conversation clearly as we drove downtown. Pete wanted to get out of the car at West Street and Canal. I drove off, but our field team observed Pete Porri going inside the Greater New York Waste Paper Association at 511 Canal Street to meet with Frank Giovinco.

It was clear to me and everyone else that Pete Porri wasn't a gangster and he wasn't a tough guy. He was one of the go-along-to-get-along carters who had learned to play by the rules of the cartel. Pete had no muscle on his own, but he paid his dues every month so he could go to the Chin's club and get muscle when the occasion arose. Hopefully this beef with Porri would get me closer to the Waste Paper Association, maybe even get me face-to-face with Frank Giovinco.

The strategy I worked out with Tony Mazziotti was to stall, never commit to anything, juggle all these different beefs as long as I could. I still wasn't too savvy in the business, but I was doing the best I could under the circumstances. Whenever I tried to ask Sal a technical question, he was of no use to me. He knows *everything* but he can't explain it articulately.

I'd say, "Sal, what's tipping fees?"

"Huh?"

"I need to know what the term *tipping fees* means. It comes up frequently and I don't really know what they're talking about."

And Sal would just stand there with his hands thrust deep in his pockets, jingling his change, and say: "You know when the guy comes in and dumps—dis-shit, dat-shit," and then walk away. That was Sally's famous line. Instead of "Blah, blah, blah," he'd say, "Dis-shit, dat-shit." Tony Maz and the rest of the field team used to crack up whenever he said it.

I started meeting Frank Allocca and Ray Polidori—along with another young Genovese associate named Danny Todisco—in the heart of

Bensonhurst, the huge Italian neighborhood of double-parked Lincolns and Cadillacs and dozens of Mob social clubs. Mostly we ate at the Americana Diner, a popular meeting place for Mob guys.

Was I nervous? Hell, yeah, but I was trying not to show it. Dealing with the Mob, it's best to put on your toughest exterior, because they prey on fear and weakness. I had to show them that I was cut from a different cloth, that I wasn't going to take the kind of intimidation they'd been dishing out to my cousin Sal. In fact, one of the first things I did was start giving them hell for the way Phil Barretti had roughed up Sal.

"What the fuck is going on with you guys? Beating up on a fifty-four-year-old man?" I said one day in the Americana. "You see Sal's condition. He's got a bad leg, he's overweight, can't defend himself. What kind of bullshit is that?"

Frank Allocca wanted me to give them the name of the guy who'd assaulted my cousin—as if he didn't know. "We can't help you, Dan, if you don't tell us his name." But of course I couldn't give up a name. What they were really doing was testing me, seeing if I was loose with the lips. These three guys at the table with me were all basically speaking for Allie Shades—an old-school gangster if ever there was one—and I was not going to start off in this thing with a reputation as a rat.

At those early meetings they laid down the parameters. They kept telling me I had to play by their rules or else. "Remember what happened to George Rutigliano? You don't want to have those kinds of problems, *do* you, Dan?" George Rutigliano was an outlaw carter who, a few years earlier, had been going around taking stops from guys in the clubs. They organized a citywide boycott against him, practically bled him to death. Rutigliano had a big transfer station on the Brooklyn-Queens borderline. When he started underbidding Association members, they locked arms and told every single garbage company to stop dumping anything with Rutigliano. He went from over a hundred trucks a day down to zero trucks a day. Finally he had no choice: He joined the cartel. That's the kind of power these gangsters had. If you were an outlaw they'd either bomb you into submission or boycott you out of business. They'd rather coerce you into joining than murder you and bring down that kind of heat. But over the years, plenty of outlaws had been shot for trying to go it alone.

To them, an outlaw is a carter who does not belong to the clubs—he's a renegade, a "midnight rider." Of course, it's an upside-down world, because to be an *outlaw* within a massive criminal enterprise is actually to be an upstanding citizen and law-abiding businessman. But to the wiseguys, they are their own world, they are their own power. They even call themselves a *government*. They recognize the Mob as a second *real* government. The other government, the government I belong to—the government of detectives, district attorneys, and judges—they call that the enemy.

I was used to surveilling hoods: Now I was the guy being surveilled. One night as I was leaving Plymouth Street, heading home to Claire, I spotted a white male with a mustache and sandy-brown hair, sitting for hours in a silver Oldsmobile parked in front of the Chambers warehouse, slumped a bit too low in the seat, pretending to read the newspaper. I got a block away and, sure enough, the silver Olds began tailing me. But I also knew how to clean myself. I led him down to the waterfront streets that run along the river. Once the Olds turned down one dead end, I knew for sure he was tailing me. I lost him, but not before getting the plate number. And later, when we ran a check with the Department of Motor Vehicles, it came back to the son of a guy from Staten Island, a former detective who'd been fired from the NYPD for taking a bribe and was now working as a private investigator.

But who was paying this PI? We were never able to determine. In recent years it's come out that retired detectives—some first-graders among them—have been hired by hoods. These multimillionaire garbage gangsters prided themselves on having former New York's Finest at their disposal. "Ricky," Tony Maz often said, "just because they're cops doesn't mean they're still blue. To them the only color that matters now is green. And that makes them even more dangerous."

Getting tailed is one thing. But I got a little more worried when the

Mob started sniffing around in person. One morning Frank Giovinco showed up at the Chambers loading dock, glancing at union cards, asking routine questions of the laborers. How well did they know this new guy Danny? Gene Fulp, the foreman and former president of the LIUNA local, was driving the forklift loaded with bales of cardboard. He stopped the lift, stepped down, tilted up his hard hat. "I've known Danny his whole life," Gene said. "Since he was five years old. Sure, he's a good guy."

Another night, just after my meeting with Pete Porri, I'm on the Cross Island Parkway, driving towards the Whitestone Bridge, on my way to see Tony Maz at a secret plant. Without warning, my Jeep starts accelerating out of control. My foot isn't near the gas pedal; I start pumping the brake. No luck. The engine's revving, steering wheel rattling, and when I glance at the speedometer, the needle's passing ninety. I swerve through the traffic, barely avoiding a rear-end collision, then fly off the highway, on the shoulder, gripping the wheel hard and trying to keep the Jeep from flipping. Blowing through clouds of dust and gravel, I finally manage to drop the transmission into neutral, turned off the ignition, and coasted to a stop. My first thought is that someone sabotaged my Jeep. Set me up for a crash. Sweat has soaked right through my shirt to my jacket. I get down on my knees to examine the gas pedal and see that the J-Bird recorder—secreted in the dashboard for my meeting with Pete Porri—has jostled loose and fallen, jamming the accelerator to the floor.

I pry the J-Bird free from the pedal and sit on the shoulder of the Cross Island for a few minutes, collecting myself before restarting the ignition.

Undercover work in general takes a tremendous toll on your nerves. But going undercover in the Mob was more stress than I'd ever experienced in my life. My wife, Claire—who was used to the strange hours and habits of my job—started noticing the changes in me. I was always jumpy, tense, irritable. The moment I got home, I had to lock myself away, listening to tapes of my meetings, typing up the DD5s. That's another huge emotional factor for an undercover detective: You're bottling it all up inside—can't even confide in family. Tony Mazziotti used to give a speech: *Guys, what you're involved with here cannot be talked about with anyone—not your wife, not your priest, not your rabbi, not your brother, not your girlfriend.*

For years I kept Claire in the dark. She knew I did undercover work, of course, but in the past, in Narcotics, that meant me posing as a junkie for the day and leaving it at work. She had no idea that I was this *deep* undercover, that I was trying to penetrate the Mafia. I tried my best to keep everything—my fears and anxieties—hidden.

In order to wear the wire all the time, I was shaving my chest and my abdomen. I don't know how many times she asked: "Rick, what's going on?"

"Nothing," I'd say. Of course, your wife knows when you're lying. But Claire also knew that I was assigned to a top-secret unit of the NYPD and she never really pressed me. I couldn't tell her the truth about my work for many years. I couldn't tell her about the bad moments, like nearly flipping my Jeep on the Cross Island Expressway, or the good ones, like the first time I got inside the Genovese paper club on Canal Street.

It was March 10, 1993, and Pete Porri had scheduled a meeting with me at the Greater New York Waste Paper Association; and to do so, he'd gotten the approval of the WPA's "business representative," Frank Giovinco. This was by far the biggest break so far in the investigation, because it marked the first time in history that a member of law enforcement had infiltrated one of the Mob-controlled trade-waste associations. Generations of detectives and FBI agents had conducted street surveillance, using zoom lenses to photograph the goings and comings of mobsters, jotting down license plate numbers and following midnight-blue Cadillacs and jet-black Lincolns. Never before had a cop or federal agent penetrated this inner sanctum of the Mafia cartel.

It was a crazy day for me. Because that very same afternoon, March 10, an undercover I'd worked with in Narcotics, Detective Luis "Louie" Lopez, was shot to death a short distance away. I was undercover as Danny Benedetto, venturing inside the West Side paper club—and as soon as I get out of the meeting, I heard that my friend Louie was killed in a spot where I used to make buys myself. It was a grocery store in Alphabet City where I used to buy bags of weed.

Louie was a great undercover, a U.S. Army veteran; whenever we saw each other we used to talk about our motorcycles. Sometimes I'd put fake track marks on him with my theatrical makeup before we went on the set to make buys, and I'd tease him about riding a "rice-rocket" instead of a Harley. Louie's murder really shook me up.

The Greater New York Waste Paper Association was located on the third floor of 511 Canal Street. The club was a loft space with beige indoor-outdoor carpet, white columns, a full kitchen area, a large pool table, and several green-felt poker tables with overflowing ashtrays. I walked to the back, past the glass-partitioned office cubicles of Angelo Ponte and Vito "Bruce" Palmeri, and was introduced to Frank Giovinco. Frank was a rock-solid five foot eight—still had the build of the all-state running back he'd been in high school. He was confident and in control, dressed in a white silk shirt and dress slacks. He never said, "Look, you gotta join us—or *else.*" He always used the word *suggestion.* He was just "suggesting" the reasons why it would be advantageous for Chambers to join. At one point Frank said that he'd heard good things about me from one of the union officials in the Plymouth Street shop.

"Yeah, who?"

"Gene Fulp."

"Oh, Gene's a helluva guy."

As nervous as I was that day, I felt a huge boost of confidence to hear that Gene—a guy who'd gone out on union junkets to Las Vegas with Frank—would vouch for me and say that I'd been around for a long time.

I sat with Frank for an hour and a half, negotiating the terms of what it would mean for Chamber Paper Fibres to join the Waste Paper Association. Frank explained that Chambers would have to "go on the board" for ninety days, during which time we'd be subject to any claims an Association member wanted to make against us. Whatever stops Sal had taken off a club member, going back five years retroactively, would have to be returned. If not, restitution would have to be paid. All the club members demanded to be "made whole." That was the term they used for their restitution, a phrase I would hear a lot in the years ahead, as these garbage gangsters expected to be paid in full. *Make me whole, Danny. I expect to be made whole.*

Frank was the first real gangster who took me under his wing. He was a tough guy, still young, but he was being brought up in the Genovese family—a knockaround kid under the Chin. Frank indicated that he would watch out for me, step in, and resolve all these beefs I was being bombarded with. He would tell me which beefs had to be paid right away and which ones could be put on the back burner. "So, Frank," I said, "how bad is it gonna be if I join up?"

"Don't worry, Dan," he said. "We'll talk to them for you. All the associations will be put on notice that you're coming in with us. But for us to accept you as a brother, you have to be willing on good faith to give the stops back or pay for them. Follow the rules, and stop being an outlaw."

The negotiations went slowly. I had to come back a few more times to meet with Frank at the WPA. On his own, Frank went and saw Frank Allocca, got the Brooklyn club's list of grievances against us. We also had him under surveillance, dressed in a black mockneck sweater and charcoal-gray double-breasted suit, going and seeing Jimmy Brown and Joe Francolino about us. Because it wasn't as simple as agreeing to join the four associations and paying the initiation dues. By taking stops off cartel members, you'd broken the cardinal rule, and you better believe they were going to make you pay through the nose. More importantly, they wanted a list of the principals in your company, so they would know exactly who they were dealing with.

If you're an outlaw, the wiseguys impose the penalties that they see fit. Generally, they want a multiple of anywhere between 30-to-1 and 60-to-1. At 60-to-1, you're paying the guy in advance what he would've made on the stop for a full five years—so if the account was worth ten thousand dollars a month, you've got to cough up six hundred thousand. Sometimes he'll want a big chunk up front, and the rest can be spaced out over the months ahead. That's all negotiable, but only on the hood's terms.

Slowly, during that whole spring, Frank was showing me the ropes, teaching me the rules that these associations have functioned by since the mid-'50s—longer than either one of us has been alive.

People talk about the Mob today being diminished by the changing values of the younger generation, and there are certainly a lot of idiots and degenerates and druggies; there are hundreds of punks who'd sooner flip than do a long prison stretch. On the other hand, especially among the West Side, there are still a lot of younger guys who are *hardcore* Cosa Nostra—and Frankie Giovinco was one of them.

He told me that the multiples I had to pay an aggrieved carter might change a little bit—30-to-1, 40-to-1, 45-to-1—but once I joined the Association, then I'd have the same protector, the same muscle in Frankie G. "*Minghia!* Because God forbid somebody tries to take anything from you," Frank said. "You're gonna get paid the same way. I don't want nobody to turn around and say, 'Oh, I'll only pay him 25-to-1.' I'll shoot him before that happens."

Frank prided himself on being very surveillance-conscious, never saying anything of consequence on the phone. When you were talking to him, he was constantly saying "Okay" and "G'head." Because he wanted you to be the one doing all the talking.

Meanwhile, every day I was with Frank, I was making some of the best recordings I made during the whole investigation. Later on, everyone—police brass, the DA's, and defense attorneys—were very curious to know why that was. "Detective, how could you record this man so clearly?" I told them Frank Giovinco had a strange habit, although it wasn't that strange among wiseguys: He'd get extremely close to you when you talked, come within a few inches of you, and keep pointing right into your chest all the time with his index finger. So the way I hooked up my wire, I always wore button shirts, and right behind the button, I could hide the tiny microphone. As Frank tapped me in the chest, he'd feel the button, not the mike, and he was always leaning right into my chest, whispering right into the button.

For months I kept stalling Frank and the guys from the other associations. As long as we were talking about joining, I figured, they wouldn't get heavy. Eventually the brass realized we were going to have to start coughing up money—paying extortion—but we were being hit with so many beefs that to try to settle them all up, in multiples of thirty or forty, that was easily tens of millions of dollars, the kind of cash that could put Chambers permanently out of business. Still, I was talking about becoming a cartel member, learning the rules from the Chin's own knockaround kid, so I figured Frank was going to keep the violence under wraps.

For violence in the carting industry, there was no place like the Bronx. The borough had always been known as the Wild West. According to Sal, carters in the Bronx wouldn't even bother going to the associations with their beefs: They'd pick up pistols and shoot it out themselves.

In the 1970s, federal agents learned firsthand about the Bronx cowboys' methods for resolving territorial disputes. For eight months, from mid-1976 to early 1977, a team of FBI men posed as garbage haulers, setting up and running a one-truck garbage and recycling company called Automated Refuse and Wastepaper Removal, Inc. As they collected the trash in the Co-Op City section of the Bronx, they drew the attention of the Mob for violating the long-standing property-rights code.

On December 15, 1976, an FBI agent named Walter Wayne Orrell was threatened and punched by carting company owner Joseph Gambino and his right-hand man, Carlo Conti, who told the agent, "I'm the guy that's gonna kill you." Joe Gambino, forty-seven, described in news accounts as a cousin of the late Carlo Gambino, the so-called "Boss of Bosses," was an underworld power in the Bronx who'd entered the country illegally from Sicily in 1957.

At the defendants' bail hearing, federal prosecutor Peter D. Sudler claimed that Gambino had "interests in virtually the entire private-sanitation industry in the Bronx" and that Conti had regularly "administered vicious beatings" at Gambino's request.[1] The Gambino-Conti case made the headlines—in a year best remembered for the summertime hysteria of the "Son of Sam" killing spree. There was even a front-page banner in the May 19, 1977, edition of the *New York Post:* FBI INFILTRATES MOB TRASH BIZ. After a three-week trial, both defendants were found guilty of conspiracy and extortion. Gambino, represented by the high-profile defense attorney Roy Cohn, was sentenced to ten years in prison and ordered to pay a fine of fifty thousand dollars. Carlo Conti was sentenced to eight years.

But that case demonstrated the difficult task faced by law enforcement in trying to penetrate the cartel's shadow fortress. As former FBI supervisor J. Bruce Mouw says today: "The Bureau put in all that time and money—we actually owned a garbage truck for a year—and we locked up, what, *two* guys?"

Nothing had changed in the Bronx in the years following the FBI sting. By the early '90s, one of the most notorious Bronx cowboys was a tall, snowy-haired carter named Louis Mongelli, who owned and operated the Mongelli Carting Company with his sons, Paul and Michael. Though they had no formal contract in place, for several years the Mongellis had serviced the Charles Green Company, a family-owned printing business located in the industrial Hunts Point section.

By May 1993, Charles Green was less than satisfied; the Mongellis were charging close to four thousand dollars a month for pickup service best described as "infrequent." Hordes of rats were breeding inside the Green warehouse, and the company began getting one-thousand-dollar

---

[1] *The New York Times,* March 3, 1977, "Takeover of a Garbage Collector Charged to Two Reputed Mafia Men"

summonses from the Department of Sanitation. As a print shop generating a high volume of paper refuse, Green turned to an established paper-recycling family, the Benedettos. After a survey, a Chambers sales agent offered Charles Green a formal contract to pick up the garbage—and said that the high-grade recyclable paper would offset the price—charging $2,500 per month.

Now, not only would Charles Green be saving money, he'd finally get his garbage picked up three times a week. In late May he sent the Mongelli Carting Company a notice stating that as of June 1, 1993, its trash-hauling services would no longer be needed.

A few days later Richard Foster, the Charles Green plant manager, received an unwelcome visitor. It was Paul Mongelli. "Look, your garbage is gonna rot," Mongelli warned. "I hope you have a lot of friends who will come to your funeral—because we're gonna plant you six feet under."

On June 1, when our Chambers driver arrived at Charles Green in the South Bronx to pick up the trash, he was greeted by a blockade: Five Mongelli garbage trucks closing down the entire street. Then a wild howling blur: Between ten and twelve workshirt-clad men piling out of Mongelli trucks, wielding baseball bats and two-by-fours, screaming that they would start breaking open skulls if anyone even touched the garbage. The driver, not being suicidal, decided it was in his best interests to drive on.

As was now routine with all such incidents, the threat was reported to me—Chambers's designated problem-solver—at my desk on the Brooklyn waterfront.

The next morning, June 2, I'm going up to the Bronx myself, wearing a transmitter and a body recorder. I'm going to join a Chambers driver with his truck, and I'm going to confront these thugs—or they're going to confront me. It's unusual for a plant manager to be on the trucks with the union guys, but I had to see it firsthand, gather evidence, and if anyone should be in harm's way it should be me, not a real Chambers employee. We go to Charles Green and I'm loading up the truck for about fifteen minutes, already getting sweaty from lifting barrels and hampers. I tell my driver, "If anything happens, go straight to the truck. If it gets real ugly, get the fuck outta here, just go—leave me here."

I'm not carrying my Glock, but I've got a nasty-looking .38 snub-nose without a handle—there's tape where the wood should be, which makes it look like a real street piece. The .38 is wrapped in a shirt and stuck in a bag behind the garbage truck seat. I'm not sure I'll be able to get to it in time.

It's 7:30 A.M. when the Mongelli truck pulls up. Out jump two very intimidating guys, both dressed in T-shirts and work boots and green work pants, while a third guy sits in the truck with a two-by-four. The first guy has longish hair, a beard, tattoos, like a biker. I later learned that his name was Tommy Oddo. The second guy with him is even scarier, a true Neanderthal, complete with the sloping forehead, single bushy eyebrow, big cheekbones, hair short and swept-back, hood-style. Six foot one, two hundred pounds, with a lean-muscled build, not an ounce of fat on him. He's half Swedish and half Italian and his name is Steve Georgison.

Georgison has me—and anyone else who crossed paths with him—*very* uneasy. Phil Barretti's main thug Raymond Ramos was feared throughout the industry as a tough guy and crazy as a loon, but this Steve Georgison is a *completely* different animal. You can see this guy's capable of the real heavy stuff at any moment.

The bearded biker-type, Tommy Oddo, is doing all the talking while Georgison is circling behind me, ominous as hell. "Pack up and get the fuck out!" Oddo tells me.

My driver does just like I instructed—heads straight for the cab of the truck. Now I'm alone with the thugs on this desolate block. I turn around, trying to keep both of them in sight, but they move as I do, very methodically, so that one is always behind me. I'm arguing with them, telling them I've got a contract to pick up the paper here. It feels like they're going to jump me at any second.

"Are you Paul?" I ask the bearded biker guy.

"I could be."

"Well, I'm Dan. I spoke to Paul yesterday. . . ."

"You're not supposed to be here," he says, blocking my way. "It's *our* stop. Not yours. Pull your truck out. . . . You're tryin' to cut our throat over here. I ain't goin' for that. You're takin' food outta my kid's mouth."

"Lemme grab a couple of these things here," I say, reaching for some carboard tubes.

"Nothing! Nothing!" They slap the stuff to the ground. "Just *leave*. Do me a favor. Please leave."

"Like I told Paul," I say, "we have a contract to satisfy and we're gonna satisfy it, until we're told otherwise."

"I'm telling you otherwise!"

"You haven't even told me who you are. How do I know who you are?"

"I don't have to tell you who I am. Mongelli is enough. Pull your truck away—and do me a favor, don't come back."

"I have to come back."

"No you don't."

"I have to."

Oddo's getting louder all the time. We're standing face-to-face and I can feel the spit flying as he shouts. I'm thinking: *This is it. I'm gonna get slaughtered here.*

"What the fuck don't you understand?" Oddo says. "This belongs to *me*. This whole fuckin' apparel center is mine—the McDonald's, the gas station across the street, this whole fuckin' complex, it's *mine*. Stay out. Stay out."

"Don't come back," Georgison says, still flexing his massive arms behind his back. "Or there's gonna be a problem here."

"What kinda problem is it gonna be?" I say.

"I don't know—but it's gonna be a problem."

"Then there's gonna be a problem."

"Where were you yesterday?" Oddo says.

"I wasn't here yesterday."

"Your truck came by and youse kept going!"

"Well, you had ten guys out here—that's why."

"There was no ten guys out here."

"That's what they told me."

"If there was ten guys here, then where were you?"

"Look, I don't normally work on the truck—I'm working the truck today 'cause I don't wanna see none of my guys get hurt."

Through this whole conversation, they're circling me like Apaches around the wagon train. It's one big motherfuck session, lasting about fifteen minutes. I don't quite know how, but I manage to talk my way out of there with my skull intact.

The next morning, June 3, I tried to finish picking up the garbage. But the Mongelli crew had been there for an hour already. When I pulled up on the block, I saw Georgison, Oddo, and about seven other guys amassing their forces, waiting for me in front of the shop with ax handles, baseball bats, two-by-fours, even shovels. We stopped the truck and I tried to talk to them through the window. This time Paul Mongelli, Lou's son, was right there in the mob doing the threatening.

"You ain't gettin' jack shit outta this fuckin' place—I told you yesterday!" Oddo yelled at me.

"Stay the fuck out!" Georgison said.

"You won't get a motherfuckin' thing outta here! Step outta your fuckin' truck! Step out *here*!"

Suddenly, Georgison jumped on the side-runner—looking like he was ready to throw a punch through the window. I told the driver to hit the gas. I felt lousy leaving without getting out and confronting them, but it would have been pure suicide.

We had two excellent detectives from the OCID Intelligence and Analysis unit, Detective Vito Aleo and Detective Joe Chimienti, hidden on the block, videotaping and shooting still photographs of all this. You can hear them talking on the surveillance video, Chimienti turning to Aleo and saying: "The smartest thing Rick ever did in his life was not getting out of that truck."

On June 9, I went back to the WPA, trying to get Frank Giovinco to step in and resolve this beef. I told him how the Mongelli crew had been waiting for us at the stop with bats and ax handles and two-by-fours; I told him I didn't want my driver to get his head handed to him. Frank said he would straighten it out, even though Mongelli was a member of the Gambino-run Queens association, which was closely affiliated with Jimmy Brown's club in Manhattan. (The Bronx was an odd borough; the way the Mob whacked up the territory back in the old days, most of the Bronx carters belonged to the association in Queens, under Gambino associate Patty Pecoraro, although there were some who answered to a Genovese faction lead by a powerful carter named Vincent "Jimmy" Vigliotti.)

Frankie G. looked across the room at Angelo Ponte, then asked me, "Do you know Angelo?" I nodded. I said I'd met Ponte a few times at his restaurant, but we really hadn't exchanged more than a couple words. To be honest, Angelo always seemed standoffish with me. Frank brought me over to Ponte, who shook my hand.

"You know Dan Benedetto, right?"

"No. I don't think so."

"Well, I met you a few times at your restaurant."

"Who's your father?" Angelo said.

"John," I said. "John from Staten Island."

Angelo was nodding, thinking about it. Remember, the Benedettos and Pontes are all from that little one-horse town of Craco, so Angelo knew the whole Benedetto family tree. Frank told him about the new beef we had, that Sal took a stop off Lou Mongelli in the Bronx. "Dan was stood off with two-by-fours," Frank said. Angelo shook his head slowly. Of course, in his eyes, Lou Mongelli's not to blame—we are.

"Sal's tough," he said. "He's got a one-track mind."

Years later, this was something the hoods and their defense attorneys tried to play up in court—that Sal and me were going around town starting fires, stirring up shit all over the place in order to advance our police investigation. But it wasn't the case. If anything, the Benedettos and their competitive instincts were causing the NYPD more headaches than we could handle. Sal and all the Benedettos were, first and foremost, businessmen. Since 1896 the family has been hauling paper and rags with one motive: to make a profit. All the Benedettos were interested in was competing for customers in the tradition of American capitalism.

Never, at any point in the investigation, was anyone in the NYPD pulling the Benedetto cart. As all these beefs started erupting all over New York City—as the Benedettos' salesmen were going around drumming up more business—we couldn't interfere. Who in their right mind would've wanted to get mixed up with a wild man like Mongelli?

Alex Fernandez was a clean-cut, husky, hardworking Puerto Rican guy—one of Chambers's best drivers. He had an eight-year-old daughter down in Puerto Rico, and she'd come up to New York for a week at the start of her summer vacation. Alex, being a single father, couldn't afford a baby-sitter, so he buckled her into the passenger seat of the garbage truck while he made the rounds. After my discussions with Frank Giovinco, it seemed that the problems in the Bronx had finally calmed down. Frank said he was going to tell the Mongellis to cool their heels.

But on the morning of June 22, as Alex went to pick up the garbage at Charles Green, the Mongelli thugs returned—Steve Georgison leading the charge. Alex tried to reason with them: "Look, I'm a working guy just like you guys." But when he turned his back, Georgison and another unidentified thug hit him in the head full-force with a lead pipe. He was beaten mercilessly and left for dead in the street.

It was the shrillness of his daughter's cry that actually saved Alex's life. Two passersby coming down Barretto Street were startled by the sound of the eight-year-old's screaming. She was inside the idling garbage truck, still buckled into her seat belt, cheeks pressed to the window, howling and pointing at her father lying helpless on the pavement, bleeding to death. Alex's skull was cracked open, his spleen ruptured; a thick mixture of blood and saliva bubbled up through his teeth. As his daughter became hysterical inside the truck, Alex slipped into a coma.

There's no doubt Alex would have died if two citizens hadn't made anonymous 911 calls. We have the official police emergency tapes:

> FIRST ANONYMOUS CALLER: I'm at 841 Barretto Street; one of the garbage guys just got hit over the head with something and he's lying here unconscious. . . . He's been hit over the head at least six times by another garbage collector . . . He didn't even have a chance, he got hit from behind.
>
> SECOND ANONYMOUS CALLER: In the Bronx. It's 841 Barretto Street. Somebody's bleeding to death. Some garbage men had a dispute and he's bleeding to death out there.

The patrolmen arrived with EMS, and they found two Spanish-speaking cops who were able to take care of the girl. She spoke no English. By the time the paramedics pulled Alex out of the gutter, he was foaming at the mouth.

I was a few blocks from Chambers on the Brooklyn waterfront when I got a beep from Sal. "Dan, we got big trouble in the Bronx," he said. I called up there, talked to Ralph, the manager of our Paper Services transfer station, who told me that Alex Fernandez was beaten halfway to death and was rushed to Lincoln Hospital.

I called Tony Mazziotti, then I raced up to Lincoln Hospital on Third Avenue in the South Bronx. Tony was already there with Detective Joe Lentini. We got as far as ICU and they wouldn't let us in to visit Alex. He was in a coma, bleeding internally, and the specialists were doing everything they could do to save him.

I just sat there in the waiting room, feeling sick. I was sick about Alex, who was only doing his job—a tough, not-too-highly-paid job—and I was sick about his little girl, who had to witness the vicious beating. I got up, paced around, stared at my reflection in the window. The guilt was really hitting me, because I knew that the Mongellis hadn't targeted Alex

Fernandez for attempted murder—he was just in the wrong place at the wrong time. I had no doubt that the beating was meant for me.

It was touch-and-go whether Alex was actually going to pull through. He was hospitalized for weeks. He'd suffered a brain hemorrhage, multiple broken bones, various internal injuries and lacerations. He needed months of physical therapy after that, suffered constant debilitating headaches and dizziness, and had permanent deafness in one ear. He left his job at Chambers as a result of the assault, and he couldn't work again—or live a normal life—for many years.

I was livid when I called up Mongelli Carting to speak with Paul Mongelli. "You knew where to reach me, Paul!" I shouted. "You know where I work. You coulda reached out for me. We coulda talked instead of goin' after my driver today. And the guy's only a driver!"

"I'm just givin' you a message from my father. He wants to have a meeting—to sit down and talk."

"Yeah, well, he should talk before he—before you guys go after my driver with baseball bats!"

The next morning at nine, Lou Mongelli called.

"Lou, why you hittin' my guy over the head with fuckin' baseball bats?"

Speaking softly now, Lou had an invitation.

"Dan, can we have *coffee*?"

I hinted—never dropping any names, of course—that I had a guy from the Waste Paper Association who was supposed to be straightening things out, settling this beef. But in reality, I now realized, Frankie Giovinco was of little use; instead of smoothing over the dispute with Mongelli, he was intentionally letting it ferment. He *wanted* it to come to a head, so that when it did blow up, I'd be thoroughly coerced and have no choice but to come running for protection, begging to join the Association.

Lou Mongelli said it was important that we meet face-to-face today, before things got any worse. I told him I had seen Paul's blockade of a dozen guys with two-by-fours. I'd seen Alex Fernandez lying near death in the hospital, and it was making me apprehensive about a meeting. Lou gave me his word that there would be no rough stuff at the sit-down. I said that Lou's son Paul had already given me direct assurances that there would be no rough stuff, but now I'd come to the conclusion that Paul's word wasn't any good and maybe Lou's word wasn't much better. Lou exploded: "Yeah, Dan? Let me tell you—excuse me—you don't want to take my fuckin' word, then I *keep* doing what I'm doing!"

Over the next few days Mongelli's threats intensified. "Look, Dan. I don't have to explain the ABCs to you, do I? This is coming to a very *short* fuse."

"I was only interested in getting Green's paper—"

"That's *my* paper! Who the fuck are you to pick up my paper without telling me? You snuck in there without my permission! You stay outta my stop—you don't touch nothin' until we rectify this whole matter with monies and my stop back. If you don't, I *do* what I gotta do—you *go* where you gotta go—you *tell* who you gotta tell! I'm tryin' to be a nice guy here! There's no more talkin'! Call me in one hour and let me know or else I'm coming to your shop, Dan, and whatever comes down, *comes* down!"

Sal and the other Benedettos overheard this psychotic screaming and they all fled Chambers—fled Brooklyn entirely. I turned around and realized I was suddenly alone in the offices. I called up Tony Mazziotti to tell him about Mongelli's threats; Tony, convinced that a violent confrontation could occur any moment, ordered a field team of detectives to set up all around Plymouth Street in case Mongelli and his people arrived—but they never came down to the Brooklyn waterfront.

Tony and I both realized that we'd come to a critical juncture in the case. Either we had to start paying "restitution" to outraged carters like Lou Mongelli and Phil Barretti and Dominick Vulpis, or the NYPD might have a murder case on its hands.

On July 16, 1993, having received even more explicit threats of violence, I drove up to the Mongelli Carting Company offices in the Bronx. I met with Paul Mongelli and personally handed him two checks, signed by Sal Benedetto, totaling $5,000.

The decision to pay thousands of dollars in extortion can't be made by an undercover detective alone. For the initial Mongelli payments, Sergeant Mazziotti had needed to get authorization from Deputy Inspector Kenny O'Brien; in the months ahead, as the extortion payments reached unprecedented levels for an NYPD investigation—sometimes as much as $80,000 a month—authorization was required farther up the chain of command. Deputy Inspector O'Brien briefed the chief of the Organized Crime Control Bureau, Martin O'Boyle, who took it straight to the desk of Commissioner Bill Bratton.

Commissioner Bratton and District Attorney Robert Morgenthau agreed to contribute funds equally, depositing the money into a Chambers Paper Fibres bank account to cover the checks Sal would be writing in the coming months. No one could have anticipated that before our case had run its course, these extortion payments would total close to $1 million.

But even by starting to pay the extortion, we still weren't convinced that we'd put a leash on Lou Mongelli. I made an appointment to see Frank Giovinco at the WPA about my concerns. Pete Porri was sitting at a poker table, still griping about his petty Weber's department store beef, but now I had much heavier things on my mind. I sat down between Porri and Giovinco at the card table, so upset with the young gangster that my language was pretty insulting.

"I got a driver that was beaten like a baby seal, Frank. What kind of *protection* are you giving me here?"

"Are you my member, Dan?"

"No."

"You're not a member. And you're not even a principal in your company. If I'm asked, 'Is Dan a member?' I can't lie. I gotta say no, and I can't vouch for you."

I told him that I now felt very embarrassed in front of my family. Look at the way this Mongelli dispute had turned out. All along, Frank's been telling me, *Relax, Dan. Calm down, Dan. Everything's gonna be fine, Dan, I'll talk to the guys at the Queens Association*—but now we've got a driver who's an invalid, and this maniac Mongelli is still threatening to murder me or someone else in the company.

Frank shrugged. "Mongelli, he's old school. He's *Barese*." (Even young wiseguys like Frank would throw around that old-country slang in conversation. Saying someone was *Barese*—technically, a person from the city of Bari, on the southern coast of Italy—was a way of saying he was hardheaded, unusually stubborn.)

The more I complained, the more I saw the rage lighting up in Frank's dark eyes. In the beginning of our talks, Frank had assured me that there was no violence in this industry. Frank said he would never stand for it.

"Well, this guy apparently doesn't listen to your association," I said. "He doesn't give a fuck about me or you and this association or the association in Queens. He doesn't give a shit about coming here to Canal Street. You told me to call and tell him to come down here and I did, and he told me he wasn't doing that. He said he doesn't belong down here."

Finally, Frank flared. "Look, nobody's going to embarrass me or this association. Believe me: It won't happen."

Pete Porri sat there grinning beside us.

"You know what, Dan?" Frank said. "I'm gonna show you how we *really* operate. Tomorrow you meet me in the Bronx. I'm gonna come see Lou Mongelli with you."

"Frank, why don't we meet Mongelli here? It'll be a lot safer."

"I'll be safe no matter what."

"Frank, we're gonna be outnumbered."

"Ain't gonna matter."

"It's gonna be the two of us and he's gonna have twenty guys there with baseball bats and ax handles."

"Listen, Dan, he's not gonna hit *me* with a bat. Lou Mongelli should be worried about me putting my hands on *him*. If he does try anything, I'll go to the stop with you on the truck—we'll have six of my guys with us and I'll give 'em all a fuckin' lesson."

The next morning I met Frank on the corner of Morris Park Avenue and Eastchester Road. We drove in our two separate cars to Lou Mongelli's office on Stillwell Avenue, parked, and walked up to the second floor. With my minicassette recorder taped inside my pants and a tiny wire run up inside my shirt, I braced myself to meet the raving madman.

But when I entered the Mongelli Carting office, I saw a radical trans-formation. The tall, slim, white-haired Lou Mongelli stood there beam-ing. "Hey, Danny! How are ya?" Yesterday Lou was threatening to beat my skull in with a lead pipe—today he was welcoming me to the Bronx, offering me fresh-brewed coffee and Arthur Avenue pastries. Of course, *now* I had Frank Giovinco by my side—young Frankie the organized-crime figure, the kid connected to the Genovese crime family.

Mongelli was moaning that I'd made the extortion check out to him personally instead of to the company, and he wanted his secretary, Louise, to type up a phony invoice saying that the Mongelli Carting Company had sold Chambers Paper Fibres a couple of tons of high-grade paper. Frank asked me to leave them alone for a few minutes. I waited while Louise typed up the bogus paperwork. The Mongelli Cart-ing Company letterhead had a bad drawing of a garbage truck and the words:

THREE GENERATIONS OF FAMILY SERVICE
SINCE 1937

After a few minutes Frank came out of the office and asked me to step into the bathroom with him. Frank turned on the bathroom faucet full blast so no one could overhear what he had to say. Once again he proved himself a well-schooled gangster: ever vigilant about surveillance.

"Look, this is what the payments are gonna be: You're gonna pay this guy two thousand dollars a month, not the three thousand a month that he wants—two thousand a month, that's it. But appease the fuckin' guy, tell him you'll work on getting the stop back to him in six months."

Frank shut off the gushing bathroom faucet and we went back to Mongelli's office. But I wasn't rolling over. "Six months? Sorry, Lou, I don't have a crystal ball. I can't tell if Charles Green's gonna even be in business in six months."

Frank returned to lecturing me. "Dan, you were wrong. You didn't have the property rights to the stop. You've got to pay Lou two grand a month."

Mongelli began moaning again, saying that it had taken him years to trick the customer into paying maximum prices and now I'd come along offering *less*.

"Youse guys screwed the fuckin' customer for youse *and* me," he said. "Youse disrupted the applecart."

Frank smiled and said that was probably the most prominent phrase you hear in the industry: *Don't disrupt the applecart*.

Just like he promised, Frank gave me an education up there in the wilds of the Bronx. He showed me firsthand how the Mob takes control of everybody. This was precisely how they'd built up the cartel—piece by piece, over fifty years—just as they'd snared me. Now Chambers was thoroughly threatened and extorted; now we were willing to become members of the Association. I didn't want to see any more vicious beatings, didn't want Cousin Sal to die of a heart attack, didn't want somebody to get shot in the back of the head.

"Okay," I told Frank, when we left Mongelli's. "We'll play by the rules. We won't disrupt the applecart."

A week later I got a call at my Brooklyn desk from Lou Mongelli.

"Danny, when can I see you?"

"What's it about, Lou?"

"Can't get into it on the phone."

I was wary, but I agreed to meet Mongelli at eleven the next morning at the Pelham Bay Diner, on Gun Hill Road in the Bronx.

I was planning on wearing the Panasonic minicassette or a digital J-Bird to the sitdown. But the night before the meeting, as I was dozing on my sofa in Staten Island, exhausted from another long day in the Chambers warehouse, I got a beep from Tony Maz.

"Dan"—no cops called me Rick anymore—I haven't been Rick for nearly a year: The chance of a slipup is too great—"we're aborting that meeting."

"Why? What's up?"

Tony explained that the supervisor of another OCID team had an ongoing investigation targeting the acting boss of one of the five families, and they'd just observed the boss with one of his button men—an assassin with a lot of hits under his belt—entering a social club in the Pelham Bay section of the Bronx. The team then observed a late-model Cadillac pulling up at the social club, and when they ran the plates, it turned out to be registered to the Mongelli Carting Company. The team didn't have a bug in the social club, so no one could be sure what was discussed. It could not have been a Mafia conversation—Lou Mongelli wasn't a made member, which precluded talking family business in front of him. Therefore, it had to be an outside beef that Lou was bringing to the acting boss.

"You understand now, Dan? Meeting is off."

"Wait a minute, Tony. Mongelli has motherfucked me and threatened me for a month. I'm gonna stand up to this guy. I'm going up there tomorrow, I'm meeting with him, I'm seeing what the fuck he wants."

"You're not going to this sitdown, Dan. It's too hot. We got Mongelli's car at a social club frequented by a boss and a guy who clips people for a living. If something goes down, I'll be jammed up—I'll lose my stripes over this thing. I have twenty years on the job—your balls-to-the-wall attitude is not gonna get me *launched*."

"Tony, I'm not trying to get you launched, but don't you understand *my* predicament? I will lose face—I'll lose all my credibility with Giovinco and the guys he's with in the WPA. I don't give a fuck if I have to punch Lou Mongelli in the face, I wanna go to the fuckin' sitdown!"

I was so angry at Mongelli I blew my stack at Mazziotti.

Tony called back in half an hour. "Okay, you fuckin' hard-on, you know what? I'm gonna let you go. But you're not wearing a body recorder. We don't know if these guys are gonna pat you down—we don't know *what* they know about you now. You're only taking a Kel."

Tony arranged to have another OCID team rendezvous at the Pelham Bay Diner on Gun Hill Road. They had photographs of the Mob assassin and they checked the place out thoroughly. So far the guy wasn't anywhere in sight. When Lou Mongelli showed up he was alone: I was watching from my parked Wagoneer, staring at my watch, still waiting for the field team to arrive on the set with the Kel booster. Without the booster, the Kel transmissions were totally useless. I waited another few minutes, until 11:10, then slammed the door of my Jeep in disgust. Booster or no booster, I couldn't keep Mongelli waiting any longer.

We sat in a booth near the door. Mongelli sipped his coffee and wasted no time in raising the issue of the attempted murder of Alex Fernandez. Of course, he didn't use any names. "You gotta talk to this guy of yours, Dan," he said. "You gotta come up with a story, not mention any of my employees. Look, it's a very *bad* neighborhood, very *dangerous* over there in Hunts Point. You never know, that guy of yours could've been robbed by some *crackheads*."

Okay, now the reason for the sitdown became clear: A day earlier, a lawyer named Tannenbaum had contacted Mongelli Carting Company on behalf of Alex Fernandez's family. That's all this sick bastard was worrying about: ducking a goddamn lawsuit.

"My guys are *union* guys, Dan. They're on my books. I can't hide them." He shrugged. "I do everything aboveboard."

"Well, I can't even talk to my guy, Lou. He's an invalid—his skull was opened up, his spleen is ruptured, his spine is fucked. What do you want me to do?"

Lou Mongelli's scowl became a smile and he changed tack: trying to play nice guy, trying to lure me into the conspiracy.

"Dan, why don't we work together?" he said. "There's some fuckin' midnight riders out here, some real fuckin' hard-ons. Why don't we band together and go after these fuckin' humps?"

6 | GHOSTS

Frank Giovinco said he was teaching me the "rules," showing me the "way things are done on Canal Street." But the funny thing was, those rules and that system went back decades before Frank was born.

The trade associations that enforced and maintained the Mob's stranglehold on the city started back in the labor upheaval of the 1920s and 1930s. They were pioneered not by Italian-American crime families but by the Jewish mobsters who influenced so much of labor racketeering as we know it today.

In the early '30s, Arthur Fleggenheimer, aka Dutch Schultz, king of the Harlem numbers rackets, put together a simple but effective shakedown of the restaurant industry. Using a lieutenant named Julius

Modgilewsky, known as Jules Martin and "the Commissar," Schultz established the Metropolitan Restaurant and Cafeteria Owners Association. Since Dutch had already taken control of the unionized waiters through the Hotel and Restaurant Employees International Alliance, every restaurateur in New York was quickly coerced by the Commissar into paying dues and fees to Schultz's association or run the risk of labor trouble.

Restaurant owners who didn't see the light found their curtains, tablecloths, and upholsteries destroyed by acid-based stinkbombs. The fearsome Jules Martin even talked the restaurant owners into signing certificates stating that they'd joined the Association of their own free will. But easy access to the treasure chest apparently undid the Commissar himself. According to the eyewitness account of Schultz's personal attorney, Richard "Dixie" Davis, Dutch murdered Martin—with a single lightning-quick gunshot to the mouth—in an upstate hotel suite, after accusing his lieutenant of pilfering $70,000 from the restaurant association's coffers. "The Dutchman did that murder just as casually as if he were picking his teeth," Davis recalled.

Dutch could master the system but not his own psychosis. The undisputed genius of labor racketeering was Schultz's less crazed contemporary, the diminutive Brooklyn gangster Louis Buchalter—generally known as Lepke, the Yiddish nickname his mother had affectionately called him in his crib. It's not likely that any other human being ever referred to Louis Buchalter again with such affection. Throughout the '20s and '30s, the name Lepke and his reputation inspired terror across America—the most cold-blooded and methodical gangster ever to hit the field of "labor relations."

Today, Buchalter is often referred to as "the Boss of Murder, Inc.," but many criminologists doubt whether this supposed syndicate enforcement arm—a crew of killers for hire, awaiting orders in Midnight Rose's candy store—ever really functioned as such. And to see Lepke Buchalter as some mere CEO of homicide is to downplay and diminish his influence on the face of organized crime. Much of industrial racketeering as we now know it today can be traced, in a direct line, back to the innovations of Louis Buchalter and his business partner Jacob "Gurrah" Shapiro.

Gurrah and Lepke were by most calculations among the richest gangsters in the heyday of the rich gangster. The headline writers of the '30s referred to them as the Gold Dust Twins. Also, less glamorously: the Gorilla Boys.

Like almost all Jewish gangsters, they got their start on the Lower East Side, in the garment industry. During the murderous strikes of the '20s and '30s, when both labor and management employed professional goons, the Gorilla Boys were in constant demand by paying customers on both sides of the picket line. Few unions could withstand the infiltration. Once a Gorilla Boy plopped his heavy heels on the desk, it was difficult to ask him to leave.

Unlike many other racketeers, Louis Lepke was not content with simple strikebreaking and extortion jobs. He had a vision of establishing long-term dominance over entire industries. And this could only be achieved, Lepke realized, if you controlled both labor and management at once. The Lepke-Gurrah mob developed "protective associations" and "factor corporations" to ensure price stability in a given industry—in effect, creating a cartel system governed by the constant threat of violence. Sometimes company owners had to be convinced to join a protective association through the use of lead pipes, car bombs, or a splash of sulfuric acid to the face—but in the tight markets of the Depression, many businessmen were only too willing to be part of a club that prevented their competitors from undercutting their prices.

Louis Lepke's gift was to recognize that the model he'd established in one industry could be seamlessly transplanted to another. Trucking was the lynchpin. All Lepke needed was to control the timely movement of goods and he controlled the whole industry. In fact, all he needed was a single corrupt Teamsters local to muscle all the other truckers into line. By this method Lepke built a massive racketeering empire. By the mid-'30s, crime historians estimate that Buchalter and Shapiro were clearing as much as $5 million to $10 million a year (the equivalent of $50 million to $100 million today), commanding an army of some two hundred fifty men, ruling over industries as diverse as dressmaking, pocketbooks, furs, leathers, baking, and motion-picture distribution.

Because few Jewish mobsters allowed their sons to follow them into the family trade, with the demise of the generation of Buchalter and Schultz—Lepke died in the Sing Sing electric chair, while Dutch was gunned down in a Newark restaurant—their plot line in the American organized crime saga ended. Lepke's former partners-in-crime, Sicilian and Neapolitan gangsters like Albert Anastasia, Vito Genovese, Tommy "Three Fingers Brown" Lucchese, "Johnny Dio" Dioguardi, and Anthony "Tony Ducks" Corallo, didn't hesitate to parcel up the bulk of the industrial rackets in New York.

And, more significantly, they didn't mess with the master formula. Under the crime families headed by Anastasia (and his successor Gambino), Genovese, and Lucchese, the technique perfected by Lepke—corrupt unions and corrupt owners' associations, joined together in a vicious circle—would be employed by the Mob, virtually unchanged, for sixty more years.

Down in the Canal Street club, you could practically sense the ghosts of guys like Lepke and Schultz. The Genovese association that we first infiltrated in March 1993 had a history stretching back almost to the time of Buchalter's walk to the Sing Sing electric chair. According to its certificate of incorporation, the Canal Street club was founded as the New York Waste Paper Removers and Packers Association, Inc., in 1946, the very year of Lucky Luciano's deportation to Italy—the year when Vito Genovese (who, in addition to gambling, narcotics, and homicide, was involved in paper recycling) began scheming to take over Lucky's crime family.

There were good reasons the West Side gangsters had been around since the beginning of time: They were the cagiest bunch going. They stayed out of the limelight. They were ultrasecretive. They didn't talk on phones.

Over the years, the Genovese crime family has produced the fewest rats of any of the crime families.

Once I got inside the West Side club, I had to be twice as cagey. I could feel them watching me all the time. It got to the point where cleaning my car of tails just became part of the daily routine.

The scariest thing about trying to maintain a double identity is that you never know who might blow your cover. In all likelihood, it's not going to be some private eye on the payroll of a mobster, tailing you around, trying to figure out where you go after work. It could just be a tiny slipup in a conversation or a random encounter you're not prepared for.

One afternoon, just as I was beginning to feel confident and accepted in my role as Danny Benedetto, I came into the Chambers office to find this elderly guy sitting there with his feet up on my desk.

"Can I help you?" I said.

"No," he said, kind of irritated. Then he snapped, "And who are you?"

"Dan."

"Dan who?"

I felt a queasy feeling in my stomach, realizing that this character might know the Benedettos personally—might even be a relation. But I tried to keep my poker face.

"Dan Benedetto."

A look of complete confusion came over the old guy's face. But before he could ask me anything else, I grabbed some dump tickets and got the hell out of the office.

I started pacing around the warehouse, thinking this guy might blow the lid off the whole caper. I went to Sal's brother and told him what happened. "Holy shit," he said, "that might be Uncle Greenie! He knows *everyone* in the family." We decided to tell Uncle Greenie that I was part of the "Staten Island crowd," the son of John Benedetto.

I stayed in the warehouse until Uncle Greenie left.

When I saw Sal the next morning, I was still pretty worried about this guy not buying my cover story. I was concerned that the word would spread through the grapevine that there was something *fugazy* about this new Dan at Chambers. Sal let loose with one of his big belly laughs. "You're worried? Don't be!" he said. "Let me tell you about Greenie. . . ."

Turns out that this old guy was actually Sal's uncle. In the years just before World War II, Uncle Greenie had some political connection who got him cushy orders when he went into the service. He was assigned to a military post in Hawaii and became a lifeguard on a Pearl Harbor beach. But when the Japanese launched their sneak attack on December 7, Greenie's cushy assignment turned into a disaster. He suffered a head injury during the bombing. He recovered, of course, but his memory was never the same.

Sal smiled. "Look, we won't have no problems with Uncle Greenie."

Every day I was in the undercover role, there was a secret danger lurking out there in the city streets. Other cops. It's not like this in an FBI operation. What the Feds can do—because they're a national branch of law enforcement—is take an agent who grew up in New York and transfer him to a deep-cover operation in Kansas City or Miami. The agent doesn't work in the area he grew up in, so chances are good no one will blow his cover.

In the NYPD we don't have that luxury. When you're deep undercover, more than anything else, you have to avoid any contact with cops. You can't go near any police facilities, can't socialize with any of your friends on the job. For years I could only have clandestine meetings with Tony Mazziotti—we'd meet in a Veterans Administration hospital in Brooklyn where we felt safe talking face-to-face.

As I said, in many ways the NYPD is like the army—there are certain rigid rules that you just can't bend under any circumstance. One is when you get Doled. The Dole is a routine drug test that every police officer has to submit to randomly—sometimes you might go the whole year without getting Doled, other times you'll get called twice in the same month. In my case they'd call OCID headquarters and tell my boss, "Rick Cowan's name popped up." Tony Maz beeps me and just like that, I have to drop everything. It sounds crazy, but that's the way it is. Doesn't matter how deep undercover you are.

If I'm in a Brooklyn diner, scheming with Frank Allocca and Ray Polidori, if I'm in the Chin's paper club with Frankie Giovinco, if I'm at Ponte's Steakhouse mingling with a bunch of hoods at the bar—doesn't matter, I have to stop in my tracks, make up some excuse, get right out there to LeFrak City as soon as possible.

It's true for every cop in the NYPD, when they Dole you, they want you *now*—a "reasonable period of time," they'll say, but you can't tell them, "I'll get there when I get there." You have to rush out there to Health Services and piss in a cup or you'll be immediately suspended from the police force.

It's the same thing with the firing range. Four times a year you have to go to the range in the Bronx for mandatory pistol requalification. But in that case, at least we were able to work it out that I could go at night, alone with Tony Maz, when there were fewer people around. We could strategize about the case, and "requal" with the Glock pistols.

All these police encounters are extremely dangerous. I've been on the job for ten years—walked a beat in Brooklyn, worked Narcotics and Organized Crime. This can blow up in my face anytime.

A chance encounter can easily kill the whole case. Say I'm in the Americana Diner in Bensonhurst and I'm meeting some of the guys from the Association. Suddenly a cop strolls in from the precinct who just met me two weeks ago when we were both at Health Services in LeFrak City taking the Dole: He's gonna blurt out, "Hey, how's it going?" And all the hoods raise up. *Why the hell is this cop saying hello to you?*

It happened to me once at this gym in Bensonhurst. I'd joined a Powerhouse Gym out there. Now that I'm hanging out with these guys every day, I'm starting to resemble a smaller version of my cousin Sal. None of these guys I was around misses *any* meals. They eat constantly. They'll meet you for breakfast and coffee, you'll sit there in the booth eating and scheming about stops, and before you know it they're bringing you macaroni for lunch. Then you go by the club in the afternoon, and they have catered Italian specialty food from Parisi's on Mott Street, the top-shelf Italian sandwiches with prosciutto and mozzarella. You'll eat that, have a few drinks, a few apricot Danish, some cannoli. Then— *look at the time*—you start thinking about heading down to Ponte's Steak-house or some other joint.

I packed on close to forty pounds in my first year undercover. I was normally around 190—I topped out close to 240 hanging out with these garbage gangsters. I was getting so fat, I couldn't hide the J-Bird on myself anymore without buying new clothes. Everything I owned was too tight.

Instead of blowing a fortune on a new wardrobe, I figured, *Let me get up two hours earlier, go to a gym when it first opens, when I'm not going to run into anybody.* I took out a membership in the name of Dan Benedetto at the Powerhouse in Bensonhurst, right across the street from Jimmy Brown Failla's social club, Veterans and Friends, on Eighty-sixth Street. I'd go there at six in the morning, catch a workout, bullshit with a bunch of these muscleheads—Brooklyn bouncers, even some wannabe wiseguys. It was going smooth for a few weeks. I started to lose the weight. A beautiful thing. Then one morning as I'm leaving, I see a guy signing in who I recognized right away. I turned my head but I couldn't avoid his eyes. He said, "Hey, how you doin'?"

"Fine"—and I kept walking.

He was a young cop who I knew from my days in the Six Seven Precinct, but he'd left the job under shady circumstances, either pen-sioned off or fired. Most of the precinct cops out in Bensonhurst are honest, hardworking guys, but you always have to be leery of a few bad apples, especially in a precinct saturated with organized-crime figures. As I left I glanced back and saw him looking closely at the sign-in sheet. I didn't know if he remembered my name or not from our time to-gether in the stationhouse. But this wasn't good.

I was concerned enough that I had to see Tony about it. We had to check this out thoroughly: It could be putting not just me but also the Benedettos at risk. I met with a good friend of mine, Detective John "Scazz" Scascia, who'd been in the Six Seven with me and was now assigned to OCID. I was certain that Scazz knew the cop I'd crossed paths with at Powerhouse. We met one afternoon on the sidelines of a Long Island football field where Scazz was coaching the varsity team, and he agreed that this former cop might be a potential problem for our investigation. Scazz reached out to a few other cops from the Six Seven, so that if this guy did start asking questions around about me, we'd quickly hear back from the precinct grapevine.

I was still pretty unnerved about this chance encounter. I didn't want this blowing up in my face a few months down the road. But Tony calmed me down. "Proceed cautiously," he said. "Wait to hear back from Scazz."

I never set foot in that gym again; I couldn't take the risk of running into the ex-cop. But later on in the investigation, at an extremely scary moment in the case, I was very glad I held on to that Powerhouse membership card.

One day I got contacted at my desk by a business located just across the street from the Chambers warehouse. It was a company called Star Distributors, and one of the owners, a middle-aged Jewish guy, was looking to have us haul away his cardboard waste. I went over to meet him, did an estimate of his cardboard output, and he gave me the grand tour of his warehouse. Suddenly alarm bells start going off in my head: Star is the name of one of the biggest pornography companies in the country. The guy was leading me down hallways, proud as can be, through rooms piled to the ceiling with porno tapes and weird lotions and dildos in all shapes and sizes and colors. Two-foot-long double-dongs. Dildos with dimples and tentacles. One dildo even had a rubber hand attached to one end that wagged back and forth. As we passed an office, the owner introduced me to his teenage daughter—very pretty and innocent-looking—who at that very moment was packaging up one of those monstrous dildos in a cardboard box.

At the far end of the warehouse, he had his own personal weight room. Thousands of pounds of plates and dumbbells, a real professional-caliber training center right inside this sicko porno factory. He gestured to one weight-lifting apparatus and asked me if I knew what it was.

"Sure, that's a Smith Machine," I said.

"That's right," he said, looking surprised.

"It's a good machine," I said. "You can work your chest, shoulders, legs, and everything on this."

"Dan," he said. "You come over whenever you want. I'll tell my people to let you in anytime, day or night. We'll catch a workout together, okay?"

But I never did take the owner up on the offer of using this weight room inside the porno warehouse. When I got back to my desk at Chambers, I did a little checking and it turned out that my hunch was right: This was the same Star Distributors that had been run by Gambino soldier Robert "Di B" DiBernardo, who'd been murdered by Sammy the Bull on the orders of John Gotti back in 1986.

By now, the hoods were calling me Danny Chambers. Most of the guys in the industry had nicknames based on their company: Frank Allocca was Frankie VA; Danny Todisco was Danny Litod; Joe Francolino was Joe Duffy; Henry Tamily was Eddie Avon; Patrick Pecoraro was Patty Marangi; and so on.

By staying away from police headquarters for so long, I got a new nickname. All the OCID detectives started calling me the Ghost. Everyone in the command knew that I was doing something undercover, but they never saw me at OCID training meetings, retirement rackets, or other cop functions.

There were days I wished I *was* a ghost. I was living the lives of three guys at once: being the full-time manager of the Chambers transfer station, getting the paper and garbage trucks rolling; playing half-a-hood, hanging out in the clubs and restaurants, scheming and scamming; doing the work of case officer, documenting my every move as a detective. The last one may sound simple, but it was actually the biggest headache.

Just keeping on top of the DD5s and the tapes was often an extra five hours' work a day. Eventually, I could no longer run my operation out of the apartment upstairs at Chambers. We had to get another place off the premises. Tony went to Deputy Inspector Kenny O'Brien and got authorization for me to use a second apartment on Cropsey Avenue in Bensonhurst—a little one-bedroom that we used to call the Crop. For many years the police department had been renting this apartment under the name Tony DeMarco. It had an infamous past. An undercover had once killed a drug dealer while making a buy in that apartment. Sometimes that made working late at the Crop a little spooky; I'd be sitting there at my typewriter, surrounded by my tapes and mountains of paperwork, thinking, *Right here on this couch a guy was shot to death.*

The investigation was getting to be so emotionally draining—there were mornings driving across the Verrazano Narrows Bridge from Staten Island that I'd pull off the expressway at the first exit, drive through Bay Ridge to this dead-end service road by Narrows Avenue. I'd park there, look out at the Narrows, breathe deeply, and try to organize my thoughts.

One dark morning, before 7 A.M., I sat in my Jeep, thinking about the Bisons. That was the name of my Little League baseball team. We had red-and-white uniforms, and we were sponsored by a New Jersey garbage company—on the back of our jerseys was stenciled a buffalo and a long Italian last name I'd rather not mention. I was only eight years old and I can remember my mother and father in our kitchen, saying: "Those garbage guys are all hooked up."

I didn't understand. "What's *hooked up?*" My parents didn't try to sugarcoat it—that was the first time I ever heard the words *Mob* or *Mafia.*

Now here I was, twenty-seven years later, in the middle of the garbage rackets, a trusted co-conspirator in the cartel, paying extortion and meeting with wiseguys. I was *inside* the machine, attempting the unthinkable, targeting John Gotti's billion-dollar-a-year candy store for a takedown.

There's no way in hell I can pull this off, I thought, staring out at the choppy water. *What the hell did I get myself into?*

Deep-undercover work is a lot like competitive wrestling: Before every big meeting—just like before every big match—you've got butterflies in your gut. It's the time before the meeting when you're nervous; once you're in there, mixing it up, the butterflies are gone. I was barely sleeping more than a few hours. I was constantly rerunning my conversations in my mind. How could I have phrased that *better*? How could I have taken it a little *further*, played it a little *dumber*, asked the question to get a more *incriminating* response for my tapes? I often had regrets—things I should have done differently. There was no such thing as small talk: Even the most routine conversation was a chance to broaden the scope of the investigation, to snag another organized-crime figure in the net.

Claire saw me tossing in bed, lost in my own thoughts. She kept asking me what was wrong, but I could never let her know what was on my mind. Looking back on it now, I don't know how she put up with it. I'm normally outgoing, a guy who likes to laugh and joke around a lot. Suddenly, I was sullen and in a fog. It happened so many times when we'd take a ride out to see our families in New Jersey. I'd be behind the wheel for forty-five minutes, we'd be almost all the way to my parents' or my in-laws', and Claire would turn to me and say: "Rick, do you realize that you haven't said a *single* word to me the whole way?"

Even my mother noticed my change in mood. Years later she told me, "Rick, you were always an easygoing kid. You never had such a bad temper until you started working on that case."

But I wasn't just bad-tempered with my family. I was constantly blowing my stack with the other detectives on the field team. Little routine things, commonplace duties of being an OCID detective, often weren't getting done, and it was making me nuts. I'd return from a meeting at one of the clubs or the Americana Diner, anxious to hear about how the photographic evidence looked, only to learn that the field team hadn't bothered to take photos that day.

Sometimes there were more serious screwups. One afternoon I was in a sensitive meeting at Allie Malangone's club, the Kings County Trade Waste Association, talking with Frank Allocca, and suddenly the receptionist at the Association is yelling: "There's a call for Danny Benedetto." I took the switchboard phone and heard the voice of a female detective on the field team, pretending to be Sal Benedetto's sister, telling me to "talk louder"—the team couldn't hear the transmissions from my Kel clearly.

Talk louder? Those two words could have got me clipped, especially in that viper's pit of surveillance-savvy, old-time Genovese hoods.

When I saw Tony Maz later, I was furious, shouting myself hoarse. I told him if that had been a male detective calling me at the club, we'd be having a fistfight right here in the street! Instead I laid into the female detective as a "fuckin' incompetent." And from that day on we had bad blood; from time to time she'd leave me my tape recordings with a note: FROM THE INCOMPETENT.

I've always liked to do things full-blast, but I'm not a real organized person—never have been. I used to help my father on welding jobs as a kid; in those days you worked at hard, physical jobs at a younger age than you can today. I'd be fourteen or fifteen on a construction site, wearing a hard hat and steel-toe boots. It would be a Friday night and I'm a typical teenager, want to get out and do what everyone does at that age, go see my girlfriend, not stand here with the sparks flying and the acetylene fuming. But my father would suddenly notice a *slight* imperfection in the job, we'd have to cut it out and regrind it, reweld it, just as per specs.

It used to drive me crazy that my father was such a perfectionist. I'd say, "Dad, no one's gonna know—it's not gonna break. Let's get outta here." "No, Rick, *I* know it's wrong," he'd say. "You gotta take pride in your work. It's a reflection of yourself."

I realized during this undercover case that I was paying special attention to every tiny detail, every little piece of evidence, dotting every *i* and crossing every *t*. I knew that down the road we would have to face some powerful defense attorneys, high-priced lawyers who could make mincemeat of even a well-prepared detective on the stand. I expected all the other cops on the team to be just as diligent and as obsessive.

I couldn't see it clearly at the time, of course, but I found myself becoming the same kind of perfectionist I used to complain about my father being when I was younger.

There was no one I could turn to for help. Tony Maz was doing as much as he could, but Tony was the team supervisor, the boss for the whole case: He had a team of a dozen OCID detectives and another dozen DA's staff to stay on top of, complex financial transactions to oversee, hundreds of pages of paperwork coming at him—*and* the brass at One Police Plaza to keep happy with monthly progress reports.

Then just when I thought I wasn't going to be able to take the pace, I met a guy who gave the case a whole new shot of life. He was Bobby O'Donahue, a thin, sandy-haired guy in wire-rimmed glasses. Bobby O wasn't with the department—he was an investigator in the district attorney's office. For months I'd heard his name but I'd never met him in person. He'd started working the case in the Manhattan plant—our eavesdropping headquarters overlooking the Waste Paper Association—and then one day in June '93 he asked to meet me face-to-face. It was a risky meeting, but Bobby was smart enough not to come in his DA's vehicle—he drove his personal car, a beat-up gold-colored Oldsmobile with grungy seats and a cracked windshield. *Perfect.* We met on a side street in Brooklyn Heights. I got in the passenger side and he laughed, shaking my hand for a long time.

"You got a pretty good grip for a ghost."

I handed him a sheet of paper with a list of five or six Mob nicknames like Butchie and Albie and Jocy Garbage. "I'm gonna need help ID'ing these subjects. See if you can get their real names and addresses, but don't stop there. Do the Con Ed checks—see who's paying the bills—"

Bobby cut me off, letting me know that he was ready to do anything I needed.

"Dan, I've been around for a month or two, watching you. I've been listening to the Kel and I understand your situation. I know you're swamped. You're frustrated. I know you feel like you need help. That's why I asked to get involved." He reached into the glove compartment and handed me a bunch of fresh batteries for the Kel. He knew that the batteries were always going dead at the most inopportune moments. Whole conversations would be lost and I'd either have to risk getting those subjects to repeat themselves or reconstruct the conversations from memory for the DD5s. Then he gave me a list of his phone numbers and told me to call him anytime—on duty or off duty.

But from that day on, Bobby took it on himself to be my contact detective. He'd meet me with Tony at the VA Hospital in Brooklyn or down at the Old Sailors' Home below Battery Park City, debriefing me after meetings. He'd swing by my Tony DeMarco apartment on Cropsey Avenue to bring me dupes of the tapes. Everytime I used a Kel device, Bobby would take the original tapes to be vouchered at the DA's office, then he'd bring me duplicates that I could listen to on my Walkman, extract the evidentiary material I needed to type up my Fives.

As the months went on, and the pace of the case got more intense— the daily scheming and scamming, the thousands of hours of taped conversations—Bobby was much more than a contact detective. He was my best friend, my lifeline to the outside world. A lot of the other cops on the field team just wanted to get home as soon as their tours finished. Understandable—we all have wives or girlfriends or kids in Little League. But Bobby was different. Bobby was a tireless, hands-on, exceptionally organized investigator. He came from a prominent legal family— his father, brother, and sister were all judges and lawyers—so he had an almost in-born ability to think like an attorney. But he was also down-to-earth enough to act like a cop. He could see I had a workload that was enough for two people, and he took the initiative to shoulder half.

Bobby'd stop by the Crop when I was pulling my hair out typing up tape transcripts and Fives. He listened to every single tape and by the end of the case, he knew all my conversations by heart: He could quote back word for word what a certain subject of the investigation had said at a certain time at a certain location; he could brief the ADAs in Morgenthau's office and save me hours of phone time. More than anyone else, Bobby gave me the room to breathe—freed me up, allowed me to move around inside my Dan Benedetto role. If Bobby hadn't come on board when he did, I probably would've gone off the deep end.

By the summer of '93, Chambers was officially on the board—proposed for membership in the Greater New York Waste Paper Association—and carters of all stripes were coming out of the woodwork. In July we won the contract to service the HBO headquarters on Avenue of the Americas. HBO had previously been serviced by Avon Sanitation, a New Jersey–based company owned by two old-timers named Joe Virzi and Eddie Tamily.

Tamily and Virzi had been charging HBO $5,400 a month. When they tried to raise the rate, the HBO executives sent out a DOS (discontinuation of service) notice and put the contract out for bids. Chambers won the contract at $3,400 a month and the HBO financial executives were delighted: They were saving two thousand dollars a month *and* they didn't have to deal with those unsavory garbage gangsters.

Tamily was less delighted, and within days he placed a call to me at Chambers.

"We gotta talk, kid."

"Yeah, what about?"

"About the TV place."

"TV?"

"Yeah, HBO."

I realized that Eddie was angry enough to come down to Plymouth Street. We still had the audio and video in place in Sal's office, but now I had to go up on a ladder into the sooty, rat hair–covered ceiling and install fresh hearing-aid batteries into the surveillance devices.

I'm just putting the ceiling tiles back in place, sweeping up the floor, when Eddie Avon shows up.

Though his given name was Henry Tamily, I noticed that he had the name Eddie tattooed in fading blue ink on his forearm. Tamily was a sixty-six-year-old Genovese associate, bald-headed, with the droopy jowls of a basset hound and an unusually large flap of flesh hanging over the crooked knot of his necktie. He came into the Chambers offices talking tough and salty. It was just me and Eddie—Sal and the other Benedettos had cleared out long ago.

"What is it?" I snapped.

"*Minghia!* You gotta pay me for the HBO stop. You can't just go out there and *take*." When Ed saw that I wasn't flinching, he tried to buffalo me. But Ed was smooth: He did it with a whisper. "Listen, it's not my stop. I'm really caretaking it for *somebody*."

"For who?"

"I'm caretaking it for Matty the Horse."

He just dropped the name of a real heavyweight. Matthew "Matty the Horse" Ianniello was a power in the Genovese crime family going back to the late 1940s: a *capodecina* who owned several garbage companies, including Duchess Sanitation and Consolidated Carting, and ran a multimillion-dollar vending racket of cigarette and candy machines, pinball games and jukeboxes. As far back as the mid-'70s, the NYPD's Organized Crime Control Bureau knew that Matty the Horse had an enormous slice of New York's entertainment economy—dozens of restaurants, bars, nightclubs, and strip joints. Approaching seventy-five, Matthew Ianniello was currently a guest of the United States government.

Matty the Horse or no Matty the Horse, I knew I had to stand my ground.

"Listen," I said, "we're a longtime independent company, we're a family business—we're talking about joining the Association, but really we want to keep to ourselves here."

"You're not gonna be able to keep to yourself, fella. You better change. That way you can have peace—you go to sleep at night and nobody's gonna bother you. Not trying to be any kind of wiseguy or threaten you or nothin', but I'm *beggin'* you, kid, I want this HBO thing straightened out."

But by now, I'd perfected my technique, learned to stay out of corners, keep all options open. In August '93, I went down to see Frank Giovinco at the Chin's paper club on Canal Street. I found Ed Tamily

sitting at a poker table with his partner, Joe Virzi. Virzi was also in his
late sixties, bald and hound-dog–faced, though I soon realized he had a
more volatile and belligerent disposition than his partner.

Everyone in the paper club was wary of the newcomer. Frank Giovinco kept patting my back when he brought me over to meet Joe Virzi
and Ed Tamily.

"Listen, young fella, this stop has got to get straightened out," Virzi
said. "Ask around about me. I'm well-known in the industry. I am your
lawyer now, kid. You come to us. Angelo, Eddie, Tony Vitale, me—we
are your lawyers. We straighten things out for you."

But for a carter who'd been in the business more than forty years,
Virzi had grown slightly careless. He snapped his fingers and yelled,
"Get me a piece of paper and pen!"

Right away, over came Greater New York Waste Paper Association
letterhead—a beautiful thing, from an evidentiary perspective—and Joe
Virzi began to juggle numbers. It was immediately apparent that Virzi
was a *wizard*. He didn't multiply on paper, didn't need a calculator. He
could rattle off complex, fractional multiples instantaneously.

"I was getting $5,400 for the HBO stop. Normally, if you're an out-
law, that's gonna cost you 60-to-1, but since you're willing to do the
right thing, it's gonna be 37½-to-1. Okay, that makes the nut $202,500.
That's a lot of money, kid." Only now did he start scribbling on the letterhead. "You can pay me $80,000 now and $122,500 over the next
year. Go past that first year, I tack on 6 percent interest."

Six percent? Virzi was charging *vig*?

"HBO is a good stop—a beautiful stop. You'll do very good there, kid."

But I was stalling—forever stalling.

"Look, Joe, I don't want to pay anybody yet. I've got a shitload of
beefs to settle. I'm gonna be on the board for ninety days"—to join the
Association, Chambers was facing a three-month claim period during
which every outraged carter that lost work to Chambers could go on
record and make a claim—"I'm gonna have beefs coming at me from all
sides. I don't want to pay anybody till I see what I'm dealing with. This
could be too much for me to handle."

Now Joe Virzi showed his true colors. Everyone in on the bidding process at HBO had been dealing with the same vice president, a friendly businesswoman named Carolyn. Suddenly Joe Virzi was venting his anger at her:

"That old black bastard!" he said.

"Who, Carolyn?" I said.

"Yeah, that old black bastard, who the hell does she think she is? She's lucky she came across you. If she didn't, she woulda went noplace fast!"[1]

They were all licking their chops. Their greed was unbelievable. These West Side guys saw Chambers as a cash cow, a meaty carcass waiting to be carved up. They knew the Benedettos had a prosperous paper business stretching back to 1896. They referred to Sal as "old money," and they'd been sharpening their blades for years.

Sal and I met with Frank Giovinco at Ponte's Steakhouse, discussed the terms of joining the club—beginning September 1. While we ate, Joe Virzi and Ed Tamily were also at Ponte's and Virzi sat himself down at our table, uninvited, and kept butting into our negotiation session. The issue that Sal was most concerned with was how far back in time claims could be made against us by members of the various associations. After all, Chambers Paper Fibres had been an independent company since 1896. Going back too far in time would obviously bankrupt the company. Frank Allocca in Brooklyn had been very specific about setting a five-year retroactive plan that would allow present members to make claims against us. But Frank Giovinco, speaking for the WPA membership, bristled at being nailed down to a specific time limit.

---

[1] HBO exacted its own brand of payback. In the years immediately following Operation Wasteland, the premium cable network would achieve its greatest commercial and critical success with *The Sopranos,* a one-hour drama following the travails of a likable but emotionally troubled New Jersey garbage gangster. ("I'm in commercial and non-putrescible waste," Tony Soprano tells his psychiatrist with a knowing smile.) But at least one HBO executive knew that the real-life Sopranos weren't always so endearing.

"Could be three years, five years," Joe Virzi said, then he laughed. "The Cigar will say, 'Where were you for ten years?'" The Cigar was well understood by both Sal and myself to be a reference to Jimmy Brown Failla, the powerful Gambino *capo*. What Joe Virzi meant was: Jimmy Brown would tell his membership, *Why the hell would you let a guy take your work for ten years before you made a beef?* It was generally understood that if a guy robbed you, you went after him right away. Joe Virzi's personal greed wouldn't let him stop from badgering Sal and me about when we could rectify the HBO beef with him.

Finally, Frank Giovinco got visibly impatient with Virzi's meddling and pressure tactics. "Excuse me," he said, and then asked Virzi to join him at the bar. After a few minutes Frank returned to our table alone.

"What happened?" I asked. "Will he be coming back?"

"No," Frank said.

Laughing, Sal said: "Frank, everybody's trying to tell you what to do."

Dead serious, Frank stared back at Sal: "They could *never* tell me what to do. They tell me what they *think* and I come to my own conclusions."

On September 15, when I went back down to 511 Canal Street, Frank began describing the list of grievances trickling in from the four associations, from Allie Shades in Brooklyn, from Jimmy Brown's Gambino club, and from the subsidiary Gambino association in Queens.

"How long is the list?" I whispered.

"Scary." He laughed.

"What's the total damage gonna be?"

"A lot of guys have been waiting with their fuckin' tongues hanging out."

Frank was trying to continue my education. If a customer contacted Chambers wanting his business surveyed, I should *always* call the carter who owned the property rights to find out what he was charging first. Then I could quote the customer a rate that was slightly above what the stop's true "owner" was getting.

But I could see that Frank was pissed off with me about something today. "More importantly, you just recently took another building off somebody—Shields."

"Yeah, Shield Die-Cutters. I knew I was going to hear something about this—"

"What are you billing the customer—you have any idea?"

"We're charging them nothing. We're getting a lot of printed bleach—"

"You know what they were getting charged, pineapple? They were getting charged a nice number. What the fuck are you doin'? You didn't take it at a good number! D'Ambrosio is getting three thousand nine hundred. You're taking it for nothin'? We ain't giving out no breaks here. We ain't gonna let the customer off the fuckin' hook, Moe. It don't happen. . . . You're making these fuckin' people fat. What's the matter with you? You gotta go in and *charge* them."

The property rights to Shield Die-Cutters and Embossers, Inc., a printing company on West Fifteenth Street in Chelsea, had "belonged" to Five Brothers Carting—an outfit run by two brothers and their father named D'Ambrosio. Five Brothers Carting had some of the premier garbage accounts in the city, including Bankers Trust, Barclays Bank, J. P. Morgan, MCI, and the Lincoln Center for the Performing Arts.

Right now, Michael D'Ambrosio, aka Mikey Five Brothers, was lingering in the shadows of the club, sipping coffee, waiting for his turn to get at me. Mikey was a thin-built, black-haired twenty-six-year-old, deeply suntanned with the heavy-lidded look of a young Al Pacino.

"He's fuckin' livid," Frank whispered in my ear. "His fuckin' jowls were scraping the fuckin' floor. . . . He's hot as a fuckin' pistol. First, you gotta know his father. His father is a real fuckin' old-time garbageman. He's screaming with the gruff voice, hollering, yelling. 'Relax,' I says, 'Dan'll do the right fuckin' thing. Just give him an opportunity.' But he ain't afraid to scuff his knuckles, Dan. This kid'll go toe-to-toe with *anyone*."

Sure, with Frank backing him up, he would. Frank called Mikey Five Brothers over to the card table and he started giving me hell over Shield

Die-Cutters. "I don't have to tell you that this is a beautiful creampuff account—especially for a paper guy like yourself," Mikey said.

The worst thing we could have possibly done with this "creampuff account," this "cherry account," was to go in and charge the customer *nothing*. In reality, of course, this was the honest, fair thing to do, because the high-grade paper we were picking up was worth a lot of money on the recycling market. But most of these customers didn't know that. The cartel members had them thoroughly bamboozled. They were used to thinking of their high-grade paper as just another form of garbage. "The problem that we're having here is, you set your salesmen on the street and they're fuckin' educating everybody," Frank said. "Everybody used to walk around with fuckin' blindfolds on. Now everybody's getting fuckin' educated. 'Ooh, ooh, ooh, this is worth something!'"

"Yeah, and I'm getting educated," I said. "'Cause I haven't been around real long. You know I was in Dom Ben, the realty part of the company. I just got into this a little over two years ago."

Frank said I had to stop underbidding the membership, because "in the end, who's the survivor? Who's the winner? The customer." The most important lesson for me to learn was to always "post up" with club members like Mikey Five Brothers. That way we could collude, get our figures straight, and at least make the bid look competitive; in this case, my salesman should have offered Shield Die-Cutters something more sensible, like $3,000 a month. That way, Frank said, "You're still the guy's hero, aren't you? You're saving him a thousand dollars a month, Dan . . . Look, I'm not turning around and telling you how to run your business. . . . [B]ut why the fuck would you take it for nothing? Michael was getting thirty-nine hundred. This guy [the customer] should be on his hands and knees, fuckin' lapping your *piscadile* over here."

I was trying to haggle, telling them that I had a binding legal contract with Shield Die-Cutters. Mikey and Frank laughed. "A contract is as good as the paper it's written on," Mikey said. He kept demanding that we work out a schedule for him to start receiving the $127,000 he claimed he was out.

"I'm not lookin' for this money in one lump—I wanna start something right away, though," he said. "And I don't think coming up with X number of dollars a month should be a problem. You're a big, big company. You guys have a lot of money. I don't know where it's hidden or where it's sitting, but my point is this: You gotta come across with something."

Everyone thought the Benedettos had a pot of gold buried there under the Manhattan Bridge. "I don't know how it is in your family, but in my family we got *them* and *those,* if you know what I mean," I said. I kept trying to tell them I had to clear everything with my uncles and cousins at the home office, the parent company, and that there were constant rifts and tensions within the family. I kept trying to buy myself a little breathing room. "It's a two-way street," I said, trying for some levity.

"Over here it's a one-way street," Frank snapped. "Do the right thing or get off the fuckin' block. It's a one-way street. There ain't fuckin' two ways here. That's all I can tell you—Canal Street runs fuckin' one way. We're gonna close down the opposite fuckin' lane."

"We're talking about Fifteenth Street here," I said, with a forced laugh.

"Yeah, we're talking about Fifteenth Street. That's what we're talking about: 443 West Fifteenth Street. Right things gotta be done. That's all I could tell you."[2]

No sooner had Mikey Five Brothers finished laying into me than Frank summoned over Joe Virzi and let the old guy loose for fifteen minutes about his HBO grievance. Virzi was demanding to know how soon I could start settling up the $200,000 he said I owed him for taking HBO.

And when I turned around, who should I see waiting in the wings?

---

[2] Years later, Patrick Dugan, head of the Manhattan district attorney's Rackets Bureau, drew an analogy for a trial jury: "If Toyota had to pay every time a customer switched from a Ford Taurus to a Toyota Camry, do you think that Toyota would be competing with Ford? Of course not. Why should it be any different in the private carting industry?" [*People of the State of New York* v. *Association of Trade Waste Removers of Greater New York, et al.*]

Phil Barretti, silver-headed, dapper-dressed in an Italian silk shirt, lounging at a table nearby, using the phone. Frank came back over and whispered: "Look, I'm gonna bring over Whatchamacallit for a couple of minutes, okay?"

"Who?"

"Phil Barretti, okay? Talk to him—nice. . . . Phil is an advocate for you. He thinks you'd be good for the industry. We wanna keep as many guys on our side as possible. I just want to put the two of youse together. Let's start airing shit out."

Barretti strutted over, shook my hand, sat down, and began listing his claims against me—starting with the "the big one," meaning One Wall Street. Also: 126 Church Street, 95 Reade Street, 51 Bowery.

"Wait a minute, Phil. You took Chase Manhattan Plaza and 20 Pine Street from me first."

"No, first *you* took One Wall—that's why we went to war."

"No, Phil, first you took Chase Manhattan. You hit first and then we hit back."

I wanted to say, *And you blew up our truck, then had your goon smack and choke my fifty-four-year-old cousin*—but I knew I had to phrase my displeasure carefully, even if I raised my voice.

"I'll tell you straight up," I said. "I was with Sal when we went to meet you once. You know how Sal is, he's a bit of a recluse—"

"Yeah, I could never meet with him."

"And the rest of my family is worse. The guy"—of course, I don't want to mention Ray Ramos by name—"kept coming down, breakin' balls, doing all this wacky shit. I asked Sal to go see you 'cause that's what I would've done. Prior to all this other nonsense, I said, 'Let's go see the guy and talk, or whatever happens happens. Can't go on like this, driver's getting fucked around—' "

"We don't have to go into it." Frank cut me off.

"I said [to Sal], 'Let's go talk to Phil' . . . and you *know* what happened. And I still hold a little in me—I shouldn't—but I still hold a little of a grudge. I was the first one he [Ramos] threatened—not Sal, *me*."

Now that I was talking about a firebombing and an assault, I'd lowered my voice to a real raspy whisper, which was showing Frank and Phil I knew how to conduct myself in Mob circles. I knew from my years doing surveillance on Allie Shades and his crew that these guys always whisper when they're starting to discuss violent crimes. "That still fuckin' gets me a little bent out of shape. I disagree with these times," I said— meaning who had started the turf war between Sal and Phil. "We were hit and hit and hit, and when we finally fought back, we got hurt over it. I know now I've made a commitment, Sal's made a commitment, things are a little different, and what's gotta be done *will* be done."

"Most importantly, the two of youse gotta coexist," Frankie G. said. "Right? I know it's hard for you to swallow what happened in the past. No one's sayin' *forget* it. But just understand, times were different then . . ."

Meaning: We were outlaws then, but now we're coming into the Mafia's garbage club.

At one point while I was in the Association, Frank was talking with a bunch of the members about going fishing that weekend for tuna off Long Island. He smiled at me then made a little joking reference to *The Godfather Part II,* when Michael Corleone had his sad-sack brother Fredo whacked while out fishing. Frank was just busting my balls in front of the guys.

"Hey, Dan," he said. "Too bad your back's out or we'd take you along. Put you at the front of the boat and have you sayin' the 'Hail Mary.'"

I was back on Canal Street a week later to negotiate with Mikey Five Brothers. I told him to bring me some invoices to show what he was billing the Shield Die-Cutters stop. That's the way you work out a beef: Get a guy to show everything in writing, the invoices and the stop's yardage, so he can't just make up some astronomical numbers out of thin air. You never take the other guy's word for anything.

I showed up at the club at 2:30 P.M. Vito Palmeri, the Chin's driver, was sitting at his desk, and Vincent Esposito, the Chin's son, was there with a bunch of other hood-looking characters. I entered the large room, where I saw Mikey Five Brothers and Sal Rutigliano standing around; meanwhile Frank Giovinco, Joe Virzi, and Tony Vitale were engrossed in a card game. Mikey Five Brothers handed me his 1993 paperwork, showing me the monthly checks he's getting out of Shield Die-Cutters. I looked at his numbers, frowning at him.

"Mike, I get the impression you want to be paid this fifty-six and change for the rest of your life."

"No, I don't want to be paid for the rest of my life."

We were waiting for Frank to finish up the card game when I noticed that on top of the big-screen TV set in the corner was a videotape of *Raging Bull*. I picked up the tape and looked at the black-and-white picture of De Niro as Jake LaMotta with his face all battered.

"This is my favorite movie of all time," I said.

All the guys burst out laughing.

"It *is*—my all-time favorite movie."

They laughed again.

"That's not *Raging Bull*."

Turns out, someone stuck something else in that *Raging Bull* box. I sat down at a card table with Frank Giovinco and Mikey Five Brothers. Frank ordered Joe Virzi to put the tape in the VCR and turn the TV volume up. Suddenly we had the sound of a porno video blasting through the club. Frank told me, "Shhh—talk low." These wiseguys always assume that their clubs are bugged, so the way to avoid being overheard by law enforcement is either to whisper or to blast the TV or stereo. In this case, they chose to whisper and blast hard-core porn.

It was extremely distracting trying to haggle with Mikey Five Brothers while there was all this humping and grunting and moaning on the tube. Mikey and I were arguing over the details of the Shield Die-Cutters beef when old Joe Virzi interrupted us, asking me what I was going to do about paying him for HBO.

Virzi was incredibly angry again—he seemed unstable. He took a piece of paper and violently scribbled two numbers: 88 and 120. Meaning thousands. "I want this," he says, circling the number 88, "in one cash payment. Then you can pay me this"—he circled the 120—"by check."

They were like a pack of panting wolves. No one could wait his turn to take a bite out of me. Virzi was still speaking and Mikey Five Brothers jumped back in, also demanding to be paid in cash only. Five Brothers wanted his first payment of $40,000 cash no later than next week.

I refused. "That's impossible, Mike. I don't have that kind of money— I just can't bring two *shoeboxes* of cash and hand them over to youse guys."

"That's what you pay when you take," Joe Virzi growled.

Virzi was not only unstable, he was slippery. Contrary to what he said at our first meeting, he and Ed Tamily now wanted me to compensate them at a rate of 60-to-1 for HBO.

"Wait a minute, Joe," I said. "First you told me that's what someone outside pays. I'm joining the club, I'm going on the board. That means I'm not an outlaw anymore. I agreed to pay you twenty-four hundred dollars in good faith while I'm on the board and I'm still gonna be penalized?"

"Yeah, Dan's right—whattaya doing here?" Frank said.

"I'm cutting his *balls* off for taking!" Virzi barked.

Frank was trying not to lose his cool. He'd been trying to ease me into the club, but these guys were all too greedy to go along with Frank's program. "Excuse us," he said, then took Joe Virzi and Mikey Five Brothers over to the kitchen, where I couldn't hear them. Now I was sitting alone at the card table, watching some guy on TV get a blowjob, and this guy, John Pasquale, was standing next to me, waiting to pounce.

Pasquale took my notepad and wrote down the stops he said I robbed from him. The addresses were 26 Wall Street, 30 Wall Street, and 693 Broadway. I had no idea what he was even talking about.

"My agreement with Frank is to go back five years," I said. "Are these stops older than five years?"

"I'll have to check," Pasquale said. "Take your time with these stops. I'm in some hot water myself. My father is Joe Pasquale. I'm sure you know him. Our families both have a good reputation. My office is a few blocks away—Atlas Paper. Stop by sometime, we'll have coffee and work it out."

Frank Giovinco, Joe Virzi, and Mikey Five Brothers reentered the room. Virzi said, "Kid, next week you'll have an answer for me, right? About how you're going to do this. You'll bring that thing with you—you know what I mean?" Sure, I knew what he meant: His first payment for HBO.

"Okay."

Frank Giovinco shot John Pasquale an ugly look. He noticed the three claims Pasquale wrote on my notepad. "No, these are older than five years. Dan, forget about this shit—you worry about this *here*." He tapped the green felt of the card table, then told Pasquale to leave us alone. "Forget about him," Frank said, disgusted, while Pasquale was still within earshot. "I'll punch *him* in his fuckin' head."

Mikey Five Brothers and I kept haggling over the porn tape. Mikey was sticking to his guns, demanding that I give him that stack of $40,000 in cash. Frank was trying to be the peacemaker, doing complicated multiplication in his head like it was nothing. Just like Joe Virzi, Frank was a whiz with mental calculations.

After every meeting I would drive through traffic and clean myself, make sure that I wasn't being tailed. I would then do two things: First, I'd meet detectives Harry Bauerle and Camille San Fillipo and turn over the J-Bird device for the purposes of downloading the microchip and vouchering the tape as evidence. (This process protects the "chain of custody," in legal terms, which must be demonstrated at the time of trial; this is true for all evidence, making it either admissible or inadmissible.) Then I'd go meet Tony Maz and Bobby O to be debriefed at different locations, rehashing word-by-word the conversations I'd just had.

That night, leaving the Association, I noticed I was being followed by two vehicles. I wrote down the license plates so we could check them with the DMV. I had to cruise around the Manhattan streets for a long time—making U-turns, sudden lefts and rights—finally losing them in the Brooklyn Battery Tunnel, before I could turn over my J-Bird and rendezvous with Tony Maz and Bobby O.

On Wednesday, September 29, I was called down to another sitdown on Canal Street in order to make my first set of extortion payments to Michael D'Ambrosio and Joe Virzi. I was extremely keyed-up for the meeting and wanted to make sure my J-Bird device was functioning perfectly.

When I was a couple of blocks away from the club, I noticed that the red indicator light on the J-Bird was going dim. For weeks I'd been getting conflicting messages from Tech Services: Did this mean it was set on Voice-activated? Or did that mean the battery was malfunctioning? I had already lost two good conversations due to technical malfunctions, and I didn't want to lose another, so I pulled my Jeep over—within a block of the club—and went out to a pay phone to call Tony Mazziotti and ADA Marybeth Richroath. But like an idiot, when I walked to the phone, I locked my Jeep door with the keys in the ignition.

I had a crucial sitdown scheduled with those organized-crime guys in minutes up in the club, and my black appointment book filled with thousands of dollars in extortion payments was sitting right on the passenger seat in plain view.

There was a garage across the street and I ran over to borrow a slim jim. I pried into the window and started working the slim jim for about fifteen minutes without any luck. OCID had a surveillance plant located around the corner, videotaping the front entrance to the Waste Paper Association night and day, and I knew that all the cops up there were having a roaring laugh over this one. In fact, Lou Balistreri, one of the field team detectives, soon came down from the plant.

"Let me try," Balistreri said.

"Get the hell outta here!" I hissed, because Louie looks like a TV version of a cop.

"If you were a real skel," he said, "you would've got in in three minutes."

Just then, from the other direction, Angelo Ponte, Joe Ponte, and Joe Virzi came walking past—and they saw Lou Balistreri walking off the block. I was embarrassed, having to tell the Ponte brothers and Joe Virzi that I'd locked myself out of my vehicle with the engine running. "I'll see you inside as soon as I can get in my Jeep."

Now the garage guy took pity: He jogged across the street and tried with the slim jim for another fifteen minutes. But he was just as incapable of breaking into a locked vehicle as I was. All the while, there was this skinny Puerto Rican kid, no older than thirteen, watching us and smiling. Finally the kid came over and asked if he could try. "Well, we've been trying for half an hour already," I said.

No exaggeration—I handed the kid the slim jim and he was inside the Jeep in seconds. I gave him ten bucks for his trouble. When I got inside the club, I told Frank Giovinco, Mikey Five Brothers, Joe Virzi, and everyone else about this kid's remarkable skill. "He must do it professionally," I said. The whole club got a good laugh.

When I first stepped out of the elevator, Frank was deep in one of his whispering conversations with Vinnie Esposito, the Chin's son.

"How's your back, Dan?" he asked. I'd been constantly moaning to Giovinco about having lower-back pain. "You want me to hit you in the back?" Frank proceeded to pat my entire back, making light chops from my neck to the small of my back. He was trying to make it look like he was doing a little amateur massage, but I was certain he was actually checking my back for a wire. "Go inside," he said. "Michael's waiting for you."

Inside the club I saw Angelo and Joe Ponte and Vito Palmeri. Standing at one of the card tables, Joe Virzi and Mikey Five Brothers were anxiously waiting to receive their first payments—their so-called restitution—from me.

"So, Dan, talk to me," Mikey said. But I cut him off, reaching for the pre-signed checks in my appointment book. "Let me give you these things," I said, "before I forget and leave with them—as if you would let me."

Joe Virzi smiled. "Naw, we got the door locked."

"Oh, I'm trapped," I said.

I handed Mikey a check for $3,633 as partial restitution for the Shield

Die-Cutters beef. He agreed he would mail me an invoice showing that this check was supposedly for the sale of high-grade paper.

When I went to hand Joe Virzi his check, made out in the amount of $2,400 for the HBO stop, he nearly gave me a heart attack. We were standing close, whispering distance, and he made a motion like he was going to take the check from me—then lunged forward, making a sudden grab with his left hand. He managed to feel right around my crotch before I could grab his wrist and pull my midsection backwards.

"What the *hell* are you doing?"

"I gotta make sure you're clean."

It was crazy: Just by a hair, by a fraction of an inch, Virzi had missed my J-Bird recorder—the metal box just slightly larger than a pack of cigarettes—taped to my abdomen above the groin. When I glanced back, I noticed Angelo Ponte and Frank Giovinco in the doorway, watching me closely. Joe Virzi nodded, satisfied that I wasn't wired. Then we sat down at one of the large tables and he accepted the first payment for his HBO grievance.

Neither Virzi nor Michael D'Ambrosio was too happy about accepting these payments by check. Cash is always king. But Virzi explained to D'Ambrosio that the checks were just my initial good-faith overtures while Chambers was "on the board" for our ninety-day probational period. After we were accepted as members in good standing, they expected me to pay them larger sums—in cash.

"What are we talking about, Dan, after the three months are up?" Michael demanded.

Virzi motioned to Michael and put his finger to his lips. He gestured to the back of the club and said, "Take him back there."

When Michael and I were in the most secluded corner of the club, sitting at one of the tables, I told him that I'd continue making these check payments of $3,633 and they would count towards the "total nut"—the total amount that he claimed I owed him.

"No way," he snapped. "If I wanted to be paid by check, I have to be paid at 50-to-1."

I told him that we'd gone around and around with these negotiations last week. It was already settled. "Frank talked to you—and you agreed," I said.

"No, I didn't understand it that way," Michael said. Then he added, with a little devious grin: "Between you, me, and the lamppost, Dan, I don't know if anyone here has conveyed this thought to you, but my point is: It *should* hurt. I *want* it to hurt. I *want* it to be difficult for you."

A few weeks later, it got even more difficult for me. Our investigation hit an unseen pothole. The pothole was named BFI.

On October 6, in a major press conference held at City Hall with Mayor David Dinkins, representatives of Browning-Ferris Industries, Inc., announced that the Houston-based trash-collecting giant would be sponsoring the upcoming New York City Marathon. BFI, the nation's second-largest waste hauler, was trying to signal a little more than its support for the New York Road Runners Club. It had come to proclaim a new dawn in the economic life of the city. No longer would New York's businesses have to pay the exorbitant carting rates—by far the highest in the nation—within the clutches of the Mafia-run cartel.[3]

"We're sending a message to the Mob," said BFI spokesman Gary Lewi, "saying we're not being run out of town."

Although New York City accounts for fully 5 percent of America's total commercial waste, it remained the only city in the United States in which no national hauler had a slice of the marketplace. That changed in early 1993, when Columbia-Presbyterian Medical Center in Upper Manhattan, which had long been using BFI to dispose of its medical waste, switched over to Browning-Ferris for its ordinary trash. The hospital dismissed its existing hauler, Louis Mongelli (owner of the Mongelli Carting Company of the Bronx), who had been charging $750,000 a year, and signed a contract with BFI at a savings of 60 percent.

---

[3] At the time, New York City's rate was $14.70 per cubic yard of commercial trash, compared to $5 in Chicago and $4.25 in Philadelphia.

William D. Ruckelshaus, BFI's chairman, was thrust into the media glare. At the time, Ruckelshaus had one of the most distinguished résumés of any chief executive in the country: He'd been the first director of the Environmental Protection Agency, had served as acting director of the FBI, and was best known as the deputy U.S. attorney general who'd resigned during the "Saturday Night Massacre" when he was given a direct order by Nixon to fire Watergate special prosecutor Archibald Cox and refused.

For more than a year Ruckelshaus had been courted by Mayor Dinkins and Mark Green. Green, the consumer affairs commissioner, had been trying to inject competition into the New York carting industry; Ruckelshaus, with his law enforcement background and "Mr. Clean" image, seemed a perfect fit for the campaign. In late '92 the BFI boss was brought to New York for lunch meetings with the editors of the country's leading newspapers and magazines. *Fortune* would later relate one conversation Ruckelshaus had with various senior staffers at the *New York Times* offices on West Forty-third Street:

> *"Hey, who picks up our garbage?" asked one* Times *man. "The Mob,"*
> *blurted a second journalist, triggering a gaggle of giggles around the table.*
> *"You think it's funny," responded Ruckelshaus. . . . "Here you are, in the*
> *financial center of the Free World, with an essential service delivered by a*
> *cartel, and you guys are all amused."*[4]

Within a matter of months, the *Times* editorial-page staff, and many colleagues in the journalistic community, had wiped off those smirks and begun to echo the somber tone Ruckelshaus set. On November 8, 1993, *The Wall Street Journal* ran an ominous A-1 story headlined "Too Good to Refuse: Browning-Ferris Bucks Mob." Its lead would become the talk of the industry for many years to come:

---

[4] *Fortune,* January 15, 1996, "How Bill Ruckelshaus Is Taking on the New York Mob" by Richard Behar

If Browning-Ferris Industries, Inc., thought breaking into the trash-hauling business here would be easy, that notion vanished in February. Dumped on the suburban doorstep of David A. Kirschtel, a company executive, was a dog's severed head. In its mouth was a note: WELCOME TO NEW YORK.

Sure, it made for good newspaper copy. A decapitation message straight out of *The Godfather*. A white-knight company galloping to the rescue of the besieged city. Bill Ruckelshaus, the young lawman who'd stood on principal in the face of presidential illegality, was, twenty years later, striding into Gotham for a showdown with the Mob.

But a few uncomfortable corners had to be trimmed to make this *High Noon* fable fit. In the first place, anyone familiar with the national waste-management industry would have a hard time sticking those Texans in Gary Cooper's boots. As early as August 1992, a *Village Voice* exposé had raised doubts about Mark Green's overtures to bring Browning-Ferris Industries—"one of the nation's worst corporate criminals"—to New York:

> *It's hard to imagine that Green hasn't heard of BFI's rap sheet. In 1987 in Toledo, a BFI official pleaded guilty to criminal antitrust charges, leaving BFI with a $1 million fine for bid rigging and price-fixing on garbage collection contracts. (The BFI regional manager at that time, Bruce Ranck, has since been promoted to chief operating officer.) In 1984 in New Jersey, a BFI vice-president pleaded guilty to antitrust charges and was charged with bribing two public officials . . . In 1983 in Atlanta, a BFI general manager pleaded "no contest" to charges of price fixing. (He was rehired by the company after his release from prison.)*[5]

And on went the list of ethical and environmental violations. One of BFI's more egregious antitrust cases was the story of Joseph Kelly, a

---

[5] *The Village Voice*, August 18, 1992, "Say It Ain't So, Mark," by Matthew Reiss.

former employee in Burlington, Vermont, who'd left BFI to launch his own waste-container roll-off business called Kelco Disposal, Inc. In 1987, Kelco sued BFI for predatory underbidding (or "low-balling"); in court, BFI salesman Richard Rudolph testified that he'd been ordered by his superior, Michael Gustin, to go after Kelly and drive the former BFI man out of business. "Do whatever it takes," Rudolph was told. "Squish him like a bug." Joe Kelly himself testified that in his days as a BFI manager he had been specifically instructed to employ low-balling tactics: to "cut the price in half," until a competitor "goes out of business—then you double the prices." The jury found in Kelly's favor and ordered BFI to pay him $6 million.

No one doubted that their intentions were to create a more competitive marketplace, but in effect, Mayor Dinkins, Commissioner Green, and the business community of New York City had welcomed a $3.2-billion-a-year Texas giant with a history of committing the same monopolistic crimes as the Mafia cartel.

And none of those journalists trumpeting BFI's bold arrival in New York realized the true reason behind Ruckelshaus's timing. *The Wall Street Journal* came closest when it noted on November 8, 1993, that BFI's biggest rival, Waste Management, the largest trash-hauling entity in the country, had "'zero' hauling business in New York City's five boroughs and zero comment on why." In fact, BFI's own founder, Tom Fafjo, said that when he'd looked at some possible New York business back in 1971, "We decided real quickly it wasn't a market we wanted to be in." After decades of being openly afraid to send even a single truck into Manhattan—BFI's few vehicles in New York were now guarded by armed private-security men—why would Ruckelshaus suddenly feel emboldened to tackle the Mafia?

In court documents and later statements made by BFI executive Philip Angell, it was revealed that Robert Morgenthau had let Ruckelshaus (with whom Morgenthau had worked with years earlier in the Department of Justice) in on our investigation. He informed the Browning-Ferris executives about a confidential NYPD undercover operation that had, by mid-1993, made substantial gains infiltrating the cartel. Without consulting the top brass in the New York Police Department, Morgenthau enlisted the help of the national waste-hauler as a corporate partner in the Mob-busting sting.[6]

For us in the NYPD, BFI's role in the investigation would become a highly charged issue. Of course, in many complex police operations, there's a kind of perpetual tug-of-war between the investigative and prosecutorial arms of law enforcement. But midway into Operation Wasteland, as our investigation was now called, the communications line between the NYPD and the Manhattan district attorney's office began to break down.

Tony Maz first got wind of the Morgenthau–BFI alliance by accident when Assistant District Attorney Marybeth Richroath made a casual remark about "the other undercover" working the investigation.

"What'd you just say?" Tony snapped.

Her words slipped out. She immediately tried to downplay it. "Marybeth, are you trying to tell me that you're running a *parallel* investigation out of the DA's office?" She was in a tough spot and knew she had to say something. She admitted that, after our case was well under way, the DA's office had inserted an undercover into BFI as a member of management, and that he was doing his own undercover operation along the same line as ours. This guy wasn't a cop, he was a DA's investigator posing as a BFI salesman.

Suddenly a whole bunch of pieces snapped into place. There had been a lot of red flags by this time. The DA stalled Tony eighty days before providing us with court authorization to get the LUDs and tolls of Giovinco's cell phone.[7] Normally you can get the LUDs and tolls in a few weeks. Marybeth was so good, sometimes she got them in a matter of days. Also, these BFI salesmen had paid several visits to the Cham-

---

[6] "Competition v. Corruption: Reforming New York's Garbage Industry," by Philip Angell, *Civic Bulletin, No. 7,* October 1996. Published by the Manhattan Institute for Policy Research.

[7] Under court order, the police can examine the LUDs (Local Usage Details) and toll calls made from a particular phone number.

bers office already, and Sal—streetwise Sally—immediately smelled one guy out. After one unsuspected visit, Sal looked disturbed, not his jolly self; he turned to me and said, "That one guy—did you get a look at him? I'm telling you, something's not right with that guy—I think he's a Fed or a cop."

When you run a parallel investigation out of the same office, the information one undercover is gathering can be contradicted by the second undercover. The worst-case scenario happens if both undercovers are wearing wires. That's common sense: If a statement is said to me in a certain way, then said differently to the DA's undercover, it's going to give the defense attorneys a tremendous opening to crack us in half. This may create a greater risk of exposure. Sal and me are both putting our lives on the line every single day. Now we find out that the DA's undercover knows all about an undercover operation at Chambers—but I don't know shit about him!

Even Tony, who doesn't usually lose his cool, was livid. As the supervisor of the case, he felt we'd lost control of our own investigation. Tony took it to his immediate supervisor, Lieutenant John O'Brien, and then they took it up the chain of command to Inspector Kenny O'Brien. They called a meeting with me at a German restaurant on Staten Island—where no wiseguys ever went—and they briefed me about the second undercover. At first I was in shock. Then I went through the roof. Tony understood the gravity of the situation and he went straight to the DA's office to complain.

Tony had already been contacted by the Feds about doing the cartel case as a joint FBI–NYPD investigation. And we both knew that the Feds would have *died* for this case. This is everything the Feds have been wanting for fifty years. Isolated wiseguys and *capos* aren't any big prize, but getting the associations that are the ruling arm of the cartel, this is the jewel in the Mafia's economic crown.

The trouble was, once you got into a deal with the Feds, you ran the risk of getting lost in the federal system. Of course, they take the upper hand after a while and it becomes much more an FBI case than an NYPD case. And while we'd gain some things with the Feds beside us—more money and resources—by linking with the FBI, we'd also lose a lot of control.

Tony was playing that as his trump card with the DA, but it was pretty much a bluff. Still, it did help us make our feelings known to Morgenthau's people. We made sure that Dan Castleman, Morgenthau's head of investigations, knew just how upset we were. They didn't stop their parallel investigation, of course, but from then on, I tried to avoid their undercover like the plague.

The one thing I couldn't avoid was the blue containers. Those Browning-Ferris Dumpsters were a dead giveaway. By civic regulation, all garbage trucks and containers in the city were strictly color-coded: Department of Sanitation vehicles were painted bright white; private sanitation vehicles and their containers were a flat army green. Most private carters owned vintage dual-tandem ten-wheel Mack trucks—often with their Italian surnames detailed in ornate scarlet or canary-yellow script. Some of those army-green trucks and containers were so vintage they looked like they'd been on the streets since the cleanup of the *Apollo 8* ticker-tape parade.

Browning-Ferris arrived in New York flashing brand-new blue trucks and containers with the corporate 800 number painted on the side. None of the local carters would do business with those blue out-of-towners—except Chambers Paper Fibres. Sal and the Benedettos agreed to let BFI dump some high-grade paper and cardboard at the transfer station. The gangsters soon had photographs taken of those *1-800-PICK-BFI* containers at our Paper Services shop up in the Bronx.

Behind the scenes, the associations were amassing their forces to keep BFI out of New York. We had our surveillance cameras aimed at the Waste Paper Association at 511 Canal Street, and on October 13 we photographed a meeting of heavyweights arriving for a sitdown. Joe Francolino came down for the Gambino garbage club in Manhattan. So did Patty Pecoraro, Francolino's associate and the head of the Gambino-club in Queens. Of course, the "big four" of the WPA were there: Angelo Ponte, Frank Giovinco, Vito Palmeri, and Vincent Esposito.

Then, only a week after that big sitdown, I got an irate call from Frank Giovinco.

"Dan, I gotta see you right away."

"What's the matter, Frank?"

He said he couldn't get into it on the phone.

The rendezvous was set for Ponte's Steakhouse at noon on October 20. When I walked in, I saw Giovinco, Mikey Five Brothers, and Anthony Vitale lounging at a large table. They'd already finished a meal of various pasta courses and were sitting with empty dishes, smoking, and having coffee. Whispering, as always, Frank launched right into an interrogation.

"People are whispering some very *bad* things about you," he said.

"What are you talking about?"

"Dan, is there some kind of *unholy* alliance here?"

"Whattaya mean, Frank?"

"Are you accepting BFI waste?"

"We're accepting some cardboard tonnage that's coming outta Connecticut. But it's not affecting any Association members."

"Is that *all* you got going on, Dan?"

"Yeah."

They were obsessed with keeping BFI from getting a foothold in the city. Mikey Five Brothers said that BFI was a "bug" that had to be crushed before it grew any bigger. Frank put it slightly differently.

"Listen, Dan, it's like with Brewster."

"Brewster?"

"Yeah, Brewster—you know, Vito." Frank was referring to the Chin's driver, Vito "Bruce" Palmeri. "Brewster's dying of cancer. And you know what they do with cancer right when they find it? They cut it out. That's just what we gotta do with BFI."

Those ocean-blue containers had definitely raised them up about my loyalties. Throughout the meeting, Frank kept tapping my chest for emphasis. As Tony Vitale rose up to say good-bye, saying, "All right, Danny, take it easy," he ran his hand leisurely along my shoulders, feeling for a wire. But there was no wire today. Luckily we'd anticipated the possibility that I might be patted down. I didn't even have a tiny Kel transmitter for Bobby O and Tony Maz to monitor the conversation, to blow the cavalry bugle if things got out of hand.

After the meeting at Ponte's, Frank got in my Jeep and I drove back to the Waste Paper Association. He ran upstairs and got me the claims list that they'd been working on.

"Here, this is Jimmy's people," he said, meaning Jimmy Brown's club on West Broadway.

Later, at the big weekly meeting at the Canal Street club, the ranting about BFI continued. The Waste Paper Association had hired a lawyer named Dave Snyder who was passing out a fifteen-page report on all the nasty business BFI was accused of doing around the country—price-fixing, low-balling, illegal dumping, poisoning the water supply. "No one has a worse track record in the United States than BFI," Snyder told the association members. The WPA was paying to have glossy brochures printed up, launching an anti-BFI publicity blitz. It was a ballsy strategy, letting the public in on a dirty secret: that BFI were even nastier criminals than the Mafia.

I was cornered at my end of the conference table. Mikey Five Brothers and Tony Vitale were talking about how BFI had staged that big phony press conference with the mayor, announcing their sponsorship of the New York City Marathon.

"They're gettin' all those fuckin' paper cups," Mikey Five Brothers groused.

"Are they waxed?" Tony Vitale said.

"No, they used to be waxed, but they got unwaxed this year so they could recycle—cocksuckers. Nobody better accept that shit— make 'em *eat* it."

Tony said that Robert Donno, the BFI subcontractor in Long Island, was so frightened that BFI had paid to brick up all his windows and

Donno was driving around in a tank. Jokingly, Tony added: "They didn't put bricks around *your* building, did they, Dan?" A wave of laughter circled the table.

"Look," I said, "I'm doing the best I can. It's not my call to make— I gotta deal with all these cousins of mine." My strategy was to put the blame on the faceless suits in the Benedettos' corporate headquarters.

Later that week I learned that the 1.6 million unwaxed New York City Marathon cups, passed out to those thirty thousand runners snaking through the five boroughs, were going to be recycled with us. The Benedettos had made a deal with BFI, agreed to buy all the recyclable cups from the marathon.

"All right," Frank Giovinco said, gritting his teeth again. "Listen, you gotta do what you gotta do. Like I always tell everybody—America's beautiful. It's a free country."

The truth is, we would've loved for the Benedettos to disassociate themselves from BFI. But the NYPD could *never* tell Sal's cousins in the home office—the corporate headquarters on Madison Avenue—to do something that was good for our investigation but bad for their business. Chambers Paper Fibres was a legitimate company with stockholders to answer to. The Benedettos and their salesmen saw that there was money to be made by hitching their bumper to BFI—even if it meant I was going to have every member of the cartel threatening me. Even if it meant incurring the wrath of a heavyweight like Angelo Ponte. Even if it meant the gangsters were going to kick us out of the club we'd been trying to infiltrate for so many years.

And that's just what happened.

Frank called me down to Canal Street, took me aside, turned up the TV set full blast—no porno this time—and whispered into my wire. "Your family's just no fuckin' good, Danny. Youse're big shots—youse're in *Crain's* magazine." (The Benedettos had recently been written up in a *Crain's* business story.) Angelo and the rest of the powers at the Waste

Paper Association had always suspected we were too legitimate to go along with the whole crooked ball game. "As of today," Frank said, "you're out of the Association. Don't worry, we'll return your dues." Which they never did, of course—the Mob's not in the business of giving money *back*. In fact, for months after we'd been kicked out, Vito Palmeri kept sending me new bills for *unpaid* dues. Frank walked me to the door, shook my hand firmly, smiling good-bye. "Listen, don't take it personal, Danny—it's strictly business."

First he had me being Fredo, "saying the 'Hail Mary'" at the front of the boat. Now he's trying to tell me that "it's strictly business." Just like Allie Shades, Frank loved quoting *The Godfather*.

I was in limbo for about a month—kicked out of the Chin's paper club, but at least I was still talking to Frank Allocca in Bensonhurst. Allocca was also pissed off about our dealings with BFI, but he didn't throw me out of his club yet. But the bad blood was brewing. Allocca called me one cold morning in February.

"Danny," he said, "meet me tomorrow at the diner. You know the place." I knew he meant the Americana in Bensonhurst; these guys were always cryptic about saying specific meeting locations over the phone.

Meanwhile we were up on Frank Giovinco's cell phone and we caught him calling Frank Allocca. "I'm in a tough spot," Frank said. "Something's come up with a friend of mine." We speculated that he was referring to Angelo Ponte. "Hey, didja ever see that kid?"

"Who?" Frank Allocca said.

"Dan."

"Yeah."

"You know which one I'm talking about?"

"Uh . . ." Allocca said.

"Danny . . . Bridges," Giovinco said. (Evidently, this had become my new nickname.)

"Yeah," Allocca said. "In fact, I made a meet with him tomorrow—"

"Good, I wanna be there," Giovinco said.

I started laughing when I heard the conversation between the two

Franks. Kind of tough for Giovinco to ask me for a favor when he just tossed me out of his club, right?

When I got to the Americana Diner, Frank Allocca and Danny Todisco—the vice president of Allie's club and one of the industry's master scammers—were both hunched over coffee cups in our usual booth.

"What a surprise," I said when I saw Frank Giovinco sitting with them.

"A *pleasant* surprise, though—right, Dan?" But Frankie G. wasn't playing the tough guy today. If anything, he was trying to smooth things out between us. "I know, I got a wicked temperament sometimes, Dan—sometimes I jump the gun a little quick. But I don't hold any grudges."

"Me neither, Frank."

We ordered our lunch. Like always, Frank Allocca ate scrambled eggs on dry wheat toast and I had my usual BLT. Danny Todisco was complaining about his weight again—so he ate next to nothing, picked at a Caesar salad. Frank Giovinco wasn't eating, either. He just stared at me, not touching his coffee or his turkey club.

Now, this was an official sitdown with the two Genovese factions in the industry. The way it works is, you put a beef on the table and the organized-crime figure makes his decision, gives his blessing. On the table today was the issue of why I'd been tossed out of the Waste Paper Association and the status of our relationship with BFI. After some back-and-forth, it was agreed that Chambers should be allowed to accept some out-of-state cardboard business with BFI, and if anyone complained I could throw around the names of the two Franks and they would straighten it out. But I wasn't supposed to have any other contact with BFI; our transfer stations in Brooklyn and the Bronx weren't supposed to accept any of BFI's work. And so it was settled. If I abided by their ruling, I would be back as a member of the Waste Paper Association. Both Franks gave their blessing.

"Dan, I wanna ask you something else," Frank Giovinco said, sliding over to the favor. "Are you bidding on 101 Barclay?"

"Yeah. The bid is due today."

"You know who's got that building, don't you?"

I nodded. "Angelo."

101 Barclay Street is an enormous office complex down in the Financial District that houses The Bank of New York. V. Ponte & Sons had been servicing it for years—it was one of Angelo's creampuff accounts. The contract had just come up for renewal and we all had to submit bid-response sheets before the end of the business day.

"Take a look at this."

Right there in the Americana, Frank gave me my first lesson in the art of bid-rigging. He pulled a folded photocopy out of his shirt pocket—it was Angelo Ponte's bid-response sheet, already filled in with figures. He slid it, facedown, across the table to me. I looked at the figures. The total was $15,000 a month.

"Dan, if you went in with these numbers, would it made you look bad?"

"No, these don't look too bad."

"Just stay around those numbers."

I'm staring at Frank, trying to look like I'm thinking this over, but all I'm really thinking is: *home run.* I'm hearing the clinking of plates and glasses and the waitress yelling right behind me—and I'm praying that my J-Bird is picking up our hushed conversation. Because this means Giovinco and Ponte are in our grasp. Under New York State law, these bid-response sheets must be sealed and notarized. Right now, we're colluding in an antitrust felony—under the Donnelly Act, a Restraint of Trade Violation—and I know that this can land both Frank and Angelo in prison.

"But, Frank," I said, "I think it might be too late. My guy's on his way to the bank right now to submit the bid."

"Can you try?"

"Yeah, let me get the hell outta here and back to the office."

Frank trusted me enough to let me keep the photocopy of Ponte's bid-response sheet. Of course, I was slipping that straight to Bobby O'Donahue to voucher as evidence. Between the folded photocopy in my hand and the digital J-Bird in my pants, we now had Ponte and Giovinco, the top two men in Chin Gigante's paper club, dead to rights.

When the meeting broke up, we all went our separate ways. But our intercepts told us exactly what Frank Giovinco did—he called his pal Mikey Five Brothers, laughing about me: "You know that kid who we kicked out of the club? He's back in the fold again. You should've seen him. He ate some humble pie." Frank also called Angelo, who sounded upset. Ponte said he'd been beeping Frank all weekend without getting a response.

"Don't worry," Frank said, "I took care of it."

But Angelo was grim. "No, it's already in."

I would've gone along with the bid-rigging scheme—if I could. The problem was, when I got back to my desk at Chambers, Sal told me our salesman had already submitted the sealed bid at 101 Barclay Street. I beeped the salesman frantically but it was too late to stop him. Of course we came in at a reasonable rate—much lower than Angelo's. This meant I now had another fire to put out. I'd now taken a lucrative account from Ponte, one of the most powerful garbage gangsters in the city, and I knew he wasn't going to take it lying down.

Frank called me down to Canal Street the next day, smoke still coming out of his ears. He told me we should have our salesman go back and resurvey 101 Barclay, tell The Bank of New York suits that we somehow made an error in our sealed bid. How the hell was I supposed to do that? I asked. Maybe we calculated the compacted yardage wrong, Frank suggested, and couldn't possibly do it for the rate we'd originally quoted.

Talk about disrupting that applecart! Now, not only was Angelo Ponte fuming at me, but the other bidder in on the 101 Barclay scheme was my old nemesis Phil Barretti. And Frank said I was making a huge mistake by pissing off those two. He told me if we didn't let V. Ponte & Sons keep this creampuff building, then Angelo would have no choice but to "hurt" me—go after my work.

On the other hand, Frank said, if I played ball, we could all be happy—and we could all stay rich.

When one of our big buildings came up for bids, Frank whispered right into my J-Bird: "You gimme a piece of paper, and I give it to him, and he'll put in the right fuckin' numbers—so that way you feel fuckin' secure, just like he wanted you to do."

I was nodding as I listened to Frank, but then I told him I doubted we could change our bid at 101 Barclay. It would look too *fugazy*—I didn't think I could talk my straight-arrow family members into going along with the scheme.

"You could talk sense into them . . . Listen to me, Moe," Frank said, losing his patience, even while he was still maintaining that cool whisper, "if there's one guy out there that you don't want to take buildings off, that you don't wanna be an enemy against, it's Phil Barretti."

"Is Barretti starting shit again?"

Frank shook his head and tried, once again, to explain the guiding principle of the Mafia cartel to me, the most hardheaded student he's ever had in his life.

"Angelo won't be bad with you, and you won't be bad with Angelo. Angelo won't be bad with Barretti, and Barretti won't be bad with Angelo—that's how the circle gets formed."

I was in the Chelsea Diner on Ninth Avenue, staring at a cold cup of coffee and waiting for the arrival of Eddie Tamily. Joe Virzi had delegated the HBO restitution duties to his partner, Ed, and I was frankly happy with the arrangement; after that crotch-grabbing incident inside the Waste Paper Association, I was leery about any face-to-face meetings with unpredictable Joe Virzi.

Now we worked on a strictly cash relationship. Tamily and Virzi didn't want any more checks made out to Avon Sanitation. No more bank transactions, no more evidence trail for the nosy IRS.

"Why should I pay Uncle?" Tamily liked to say with a laugh.[8]

Around 2:45 P.M., Tamily pulled up in front of the diner in his black Avon Sanitation pickup truck, wearing a dark gray fedora and chewing a soggy cigar. I had the $8,000 in my jacket, the J-Bird taped up tight

---

[8] Tamily and Virzi often discussed ways to make the extortion payments appear to be tax-deductible; they told Dan that he would "never get caught" and claimed to have cut their own tax bill from $600,000 to $30,000 a year with such schemes.

inside my pants, the wire strung up the front of my shirt with the microphone secured behind a button. I didn't need the Kel transmitter or surveillance team when dealing with Ed Tamily. Tamily liked to talk tough but—physically speaking—he was relatively harmless.

Eddie was smiling like a kid on Christmas morning when he opened the plain white envelope stuffed with $8,000 in crisp hundred-dollar bills. Untraceable cash.

"It's all there?"

"Yeah, Ed—whattaya think, I'm cheatin' ya? Count it if you want."

He licked his thumb and started fanning through the faces of Ben Franklin. He said he was glad we were straightening this thing out: It meant Ed and Joe wouldn't have to go on the warpath again, and go after any of our work.

On the subject of warpaths, I told Ed how I'd screwed up the 101 Barclay bid-rigging scheme, how I'd tried to do the right thing, tried to rig the bid for Angelo, but I just couldn't catch my salesman in time.

"Get rid of your salesmen!" Eddie said, shaking his head. "They're only gonna hurt you. Listen, if you're gonna be with friends, you're not gonna be alone. If you want to be alone, I can't help you."

He told me I should just go to Angelo Ponte and apologize. When I said that Angelo always seemed "cold and distant," Ed told me to pay Ponte a visit at his paper mill in New Jersey, work things out *mano a mano*. "It's a give-and-take and everybody knows what's right and what's wrong. And everybody's gotta bend to the fact—'Okay, I know I been wrong—but don't kill me . . .'"

"Right."

"Okay? 'Don't *kill* me. Let's sit down and work something out.' . . ."

I told him that down at the club they were moaning at me, "'Why'd you go in on the bid?'"

"Once you get involved," Ed said, meaning being a member of the club, "you have bids, and you know who's in those bids. You see it's a fellow member, okay? And you do respect each other." Everybody in the cartel works hand-in-glove.

Of all the West Side guys, Eddie Avon was by far the best conversationalist. We made a beautiful threesome—Eddie, me, and the J-Bird. That afternoon we sat in the pickup truck for over an hour with the windows rolled up, Eddie talking my ear off.

Ed Tamily had one of those ancient-sounding New York accents, like Art Carney on *The Honeymooners,* pronouncing *curb* as *koib* and *whores* as *hooahs.* He talked about how he'd been in this industry since 1948, how he'd seen it all—known all the old West Side crew, even been friendly with Vito Genovese.

I told Ed that for decades my family had been getting by alone, staying away from the West Side and their association, just "out there by ourselves."

"Well, now you don't have to be," Ed said. "If you think you're gonna get away with it, that you don't have to pay, and say the hell with everybody, in the long run you're gonna *pay.* I'm talking to you as a friend now, nothing to do with the business, this is human *beans.*"

But now the industry was changing—and all the old traditions were going out the door. Now BFI was trying to bust into town, underbid everybody, make all the old cartmen work for *nothin'.* And here was the problem, Ed said: The Benedettos were being used as pawns. We shouldn't even be talking with those treacherous Texans.

"Don't let BFI use you. Don't let them use you. You got too much class."

"It's causing me a lot of headaches with my uncles and other relatives. It's been a real pain in the ass."

"Yeah, because we're all Italians, and we've got these big—whattaya call these people that come outta there? Whattaya call those, uh, Protestants? Whattaya call 'em?"

"Whattaya call 'em?" I really had no clue what he was getting at.

"Yeah, whattaya call 'em—they have a name for 'em. You find 'em upstate. You find 'em in Ridgewood, where I live. They're *executives.* Ah, that's stupid—my brain is wearin' out. How many Protestant religions that's uh, white Anglo-Saxon, y'know?"

"WASPs?" I yelled out.

"The WASPs!"

"WASPs." I nodded now, laughing.

"That's who you're doing it for, kid. The fuckin' WASPs! Y'understand?"

"Yeah."

"They want you. All right? After—they gonna spitcha out."

"I know, I know. They're using us. . . ."

"So you tell your uncles, your father, or anybody there—you can't do it. You cannot go against your *brothers*. You can't go against them and that's it."

All over the country, the majors had run the small family-run companies out of business. But they weren't going to get away with it here. Not in this town. Those cowboy-hat–wearing WASPs from Browning-Ferris Industries were making a big mistake, Ed said, convincing Mark Green and David Dinkins that New York was run by a bunch of Italian gangsters.

"Because they got that stupid Green and this last mayor. They went and talked to 'em and said we're all gangsters."

"Right, of course. If you pick up any of the papers, or you talk to anybody—'Oh you're in the garbage business?' Right away they think you're in rack—racketeering—"

"Me, I'm with Giuliani."

"—they think you're the Mafia."

"I'm in Giuliani's transition team, me."

"You are?"

"Yeah, and I tell him, 'How do you have *me* here? I'm in the garbage business—I'm a gangster!'"[9]

"And *him* of all people . . ."

"Let me tell you, Danny, they didn't know how powerful we were. They thought we were just Mafia."

---

[9] Tamily's assertion that he had a role in newly elected Mayor Giuliani's transition team was relayed to the chief of the Organized Crime Control Bureau and to New York City's Department of Investigation.

"They thought everybody was the Mafia."

"Yeah, but in the meantime they find that it's not the Mafia. You're dealing with human *beans*. Y'understand? I'm not the Mafia," Ed said.

"I'm not the Mafia," I said.

Oh, sure, Ed admitted, there were a *few* mobsters around.

"But maybe a thousand of one percent that's any gangsters in our business. Y'understand? There's nobody. You can't tell me one company. Tell me *one* company—" He didn't even let me open my mouth. "Well, there's *one*," he said. "The president of the New York Association. That's Duffy—Joe." He was referring to Joseph "Joey Cigars" Francolino, newly elected boss of the Gambino garbage club. Within the industry, Francolino was widely known as Duffy, because he owned Duffy Waste Removal.

"Yeah, Duffy. He does some business with us," I said. "You hear about him. 'He's in the Mob. Stay away from his stops.'"

"Yeah, yeah, but Joe could help you a lot—if you *know* him."

Ed told me that Francolino was taking over the reins of power once Jimmy Brown went away. Right now, Joe Francolino was organizing a campaign, trying to get everyone to send letters on behalf of Jimmy Brown.

"He wants us to send letters to the law that Jimmy is a good person. That he's worked with us for thirty-five years. He's good at negotiating. He wants everybody to write a letter to the parole board—for Jimmy. He's going away."

"He went to jail?"

"Yeah, he's goin' in—not yet. They're gonna be sentenced in June."

It didn't look good for Jimmy Brown: They'd nailed him for conspiracy to murder his soldier Thomas "Tommy Sparrow" Spinelli. Jimmy Brown was either going to turn eighty or die inside federal prison. Tommy Masotto—who'd been the treasurer of the Gambino club before he got sentenced for torching that FBI plant in Long Island—had tried to use the club membership to organize a similar letter-writing campaign on his own behalf. A lot of good it did him—Tommy Masotto was another one who was likely going to die inside the federal pen.

"Yeah, Tommy Masotto, my cousin went to school with him."

"He's a jerk, he's a jerk," Ed said.

"He's Mafia."

"No, he's nothing, he's nothing. That's a big *ploy,* y'know. He knew people. That's all he was. He wasn't Mafia. He wasn't never made a button man."

I furrowed my brow—that was the well-honed expression: Always elicit more detail.

"That's Mafia—a guy that's *made.* That's gonna go out and kill you. I'll tell you something: The only people down there that's got any clout after Jimmy goes away is Duffy. The rest of 'em are wannabes."

What about Frank, I wondered, *the old guy running Brooklyn?*

"No, the guy that runs Brooklyn wears dark glasses. He's just a front, Frank Allocca. He's a front man. He's no gangster."

Ed Tamily was giving me his own kind of education. Sure, he liked the weight of that eight Gs in his jacket pocket—he wanted to feel that weight every month from now on. He said he was going to look out for me, make sure I didn't get myself hurt. He warned me that I was playing a dangerous game, creating all this mayhem, taking stops from club members all over town, having conversations with those cowboy WASPs. It was a lucky thing that I was so young and inexperienced, that I could always plead ignorance by saying my family had always been "independent," had never played by the club rules before now.

"Well, I don't know," I said. "I had problems last summer. A guy come after me and fuckin' did my guy—opened my guy's head up. He tried to kill him. He was in a coma. It was meant for me. The guy's driving a truck for a living. I mean, I got the stop, and he tried to come after me with pipes and everything."

Sure, Tamily said, but that was a *personal* beef, right? That wasn't violence sanctioned from *above*—that didn't come from the powers that be.

"*Minghia,* in the old days there woulda been no talking. They woulda blown your head off. Twenty-five years ago? *Fuggetaboutit!* You woulda probably been shot for nothin'. *Nothin'.* Things were crazy in those days. . . ."

7 | JIMMY BROWN, JOEY CIGARS

They have the look of Capone's men. They are sleek, often bil-
ious and fat, or lean and cold and hard. They have the smooth
faces and cruel eyes of gangsters; they wear the same rich
clothes, the diamond ring, the jeweled watch, the sickly-sweet-
smelling perfume.

—ROBERT F. KENNEDY, *THE ENEMY WITHIN*

By the spring of '94, we'd gathered excellent evidence against many
key players in the Mob cartel. We could make a case against Phil Barretti for the firebombing on Plymouth Street and a laundry list of other
criminal acts. We could collar Lou Mongelli and his son Paul for extortion, coercion, and restraint of trade, and we had their main leg-
breaker, Steve Georgison, for attempted murder. We'd gathered good
racketeering evidence against the main powers in the Waste Paper Association, Frank Giovinco and Angelo Ponte.

There were some people in the Manhattan district attorney's office
who saw this as a good haul, felt it was time to take the case down.

Personally, I was dead set against it. True, I'd made strides in infiltrating the two Genovese clubs—despite my falling-out with Frank and

Angelo over our dealings with BFI. But I didn't feel we were even
halfway to the finish line. I knew that the most powerful Genovese
gangster in the industry was Alphonso Malangone, and we had no solid
evidence against him. Taking the case down now would mean letting
Allie Shades go scot-free.

More importantly, I'd got nowhere near the biggest catch of the investigation: the powerful Gambino association, Jimmy Brown's club.
And getting me close enough to gather evidence against those Gambinos wasn't going to be easy.

You have to keep in mind that although the Genovese and Gambino
crime families at this time were on par with each other in terms of
overall strength and clout, within the city's private sanitation industry
the Gambino faction *always* had the loudest voice.

To understand why that was, we have to go back a bit—back to those
"crazy old days" Ed Tamily liked to talk about, back when a guy could
get his head blown off "for nothin'." Back to the reign of a tiny empire-
builder that the newspapers called "the Little King."

You are not that tough. Don't think you are too tough that we can't take
care of you." The scene was the 1952 Teamsters convention in
Rochester, New York. Bernie Adelstein, the little one-legged union
boss, stood glaring up at Johnny Acropolis. "Tougher guys than *you*
have been taken care of," Bernie added with a sneer.

John Acropolis, by all accounts an honest, straight-arrow truck driver
and the president of Westchester County's Teamsters Local 456, did not
appreciate being threatened by anyone, least of all by Adelstein, this
slick-dressed, mustachioed five-foot-two-inch so-called business agent
dispatched by his Mafia masters in their Park Avenue high-rise.

"Too bad you're a cripple," Acropolis replied, "or I'd flatten you
right here."

Bernie Adelstein had come to the convention with his colleague Joe
Parisi. Parisi, secretary-treasurer of Teamsters Local 27—from which

Adelstein's Local 813 had only recently been spawned—was a trade unionist with a distinguished record: convicted of rape (he served two and half years in Sing Sing), arrested and indicted eleven times for murder, coercion, felonious assault, and robbery with a handgun. Within law enforcement circles, Joe Parisi was described as a "former member of Murder, Inc.," a professional killer who had been called upon, from time to time, to dispatch victims at the behest of Charles "Lucky" Luciano, Louis "Lepke" Buchalter, and Albert "the Lord High Executioner" Anastasia.

In 1951 and '52, the garbage business in Yonkers—the Westchester County suburb just north of the Bronx borderline—was in turmoil. For over a year the mobbed-up Teamsters locals headed by Adelstein and Parisi had been trying to muscle John Acropolis and his friend Eddie Doyle, secretary-treasurer of Local 456, out of lucrative trash-hauling contracts, including the Safeway supermarket chain and the Yonkers racetrack. Businessmen who sided with Acropolis and Doyle were threatened, their stores picketed, their equipment and property torched.

Acropolis and Doyle's holdout Teamsters local faced an intense gangland onslaught: Bernie Adelstein and Joe Parisi on the union side, and on the management side, Nick "Cockeye" Ratteni, president of Westchester Carting Company, described by the U.S. Attorney General as "a chief lieutenant of Frank Costello" and a man who'd already spent seven and a half years in Sing Sing. Cockeye Ratteni's partner in Westchester Carting was an equally sterling business personality: a certain Joseph Feola, aka Joey Surprise. Feola had been convicted and sentenced to death for the murder of one police officer and the wounding of another. He narrowly escaped the electric chair when the conviction was reversed on appeal, and Joey Surprise ultimately got away with a manslaughter plea. After their years together behind the walls of Sing Sing, Cockeye quickly put his pal Joey on the books at Westchester Carting as an "efficiency expert."

The double-barreled labor-management squad was quickly tiring of the hard-to-scare Johnny Acropolis and Eddie Doyle. Things came to a

head at the '52 Teamsters convention. When Acropolis and Doyle retired to their Rochester hotel room, Joe Parisi paid them a late-night
visit. "Gee, I don't want to argue with you no more," Parisi said. "I have
a bad heart. I am not going to argue with you. There is other ways of
taking care of you. We can see that it is done."

Later, Eddie Doyle received a phone call that was even more explicit:
"Four of youse're gonna die."

Johnny Acropolis didn't take such threats lightly. "Don't park the car
when you go home in a dark spot," he advised Doyle. "Make sure you
park it out in front of your house."

We'll never know why Acropolis didn't listen to his own advice.
Three weeks after the Teamsters convention, he left his car a few blocks
from his apartment house at 1080 Warburton Avenue and walked home
with his keys in one hand and a freshly dry-cleaned suit in the other. At
2:30 A.M., as he opened his front door and turned on the parlor light,
he was shot point-blank in the head.

His murder was never solved. Organized-crime investigators first
gained insight into the motives for the killing in November 1957, when
the Senate Select Committee on Improper Activities in the Labor or
Management Field began its week-long inquiry into the New York
garbage rackets. Eddie Doyle, who'd by now stepped into Acropolis's
shoes as Local 456 president, was sworn in as one of the committee's
few cooperating witnesses, bravely telling Senator McClellan why he
believed his good friend must have known his killer personally. "Acropolis had very fast reflexes—he was an athlete—and no one could have
gotten him who didn't know him. The indications were he was bringing someone in his house with him. He had turned on the parlor light
and was shot through the head—and shot again when he was lying
down."

CHAIRMAN McCLELLAN: Was anyone ever apprehended for his murder?
MR. DOYLE: No one was ever apprehended.
CHAIRMAN McCLELLAN: Are you personally still apprehensive about
    your safety?

MR. DOYLE: Well, I dunno—you gotta die sometime, Senator. You
can't live forever.

By the time of the McClellan hearings, hit-man–turned–union-man
Joe Parisi had died of a heart attack. And seven gangland witnesses, including Joey Surprise and Cockeye Ratteni, were mysteriously missing
when committee counsel Bobby Kennedy tried to summon them down
to Washington.

Bernie Adelstein chose not to lam. He arrived on Capital Hill, showing off his perfect pencil mustache, gold cuff links, and diamond pinky
ring in the Senate hearing room—and in a photograph plastered on the
front page of the November 17 edition of *The New York Times*. The
story read:

> *Mr. Adelstein, a man in his fifties with a record of four arrests on mi-
> nor charges, but no convictions, arrived in an indignant mood. In a pre-
> pared statement, he implied that the committee was trying to destroy his
> reputation. This, he said, has caused him and his family great pain. His
> indignation, however, occasionally yielded to grins as the committee con-
> fronted him with new evidence, including three wiretapped conversations
> about his conduct. Mr. Adelstein vigorously denied that he had threatened
> John Acropolis, Yonkers' Teamsters leader, three weeks before he was mur-
> dered in 1952.*

The committee's investigators noted that in addition to his $35,000-a-
year union positions (as "secretary-treasurer" and "business manager" of
Local 813 of the Private Sanitation Union, International Brotherhood
of Teamsters, and a similar post with the Cooperage, Drum and Con-
tainer Workers Local of the Coopers' International Union of North
America), Bernie Adelstein was the custodian of a "dance fund" that
raised money every year through the sale of five-dollar tickets that every
union member was forced to purchase. The senators noted that 10,000
such tickets were printed—although the dance itself held only 1,750
people. Union records further indicated that from the dance fund's ex-

pense account, Mr. Adelstein had spent $5,889 on an air-conditioned 1956 Cadillac, made payments on a $10,000 personal annuity, and purchased a substantial quantity of liquor from a store owned by Mr. Adelstein and his wife.

By any measure, '57 was proving to be a bad year for the Mob, the worst public-relations disaster since the Castellammarese War.[1] Since the mid-'50s, a bloodbath had been brewing in the streets of New York, pitting two power-mad killers against each other. Gangland simply wasn't big enough to contain the ambitions of Albert Anastasia and Vito Genovese. Since Lucky Luciano's deportation to Italy in 1946, Frank Costello—known as the Prime Minister of the Underworld, due to his numerous upperworld connections to politicians—had been serving as boss of the *borgata,* and Don Vitone, as Genovese preferred to be addressed, could not abide playing second fiddle to Frank. He wanted to displace the Prime Minister but was wary of making a move as long as Costello had the protection of his old friend and ally Anastasia.

On the night of May 2, 1957, Genovese struck. He dispatched a square-jawed, crew cut–wearing former prizefighter named Vincent "Chin" Gigante to assassinate Costello in the lobby of the Majestic apartment building on Central Park West. The three-hundred-pound Gigante made a mess of the job, rushing into the lobby, standing four feet away from Costello, and shouting, "This is for you, Frank!" The

---

[1] An internecine Mafia conflict of the late 1920s, the Castellammarese War pitted two New York Mob factions, one loyal to Giuseppe "Joe the Boss" Masseria and the other loyal to Salvatore Maranzano, against each other. After the murders of both Masseria and Maranzano, a younger generation of gangsters, lead by Lucky Luciano, Vito Genovese, Frank Costello, Joseph Bonanno, and Meyer Lansky, emerged as the powers in the newly Americanized Mob. The Castellammarese War—so named for Maranzano's birthplace, the Sicilian town of Castellammare del Golfo—is often seen by experts as the dividing line between the old clannish "Mustache Pete" generation of Sicilian Mafioso and that of Young Turks like Luciano who preferred to surround themselves with non-Sicilians like the Jewish Lansky and the Neapolitan Genovese.

Prime Minister was startled, turned his head, and the bullet merely grazed his scalp. Gigante fled in a car driven by Thomas "Tommy Ryan" Eboli and was soon arrested. But Costello, head bandaged beneath his fedora, refused to identify the gunman in a police lineup; a doorman at the Majestic would, but Gigante was ultimately acquitted at trial. Thirty years later, this chubby-cheeked young hit man would again be in the front pages, considerably gaunter and grayer, transformed into the Mafia's wariest don, the unshaven, pajama-wearing "Oddfather."

A month after the attempted hit on Costello, it was the Anastasia crime family's turn to be shattered by gunfire. The first casualty was underboss Frank Scalise, better known as Don Cheech, a mafioso whose résumé stretched back to the era of the Tommy gun. (Organized-crime experts today theorize that Frank Scalise and his brother Joe were two of the out-of-town "talent" brought to Chicago by Al Capone for the St. Valentine's Day Massacre.)

The underworld grapevine had it that Scalise, no doubt with the approval of Anastasia, was selling off buttons in the crime family for $50,000 a pop—an unforgivable offense. Anastasia feared that Vito Genovese would use Scalise's greed as a pretext to move against him and gave the contract to his trusted *capo*, the garbage-rackets boss and fruit merchant Vincent "Jimmy" Squillante. Luring his target to his Bronx fruit stand, Squillante gunned down Don Cheech amid the rolling peaches, plums, and pears.

The fruit-stand assassination scene would later be borrowed by Mario Puzo and Francis Ford Coppola in *The Godfather*. But unlike the fictional Don Vito Corleone, Don Cheech Scalise didn't walk away from his wounds. Within weeks Frank's grieving brother Joe could be heard vowing revenge. According to Joseph Valachi's account of the internecine war, as related to journalist Peter Maas, Squillante invited the younger Scalise to a party at his home in the Bronx, where Joe was murdered, chopped up, bagged, and hauled away in one of Squillante's own garbage trucks.

Little Jimmy seemed to be everywhere in that year of Mafia mayhem. At 10:20 A.M. on Oct. 25, 1957, the garbage czar was in the barbershop of the Park-Sheraton Hotel in midtown Manhattan, settling down comfortably in Chair 4. Next to him, in Chair 5, sat Albert Anastasia, having his hair clipped, chatting with barbershop owner Albert Grasso, and awaiting a shave. Two men wearing black masks casually strolled through the hotel lobby door. Without warning, they blasted the Lord High Executioner, an accomplished murderer in his own right (five times Albert had escaped the electric chair when witnesses against him mysteriously vanished). One gunman was firing a .38-caliber pistol, the other a .32, the slugs ripping open the Mad Hatter's head, neck, kidney, and spleen. Anastasia, reared like a wounded elephant, and crashed to the floor, dead.

Jimmy Squillante—described by an eyewitness as a "jockey type" with thick eyebrows and coarse "Italian" features—was heard to say, "Lemme outta here!" before fleeing the bloody barbershop.

Squillante stonewalled the NYPD detectives who questioned him about Anastasia's murder, and three weeks later, down in Washington, D.C., he similarly stonewalled Bobby Kennedy and the senators of the McClellan Committee. Anastasia's untimely murder prevented his own date in the Senate hearing room, and Squillante's arrival before the committee prevented his making an appearance at a supposedly top-secret convention scheduled that same week in bucolic upstate New York.

On November 14, in a sleepy town called Apalachin, a small army of mobsters, chauffeured in brand-new Cadillacs, was converging from all over the U.S. The flashy visitors drew the attention of local cops, who raided the nearby estate of Joseph Barbara. Dozens of gangsters escaped through fields and brambles, but the sixty-two who were detained for questioning—including bosses Carlo Gambino, Vito Genovese, and Joe Profaci—all claimed, with straight faces, that they were simply coming to visit their dear sickly friend Joe Barbara.

Crime experts immediately saw the conclave as an attempt to prevent an all-out shooting war in the wake of the Anastasia murder. Vito Genovese was believed to have orchestrated the mass sitdown so he could declare himself *capo di tutti capi*. Instead, the aborted meeting lead directly to Genovese's downfall: Set up by Meyer Lansky, Carlo Gambino, and Lucky Luciano on a bogus drug rap, Don Vitone would die, embittered and betrayed, in the federal penitentiary.

In later years Apalachin would come to be seen as the Mob's watershed moment—an embarrassment so public that even the willfully ignorant J. Edgar Hoover couldn't deny the existence of a powerful national syndicate of Italian-American crime families. But most news accounts of the Apalachin arrests were trumped by the even bolder headlines about the revelations in the Senate's garbage-rackets investigation.

In one stunning day of testimony, Jimmy Squillante had been fingered by undercover federal narcotics agent Joseph Amato as a "member of the Mafia," an organization described to the committee as "an underground society of killers, supposedly based in Sicily—also known as the Black Hand." Six years before Joe Valachi's Senate testimony about his life as a Genovese button man, Agent Amato provided the first public linking of a millionaire racketeer to a secret underworld society called the Mafia. Amato claimed that Squillante not only controlled a vast trash-hauling empire in New York but was also a high-level figure in the Mafia's international drug trade, though Jimmy "wouldn't touch narcotics himself—he's too big for that."

When Squillante's testimony began on November 15, he invoked the Fifth Amendment against self-incrimination 111 times. Occasionally he seemed ready to speak his mind, wagging his finger at Chairman McClellan and the other senators who were clearly trying to bait him. "It's nothing but a shakedown, isn't it?" McClellan demanded at one point, referring to a war chest of some $57,855 Squillante had raised from New York City carters, charging each $250 per truck "for the defense of Vincent J. Squillante (in any shape or form)." The chairman sarcastically noted that Squillante had used $17,213 from the defense fund to pay his personal state and federal back taxes.

In a sidebar to its front-page coverage of Squillante's testimony, *The New York Times* provided a character sketch, and a dose of armchair psychoanalysis, of this minuscule forty-year-old East Harlem–born mobster.

THE LITTLE KING OF CARTING

Perhaps one fact more than any other explains Vincent James (Jimmy)
Squillante. His godfather was Albert Anastasia, the Executioner for Mur-
der, Inc., who was recently murdered. . . . By almost any standard, he is
an unimposing figure. For example:
Size. Below average. He is 5 feet 1½ inches tall and weighs 122 pounds.
Appearance. Unimpressive. He used to wear string ties of the Senator
Claghorn type but lately has given them up in favor of more conservative
gray ties with black figures against white-on-white shirts. His hair, once ar-
tistically long, is crew cut. He occasionally affects sunglasses.
Criminal record. Second-rate for a man reputed but never proved to be
an important figure in the Mafia-run international dope traffic. He has but
a single conviction. In 1953 he pleaded guilty to a charge of having failed
to file his 1948-49 Federal income tax.
Business career. Undistinguished until he entered the garbage-collection
business in 1950. Before that he had been a commission fruit merchant in
the Bronx, according to his own description. More impartial observers have
called him a small fruit peddler. . . .
One interpretation of Squillante is that he has an inferiority complex
which he appeases by thinking of himself as the "Messiah" of the New
York carting industry. He manifests this quality also by gratuitously cor-
recting the mistakes of others.

Through the testimony of Senate investigators and cooperating witnesses, the committee was able to piece together how the Little King of
Carting had built his $50-million-a-year empire. Using Bernie Adel-
stein and Joe Parisi as his labor muscle, and Joey Surprise and Cockeye
Ratteni as his management muscle, Jimmy had taken over Yonkers in
1952, crushing the Acropolis-Doyle resistance along the way. Then, in
a flanking maneuver, Jimmy overran Long Island, where he had little
trouble strong-arming the lucrative carting industry in Nassau and Suffolk counties.

On July 1, 1956, the City of New York handed Squillante the keys to its kingdom: By passing a law that required every business in the five boroughs to contract private waste-haulers, the city council gave Squillante free rein over the entire New York metropolitan area.

In one of his pronouncements from the committee chair, Senator McClellan described the trash kingpin as "a person with an underworld background and no previous experience in the labor management field," who was able, through violence and the threat of violence, "to establish a stranglehold on industry trade associations for his own personal profit and that of his associates, a number of them prominent hoodlums."

Squillante and his cronies were perhaps best characterized by the remark of one committee witness: "In the garbage industry we don't get Harvard alumni and Yale graduates."

But the original garbage gangsters did have their own "professor." His name was Casper Donald Modica, and he was officially listed as the "educational director" of the Greater New York Cartmen's Association. Five foot five, thickset, and white-haired, Modica had been an instructor of philosophy at New York University from 1939 to 1943. (Although he had never formally earned the title of professor, within the confines of the Cartmen's Association, he was respectfully referred to as "the Prof" and "the old Pro.") Prior to his move to academia, Modica had been convicted of practicing medicine in Delaware without a license and for attempted grand larceny in Queens County, for which he was sentenced to two and a half years. Seated before the McClellan Committee, introduced as an expert in "industrial psychology" and "labor and management problems," the Professor chose to recite the Fifth Amendment throughout the day.

Long Island carting executive John Montesano, who'd once been summoned to the Park Avenue offices of the Cartmen's Association and threatened by Jimmy Squillante, related his own observations to Bobby Kennedy:

MR. MONTESANO: We went all the way to New York, and while we
    were there on three different occasions, I saw this young boy come
    in, and it seemed to me that the Professor was tutoring him. . . .

He had a blackboard and he had all kinds of symbols and numerals
and different things. It didn't bother me at first, but after the third
time I said to myself, "Who is this fellow?" I asked Beansie Fazula,
"Who is this fellow?" And he turns around and tells me, "That is
Albert's boy." I drew my own conclusions after that.

MR. KENNEDY: Just on the basis that it was Albert's boy? Didn't he say
Albert who?

MR. MONTESANO: Well, it was common knowledge. I mean, after a
while I found out that Jimmy was supposed to be—this is later, after
I got out of the organization.

MR. KENNEDY: Jimmy was what?

MR. MONTESANO: Linked to Albert Anastasia.

In addition to tutoring "Albert's boy," the Professor was known for
schooling some of gangland's best and brightest: the sons of Vito Genovese, Willie Morretti, and Joe Adonis. Surrounded by reporters in the
Senate hallway after his appearance, Modica said that he'd been tutoring
his pupils "in philosophy from Socrates to the moderns." "What about
Machiavelli?" one reporter called out. The Professor replied that he had
always urged his boys to avoid Machiavelli, believing that "a philosophy
that the ends justified the means [is] immoral."

The committee made note of the fact that during the Professor's
tenure as "educational director" there were a "startling number of
phone calls" from Anastasia's fortresslike home in Palisades, New Jersey,
to the Cartmen's Association on Park Avenue. "It was understood that
Modica was in the office of the cartage industry as a representative of
Albert Anastasia and to make sure that Anastasia's interests were being
protected," Bobby Kennedy concluded. "To quote from one of the
witnesses: 'I would say he was a watchdog.'"

In addition to his duties home-schooling gangland princes and keeping the Lord High Executioner abreast of things, the Professor found
time for a little literature. He edited an industry paper called *The Hired
Broom* in which one of his own poems appeared: "Out of Garbage,
There Grows a Rose."

Mobster Vincent "Jimmy" Squillante, the kingpin of New York's private sanitation rackets, wags his finger at Robert Kennedy and the McClellan Commission in the U.S. Senate, November 15, 1957. Squillante invoked his Fifth Amendment right 111 times during his testimony. (© *2002 AP Wide World Photos*)

Bernard Adelstein, who reigned as boss of Teamsters Local 813 from the mid-1950s to the mid-1990s, during his testimony before the McClellan Commission. (© *2002 AP Wide World Photos*)

Adelstein and his unionized drivers could shut the entire metropolis down. The seventeen-day garbage-hauling strike of 1981 forced New York City mayor Ed Koch to declare a citywide health emergency. (This is an aerial view of West Broadway in Manhattan.)
(© The New York Times/*Keith Meyers*)

Albert "The Executioner" Anastasia, the psychopathic boss of what would later be known as the Gambino Crime Family. Anastasia and his *caporegime* Jimmy Squillante established the "property rights" law of the cartel, which would remain unchanged for nearly a half-century.
(© *2002 AP Wide World Photos*)

Vito Genovese, Anastasia's equally homicidal rival, was the boss of a powerful, secretive crime family known in New York mob circles simply as "The West Side."
(© *2002 AP Wide World Photos*)

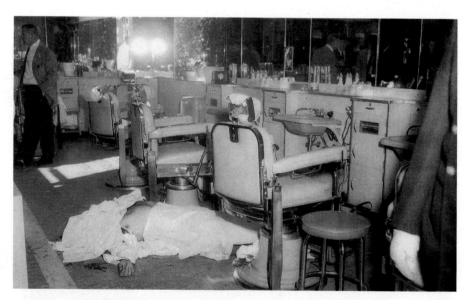

The most famous murder tableau in organized crime history: Anastasia lies assassinated in the barbershop of the Park Sheraton Hotel, October 25, 1957. Three weeks before he and Jimmy Squillante were to be called before the Senate racketeering hearings, Anastasia was shot repeatedly, while sitting in chair no. 5; Squillante, sitting in chair no. 4, fled the crime scene, muttering, "Let me outta here!" To this day, the Anastasia murder is unsolved, though most experts see the hand of Carlo Gambino, who took over as boss of the crime family. (© *2002 AP Wide World Photos*)

Disheveled and feigning madness, Vincent "Chin" Gigante (right), the long-reigning kingpin of the Genovese Crime Family, leaves his apartment with his son, Vincent Esposito, during Gigante's June 1997 racketeering trial. Esposito played a key, though well-shadowed, role in the Chin's "paper club," the Greater New York Waste Paper Association on Canal Street. (© 2002 AP Wide World Photos)

Gigante's bitter rival John Gotti, smirking and in full "Dapper Don" bloom, leaves Manhattan Federal Court in 1990, accompanied by his brother Peter Gotti, on the right. (Robert Rosamilio/ New York Daily News © 2001 Daily News, L.P.)

Cops and cartmen on the Lower East Side, circa 1900.
(© *New York City Municipal Archives*)

Many private sanitation companies began as single horse-and-wagon operations on the Lower East Side. Well into the 1990s, the millionaire lords of New York's waste-management industry continued to refer to themselves as "cartmen." (© *New York City Municipal Archives*)

Before he began his undercover role as Danny Benedetto, Detective Rick Cowan spent two years covertly investigating the powerful Genovese capo Alphonso "Allie Shades" Malangone (right), a self-described "gangster and hoodlum" who had interests in illegal gambling, loan-sharking, and Wall Street stock manipulations, and who ruled as kingpin of the Brooklyn private sanitation racket. (*Courtesy New York County District Attorney's Office, exhibit at trial*)

The property rights to 55 Water Street had belonged to Angelo Ponte (left), a multimillionaire garbage executive, restaurateur, and real estate mogul. Honored by the Catholic Church as a Knight of Malta, Ponte was one of the bosses of the Waste Paper Association on Canal Street. (*Courtesy New York County District Attorney's Office, exhibit at trial*)

55 Water Street, one of the largest privately owned commercial office complexes in the United States, was the subject of a bid-rigging scheme involving NYPD undercover operative Danny Benedetto. (© *Olegna Productions, Inc.*)

Genovese associates Henry "Eddie Avon" Tamily (left) and Joe Virzi (below) "owned" the property rights to HBO headquarters on Avenue of the Americas in Manhattan. Tamily's covertly recorded remarks to Detective Cowan provided strong evidence about the Mafia's control of the garbage rackets.
(*Courtesy New York County District Attorney's Office, exhibit at trial*)

In the years after Detective Cowan's investigative work, HBO would achieve its greatest commercial and critical success with *The Sopranos*, a saga of fictitious garbage gangsters in New Jersey.
(© *Olegna Productions, Inc.*)

Joseph "Joey Cigars" Francolino, the Gambino soldier who stepped into the role as kingpin of the industry, after James "Jimmy Brown" Failla's imprisonment in 1994. Francolino, who was personally inducted into the *borgata* by John Gotti, was typically decked out in hand-tailored suits and expensive jewelry, but in this mug shot, having turned himself in to the NYPD, he was clad in his "going to jail" clothes. (*Courtesy New York County District Attorney's Office, exhibit at trial*)

Francolino owned a Manhattan-based garbage-hauling company and came into conflict with Danny Benedetto over the rights to the Century 21 department store, located across the street from the World Trade Center. (© *Olegna Productions, Inc.*)

Philip Barretti, one of the city's wealthiest garbage executives, set the entire investigation in motion by violently trying to enforce his rights to One Wall Street, the Bank of New York Building, formerly known as the Irving Trust Company Building, a jewel of Art Deco architecture soaring over the heart of New York's financial district. (*Photo of Barretti courtesy New York County District Attorney's Office, exhibit at trial; photo of Bank of New York Building by Berenice Abbott © Museum of the City of New York*)

James "Jimmy Brown" Failla, the diminutive Gambino family *caporegime* who reigned unchallenged as boss of the family's garbage rackets, after the demise of Jimmy Squillante in the late 1950s. Jimmy Brown—who earned his nickname by frequently dressing in dull shades of brown—was so surveillance-conscious that he virtually never spoke an audible word indoors, preferring to conduct all business on "walk-and-talks." Here, he is caught leaving the West Broadway headquarters of the Association of Trade Waste Removers of Greater New York, at the time of his murder-racketeering trial in 1993. (© *Philip Greenberg*)

Alphonso "Allie Shades" Malangone (on right), conducting a "walk-and-talk" meeting in Bensonhurst, Brooklyn, with Bonanno crime family capo Anthony Spero. Spero, the onetime acting boss of the Bonannos, would later receive a life sentence in a Federal murder case. (*Courtesy New York County District Attorney's Office, exhibit at trial*)

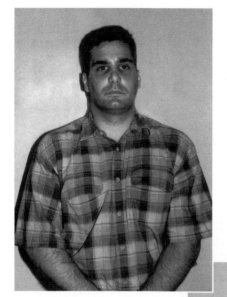

Frank Giovinco, an up-and-coming Genovese gangster, was inserted into the Waste Paper Association on Canal Street to wield a disciplinary whip over the industry. (*Courtesy New York County District Attorney's Office, exhibit at trial*)

Patrick "Patty Marangi" Pecoraro, a Gambino crime family associate being groomed by Joe Francolino, and the president of the Queens County Trade Waste Association. (*Courtesy New York County District Attorney's Office, exhibit at trial*)

Steve Georgison, a Mongelli Carting Company employee, was convicted for the vicious, nearly fatal assault on a Chambers Paper Fibres employee. (*Courtesy Bronx County District Attorney's Office, exhibit at trial*)

Two Gambino family gangsters, Tommy Masotto (middle foreground) and Johnny Drago (left, in dark suit) arrive for a meeting at Jimmy Brown's club on West Broadway. Masotto would later be sentenced to twenty-one years in Federal prison for ordering a firebombing of an FBI surveillance post on Long Island. (*Courtesy New York County District Attorney's Office, exhibit at trial*)

Detective Cowan, in his Danny Benedetto role (right), strolls down West Broadway outside Jimmy Brown's club, during a "walk-and-talk" with Patty Pecoraro. (*Courtesy New York County District Attorney's Office, exhibit at trial*)

Detective Cowan (center) at NYPD headquarters after being promoted to Detective First-Grade by Police Commissioner Bill Bratton (second from left). (*Private collection*)

The Chambers warehouse location on the Brooklyn waterfront, directly under the Manhattan Bridge. (© *Olegna Productions, Inc.*)

A Chambers Paper Fibres packer truck arrives at the Chambers transfer station on Plymouth Street in Brooklyn. The firebombing of a similar truck in May 1992 launched Detective Cowan's unexpected undercover odyssey. (© *Olegna Productions, Inc.*)

Many crucial meetings during the investigation were conducted in the Americana Diner in Brooklyn. (© *Olegna Productions, Inc.*)

Frank Allocca, owner of VA Sanitation, a World War II veteran, a Genovese associate and the president of the Kings County Trade Waste Association. (*Courtesy New York County District Attorney's Office, exhibit at trial*)

Vincent "Jimmy" Vigliotti, a Genovese associate, owned a string of Bronx-based companies, one of which hauled waste from the *New York Times* building on West 43rd Street in Manhattan. (*Courtesy New York County District Attorney's Office, exhibit at trial*)

Frank Allocca (smoking) with Rocky Cimato, Alphonso Malangone's chauffeur, outside the Kings Country Trade Waste Association office.
(*Courtesy New York County District Attorney's Office, exhibit at trial*)

Danny Benedetto (right) engages in a "walk-and-talk" to resolve a dispute with Frank Allocca in Bensonhurst, Brooklyn.
(*Courtesy New York County District Attorney's Office, exhibit at trial*)

New York Police Commissioner Bill Bratton (seated, left) and Manhattan District Attorney Robert Morgenthau (seated, wearing glasses) announce the unprecedented arrests of "Operation Wasteland" at a packed press conference, June 22, 1995. (*Private collection*)

Meanwhile, at One Police Plaza, the "daisy chain" of shackled suspects arrives: Frank Giovinco (not pictured) leads the way, followed by Philip Barretti (foreground), Frank "Frankie VA" Allocca, Alphonso "Allie Shades" Malangone, and Michael "Mikey Five Brothers" D'Ambrosio. (© *1995 Helayne Seidman Photo*)

The future wasn't so rosy for the Little King. Although the McClellan hearings couldn't lay a glove on him, Squillante, like Al Capone before him, soon suffered a knockdown at the hands of the IRS. On November 27, 1958, a federal court revoked Squillante's probation in his tax-evasion conviction. "He is not redeemable, not tractable and further rehabilitation efforts would be a waste of Government funds and time," probation officer Donald Stewart had argued.[2] As proof that the garbage boss was an incorrigible liar, the court tried to debunk one of Squillante's loudest boasts—that he was the godson of Albert Anastasia—by introducing Squillante's original baptismal papers from St. Ann's Roman Catholic Church on East 110th Street. The late Umberto Anastasia's name was not listed anywhere among baby Vincenzo's sponsors.

"He is a man who for some years has traded on the false label that he was the godson of Albert Anastasia," argued chief assistant U.S. Attorney Arthur Christie. "He strong-armed his way up to the top of the garbage-collection racket. Like an octopus, his grubby, avaricious tentacles have extended from New York to Westchester to Nassau and Suffolk Counties."

In sentencing, Judge Irving R. Kaufman berated the trash kingpin for running a citywide criminal monopoly and for sitting as a judge himself in the carting industry's kangaroo court, but Squillante's freedom was revoked simply for keeping poor company: "The probationer's associates and consorts, both socially and professionally, reads like a 'Who's Who in the Underworld.'"[3]

Squillante was slapped with a year-long stretch, and while held at the Federal Detention Headquarters on West Street, he found a new class of friend. His cellmate was the recently convicted Soviet master spy Colonel Rudolph Ivanovich Abel, who'd been sentenced to thirty

---

[2] *The New York Times,* November 27, 1958, "Squillante Cited as Incorrigible"
[3] *The New York Times,* November 28, 1958, "Squillante Gets Year in Tax Case; Judge Berates Garbage Racket"

years. Squillante, evidently in a patriotic pique, resented being imprisoned alongside the communist, and requested that he be released into general population. The warden repeatedly refused: Unpopular Jimmy had been receiving too many death threats. During one visit, James B. Donovan, Abel's attorney, asked the cultured KGB spy—who was fluent in five languages and an accomplished musician, painter, mathematician, and cryptographer—how the two cellmates were getting along.

"Quite well," Abel replied. "I am teaching him French."

"Rudolf, what in a heaven's name would a gorilla like Squillante do with a knowledge of French?"

"Frankly, I don't know, Mr. Donovan, but what else could I do with the fellow?"

Of this teacher-student relationship, *The New York Times* wrote: "Squillante had only started on active verbs when he was transferred to Lewisburg."

But the Little King had little time to show off his newly acquired education. After his release, Jimmy was a hunted hood. First the NYPD hauled him in as a material witness in the unsolved Anastasia murder, and when he again stonewalled, they slapped him with a vagrancy charge.

Then he was prosecuted and convicted, along with his brother Nunzio Squillante and Bernard Adelstein, on charges of extortion in relation to the Long Island garbage industry. On February 18, 1959, Squillante received a sentence of seven to fifteen years in New York State prison. All three men's convictions were overturned on appeal, but the Little King soon found himself facing a fresh extortion case in Nassau County, scheduled to go to trial in November 1960.

On October 21, Squillante's lawyer, Nicholas Castellano, Jr., announced at a bail hearing in Mineola, Long Island, that his client had been reported missing. "If he were alive he would be here today," Castellano claimed. "He had everything to gain by staying around."

Vincent J. Squillante had last been seen in the Bronx at two P.M. on September 30, 1960, driving a car owned by his brother-in-law. The NYPD was notified that the car was also missing.

On June 12, 1962, the *Daily News* reported that Squillante—along with other "missing and presumed dead" mobsters Anthony "Tony Bender" Strollo and Joseph "Joe Jelly" Gioielli—had most likely been the victim of "the crushout," the latest gangland innovation in unwanted corpse disposal:

> *You'll find one in almost any auto graveyard. It's a 12-foot-high hydraulic press with a steel pit underground and two powerful rams, one of them packing a wallop of 1 million pounds. You can stick the body of a Cadillac into the pit and in 90 seconds smash it into a cube of metal 36 inches high, 24 inches long and 24 inches wide. . . . It's the most diabolical device since the late Hymie Weiss of Chicago invented the one-way ride back in the rip-roaring days of Al Capone. In fact, it's an improvement on the one-way ride, but an improvement that's downright revolutionary. . . . The hydraulic press assures a perfect crime—no corpse, no fingerprints and no heat from the cops and feds. A mobster, thus executed, never, in a sense, really dies—he simply vanishes.*

Years later, Anthony "Nino" Gaggi, the fearsome Gambino *caporegime* from Bensonhurst, would raise doubts about this prevailing theory that Squillante had been crushed into a "cube of death" because his high-profile legal troubles were drawing too much attention for Carlo Gambino's taste. Gaggi—a proud cousin of the murdered Frank and Joe Scalise—claimed that he'd personally taken revenge on Don Cheech's murderer. "We surprised [Squillante] in the Bronx," Gaggi told his nephew Dominick Montiglio, as recounted in Gene Mustain's and Jerry Capeci's book *Murder Machine*. "We shot him in the head, stuffed him in the trunk, drove to 10th Street and threw him in a furnace."

Whatever the gory details of his disappearance, tiny Jimmy left behind big footprints, both in the underworld and on the economic landscape of New York City. In the midst of the McClellan Committee's revelations, the office of New York State Attorney General Louis Lefkowitz vowed to crush the "rubbish ring" by prosecuting all the top gangsters under the Donnelly Act. But the machine Squillante put in place proved impenetrable to law enforcement—not just Lefkowitz but repeated attempts by Brooklyn and Manhattan district attorneys and waves of federal investigators. A few frontline troops might fall here and there, but the cartel was untouched.

Jimmy Squillante had styled himself a "messiah" but, as his on-site Professor might have told him, he was really more of a Caesar. Like Julius, he laid the foundations for an enduring empire before falling to assassination.

And it would be up to his successor, another little Jimmy, to grow from his position as Don Carlo's chauffeur and bodyguard into one of the Gambino family's longest-reigning captains—the commander who would lead the cartel through more than three decades of prosperity.

Forty years had passed since the unsolved murder of Johnny Acropolis. The country had survived the JFK assassination, the Vietnam War, and Watergate, seen the end of the Cold War and birth of the Information Age. But in this strange New York garbage empire, little had changed since the Eisenhower era. Bernie Adelstein—tiny, one-legged Bernie who'd snarled at Bobby Kennedy in the Senate—was still calling the shots in Local 813.[4]

In late November 1993, I got a message at my desk at Chambers telling me to be at a crucial industrywide meeting at the Sheraton on Monday, November 29 at 11 A.M. Local 813 was calling another city-wide strike and I was told that it was imperative that everyone—a principal from every carting company—be in attendance.

I was running late and when I got to the Sheraton the meeting was

---

[4] In 1992, at the age of eighty-four, Bernie Adelstein was formally removed by the U.S. Justice Department as president of Local 813, after fifty-five years as a Teamster. Charged by court-appointed Teamsters Investigations Officer Charles Carberry with being an associate of known mobsters James "Jimmy Brown" Failla, Anthony "Tony Ducks" Corallo, and Matthew "Matty the Horse" Ianniello, Adelstein was removed from the Local 813 presidency, though his two sons remained active as Local 813 officials.

well under way. I strolled through the revolving doors wired with my
J-Bird—no Kel transmitter, no other cops in the vicinity. Whatever
happened inside, I'd have to wing it.

I took the stairs up to the second-floor Imperial Ballroom. But when
I tried to get in, the door was blocked by a moveable wall named Carl
Bivona. Carl was the owner of Bivona Carting and a prominent member of Allie's Malangone's Brooklyn club. He was a six-footer, well over
350 pounds, with a pumpkin-sized head and an 11 A.M. case of five-
o'clock shadow. He was the meeting's sergeant of arms, but he looked
more like a pro wrestler stuffed into a black mock turtleneck and a
Big-n-Tall blazer.

"Where you goin'?" Bivona barked. "Who're you?"

"I'm Dan Benedetto from Chambers. I was told by Frank to come."

"Sign in."

I wrote my signature at the front desk—I'd been practicing my
Danny Benedetto scrawl to get it just right. When I opened the door, it
was a plush-carpeted ballroom with giant chandeliers, filled to capacity
with hundreds of stogie-chomping carters. Every garbage gangster and
company owner in the tristate area was packed into that one room. And
there was so much smoke, the place looked like it was on fire.

At the center of the dais sat Jimmy Brown Failla and Allie Shades
Malangone. Flanking Jimmy and Allie were all the top organized-crime
figures in the industry and their close associates—on one side, the Gambino guys: Joe Francolino, Patty Pecoraro, Johnny Drago, Mike Marone;
on the other side, the West Side crew: Frank Allocca, Ray Polidori,
Danny Todisco. Then at both ends of the stage, like bookends, were two
muscular bodyguards: bent-noses in double-breasted suits.

I'd never covered a meeting like this. To my knowledge, no NYPD
detective or FBI agent had ever been *near* anything like this. It was all
the king's men—together on one stage.

As soon as I took a seat at the back of the ballroom, it felt like all eyes
were on me. Most of these old-timers had known each other for
decades, and here I was, some fresh kid—Danny in the lion's den.

But they didn't stare for long. Jimmy Brown was at the podium, and every wiseguy, association president, and company owner was listening to the boss. Frog-faced Jimmy was growling into the microphone.

"Listen, men. You gotta keep your trucks rolling. Keep 'em rolling no matter what. If you don't, you'll give these bastards BFI a shot to come in."

In the old days the Teamsters would've had their strike, the tons of garbage would have piled up, and in a week or so both sides would've settled—another shakedown at the taxpayer's expense. But with Bill Ruckelshaus threatening to make inroads into the city—that front-page *Wall Street Journal* article had just come out about the BFI executive waking up to the severed German shepherd's head on his doorstep—Jimmy Brown couldn't afford to let any kind of strike action go forward.

Even though this was a meeting of management, a lot of the company owners in attendance also doubled as union men. They were card-carrying members of Adelstein's Local 813. So if they went on strike, they'd only be striking against themselves.

"Keep the trucks rolling, boys!" Jimmy kept saying. "Hey, if I was a *younger* guy I'd be right on the trucks with you—riding shotgun!"

Everybody in the ballroom cheered— *"Yeah, Jimmy!"* Everyone worshipped that little sour-faced, seventy-two-year-old gangster. Jimmy Brown was the legend: He'd been Carlo Gambino's driver and bodyguard. *Old* school? Jimmy was one of the Gambino family's biggest earners when John Gotti was still a grammar-school bully.

At one point Jimmy said, "Guys, I'm up here speaking to you as—" He turned to his lawyer, Sal Spinelli. "Hey, Sal, what's the position you gave me again?"

"Jimmy, you're an administrator," said Spinelli.

"An *administrator*—that's the word. Yeah, I'm an administrator."

Now everyone let out a huge laugh, braying like this was the greatest stand-up routine they'd ever heard. And it *was* pretty comical. Because everyone in the ballroom knows that Jimmy Brown's no *administrator*. And he's no fucking comedian, either. He's one of the biggest wiseguys in the city. A feared gangster, even among other gangsters.

At this very moment, in fact, Jimmy Brown was out on bail, awaiting trial in federal court on charges of conspiring to murder Tommy
Sparrow. Thomas "Tommy Sparrow" Spinelli was a soldier in Jimmy's
crew who made the mistake of going before a federal grand jury investigating carting and property rights. When Jimmy got wind that Tommy
Sparrow was going to talk, he told John Gotti about it. Gotti gave the
contract to Jimmy Brown, who did the "work" in Brooklyn with the
help of Louis "Louie Fats" Astuto and Sammy "the Bull" Gravano.[5]

Keep 'em rolling? Jimmy hardly needed to say it twice. Who the hell
was going to defy him? Jimmy and Allie Shades were calling all the shots:
controlling the companies, controlling the associations, controlling the
union men. Jimmy Brown and Allie Shades had the entire city in a vise.

I'd only been listening to Jimmy talk for a few minutes when I noticed some activity on the stage. Allie Shades, as always in his dark
glasses, started whispering something in Frank Allocca's ear. Then Frank
Allocca called over one of the bodyguards and whispered something in
his ear. Then the bodyguard came straight to the back of the ballroom,
eyeballing me the whole way, and whispered something in Carl
Bivona's ear. They both checked the sign-in book. I watched as the
bodyguard reported back to Allie.

It had me nervous—but I was also impressed. From all those years on
the Pastels Disco surveillance in Bay Ridge, I knew that Malangone was
savvy. But there had to be three hundred guys in that room, and Allie
spotted me at the back, singled me out, sent his muscle to check up on
me. Allie Shades didn't take any chances.

When the meeting broke up and I drove away from the Sheraton, I
circled around in the Manhattan streets, cleaning myself. Right before
the entrance to the Brooklyn Bridge, I veered off and swung to a stop
in front of Downtown Beekman Hospital. I loosened my brown leather

---

[5] In a typically perverse Mob twist, Tommy Spinelli's own son, Sal, onstage in the Sheraton ballroom, remained Jimmy Brown's confidant and lawyer. He apparently saw no conflict of interest in serving as the attorney for the man accused of murdering his father.

belt, unzipped my pants, and ripped the thick wad of sterile gauze and surgical tape from my crotch.

In a few minutes I saw Detective Joe Moore strolling down from his office at One Police Plaza. Joe was in his mid-fifties, gray-haired, a second-grader dressed in black slacks and a herringbone blazer. He had the Gambino desk at the Intelligence and Analysis section of OCID. He got in my Jeep and we did the chain of custody for my J-Bird.

"Joe, you'll never believe who I was just with."

"Try me."

"Jimmy Brown."

"Holy shit."

"Yup. I was at the Sheraton for an industry meeting—I just left Jimmy Brown, Joe Francolino, Allie Shades, Johnny Drago—"

"Enough—don't tell me any more. I don't want to know this shit. I don't *need* to know. . . ." Joe slipped the J-Bird into the side pocket of his herringbone blazer.

"Take it straight to Tech Services," I said. "They'll download it and Harry and Camille will pick it up."

"Take care of yourself," Joe said, getting out of my Jeep. "Jimmy Brown, Joey Cigars, Allie Shades—you better watch your ass. Dan, you're with the heavyweights now."

But to be honest, I didn't get near those heavyweights again until the spring of 1994. The first Gambino I came in direct contact with was Patrick Pecoraro, aka Patty Marangi. Patty was the head of the Gambino-run association in Queens, a hood coming up under Jimmy Brown and Joe Francolino. Patty P. was not the handsomest character: swarthy, thick-lipped, balding, a dapper gangster with a gruff voice and the build and disposition of a bull walrus. He ran the Marangi Group, a string of interconnected Bronx- and Queens-based companies (V. Marangi Carting Company, Delmar Waste Services, Delmar Recycling Corp., Delmar Transport, Inc.).

Patty was the carter who picked up the mountains of stale hot-dog buns, plastic beer cups, and baseball-related rubbish at Yankee Stadium, and the heaps of paper cups and corrugated cardboard from the scores of Starbucks coffeehouses that had been springing up like mushrooms all over town. But it was a dispute over another popular chain that had Patty Marangi butting heads with me.

D'Agostino supermarkets, founded in 1932 by Nicola and Pasquale D'Agostino, immigrant brothers from the Abruzzi region, was a New York retail institution and a proud page in the story of Italian-American entrepreneurship. It began in the Great Depression as a little family gro- cery on Lexington Avenue at Eighty-third Street, and it had grown, by the mid-'90s, into a string of twenty-three high-end supermarkets spread out from Park Slope in Brooklyn to the Upper West Side of Manhattan to Rye Brook in Westchester County.

Everyone in the industry called the stores D'Ag. For decades the Benedetto family had been picking up the bales of corrugated card- board at seventeen D'Ag locations. In May of '94, all the D'Agostino outlets decided to throw their recycling and garbage business our way. Almost overnight I knew that a score of mobbed-up carters would be screaming that they'd been *robbed* of their D'Ags.

On May 26, I asked Frank Giovinco to come meet me at our Paper Services shop in the Bronx. Frank showed up driving his brand-new Lincoln Town Car, and since it was a hot day, he was wearing a dark- blue matching shorts and shirt set. I was dressed in my typical pressed khakis, button-down shirt, wired with my J-Bird.

"You're very relaxed, Frank," I said.

"Today I am," he said.

"That's good, because the war's about to break out."

We went on a long walk-and-talk, the classic wiseguy way of mak- ing sure you're not being recorded or overheard. I told Frank about the D'Agostino situation, that I knew the shit was going to hit the fan any minute. Frank remained calm, telling me that he thought I was mis- taken: His own understanding was that all the various carters were going to keep all their D'Agostino locations. I shook my head and told him that I had some very up-to-the-minute information that all the D'Ags were coming to Chambers. I knew that there was going to be a bad reaction from the club members. Frank said he'd look into the situation and then get back to me.

As we did our walk-and-talk Frank watched all the packer trucks rolling into our shop; Sal had just leased some brand-new Mack packers, so it looked like we had quite an impressive fleet. "Got a few trucks, huh?" Frank said, eyes practically flashing with dollar signs.

"Yeah," I said.

"Spoke to Angelo yesterday," he said.

"All right."

"He appreciates you comin' to him about 55 Water."

"Right."

Chambers had been asked by 55 Water Street, one of Angelo's premier accounts, to submit sealed bids for the garbage and paper contracts. This time I followed Frankie's rules, did the right thing, and told Angelo about the approach in advance.

Frank narrowed his gaze at me. "I'm gonna tell you the question he asked, though. I says, 'Ya know, Dan feels a little slighted because you won't speak to him.' Angelo's sixty-eight years old. I'm a young guy, you're a young guy. I've been in jail, I've been outta fuckin' jail. I couldn't give a *fuck* if I go away for the next hundred years. That's the way I gotta think. In order to have the kind of conversations I have, as careful as I could be—and you can see when I'm on the phone, I don't say a fuckin' word—"

"I try to be careful too," I said. "In this business you gotta be careful."

"So now, his question to me was—and I want you to take this as a compliment—he says, 'If we pat him down, I'll talk to him.'"

I was taken aback for a second, then showed Frank a flash of my bad temper: "Look! My family's been here for—"

"Let me finish. He says to me, 'Do you trust him?' I says, 'You know me. I don't trust anybody. But if you ask me right now, off the top of my head: 50-50.' I gave you 50-50. You can take that as a compliment. You go home at night and you hug yourself. Because I don't trust anybody. I think you're a good guy. . . . I says, 'Dan's a good guy.' You know what he says to me? 'Okay, we'll see. I'm gonna sit down with him.' So he's gonna sit down with you. It's just that he's sixty-eight, sixty-nine years old. Knock on wood, this fuckin' guy's been in the street for how long? He built an *empire*."

"He did—I'll grant him that."

"This is why he's leery. He says, 'I worked all these years—' "

"I mean, he knows my family, and he says something like that? That's the lowest fuckin' thing to say. It really is. It sickens me he said something like that."

"You have to understand the reputation your family had," Frank said.

"I know, I know, my family—"

"You know the reputation? The reputation was going back thirty or forty years ago—this is always the story—thirty years ago somebody got killed and you're fuckin' hooked up with the, uh, law."

Okay. This was a true story: Decades ago one of the Benedettos had been killed. Coincidentally it was another Salvatore Benedetto, who'd been murdered during a payroll holdup. (Just like the family recycled paper, they recycled boys' first names.) It wasn't a Mob-related crime, and like any normal citizens, the family cooperated with the cops who were investigating the murder. But with these mobsters, these hoods with elephant memories, this had us forever branded as do-gooders, as snitches.

I was so hot now, I was yelling at Frank during our walk. "My family member got killed! My cousin—Sal's cousin Sal got killed in a robbery! What the *fuck*? How does that bring us with the law? It was a *robbery*! I mean, what the fuck? . . . We've been independent, we've fought the current on our own, and we always will. We'll never stoop to fuckin' shit like that! Never!"

"I like you, Dan—"

"I will walk away and quit the business, I swear to God, before I'd—"

"Angelo sees you're a good guy," Frank said. "I tell him you're a good guy. I'm gonna put the two of youse together and you air out your differences. The two of youse sit down and you work it out."

A few days later, Frank stopped by my office on Plymouth Street in Brooklyn. I cleared Sal and the other Benedettos out and had a private meeting with Frank, recorded by our hidden videocamera in the ceiling. Frank stood staring at the old photographs of the Benedettos back in the early 1900s and during the Great Depression, at the old horse-drawn carts and the vintage flatbed trucks down on Cherry Street. "These are some beautiful pictures," he said. "Some gorgeous pictures."

"The real old times," I said, nodding.

There was one group shot of some of the older Benedettos that made Frank laugh. He pointed out one of my distant, heavyset, long-dead relations. "He looks like you—there's a resemblance there."

"Yeah, I look like him more and more, the heavier I get."

But Frank wasn't just making small talk. He was casually quizzing me, trying to trip me up. "How are you related to Sal?" he asked.

I'd known Frank for more than a year and a half, and this must have been the third time he'd asked me that same question. It had come up during one early meeting, in the summer of '93, and later, in Ponte's Steakhouse, when we were negotiating the terms of joining the Association. The minute Sal went to the bathroom, Frank asked again, "How are you guys related?"

Now, Frank Giovinco was no dummy, and he didn't have amnesia. He was carefully watching my facial expressions for any tics, to see if there was any hesitation, any change in my story.

"My father's brother's uncle," I said, without flinching. "He's on Dominic's side, I'm on Paul's side. We're cousins, just on different sides."

Frank's real purpose for coming down to Brooklyn wasn't to test me on the Benedetto family tree; it was to bring me the numbers Angelo wanted me to put in on my bid for 55 Water Street. After we'd screwed up the bid-rigging scheme for 101 Barclay Street, Frank and Angelo wanted to make sure that everything went off without a hitch on 55

Water. Located near the South Street Seaport, 55 Water Street is one of the biggest privately owned office complexes in the United States. As far as the garbage and paper-recycling business goes, it's one of Angelo's creampuff accounts.

While we were talking, Frank crumpled up the piece of paper with Angelo's numbers written on it. Then he whispered exactly the amounts he wanted me to put in my bid response sheet. I scribbled as Frank spoke: *Dry Waste: 40 yards x $35.00 per yard x 22 days per month. Fixed Monthly Fee: $30,800 per month. Charge for Additional Pull: $1,400 per pull . . .*

Frank was especially cautious today, speaking so softly and so close to my ear that you could barely hear his voice on the surveillance tapes. I offered to toss the piece of paper with Angelo's bid numbers in our wastepaper basket where I could retrieve it later, but Frank thought better of leaving that evidence behind. He grabbed the sheet of paper and, glancing around, began tearing it into pieces. As we walked out of the office he continued shredding it into tiny bits of confetti and then stuffed them back into his pants pocket.

"You never heard of fuckin' Oliver North?" he said, looking back at me with a sarcastic smile.

On June 6, in order to resolve the brewing D'Agostino beef, Frank brought me to a meeting at 510 Faille Street in the Bronx, headquarters of the Marangi Group. We had the sitdown at a polished circular oak table in a spacious conference room on the third floor. All of a sudden I found myself staring at representatives from all the four Mob-run associations. Frank Giovinco was speaking as "business representative" for the Chin's paper club, the Greater New York Waste Paper Association; speaking for Alphonso Malangone's garbage club, the Kings County Trade Waste Association, were president Frank Allocca and vice president Danny Todisco. Patty Pecoraro was doing double duty, representing the Gambino-controlled Queens County Trade Waste Association, of which he was president, as well as Jimmy Brown's club, the Association of Trade Waste Removers of Greater New York.

Also present was Vincent "Jimmy" Vigliotti, an influential carting executive, speaking for the Genovese faction in the Bronx. Jimmy Vigliotti was an enormous guy, as wide as a refrigerator, with three chins and a close-trimmed stubble of salt-and-pepper mustache. For many years he'd picked up the rubbish and recycled paper from *The New York Times* on West Forty-third Street. But Vigliotti was better known to the NYPD for another affiliation: Liborio "Barney" Bellomo, the power-house Genovese *caporegime* rumored to be stepping up front as the fig-urehead boss of the family in order to deflect law enforcement attention from the Chin. Barney Bellomo liked to spend his days in a sweatshirt and work boots, drinking coffee and reading the *Daily News* at Du-Rite Carting, Vigliotti's company on East 138th Street in the Bronx.

Jimmy Vigliotti was the largest man in the conference room, but it was Patty Pecoraro who carried the most weight. He dominated our conversation through sheer facial expression: Like any cagey mobster in the presence of a guy he's never met, Pecoraro said next to nothing to me all afternoon. Occasionally he'd whisper his comments in Frank Giovinco's ear and at one point he barked angrily at me: "Dan, you can't be goin' against everybody like this!" Mostly Patty—in his black mock turtleneck, gray double-breasted suit, and pinky ring—sat glaring like a rotund king from his well-cushioned executive's chair.

Meanwhile, back downtown at One Police Plaza and One Hogan Place, the Manhattan district attorney's office, this Bronx meeting of the four association representatives was seen as another evidentiary breakthrough. D'Agostino was a citywide beef and it led to a citywide response—providing proof that a group of diverse organized-crime fig-ures was acting in concert, functioning as a massive, unified criminal enterprise.

Paying off all the carters who had made D'Agostino claims wasn't going to come cheap. At a rate that varied between 35-to-1 and 40-to-1—depending on whether the payments were made by cash or check—the supermarket beef would prove to be the biggest single shakedown of our whole investigation. The judgment we arrived at during our Bronx sitdown was that I would cough up $60,000 per D'Agostino su-permarket—a total of $1,380,000 in extortion.

But the D'Ag confrontation served an even bigger investigative goal: It led me into the fold of the Gambino crime family. On June 28, three weeks after my meeting at Patty Pecoraro's Bronx offices, Patty asked me to come down to Jimmy Brown's club at 180 West Broadway.

It was the hub of power in the industry. It had been the power club in the days of Jimmy Squillante—under its original name, the Greater New York Cartmen's Association—and it remained the power club under Jimmy Brown.

My first day venturing into Jimmy Brown's club, I don't dare wear the J-Bird. This club is legendary in Mob circles. The FBI has had it under surveillance for decades. Every Tuesday afternoon is the big weekly meeting of the membership, and all the industry powers are expected to attend. Patty Pecoraro and Frank Allocca told me to meet them there at 3 P.M.

I really don't know what they want to see me about, but I'm excited. Jimmy's club is located inside a tan-brick building on West Broadway in TriBeCa, just a few blocks to the east of Ponte's Steakhouse. Downstairs, there's a luxury car dealership—Provenzano Motors—with a parking lot packed with Porsches and Jaguars and Mercedes-Benzes. The mobsters would generally show up in brand-new Mercedes 500s that looked like they'd just come out of the dealership.

Jimmy's club is on the second floor. I take the stairs up, ring the bell, and see the club's surveillance camera peering down at me from the ceiling in the hallway.

"Who is it?"

"I'm Dan Benedetto," I say into the intercom. "I'm here to see Frank Allocca and Patty Pecoraro."

They've got me waiting for about two minutes before the door opens. It's this big Bronx carter named Mike Cammallare. Distinguished-looking, about six foot three, muscular and tough, big hands and a fighter's busted nose. He's wearing a double-breasted blue suit and a royal-blue tie. "Come in," Mike grunts as I slide past.

When I look around the club, I know that I've finally arrived. *This is the big time—as big as it gets.* It's all the guys who'd been on the stage at the Sheraton Hotel, all the garbage gangsters in Brioni and Armani suits and the brightly painted silk ties dripping down their white-on-white shirts, sitting at green-felt poker tables, chomping cigars, sipping demitasse. They all look up at me as I enter, not saying a word, all hush-hush in the card games. Across the room I see a couple of familiar faces—Danny Todisco and Frank Allocca.

"Hey, Danny!" Frank yells. "How you doin'? Siddown."

I sit down at this big round table, next to Allocca and Todisco, run my hand along the polished wood. Someone brings me a little demitasse, asks me if I want some pastries. Jimmy Brown's club is famous for its pastries. Every day Jimmy personally brings in a box of fresh-baked Italian delicacies from Mulberry Street. Across the room, in a glass-enclosed office, I catch sight of Jimmy Brown. I've surveilled him for years, of course, but this is my first time up close. He's a short guy, about five six, with a Buddha belly. Gray hair combed straight back. Little beady eyes that cut right through you. You can see why they call him Jimmy Brown: He's almost always dressed in dull shades of brown. Brown suit. Brown fedora. Brown tie. Brown friggin' shirt, even.

Jimmy's sitting there holding court behind his big desk. Next to him is Joe Francolino. These two wiseguys represent the two different generations of Gambino power. Jimmy's the old Cosa Nostra—not only was he Don Carlo's chauffeur, but at various times over the years he's been acting boss of the *borgata*. Jimmy Brown was one of the *capos* waiting inside Sparks Steak House on East Forty-sixth Street when Paul Castellano was taken out by Gotti's hit men. In April 1986 the Chin and Anthony "Gaspipe" Casso, the Lucchese boss, planned to retaliate for Big Paul. They planned to kill John Gotti and Sammy the Bull and install Jimmy Brown as boss of the family. They knew that Gotti and Sammy were supposed to come to a meeting at Veterans and Friends, Jimmy's Bensonhurst social club, and they planted a remote-control car bomb. But at the last minute Gotti changed his plans, didn't come to

Jimmy's club. And when the bomb blew up half of Eighty-sixth Street, it killed Gotti's first underboss, Frank DeCicco, instead.

Jimmy's got a squashed-looking face, and he's always chewing and puffing on cigars, from the moment he rolls out of bed until the moment he falls asleep. Of course, that accounts for his other nickname: the Cigar.

Joe Francolino smoked constantly too. These guys must have had thousand-dollar cigar bills each month. You'd hear two carters talking— "I saw the Cigar yesterday." "Which Cigar? The Big Cigar or the Little Cigar?"—and you'd know they were talking about Jimmy Brown and Joey Francolino.

As old-fashioned as Jimmy Brown was, with his bad-fitting brown suits and musty fedoras, Joe Francolino was the *GQ* gangster, modeled after the Dapper Don. Whenever I saw Joe, he looked just like his big-mouthed boss on Mulberry Street: the slick double-breasted suits, cashmere mock turtlenecks, and silk shirts. Like Gotti, he was a wiseguy who never wore the same suit twice.

The door swings open slowly and Patty Pecoraro and Frank Allocca are summoned into Jimmy's office. I spot Johnny Drago in there, a gray-haired old-timer who runs the Queens association with Patty P.

So now I'm sitting there at my poker table, staring at an empty espresso cup and an ashtray heaped with cigar butts, talking with Danny Todisco about this ongoing Fayva Shoes beef that I'm still trying to settle. The activity in Jimmy Brown's office is pretty quiet and low-key— the door is shut tight and the double-paned glass in the window makes it practically soundproof.

Suddenly, a loud and heated argument erupts between Angelo Ponte and Patty Pecoraro.

"I'm only tryin' to do what's right for everyone!" Patty shouts.

"So am I!" Angelo shouts back.

I have no idea how much trouble I'm in until I hear this demented screaming: "Fuckin' *Danny*! He's a *liar*! *Cocksucker*!"

I look up, and just to the right of Jimmy Brown, I see Angelo—

who's not red in the face, he's *purple*. Ponte's about to blow a gasket in there, screaming *"Danny!"*

I glance over at Danny Todisco, whom I've known for a couple of years now. He's a good-humored guy—beefy and bald, always scheming, got all kinds of companies, most of them bogus. We're around the same age and we're both named Danny—I shrug at him.

"You think they're talking about *me*?" I whisper.

"I hope so."

"If you see a flash going out that door, it'll be me gettin' the hell outta here."

"Well, just don't stop short, pal. I'll be right behind you."

We're kidding around, but the truth is, I'm shitting myself. This is bad, having a guy like Angelo Ponte pissed off. In some ways it's a scarier situation than being surrounded by Mongelli's lead-pipe and ax-handle crew in the South Bronx.

Angelo's a Knight of Malta, a friend to senators and congressmen, a much higher-caliber character than someone like Barretti or Mongelli. He's not straightened out like some of the guys in the room with him. Jimmy Brown's a *capodecina* in the Gambino crime family, and John Gotti personally gave Joey Francolino his button—which makes both those guys completely untouchable. No civilian can put his hands on them without signing his own death warrant. But in his own way Angelo Ponte seemed just as powerful and untouchable.

I was in shock. Angelo himself, face-to-face with Jimmy Brown, howling my name. When I glance at him, it looks like his temples are going to burst.

Now I see Patty Pecoraro leaning over the desk, yelling right back in Ponte's face. And it looks like Joe Francolino's going to have to jump in and separate them, and then Jimmy Brown turns to Ponte, and says something I can't hear—and the arguing stops immediately.

The whole place goes dead, the door flies open, they all file out. Ponte is glaring at me, red as a tomato. He gets on the phone, staring me down from across the club. Now Joe Francolino—whom I've never formally met—comes over and sits down at the table to my right, smooths out his silk necktie. Johnny Drago sits down on the other side. Patty Pecoraro and Frank Allocca sit down at my table on either side of me. I'm completely surrounded. Nobody says a word.

Jimmy Brown's the last guy out of the office. He walks slowly with a cane, comes around the table with a guy named Louie, and stands directly behind me, next to the little kitchenette. He doesn't go over to the coffee, cake, and cannoli. I can't turn around—it wouldn't look right—but I can feel him close, standing right behind me. And all I keep thinking is that, although this guy might *look* like a little old Italian grandfather with a metal cane, he's actually a gangster with a reputation for clipping people going back fifty years: Even as he's standing there behind me, he's out on bail, appealing his conviction for the Tommy Sparrow murder.

Jimmy's the ultimate garbage gangster, but he's also involved in all the other Mob rackets, like gambling, shylocking, and he's got a big crew out there that would kill for him in a heartbeat. He almost never says a word indoors. If he has to conduct Mob business, it's during walk-and-talks out in the TriBeCa streets or on the sidewalk outside Veterans and Friends in Bensonhurst, where he can't be overhead. When the feds prosecuted Paul Castellano in the '80s, they had Jimmy Brown going to Big Paul's "White House" in Staten Island all the time, being present for hundreds of serious Mob-related conversations. But they couldn't touch Jimmy, because on all those tapes, he almost never made a sound.[6]

Right now he's standing about six inches behind me, breathing on my neck. Louie steps up from behind me and says: "You're Dan, right?"

"Yeah."

"Dan, I see you got the new Motorola flip phone."

"Yeah."

"Could I see the thing?"

"Yeah . . ."

---

[6] Accused of being a *capodecina* in the Gambino family and engaging in a pattern of racketeering, loan-sharking, and extortion, Failla was acquitted on all charges in federal court in 1987. As ex–NYPD detective Ralph Salerno observed, the case against Jimmy Brown fell through because he always followed a maxim learned from Carlo Gambino: "The man who says the least is the most powerful."

I hand over my Motorola and I can see that Jimmy Brown is right there examining it too. This poses a problem. Because that's where our microphone and transmitter are—built right into the cell phone.

I hear Louie flipping it open and beginning to dial.

"Hey, Dan, this thing don't dial."

Joe Francolino and everyone at the poker table are staring, wondering what's going on.

"Uhh . . . I got a code on that so I don't get cloned and somebody runs up my phone bill. Whattaya gotta make a call?"

"Yeah."

There's a bunch of phones in the club, and all these guys have their personal cell phones, but this *goombah* Louie just has to use *mine.* I uncode it and give it back to him. I can't turn around, but I hear him opening up the phone, actually taking it apart, unsnapping things. The transmitter is right *there*—he's staring right at it.

Meanwhile, I know that Tony Maz and Bobby O and the field team are out in the street listening, hearing the wiseguys taking apart the phone. They later told me they were preparing to call in backup, because they thought for sure I was in trouble and our mike was found.

I'm trying my damnedest not to let Jimmy Brown and Francolino see me sweat. But if they do find the transmitter, the first conclusion they're going to jump to is not that I'm an undercover cop or an FBI agent; they're thinking that I really *am* one of the Benedettos who's cooperating with the government—and that could easily get me killed.

Jimmy Brown and his boys must have some inkling that it's possible to put a mike in a cell phone—but they don't really understand our newest surveillance technology. Luckily we're still a step or two ahead of them. Louie snaps the Motorola back together, makes the outgoing call, and gives it back. That calms things down. Saves my ass—for a moment.

But it still doesn't get me out of the jam with Ponte, who's sitting about fifteen feet in front of me, muttering under his breath. The way he's holding the phone, he's making the sign of the *malocchio,* the Italian horns, with his pinky and index finger extended. That's an ancient curse, from the Old Country, meant to bring the evil eye down on you.

I know precisely why Ponte is pissed—and once again I've got BFI to thank for it. Over the past few weeks, in various meetings and cryptic phone calls, Frank Giovinco—acting as Angelo's buffer, of course—has prodded and coached me in the bid-rigging scheme for 55 Water Street. I agreed to go along with the program, and this time everything went smoothly. Or so I thought.

Little did I know, while I was scheming with Frankie G., Angelo's son, Vincent, was talking directly to the building manager at 55 Water Street, offering him a bribe in order to get a last-minute peek at all the sealed bids—what's known as the undertaker's look. If you get the undertaker's look, you can slip in a winning bid that looks reasonable, but it's just slightly less than the others, and you keep your stop. The building manager at 55 Water Street accepted the Pontes' bribe of $10,000.

But what Angelo didn't know—what *I* didn't even know—was that this building manager Paul Vassil didn't even exist; he was actually an NYPD detective named Harry Bridgewood, who'd been planted in the building manager's job by Morgenthau's office.

Ponte had been charging 55 Water Street an unbelievable sum: $94,000 a month. That's a guaranteed million and change a year, and bear in mind, most of the waste coming out 55 Water Street was recyclable paper—which of course Ponte would turn around and sell at even more of a profit. Talk about a beautiful thing.

Now with BFI looming in the picture, Angelo knew he had to cut his price significantly. All the guys who were in on the scheme, including me, submitted notarized bids that were in the neighborhood of $50,000 a month. But Bridgewood, the undercover, though he accepted the bribe, would not give Angelo the undertaker's look. And the winning bid from Browning-Ferris Industries? *$5,000 per month.* How does that look now? If that's really the fair market rate, then for years Angelo Ponte has been overcharging 55 Water Street to the tune of nearly 2,000 percent.

That's why Angelo's livid with me: Not only did I "steal" 101 Barclay Street from him, now he's blaming me for screwing up an account that's been bringing in $1,128,000 annually. He's holding *me* personally

responsible because, even though I went along with the bid-rigging
scam, he's convinced that the only reason BFI could get the bid so low
is because we're allowing them to dump at our Plymouth Street transfer station. This goes back to that "unholy alliance" Frank Giovinco
asked me about at Ponte's Steakhouse a year earlier. Everyone else is
boycotting BFI.

Patty Pecoraro looks at me and whispers: "Listen, Dan, are you still
accepting some BFI shit?"

"Yeah. We got a little bit of paper coming from 55 Water Street."

"That's the problem here: Ponte just lost that stop. And when the
stop was asked how BFI could do it so cheaply, they said 'cause they
could dump the shit right over the bridge with you."

This was absolutely absurd, of course. There was no way that allowing BFI to dump nearby at Chambers could have offset the collection
rate from $94,000 to $5,000 a month. Even if BFI's number was a lowball bid—which it certainly appeared to be—you couldn't account for
that huge discrepancy by saying it was all *our* fault by having a nearby
transfer station just across the bridge in Brooklyn!

"Look, Patty. Angelo asked me to do the right thing, which I did. I
put the numbers in that he wanted—but how can I control BFI? It's an
outlaw company, a national company in Houston. I can't control what
they do."

"Is that right?"

Actually, it was. BFI wasn't just an outlaw carter in the sense that
Chambers or some of the local Italian family-run companies had been
outlaws. BFI was a faceless corporate entity that couldn't be easily mus-
cled. Not that the cartel didn't try. Trucks of goons were tailing and intimidating BFI drivers. Somebody was sabotaging the 55 Water Street
recyclable paper, putting bottles and garbage into it, so BFI would get
jammed up with summonses and fines and the paper would have no recyclable value to Chambers.

Patty gets up and walks over to Ponte and they whisper a few words.
Then he comes back to me. "Dan, it's either you can do this thing or
you can't—you gotta let me know. Either we're gonna go *one* way, or

we're gonna go another. You're gonna be with *us*—and we're gonna fight these bastards all the way—or you're gonna be *against* us. Can you get rid of BFI or not?"

"I'm working on it, Pat."

The meeting is turning into my worst nightmare. Here I walk into Jimmy Brown's club dressed like a real hood, feeling like a big shot, figuring I'm doing very good for myself. I show up in the light-green dress pants, neatly creased and cuffed, an Italian silk shirt, nice gold jewelry, and a diamond pinky ring that these guys wear. Figuring things are going in the right direction, I step inside, and suddenly I'm getting harpooned from all angles.

Joe Francolino, Johnny Drago, Patty Pecoraro—everyone's staring at me. Frank Allocca sticks his finger in my face. "Dan, we warned you: The BFI thing has to end—*now*. No ifs, ands, or buts."

Even though this is technically just one beef about Ponte and BFI and 55 Water Street, the Gambino club membership is treating it like the bombing of Pearl Harbor. Because they know that if BFI and the other majors get a foothold, it's the end of their beautiful thing. For nearly a half-century, from the days of Jimmy Squillante, these guys have had a license to steal. And they aren't about to give that up without going to war.

Thanks to the loss of 55 Water Street, Angelo Ponte is now personally losing more than $1 million a year. But to the leaders of the cartel, this means potentially losing hundreds of millions. In the Mafia, guys get whacked out all the time over a lot less money, a few grand. Would they hesitate to clip me and Sal over *hundreds of millions?*

"Can you get rid of them, Danny? Yes or no?"

"I don't know, Frank . . . I'm trying my best here. . . ."

"No, you *gotta* get rid of 'em."

I left Jimmy Brown's club soaking wet, feeling like I'd run the gauntlet. And then the whole drive back to work, I noticed I was being tailed. A black Chrysler New Yorker with two guys in it kept following me from

Jimmy's club, through the Battery Tunnel, through all the cobbled side streets right down to Plymouth on the Brooklyn waterfront. I didn't try to lose them. Instead of cleaning myself and going to meet Tony Maz and Bobby O at the VA Hospital, I made everything look normal by going back to Chambers Paper Fibres and staying there. They parked two blocks from the warehouse, facing us. I got behind the wheel of a packer truck and pulled it inside, closing the bay doors. I knew it wasn't the private eyes from the Association. We'd often seen the feds out in front of Jimmy Brown's club; the FBI had just started driving those brand-new Chrysler New Yorkers. In all likelihood, the feds had been on their usual surveillance duty in front of Jimmy's, then tailed me, convinced I was some new gangster on the scene.

A few months later I had a chance to ask Joe Francolino what happened in that closed office when Ponte started going into convulsions. I'd been dying of curiosity. Francolino laughed. He told me that Jimmy Brown just turned, glaring at Angelo, and said: "Shut up! Don't make me kick you in the *balls*. . . ."

B y the summer of '94, the heat coming off Canal Street was unbearable. All the Waste Paper Association powers—led by Angelo Ponte and Frank Giovinco—were amassing their forces against me. On July 7, Frank G. was so angry about everything that had happened with 55 Water Street and BFI, he came down to the Chambers warehouse with a couple of leg-breakers, asking shop foreman Gene Fulp if anybody had seen me around. Then, on top of it, Phil Barretti started sending yet another goon. He wasn't employing the Puerto-Rican tag team of Ramos and his partner anymore; Phil dispatched a fierce Italian-looking guy, some two-hundred-fifty-pound enforcer with twenty-inch bodybuilder's biceps, driving a red Barretti pickup truck.

On July 13, Frank Allocca, Danny Todisco, and Phil Barretti asked me to meet them at the "usual" diner, the Americana. By now I had plenty of experience straightening out beefs with Frank Allocca and the leaders of the other associations. In fact, I had a reputation for being such a tough negotiator that during one of our earlier Americana Diner sit-downs, Frank had sarcastically teased: "You sure you're not Jewish?"

"No, Frank, on both sides, my family goes back to the Old Country. One hundred percent from the boot."

Today, with Phil Barretti sitting across from me, I decided to show these guys just how tough a negotiator this *paisan* could be. I angrily asked why Phil had repeatedly "sent guys" down to the Chambers warehouse during the day and in the middle of the night, obviously for the purposes of intimidation. At first Barretti denied that his people had gone inside our warehouse, but finally he admitted that he had told his guys to go down to Plymouth Street, though only to "watch youse guys."

That sitdown was so tense, everyone's tempers were flaring. Frank Allocca was grumbling at me, chewing his scrambled eggs on dry wheat toast. Barretti was glaring at me and I was glaring back at him. I was frankly sick of his bullshit. "Phil, what's with you sending those fuckin' thugs into my warehouse?"

"I'm in this business to make money," Phil said.

"So am I, Phil."

"You're trying to make money off of me, buddy. If you think you got a headache with me, you're gonna have a fuckin' headache you ain't gonna *believe*. I'll tell you that right now. You take my fuckin' work, I ain't happy about it."

"I'm gonna have a fuckin' headache, Phil?"

"You're gonna have a fuckin' headache, you keep fuckin' with me!"

That was it. We both started to lean forward, as if to get out from the booth, but I was pinned into my seat, and Frank Allocca grabbed us both by the forearms and held us. "Keep it down!" Frank shouted. I was surprised at how strong his grip was.

I was so mad, I felt like hauling off and belting Phil. But I'm glad Frank Allocca held us back—it would have been a big problem for the case if there'd been a fistfight in the Americana. As an undercover, you always have to remember that you're supposed to be the victim here—

you're supposed to be the guy getting coerced and extorted by the Mob. If you cross the line and become the aggressor, it will look bad at trial, like you're the badguy.

Phil and I sat there staring at each other while Frank Allocca's lecturing us, telling us to calm down. "What the hell's wrong with you guys?" I knew what was wrong with Phil—he wasn't used to running into this kind of resistance.

A few days earlier, Cousin Sal had been solicited by the Century 21 department-store chain to pick up the recycling and garbage at their flagship store on Cortlandt Street across from the World Trade Center and their Brooklyn store on Eighty-sixth Street in Bay Ridge. Turns out that Phil had the property rights to the Brooklyn store. I thought he also had the property rights to the Manhattan store.

"Look, you're gonna give me that Century stop back," he says, then he spits a sarcastic laugh into my face. "Wait'll you see who the *other* guy is. The guy who's got the other stop—he's a friend of yours too."

"Who we talkin' about here, Phil?"

"Joe."

"Joe who?"

"Francolino," he whispers.

"Yeah, Joe's a customer of mine—he dumps at my facility."

"Well, he won't be for long!"

Behind the scenes—as it was later shown in court—Barretti reached out to Joe Francolino, let him know about the problems he was having with me. And the very next day Francolino came down to Chambers looking for me. I was running around town—of all the times for me to be out of the office. Sal was left alone to deal with the biggest wiseguy in the industry. Sal only knew the name Duffy from the army-green trucks with pink writing on the side, trucks dumping recycled paper with us every few days. He didn't even know what Joe Duffy looked like in person.

Joe Francolino strolled right into the warehouse, through an open bay door, followed by his son—yet another Danny—who was holding a large ledger. He came in and he sandbagged Sal—the elusive Sally

Skates. This was Joey Cigars in person, not calling on the phone. Sal couldn't pull the usual bobbing and weaving routine. And he couldn't roll with "dis-shit, dat-shit" now.

"Sal," Joe said, "I see we got a problem here."

"Yeah? We do?"

Francolino told his son to open up the ledger. "Look, I'm out forty-eight hundred dollars a month with Century 21. Sal, I wanna know what your intentions are."

Sal's intentions were to shit in his pants.

For more than a year now I'd been the guy on the firing line, and when the Benedettos took stops from the cartel, I was out there with a target on my head. Sal had some sympathy for what I was going through, but the rest of the Benedettos in the corporate offices on Madison Avenue, they didn't give a damn. But now Sal saw for himself what I'd been dealing with: He was staring at Joey Cigars in his flashy suit and pinky ring, staring at a made member of the Gambino crime family. Joey Cigars was three feet away, demanding to know what Sal's intentions were.

Sal told Joe he'd pay him the $4,800 a month *and* give him back the stop when the contract expired. A beautiful thing. It was a much better deal than I was giving any of these gangsters.

When I got back to the office, Joe was gone, but Sal was still shaking. I debriefed him, taking notes for the DD5. Sal just wanted to appease Joe and get him the hell out of his office. He told me the details of the deal he'd offered.

"What the hell?" I said. "What kind of deal is that? Sal, you folded like a card table! I'm gonna have to start calling you Laydown Sally."

"Well, you left me alone here, Dan—what was I supposed to do? He's intimidating. I mean, how you gonna say no to *this* guy?"

Meanwhile, up in the Bronx, we had more mayhem. This time it wasn't Lou Mongelli and his bat- and lead-pipe-wielding goons. Now our problem was Vince Promuto, a former NFL offensive guard turned garbage-hauler. In the 1950s Vince had been a standout football and track-and-field man at Holy Cross; drafted by the Chicago Bears, traded to Washington, he started for the Redskins from 1960 to 1970, was team captain and the personal protector of quarterback Sonny Jurgensen. After his football career Promuto earned a law degree and went to work for the federal government in Washington. At this point, well into the 1990s, he remained one of the most popular retired Redskins, holding the distinction of being the last captain of a team coached by Vince Lombardi. (Promuto once described Lombardi's "rooster walk" conditioning drill as "the worst thing I've ever been through.")

In August 1994 a turf war broke out between Vince Promuto and our manager of the paper services transfer station in the Bronx, Ralph Coppola. Technically, Promuto was an outlaw—his company didn't belong to any of the Mobbed-up associations. But Vince really didn't need the cartel. Whenever problems arose, Vince took matters into his own hands.

In August we had a Chambers truck hijacked, the driver tossed out on his ass in the street. Message sent: Chambers gets its truck back when Big Vinnie gets his stops back. Immediately, Ralph called me up, breathless, complaining that Promuto had one of our trucks. "Vince wants me to meet him at his yard," Ralph said. "He says he just wants to talk but I don't wanna go, Dan—he's gonna pound me into submission."

So, on August 11, I drove up to the Bronx to see Patty Pecoraro at his Delmar offices. Jimmy Vigliotti was also there. I figured that maybe these powerful Bronx carters—one a Gambino associate, the other a Genovese—could step in and straighten out my Promuto problem. In his thick, old-time New York accent, massive Jimmy Vigs made a classic, cryptic wiseguy reference to me: "Danny, your friends in Brooklyn are the same as my friends in the Bronx, who are the same as our friends in New York." Translation: We're all hooked up with the Genovese crime family. My friends in Brooklyn meant Frank Allocca and the boys with Allie Shades; Jimmy's friends in the Bronx meant Barney Bellomo and his Genovese crew; our friends in New York meant Angelo Ponte and Frank Giovinco and the Chin's club on Canal Street. But as with most hard-core Mob conversations, you had to read between the lines to grasp the meaning.

We were still struggling to work out the terms—what Patty Pecoraro called "the program"—of my monthly D'Agostino's payoffs. Now I implied—but didn't directly state—that maybe my latest case of *agita* was the result of Patty and the boys sending a message to me through Vince Promuto.

"We don't need Vinnie Promuto to come after you," Patty snapped. "If we wanna come after you, we'll come after you."

Vigliotti smiled, spilling out of his chair, nodding and stroking his stubbly mustache. "Vinnie is a strange animal."

"Danny," Pecoraro said, "I'll be honest with you. No one speaks for Vinnie. You say one thing, he says the opposite. Watch—I'll show you how Vinnie is." He turned to Vigliotti for assistance. "Jimmy, you be me and I'll be Vinnie."

Backlit and in profile, with his double chin and shiny bald head, Patty Pecoraro was a dead ringer for Alfred Hitchcock.

"I'm gonna be Vinnie?"

"No, I'm gonna be Vinnie! You be me."

"Whattaya want me to say?"

"Say anything, I don't care. Say the sky is blue."

"Vinnie, ain't it a beautiful day out? Look how beautiful the blue sky is."

"No, it's not beautiful! And it's not blue—it's *black*!"

Patty's chins quivered with mock rage. I couldn't keep a straight face. The conference room boomed with the sound of these big garbage guys laughing.

"You understand now, Dan? Vinnie is a strange bird. In fact, there's only one guy who can talk to Vinnie."

"Who's that?"

Patty dropped his voice to a respectful whisper and put his mouth directly to my ear. "Joe."

I'd been surveilling Joe for years now—I'd personally snapped pictures of Joey Cigars and Jimmy Brown meeting Allie Shades on Eighty-sixth Street in Bensonhurst. I'd sat a few feet away from Joe in the Gambino garbage club, and of course I'd had that awkward encounter in the Ponte's Steakhouse men's room when the Kel transmitter burned my groin early in the investigation. But Joe Francolino had never spoken a word directly to me.

On August 16, 1994, I went to Jimmy Brown's club on West Broadway to meet with Patty Pecoraro. This was a transitional period for the Gambinos: Soon Jimmy Brown was set to ship out to Texas and start serving his federal sentence for the murder of Tommy Sparrow. And Joey Cigars was settling into his new position on the throne.[7]

When I entered the club, Patty Pecoraro was waiting for me at a poker table, lounging back, trying, without luck, to fill in an ace-high straight. As always, Patty was dressed to a tee—even in this August heat he was wearing a black silk shirt and blue double-breasted suit. I started to speak, but Patty put his finger to his lips and mouthed the words *Talk low*. Nat King Cole's "Mona Lisa" was booming through the speakers. They had the club radio tuned to an oldies station. Twenty garbage gangsters were scattered around the room, engaged in various card games and hush-hush scheming.

I nodded and whispered. "You speak to him about the problem?" The NFL lineman–sized problem in the Bronx.

"Not yet," Patty said. "Wait for Joe to finish his card game."

I handed over three checks totaling $24,000, signed by Sal Benedetto and made out to Pecoraro's Delmar Recycling, to Jimmy Vigliotti's ABC

---

[7] During his murder and racketeering trial in Brooklyn federal court, the frail-seeming Jimmy Brown had created a memorable media spectacle. When the crowd of reporters and photographers surrounded him at the courthouse, Jimmy lost his famous close-mouthed demeanor. "Get the fuck away from me!" he repeatedly shouted, swinging his two metal canes fiercely at any newshound in his vicinity.

Recycling and to a third company, Cameo Carting. These were our first
month's restitution for having taken the accounts at D'Agostino supermarkets. Patty slipped the checks into his suit pocket with a nod.

"I gotta get a hold of everybody and make 'em bill you," he said.
"But change the bill—like one month thirty-eight hundred, next month
thirty-seven hundred, you know what I'm sayin'? This way it's not con-
sistent. We don't want to show no consistency, all right?"

"Right. No consistency."

Patty snuffed out the nub of his cigar and told me to sit tight.

In a few minutes Joe Francolino strolled over with his freshly lit cigar
and his flashing pinky ring. We were formally introduced for the first
time. I mentioned that I'd spoken to Joe's son on the phone the other
day about that awkward situation—

"It's not awkward really," Joe interrupted. "You have something of
mine. But we got that straightened out with your uncle—as far as that
goes. Your uncle said he's gonna pay me every month. Sal's your uncle?"

"Actually, no, he's my first cousin—everyone thinks he's my uncle."

Joe was aware of my problems with Phil Barretti. I tried to laugh it off.

"Yeah, I've had a lot problems with Phil—he took things off my
family first. I'm not giving in to his bullshit—Phil's bullshit or Ponte's or
anybody else's. This is my end of the business, Joe. I'm not going to be
hypocritical and two-faced. I'm not some Lay down Sally here."

Joe smiled, seeming to appreciate the show of backbone. "I already
talked to Philly," he said. "Today, Philly's a *different* Philly. You go see
Philly and it's gonna be straightened out. You have any problems with
Philly, you come see me."

Jimmy Brown came out of his office, hobbling along on his metal
canes, and growled his good-bye to us.

"Good-bye, Jim," Joe said.

"Good-bye, Jim," I said.

The last time I'd been in Jimmy Brown's club, Angelo had been
screaming like a maniac about me. Joe sighed, nodded, remembering
that unpleasant scene. "Yeah, we got our hands full with Angelo."

"I got my hands full with him. You know why? It's all for Angelo and nothing for me."

"Yeah, we're aware of that, but we're working on that. You got my word—because we're fed up too."

I told Joe that I was pretty concerned about the bad blood between me and the Canal Street club. I mentioned that Frank Giovinco had come down to the Chambers warehouse in Brooklyn. "He brought a couple of guys with him—asking for me. They were looking to start something. This problem ain't going away."

"I'm gonna see Allie tonight at eight o'clock," Joe said. "I'm gonna mention that, okay? They came down by you?"

"Yeah, they came down by me, asking my shop guys where I was. My cousin was so scared that he locked himself in a loft upstairs and wouldn't come back to the office."

Francolino stared at me. I fidgeted with my gold watch. I felt bad complaining to Joe, but I had to do something to prevent Frank Giovinco and his guys from confronting the Benedettos. This was a potentially volatile situation—getting a heavyweight Gambino soldier like Joe to take a beef to a heavyweight Genovese *capo* like Allie—and I sure as hell didn't want it to recoil in my face. The last thing I needed was an even more agitated Frank Giovinco.

"Joe, listen, I don't want you to throw any names around. Because then I'll be in more trouble. . . ."

"No, you're not gonna get in trouble," Joe said. "I'm gonna get you *outta* trouble. Don't worry about that part, I'm gonna settle it tonight with Allie."

For now, Joe said, we had our own thing to settle.

"Whattaya wanna do about Century?"

I handed over a check for $4,800, signed by Cousin Sal. "To be honest, Joe, it's not what I would've done—it's not the deal I would've made—but I know that's the agreement you and Sal worked out."

Joe gave me a strange look, like, *The balls on this guy!*

He nodded and said he'd get me a receipt to show that Duffy Waste

Removal had sold the Benedettos $4,800 worth of corrugated card-board.

"As far as I'm concerned, as far as my friends are concerned, and the membership in Queens, you're doing the right thing, Dan. Rome wasn't built in a day. But you've got an ally here. Like I said, tonight I'm gonna handle that situation, and nothing else is going to happen."

"Joe, I'm a little concerned that these guys will be pissed off and I'm gonna have an ugly situation down at my office."

"That's not gonna happen, Dan. We're not gonna have that, you understand? That's *out*. Take my word for it. They might call for you, they may wanna see you, but they're not gonna come down and use any tough-guy tactics after *I* talk to 'em, okay? From now on, you got any problems with anybody, you tell 'em to come see *me*. You tell 'em, 'Go see Joey.' "

And Joey proved as good as his word. There were no more tough-guy tactics. Joe spread the word that I was now a member of the New York Association—therefore under Francolino's personal protection—and that held Angelo Ponte and Frankie Giovinco at bay. All the garbage guys who'd been bleeding us dry for two years—Dominick Vulpis, Frank Allocca, Danny Todisco, Ray Polidori, Joe Virzi, Eddie Tamily, Michael D'Ambrosio, Jimmy Vigliotti, Anthony Vitale—had to cool their heels now or risk Joe Francolino's wrath.

Joe demanded that I give him a complete list of the claims against Chambers. Then, one by one, he started straightening them out. He told me exactly who to pay and who not to pay. Certain "Joe Schmoes" he didn't want me to even acknowledge—the Five Brothers clan, for instance. Francolino had been friendly with Mikey Five Brothers's father, gruff old Pauly Five Brothers—one of the industry's real old-timers—but for the sons he had nothing but contempt. Joe once caught young Pauly, Jr., raising his hand to an older man, and that kind of behavior wasn't tolerated in Joe's universe. "He's a fuckin' snot-nosed cock-sucker," Joe said about the incident. "I blasted him good—I says, 'You walk off!' "

Francolino was such a commanding presence. He had the kind of confidence that came from knowing that his power in the industry was unquestioned, that his word was absolute. Everyone knew that Joe was the direct successor to the two legendary Jimmys, only the third gangster in fifty years to sit at the top of the heap.

When Joe learned about my latest beef up in the Bronx, he quickly took Vince Promuto by the horns. There would be no more hijackings, Joe vowed. Promuto and Francolino had a long-standing relationship; Joe had in fact purchased his first garbage truck years ago from Vince's father.

Next, Francolino set about bringing Phil Barretti to the table. He scheduled a sitdown between me and Phil at Giando—fittingly, the same Brooklyn waterfront restaurant where Phil had sent his goon, Ray Ramos, to rough up Sal two years back. In Giando, over red wine, we finally resolved One Wall Street, the beef that had started it all.

"I don't care what bullshit happened in the past," Joe told us as we sat down to a 3 P.M. meal. "I'm a bit of a judge here and I know that everybody's got his rhyme and reason. But as of today, we're moving forward." He wanted me and Phil to shake hands, and we all raised glasses of wine and said *salut'*.

"Put it all on the table," Joe said. "If I sit down neutral, and you're right, you're gonna win." Francolino was highly critical of the arbitrary fashion in which Angelo Ponte settled his disputes on Canal Street. "All fairness to Angelo—I mean, we'll eat and drink and go away together—but when it comes to business sometimes he is not a hands-on type of guy. Sometimes he's all over the place. Sometimes he jumps the gun. I mean, you wanna be the judge, the jury, and then you'll sentence the guy? That's not a fair trial. The guy's gotta sit down and defend himself, you know what I mean? So before anybody starts throwing accusations or insinuating and what have you—before you start labeling a guy, we could have a more gentlemanly-like business. Say, 'Phil, can you maybe have time for coffee?' and you find out what the problem is and you get the facts."

Phil and I proceeded to lay our facts on the crisp white tablecloth.

We ran through the years of cross-complaints. We exchanged bills and invoices. The evidence clearly showed that Barretti had taken one of Sal Benedetto's premier accounts, the one-million-square-foot Chase Manhattan Plaza, a full two months before Sal had taken One Wall Street from Phil. The official rubbish survey I brought as evidence showed that there was not $8,000 worth of compacted waste coming out of One Wall Street, as Phil had always maintained, but closer to $3,500. When Joe saw the evidence, he was decisive. "Look, we're going to put this to rest," he said.

His ruling was that I would have to pay Phil $1,750 a month, half of what Chambers was charging One Wall Street. Phil jotted down the figure. "Is that fair?" Joe asked. We both agreed that it was. The agreement was sealed with another handshake. No more bad blood between the Barrettis and Benedettos.

Francolino assured me that he was always going to be my protector. "I'm not gonna put you in the jackpot, Dan. And for whatever reason, God forbid that something happens that you wind up in the jackpot, I'm gonna be there to help you. In other words, I don't run away and desert my obligations or desert a situation that I created. I'd never throw you in the water to sink or swim, Danny—on the contrary, I'm gonna be there with the life jacket."

"Yeah, because I might need a life jacket with Mikey Five Brothers."

"Don'tcha worry about it."

"I might need a life jacket, Joe. I mean, I'll stand my ground, but the bottom line is I'm gonna need—"

"Stand your ground."

"—a life jacket."

"Listen, Danny, anybody bullies my member, it's like they're bullying me. And let 'em come bully me and see if they get away with it. If they bully me, then they could bully you or they could bully Philly. But first you have to get past me. And you're a helluva man if you can get past me. 'Cause you know how you're gonna get past me? You're gonna get a steamroller."

"A what?" I said.

"A *steamroller,*" Joe said.

"A steamroller," Phil said.

Phil and I laughed. Joe didn't crack a smile.

"And I don't want to sound egotistical in any which way, but I have to try to make you understand: This is factual. Go check it out. I wanna see anybody defy me. I'm the fuckin' lawyer here. Believe me when I tell you, I'm a Philadelphia lawyer. You're not gonna win too many arguments with me—you're not gonna win 'em if I don't want you to win 'em."

That summer, the tension between Joe Francolino and Angelo Ponte got bad enough that Joe ordered me to stop paying any of Ponte's Waste Paper Association members. "You hold off on all of those paper guys," he said, laughing. "Let 'em go screaming to Angelo."

Unwittingly, Francolino's order perfectly suited the direction of our investigation: There was really no need for me to further infiltrate the Chin's paper club; we had plenty of evidence to lock up all the principal Mob figures on Canal Street.

There was only one of the "old paper guys" whom I continued to meet regularly—actually going against Francolino's explicit instructions. Eddie Tamily's conversations were priceless. Tamily couldn't stop talking about subjects he should never have started on. Ed's language was so colorful—and so evidence-rich—it was worth the $8,000 a month in extortion just to let him talk.

Within the highly surveillance-conscious Genovese crime family it was prohibited to even utter the boss's nickname. Mobsters were instructed to point at their chins when referring to the boss.

Just mentioning the names Chin or Gigante could be a death sentence. I'll give you an example: Before my undercover role as Danny Benedetto, I debriefed an unsavory gangster named Peter "Fat Pete" Chiodo, whom I had arrested during our Painters District Council 9 investigation. Pete was a five-hundred-pound Lucchese *capo* who'd somehow managed to absorb thirteen point-blank gunshot wounds in a 1991 assassination attempt and live to tell about it. After that, the wheelchair-bound Chiodo became a government informant and vanished into the Witness Protection Program.

Fat Pete told me that during a meeting inside Veterans and Friends, Jimmy Brown's social club, he had casually mentioned the Chin during a card game with Allie Shades. Allie turned suddenly red, stood up, and told Fat Pete to come outside. "Don't *ever* say that name," Allie barked at Pete as they walked on Eighty-sixth Street. "Whattaya tryin' to do, get me clipped? That's a *killing* offense!"

Most of these West Side guys were so cagey that to actually catch a Genovese wiseguy or associate on tape talking about Chin Gigante was unheard of. But near the end of August '94 we caught such a break. I'd come by Ed Tamily's paper-recycling shop on East Third Street to hand him his HBO extortion payment of $8,000 in cash.

This was the first time we'd ever heard anyone talk about a "point system," a secret percentage tribute going to the Mafia bosses that ran the cartel. But old Ed Tamily had his own curious way of referring to mobsters. He liked to call them "banana noses." Joe Francolino, Allie Shades, and Jimmy Brown were all banana noses in Eddie's book. Frank Giovinco, for example, wasn't a banana nose yet because he wasn't officially made. "He's a knockaround kid," Ed told me. "They're bringing him up. But he ain't got his button yet."

One of the primary reasons Frank was so pissed off with me, Tamily explained, was that when I first joined the Canal Street Association, Frank had been resolving various beefs for me, but I'd failed to show appropriate respect, failed to pay the required tribute. Eddie rubbed his thumb and index finger together to indicate the cash that Giovinco expected, money he was in turn expected to "kick upstairs" to his own boss.

"So Frank's pissed off that I never paid him?" I said.

"Right."

"Well, why didn't he ever tell me? I mean, how am I supposed to know this? He doesn't tell me. Strange guy sometimes."

"Don't worry about it, Dan. 'Cause he don't know how to come up to you. He don't know what to say. Because he didn't know himself—

because people pushed him, like Ponte and the rest of 'em. Oh, you're making money. Where's the percentage? You gotta give to the *big* boss. You can't keep it all yourself. You gotta share it."

"So, he gives it—Ponte's a big boss?"

"No. The Chin."

"The *Chin?*"

"Yeah. Gigante."

"Gigante?"

"He's the head of the Association."

"Shit. He's the biggest wiseguy around."

"Yeah. He's the head of the Association."

"Are you sure?"

"Listen to me, I know what I'm talking about. Let me tell you something, I have no respect for nobody. The only thing I have respect for is what's right and what's wrong. It has to be done—you gotta pay. And that's the respect: *dollars.* Nothing else. You understand? And you don't wanna be involved with these fuckin' banana noses, Dan. You don't wanna have nothin' to do with them."

"How do I—how do I not do that?"

"You do it this way—*dollars!* You get rid of it with this—*dollars!*"

"I know that. . . ."

Tamily began to laugh through the cigar smoke. He pointed at my temples.

"Dan, you're getting old. You see how many white hairs you got?"

"Yeah, I'm—I'm getting gray. I just got a lot more gray when you said Gigante's involved."

"He's the boss here. He's always been the boss."

"He's the boss. But I mean, if I don't pay—"

"Before that, it was Genovese."

"But if I don't pay him, a guy like that, they're gonna do something."

"Fuggedaboutit, fuggedaboutit. . . ."

A little later Tamily was even more explicit about these "points"—the Mafia tribute system. He said this was the reason he preferred to settle his beefs *mano a mano,* behind the backs of the Association leaders

and wiseguys like Jimmy Brown and Joe Francolino and Allie Malangone. That way he didn't have to pay the banana noses their points.

"What's a point?" I said "I know it's a percentage, but—"

"*Minghia!* For every dollar—for every dollar you pay a penny. All
right? For every hundred dollars you pay a dollar. For every thousand
dollars you pay ten dollars. Okay? And if you spend a hundred thousand dollars, it's a thousand. *Capice?*"

"Yeah, *capice.*"

"I'll tell you why, I'll tell you why—Dan, you wanna pay points?"

"Do I wanna pay points?"

"Yeah. You wanna pay to these banana noses?"

"No."

"Well, this is what they're doing here. Let me tell you how this works
at the Association. Say you take ten thousand dollars' worth of stops from
me. We gotta pay two points. You pay a point and I pay a point, okay?
That's what it's all about. You gotta pay a point to this guy—the Chin."

"I don't know about a lot of that stuff. . . . But—I mean, this Gigante's like the biggest wiseguy—"

"Yeah, he's—"

"He tells you, you gotta pay a point?"

"He sends Frank. He don't wanna know nothin'."

"Oh, he sends Frank?"

"Angelo Ponte too."

"Ponte had to pay a point?"

"Yeah."

"He had to pay a point to the Chin?"

"Yeah, yeah, yeah. He don't—Chin don't wanna know nothin'. He's
a banana nose. He ain't got no friends."

Ed Tamily also explained to me another of the cartel's unwritten rules:
How the Genovese crime family got cash directly from the carting
companies through their control of LIUNA Local 958, where Frank
Giovinco used to work as an organizer.

"And you got—what union you got?" Ed asked. "958?"

"Yeah," I said. "And [Local] 27."

"Huh?"

"We got [Locals] 27 and 958. Now one of them is trying to absorb the other one. There's problems with that going on."

"But that's what you should do," Ed explained. "You should go to Frank. He's 958. He used to be a—he used to work [with them]."

"Yeah, right. I know that. . . ."

"You guys don't pay no cash to the union like we pay," he said. "In other words, we got—let's say we have eight, ten employees. [It's] costing us five thousand dollars every year that we gotta send to the Chin."

"Oh, yeah? But then what's that—what does that do for you?"

"That helps you in the union. It keeps the things kind of low. You know?"

"But what does the, uh—?"

"Costs," Ed said. "Operating costs."

Operating costs. I had to smile when Ed said that. That's what guys like Ed and Joe Virzi called those cash payoffs to the Chin.

Just as the name Dan Benedetto began circulating with the top bosses in the Mafia cartel, my alter ego had also become a topic of considerable discussion among the top bosses in the New York Police Department and at City Hall.

Mayor Rudolph Giuliani was briefed about the expanding scope of Operation Wasteland: It was now the largest and most complex organized-crime case ever undertaken by the New York Police Department. The mayor was informed that a New York Police detective had now infiltrated the upper echelons of the Mafia cartel, that an Irish cop, posing as an Italian-American, had gained the confidence of the top-ranking Gambino wiseguy running this $1.5-billion industry. By August 1994 the NYPD and the New York County district attorney's office were jointly paying out more than $80,000 a month in extortion and dues to the various Mob-run associations. But Giuliani, the former Mafia-busting U.S. Attorney for the Southern District, knew that this was taxpayer money well spent: The fines and forfeitures in such a sweeping racketeering case could potentially bring in tens and even hundreds of millions.

In the feverish pace of the investigation, I came out of my undercover role to make a rare appearance at One Police Plaza. All the big brass were gathered in the commissioner's office on the fourteenth floor for the top-secret presentation: Commissioner Bill Bratton; First Deputy Commissioner John Timoney; Deputy Commissioner Jack Maple; Chief of the Department Louis Anemone, Chief of the Organized Crime Control Bureau Martin O'Boyle; Lieutenant Greg Longworth.

Making the presentation for OCID were Inspector Kenny O'Brien, Deputy Inspector John Regan, Lieutenant John O'Brien, Sergeant Tony Mazziotti, and me. We had elaborate flow charts and an enormous map depicting New York's five boroughs with movable Velcro-backed garbage trucks indicating the carting companies and black-trench-coat-and-fedora–clad silhouettes representing the mobsters. We gave an overview of the investigation, going back to the night when I first broke into Allie Malangone's club, Pastels, to get our surveillance bugs in place.

I should explain something about Deputy Commissioner Jack Maple, now deceased. He was a legendary figure in the department, a former transit cop credited with transforming the entire city with his CompStat program, a system of tracking crime statistics and holding individual commanders accountable for any spikes in their precincts. Jack Maple had an extravagance and flair that was unusual for a cop; he liked to wear homburgs, bow ties, and spats. He also had a well-documented taste for nightlife, was often seen rubbing shoulders with the celebrities at Elaine's. When Jack Maple heard the first mention of Pastels Disco, he smiled at us.

"You mean the place in Bay Ridge? Oh, I've been there a time or two."

Commissioner Bratton shot him an icy look—like, what was his deputy commissioner doing in the nightclub of a notorious Genovese wiseguy? But that was just Jack Maple, man about town.

The commissioner began to address me as Detective Cowan, but he soon picked up on the fact that Tony Maz and everyone else was calling me Dan. It came my turn to take the floor and I described being surrounded by the pipe- and bat-wielding thugs in Hunts Point. I briefed the brass about the vicious attempted murder of Alex Fernandez. Lieutenant John O'Brien played selected tape recordings of Lou Mongelli's maniacal death threats to me. O'Brien stood at the map and pointed to the little black fedora-wearing figure Velcroed in position at 180 West Broadway: Joe Francolino, aka Joey Cigars, aka Joe Duffy.

"Commissioner, Dan has now become a trusted confidant and co-conspirator of Joe Francolino, the most powerful gangster in the carting industry."

When the presentation finished, the commissioner shook my hand. "Keep up the good work, Detective," he said, smiling, correcting himself. "I mean—*Dan.*"

For more than two years now, I'd managed to keep my two lives separated. Then the firewall was breached. It was my own stupid slipup. My wife was nine months pregnant—her due date was any day—and I was so excited I couldn't keep it to myself. We'd been trying to have a child for years, and it had been a difficult pregnancy, which wasn't made any easier by the overwhelming demands of the job.

When Claire gave birth to our son Ricky, I was so happy, I could barely contain myself. Sal's sister was laughing at me. She knew something was up, so I told her the truth: "I've got a newborn son." Pretty soon all the Benedettos and the working guys in the shop are congratulating me, slapping me on the back. Then next thing I know, one of the guys who dumps paper at Chambers is yelling out the window of his Mercedes: "Danny! Congratulations on the baby!"

By this time I'm so deeply entrenched in the role that I'm hanging out with the guys every day and night. We're socializing, having drinks, eating and scheming all the time. How's it going to look that I have something as momentous as a firstborn son and don't even mention it? This is going to raise *somebody* up pretty fast.

Of course, as an undercover, the last thing in the world you want is to let these gangsters know anything about your personal life. But since the cat was out of the bag, I figured, *maybe this can work for me.* Before the word could spread any further, I went down to J&R Tobacco and bought all these boxes of cigars. Te-Amo Toro Lights, the same brand Joe Francolino smoked. My plan was to show up at all the clubs, drop the cigars off, then make a big announcement to everyone that I now had a baby boy named Danny.

But I saw I'd created another problem. I asked Tony Maz about it after one of our debriefings at the VA Hospital.

"What's the matter, pal?" he said.

Tony was a pack-a-day Marlboro man—most days on the job, he even wore a black Marlboro baseball cap. I'd never smoked anything in my life. We split open one of the Te-Amo boxes and sat in the parking lot of the VA Hospital in Brooklyn for over an hour, dirtying up the windows of his car. "Just clip a little hole in one end," he said. "You should buy a proper cigar clipper, but you can use a pen knife, or if you have to, tear a little hole like this . . ." Tony got his Te-Amo flaming, took a leisurely puff, leaned back, savoring the flavor of the smoke. "Now just hold the smoke in your mouth—don't inhale it past the throat, pal, or you'll have problems." I felt like a kid in high school, learning to smoke with an older brother. By the end of the evening my throat was sandpapered raw and I was hacking like a madman.

The next day I made all the rounds, dropped the cigar boxes off at all the clubs, and announced that I had a nine-pound dark-haired Danny Boy. We all lit up the Te-Amos, everybody was cheering, calling me proud papa. Ed Tamily looked a little sad, remembering his own kids. "This is the best part," he tells me. "You know, when they're like five or six months and they crawl all over you in bed. . . ."

Later, I started leaving my little guy's car seat in the Jeep, and a couple of his toys lying around. On a trip to Florida, I found this Mickey

Mouse from Disney World with my son's alias—DAN—in big letters on the front. I left that sitting on the console of the Jeep. One day I was giving Joe Francolino a ride to lunch and he picked up the Mickey Mouse and laughed.

It's just a few little details—Te-Amo Toros, the car seat, the Mickey Mouse with your kid's name on it. But those few little details fit into place to show you have a family life, a life outside all this scheming and scamming. It's the little details that make you seem more real.

On the other hand, having these guys know any little personal details made the case even more unnerving. From then on, Ed Tamily kept bringing up my son in our conversations, often with an implied warning of violence to come.

"I don't wanna see you getting old like you're getting now," Eddie said. " You got a beautiful kid, you're married, you got a nice life ahead of you. You wanna go to sleep at night, not thinking some cocksucker's coming after you. . . ."

On the afternoon of August 26, 1994, on a windswept Long Island golf course, the delicate facade protecting the entire investigation came crashing down. Sal had a distant cousin named Joe Benedetto who'd long ago left the New York area. Joe had worked for several years with the rest of the Benedettos in New York, but he'd relocated to Chesapeake, Virginia, and started his own recycling company called Tidewater Paper Fibres. Over the years Tidewater had grown into a prospering business, the biggest private recycling interest in Virginia. In the late summer of '94, Joe Benedetto—known to everyone as Tidewater Joe— returned to the New York area for a vacation. On August 26, he attended the annual Recycling and Garbage Industry Golf Outing, held at the South Shore Country Club, in Hamburg, Long Island.

Tidewater Joe was just finishing up on the front nine when he was surrounded by some heavyset carters in snappy golf shirts and caps. Tony Vitale from the WPA flashed a knowing smile.

"How's your cousin Dan doing? You know we took him into the club."

"Who you talking about? Dominic?"

"No, Dan."

"Little Dom?"

"No, Dan—Danny at Chambers. Danny Benedetto in Brooklyn!"

"Jeez, I'm trying to think of everybody out there in Brooklyn," said Tidewater Joe, "but I don't know any *Dan* in the family." Joe stood there, leaning on his putter, mulling it over for a while. "I know for a fact that there's no Danny at Chambers."

Tony Vitale and the other carters circled tighter. Suddenly the mood on the golf course was dark. "Joe, so what you're telling us, then—if there's no Dan in Brooklyn—you're telling us that Dan's an undercover *FBI agent?*"

Tidewater Joe realized he'd stepped into something, and he started backpedaling fast. "I'm not telling you that."

"Then what *are* you telling us, Joe?"

"I don't know what I'm telling you, but I'm not telling you *that*."

Tidewater Joe was so shaken, he left the country club immediately, right in the middle of his golf game. Before he'd even got to his car, he had his cell phone out, dialing Cousin Sal on Plymouth Street.

It was around 4:30 P.M. and I was pulling my car into the back of an apartment building in Staten Island, the parking lot where I switched from my Dan Benedetto Jeep into my Rick Cowan Chevy pickup. I get beeped from the office in Brooklyn. I can hear right away that something's very wrong with Sal.

"Listen, I've got some bad news. I just got a call from my cousin Joe—Tidewater Joe from Virginia. He got surrounded today in Long Island by Tony Vitale and the rest of 'em."

"What happened?"

"They asked about you and he told 'em he don't know no Danny Benedetto."

"He told them what? Stop fuckin' around, Sal."

"I'm not fuckin' around."

I shut off my engine and tried to deal with this bombshell.

"Sal, listen to me. As easy as these guys could grab me somewhere, they could grab you somewhere. They all know you too well—they know where to find you. Stay put—don't leave the office. We gotta nail down our story quick. Any minute somebody could put a gun to our heads."

"Lemme think—lemme think—"

"This is not going away, Sal. This is gonna escalate. This is gonna get ugly."

We sat there trying to work out an alibi. How the hell could we explain the fact that one of our own blood relatives had claimed I don't even exist? There was no way to explain it—I'd have to pull out of the undercover role immediately. Yes, we'd have to deep-six Danny. Just when I was starting to get close to Joe Francolino! I was so pissed off, I lost my cool with my cousin.

"You gave me this goddamn John Benedetto for a father! Sal, I always told you that would not fly! He's too fuckin' old to be my dad."

I thought we'd lost our cell connection. The phone was dead for a long time.

Then Sally Skates came through once again.

"There's one other Benedetto who's been out of the New York area for decades," he said. "No one has talked to this guy for years. He's a cousin of Tidewater Joe and me and everyone. This might work, y'know—nobody can check it out. . . ."

He told me his story. It was wacky—possibly just wacky enough to work. The cousin Sal was referring to was a Paulist priest named Robert Benedetto. Back in the '60s he was known as "the hippie priest"—he'd organized a rent strike and was featured in the *Daily News* as this radical, long-haired, flower-power priest leading a bunch of wayward women in the East Village. Our story was that Robert Benedetto had an illegitimate son. Of course, this would have created a scandal, and that's why he'd left the Church. He'd married a nun, they'd run off together, moved to California.

"Are you okay with it?" Sal said.

"What choice do I have?"

"Okay, but I gotta call Tidewater Joe and tell him our story—"

"You do that, Sal."

I hung up the phone and looked at myself in the rearview mirror.

I was now the family embarrassment. The skeleton in the closet. The bastard son of a hippie priest.

It didn't take long before Angelo Ponte launched his own investigation into my "real" family connections. He telephoned Johnny Tuzzio, now retired and relaxing on his Bensonhurst stoop. Angelo had known Johnny for fifty years—and he knew that Johnny had all the Benedetto family dirt.

"Is he real, Johnny? Tell me—is he real?" Angelo asked.

"Sure, he's real," Johnny said.

"How long have you known him?"

"I've known him for years. He's Sal's second cousin. Sure, Danny's one of the Staten Island crowd. . . ."

Then Angelo called down to Virginia and started questioning Tidewater Joe. (Tidewater Joe called Sal immediately to report it.)

"Do you hear what's going on up here, Joe?" Angelo asked. "Everybody's worried about this thing. Tell me—is Dan real or a *phantom?*"

On the muggy afternoon of September 12, I was alone in the Chambers offices. All the other Benedettos had left Brooklyn for the day; it was just me and the damn rats scampering through the warehouse. I was waiting for one last shipment, a tractor-trailer bound for a paper mill in Canada, before I could close up shop.

Around 5:30, I got a page. I didn't recognize the Manhattan phone number. When I dialed, a woman's voice answered.

"This is Dan Benedetto—I just got beeped."

The woman didn't say another word: It was Joe Francolino on the line.

"Danny, how's it going?"

"It's going good, Joe."

"When am I gonna see you?"

"I'll see you tomorrow at the club."

"No, Dan. I wanna see you tonight."

Now it hit me: The Mob grapevine had reached Joe.

I said that I still had some work to finish up, that I didn't know when I was going to get out of the office. But Joe told me he wanted to see me as soon as possible. He told me to meet him at a restaurant called Pierino's on Reade Street. When I said I didn't know where Pierino's was, Joe gave me precise driving instructions, even telling me which parking lot to use. "Okay," I said. But I still needed to buy myself a little time to call Tony Maz and the field team.

"Joe, listen, I'm waiting for a big load of paper going to Canada. The minute that leaves, I'm outta here."

"As soon as you can, Dan."

I reached Tony Mazziotti at our plant right off the Cross Island Expressway in Queens. Tony didn't like the sound of this one bit.

"No fuckin' way," he said. "You're not going. This could be a setup."

Bobby O'Donahue, on the other line, was equally adamant. "It's a Mobbed-up restaurant—they can whack you in there, take you out with the garbage, and nobody will see a thing."

"But if I don't show up, he'll *know* I'm a cop and the case is over."

As usual, Tony aimed for a compromise. "Okay, stall him," he said. "Just give me two hours to get there with the field team."

"Forget two hours, Tony. Joe's not stupid. If I take two hours, he'll know I'm calling for backup. It won't look right. The best thing I can do is get there the soon as possible and make it look natural."

There were so many unknown factors going into that meeting. Tony and Bobby and I were trying to play every angle in our minds. The only thing we knew for sure is that we had Joe Francolino calling me on the carpet, that I had to be ready in forty-five minutes, had to know exactly what to say and how to pull it off. The consequences of not pulling it off could have been anything from, "Get the fuck outta here—you're full of shit," to "Let's take a walk," and somebody's waiting there to take me out.

In a way, it wouldn't have been so bad for Joe to think I was a cop. Traditionally—it's not really true today—but traditionally the Mob really doesn't go after cops, doesn't sanction the open killing of a cop. But you better believe they would kill Sal Benedetto for allowing a cop to operate within his organization. So our biggest risk was not Francolino thinking I'm a cop; it was Francolino thinking I'm really a Benedetto who's started collecting evidence against the Mob. Because once you take off the protective shell of me being a cop, these guys wouldn't think two seconds about killing a carter who's been cooperating with law enforcement.

I drove across the Brooklyn Bridge and up through the Financial District to Reade Street, then pulled my Jeep into the parking lot that Joe had described. It was a small lot, only about half full. The back of the lot led to a little narrow alleyway, a dark passage that connected straight through to Chambers Street. I pulled up to the booth, rolled down the window—expecting to be handed a ticket—but instead the guy asks me:

"What's your name?"

Since when does a parking attendant ask your name?

"Dan."

He nodded, told me to leave my Jeep in the very back of the lot near the alleyway. "Lock it up," he said. "Take the keys." The way my Jeep was parked in the dark corner of the lot, it would be easy to take a slim jim and start going through my truck, looking for any kind of incriminating papers.

I hurried up the block to Pierino's, knees feeling like rubber. It was exactly 6:15 when I walked into the restaurant. The place was deserted. There was no maître d' at the door. There was no bartender behind the bar. I looked into dining room and I didn't see a soul. I suddenly felt like Luca Brasi stepping into that bar when the Tattaglias gave him the Sicilian necktie in *The Godfather*.

When I walked downstairs to look around, I saw they had a second dining room, and then—*bam*—rounding the corner, coming out of the bathroom, I walked square into Joe Francolino. My stomach flip-flopped, but I think I managed to keep my composure.

"Danny, how are ya?"

"I'm good, Joe. Listen, thanks a lot for straightening out that situation with Vince Promuto."

"No problem. I went and saw Vinnie and told him you're a friend of *mine,* and he had to straighten this out."

We went upstairs. Joe found the bartender and ordered a couple of martinis. Then Joe walked behind the bar, picked up the house phone, and made a call. I couldn't hear much of the conversation, just a few bits and pieces: "Yeah, he's here. . . . There's no problem. . . . Yeah, why don't you stop by. . . ."

We sat down together at a secluded table at the back of the dining room. It started out as a typical dinner. Joe didn't see anything that suited him on the menu, so he started dictating precise directions for the chef: a combination of various pastas, a little penne marinara, some spinach ravioli. "But no seafood," Joe said. "I don't like anything that moves."

I had no appetite at all—if anything, I was now queasy—and I jabbed my finger at the page of appetizers. The waiter had been singing the praises of the *mozzarella di bufala.*

"Okay, I'll get that bufala mozzarella."

The waiter had an accent like he just flew in from Naples last month. "What about for your main course, sir?"

"No, I'm just gonna go light. I'll just have—you sold me on the bufala mozzarella."

Joe's staring at me in disbelief. "Danny, that's all you eat? Fuggedaboutit. Order something else. Fuggedaboutit."

"No, the bufala mozzarella—that's fine. What's that come with? It's, uh, beef with mozzarella?"

"No, no," the waiter said, "it's just fresh slices of mozzarella served on top of tomato, with roasted peppers and basil."

I had eaten buffalo meat—a bison steak—in a Staten Island restaurant about six months earlier, and with my thoughts racing a thousand miles an hour, I didn't even realize how dumb I sounded. But when the case finally came down, it seemed like every media smart-ass was there to remind me. All the crime reporters from the New York *Daily News* to the London *Times* got a huge kick about how I was supposed to be from a big family named Benedetto but I didn't have a clue what an Italian delicacy like *mozzarella di bufala* was.

"You're kiddin' me," Joe said, shaking his head. "How can you—? Fuggedaboutit. You gotta order something else, Danny. You won't be able to walk outta here, you'll be so weak."

"I'll have the lobster."

"The one-and-a-half-pound lobster?"

"Yeah, the one-and-a-half-pound lobster. Steamed."

So much for going light.

Joe was in full John Gotti mode: a charcoal double-breasted suit, white-on-white shirt, black-and-red silk tie with matching silk pocket square. As he rested his arms on the table his gold cuff links flashed in the overhead light.

A guy named Lou came over briefly. Joe introduced us. I recognized his face from the club. Joe told Lou that there were two nice-sized TV sets downstairs, and now that it was football season, they should maybe get a little Monday-night thing going, maybe have a little pool.

"We got guys to take the action?" Lou whispered.

Joe shrugged. "Why not?"

My favorite Italian love song was coming through the speakers—Al Martino singing "I Have But One Heart." A great romantic ballad, sung half in English, half in Italian—but I can think of plenty of people I'd rather be sitting there listening to love songs with than Joey Cigars.

Sipping his martini, in the most casual manner possible, Joe said:

"Somebody had told me that there was a relation to the Benedettos . . . a Joe Benedetto. . . ."

I reacted innocent at first. Sal had a brother in Chambers, also named Joe. "Joe Benedetto? He works with me at Chambers. He's Sal's brother."

"Well, he says he doesn't know no Dan Benedetto."

"Joe Benedetto?"

"He didn't say this to me. He told it to somebody else."

"Oh, you're talking about Joe Benedetto from Tidewater Paper. That's Tidewater Joe—he's down South. He was a part of D. Benedetto, Inc., years ago, but he left. There was a rift in the family. I know who he is but he doesn't really know me. . . ." I was talking too fast now, but I couldn't slow down.

"Are you a nephew to Sal?"

"I'm a cousin of Sal."

"So how is that relation?"

"I'm the son of John Benedetto, who was first cousin to Sal. So I'm second cousin to Sal—and I'm a—third cousin to Tidewater Joe."

"This Joe who used to be involved in the business, he no longer is involved in the business, so he doesn't know you?"

"Yes, they parted ways—"

"Why couldn't he have checked it to find out that you are a relation?"

"He ought to have. He really ought to have. I don't know him—I don't know his kids. He's got three or four kids. I don't even know their names. All I know is that one of them—"

"Yes, that's feasible."

"—all I know is it's a tremendous family and one of them—all I know is one of them—I don't know who it is—but one of them's getting married in Italy in October."

"Getting married to who? In Italy?"

"They're getting married in Italy."

"In Italy, in October?"

"Yeah—"

"Now, you don't mind me asking you all these questions?'

"No, I don't."

"Because I'm in a position where I have to—"

"Absolutely, that you should know and—"

"I have to say, 'Hey, don't you worry and feel comfortable—Dan's checked out and verified.' And I can't do that unless I do it."

"Right."

"I'm not gonna *lie.*"

"By all means. You check it out. You should—y-you sh-should."

"Do you know Tommy Masotto?"

"I—yes. I know his son. I know Tommy—when I was with Dom Ben, when Tommy was, y'know. Sal's really met with Tommy and—"

"So you know Tommy and you know his son?"

"Y-y-yeah."

"How long?"

"To make you feel a little better, to know that I'm straight—shooting straight—"

"You gotta be straight with me, Dan, cause once you—"

"I am."

"—once you're not, I gotta walk away."

"Right, and I realize—" I had my Motorola cell phone flipped open and I was trying to dial Sal's number. No signal. "I can't get through on this telephone."

"Whattaya need? You have to make a call?"

"Yeah?"

"Go over there—to the door. There's a phone there to one side."

"Joe, you wanna come to the phone with me?"

"Why? You want me to verify something?"

"Yeah, I'm gonna ask my cousin something and if it's all right to—if I was gonna tell you something, would you keep it between us? 'Cause he probably wants to talk to you on the phone with me."

"No, no, no, no. You don't have to be on the phone with anyone to verify. That's not necessary. But you have to—don't feel uncomfortable. Understand why I'm doing this, okay? I have to put a stamp on the situation. If I'm gonna go to bat for you—and I have done so—"

"You have."

"—up until tonight."

"Yes."

"Because I gave you my word, and because you've been honorable up to this point. And I wanted to have a continuous relationship. And hopefully, everybody winds up being happy. And we're all—everybody's making money."

I picked up my cell phone again to dial Sal. Still no freakin' signal.

"What were—who were you going to call? For me to talk to?"

"I was just gonna call my cousin Sal. I was gonna ask him if it was all right to let you in on a family skeleton. Just 'cause my family—I mean, everyone who knows my family can tell you they're straight shooters. They're independent and on their own. They like everything just right, squeaky clean, and because there's a couple things—I—I promised that I would not say certain—certain things when I worked with the family. And you know, it's out of place for me to really say—it's sort of an embarrassment. If you want to go into this—and you could check this out—see, I've told people that my father is John, okay?"

"Because . . . there's like a little controversy when somebody puts something in front of me that—that they never heard of you—they don't know you. And I'm not an *alarmist,* you know?"

"Mmmm-hmmm."

"I'm not paranoid. But I'm *careful.* And if somebody asks me, 'Joey, would you check out what I told you about?' Now the burden is on *me.* They're relying on me to make sure that everything is in order. Sometimes I like to back off and not get involved in certain situations. But then I won't be doing my job. If it's asked of me and it's expected of me, you know I'm not here to dupe anybody. I'm here—"

"Mmmm-hmmm."

"—I'm here to make things work. I try my best. I don't walk on water, like I said. And I don't work miracles. But if anybody can help anybody, it's me. That's just where it's at. Because everybody knows that I don't bullshit. I don't do anything for a pay. I mean, somebody comes to me for my birthday or Christmas, I don't get blisters. I'm not allergic, y'know? But you can't buy me a suit and you can't buy me a pair of shoes for me to go to bat for you if you're wrong. You know what I mean?"

"Yes."

"So when I sit down with you and somebody else, and I say, 'You're wrong,' you'll know that this guy didn't fuckin' buy me a suit. I got more suits in my closet than I can ever wear. A guy wanted to buy me a pair of shoes. He said, 'I want to buy you a pair of shoes, because you know, you helped us out—' I said, 'Let me tell you something. You wanna come to my house? See—'"

I laughed out loud. " 'See all my suits and shoes?' "

"But now we've started the wheels in motion and I've been making inquiries with certain people and everybody's a little skeptical."

"Right."

"When this came back with Joe making the statement to the effect that he doesn't know any Danny Benedetto, a couple of times—"

"It's very— I'll tell you, it doesn't surprise me that he doesn't know me, or if he was—"

"Or he doesn't 'know of any' or 'I don't think there's any' or 'there isn't any' and words to that effect. And everybody's asking."

"Okay, well, that—that *does* surprise me. But, I mean, I've been around a long time. People know me from the business."

Joe was sipping his martini; I was gulping down my wine. Joe summoned the waiter with the bottle and told him, "You see my friend's glass there? It *never* gets empty." By now I was sure Joe could see the effect of all that red wine.

He stared hard at me, almost through me, with an expression that said, *Okay, if you are the law, kid, then this is my statement to you:*

"I mean we're really, truly 100 percent not doing anything or saying anything or having a conspiracy in any which way that's totally illegal. I think that our conversation is pretty much leaning toward the right thing to do with carters that are—that are being hurt. What I'm doing is saving legal fees. I have a job and if you want to convict me of that, then convict me, because I'm gonna be doing that as long as I'm around. But I have to be very careful because I don't want anything to be misconscrewed as well."

"Right."

"We're not plotting anything—I don't think. And I don't want it to sound at all illegal. Pretty much everything's aboveboard. But I just met you. I just met Sal. Tommy mentioned Sal—that he knows Sal. And Tommy's opinion of somebody—that would be my opinion. So I don't doubt Tommy's opinion. No matter what, I'm gonna go with Sal. I have no problem with Sal. He's acknowledged me and I respect that. And I feel as though it warrants for me to take an additional step forward on your behalf because of the welfare of our industry. It's in everybody's best interest. It's not a one-sided thing. There's no fee here, you know. There's no charge, you know what I'm sayin' here?"

"Right, right."

"I'm not gonna send you a bill."

"I understand."

"As far as we're concerned, as far as being a member with us: You're not forced to be a member with anybody."

"Right."

"It's your decision."

"Right."

"You could be a member—of *China*."

Joe drifted from questioning my identity for a moment and started to hit me with some detailed industry questions, relating to the various classes of truck licenses—Class Ones, Class Twos—and how many of each type I had. Class One licenses were for trucks hauling putrescible waste. Class Twos and Threes were for trucks hauling recyclable waste. There were some subtle points pertaining to the Gambino and Genovese club bylaws within Brooklyn and Manhattan, and he was trying to test me—trip me up. When you joined a club, your dues were calculated on a per-truck basis. Luckily, I'd not only done my homework early on in the case, but by this point I really *was* an experienced garbage and recycling executive. I could talk the talk with anybody. Even Joey Cigars couldn't throw me off track. He took another sip of his martini and leaned toward me to intensify the interrogation.

"You're actually a Benedetto?"

"Yes."

"Your last name is Bene—Benedetto?"

"Benedetto. I mean—I'm—yes, I'm one of the Benedettos."

"You have that on your driver's license?"

"Yeah."

"Gimme your license, and then we'll go forward. You don't have to gimme no phone call."

"I have tried to do the right thing," I said. "I mean, I belong to a gym—" I handed him my Powerhouse Gym card, from the branch across the street from Jimmy Brown's social club in Bensonhurst. Then I gave him my New York State driver's license.

Joe held the driver's license photo up to the light, squinting at it. "Good thing you took off that beard." And he laughed—wiseguys hate any kind of facial hair. "This don't even look like you."

"Here I am." I also handed him my Blue Cross health insurance card and my Dan Benedetto MasterCard—a useless piece of plastic: The damn thing never worked when I needed it.

"You live in Staten Island?"

"Yeah."

"How do you like that? You guys have work out there?"

"A little bit. Yeah, we got *The Staten Island Advance*."

"You're kidding. *Staten Island Advance*? And what is that, bids?"

"Uh, no we just have it—we've had it for a long time."

"That's not bids?" Joe was testing me again—and actually, I slipped up here. The newspaper on Staten Island *was* a sealed-bid account.

"Phil—Phil tried to get it off me, a while back, but that's a long time ago. . . ."

"That's not bids? Okay, let me ask you something."

"Yeah."

He was staring harder at my license. "I never seen one like this. You know, just out of curiosity—just for conversation, I never seen a license—"

"This is one of the newer licenses," I said.

"That's what they gave you when you renewed?"

"I had to get my picture."

"No, the picture I know," Joe said. "I know the picture. I just re-newed last year. It's a different license. That was in '93. Danny, this is un-believable. This doesn't even look like you."

"I was a lot heavier then too. I've been trying to diet. Slimfast, y'know. There's so many diets. . . ." I was starting to show a little anger now. "All I gotta say is, y'know, I wasn't one to stand behind a door. I wasn't one to stay locked in the office like Sal. I try to do the right thing. I'm try-ing to work things out. And I can't get out from under—my family, it's got this thing, like we're stig-stigmatized—and I can't get out from un-der it. And now you tell me people are saying, 'Oh, I don't know him,' and 'He's making things bad for me.' I mean, how would *you* like it if someone comes up to you and says, 'Well, I don't know you'?"

"The only reason why that came about is because this Joe Benedetto says he doesn't know of any—as far as he's concerned, there's no Danny Benedetto in his family. So that opened up a lot of eyes. And it was brought back to me and told to me. And I said okay."

"That is strange and you should be alerted and, y'know, be careful," I said. "But I mean, that's not the case. And I don't know what to say. I really don't."

"Then don't. Let's—let's—I'm not an alarmist, okay?"

"It's uncomfortable. It's hard. I-I feel uncomfortable. Hearing things like that."

"As long as I'm convinced, okay. I mean, if I'm convinced— Hey, you have to have a little faith in *somebody*. When I told you that nothing was going to happen to you as far as your concern about Frankie, I said, 'Don't worry about it.' And if I didn't feel as though I could've been pro-ductive in that area, I wouldn't've made that statement. I would've said to you, 'Lay low for a while until I straighten it out.' I would've said, 'I don't know if I can help you in that area.' If that would've been the case, that's what I would've said to you. But I didn't say any of that. I said to you, 'Don't worry about it. Nothing's gonna happen. And let that be a bad dream and whatever. Don't even mention it no more. Don't even bring it up.' "

"Right."

"It's a dead issue. It's finished with. It was misconscrewed. It shouldn't have never happened the way it happened. Things like that can be misconscrewed. So again, I'm not gonna give you false promises. I'm not gonna mislead you. I'm not gonna give you any shit. But I'm telling you this like it is. Sometimes you may not like what you hear."

"Well, I'd rather hear it that way."

"You're gonna hear it *regardless*," Joe laughed. "Whether you like it or not."

I've interrogated a few gangsters and badguys in my life, and I have to say, I was pretty impressed by Joe's technique. He was talking in looping circles, making chitchat for a few minutes—then, like a hawk catching an updraft, waiting to swoop down on a mouse, he'd suddenly get very specific, trying to trick me with details, trying to catch me in a lie.

Self-confidence is the quality you need more than anything else to be a good interrogating detective. Joe Francolino was the most confident man I've ever met in my life. His whole demeanor, his manner of dressing and speaking, shouts *power.* When he sits down to eat, it's like he owns the entire restaurant: In fact, our waiter did nothing but stand to one side and wait for Joe to look his way. Joe wants to make a call? Fuck it—he just walks behind the bar and grabs the phone. Big-screen TVs downstairs? Fuck it—let's start taking a little Monday-night action. The whole world was Joey's for the taking. They didn't even bring his dinner on a *human*-sized plate—that was for Joe Schmoes at the next table. Joe Francolino's special meal arrived on a yard-long serving platter.

While we were eating our main course, the hostess came over and told Joe that someone wanted to say hello.

Joe glanced up. "Oh, there's Angelo at the bar. Excuse me, I'll take my drink."

I hadn't seen him come in, but now I noticed the gray-haired man that Ed Tamily liked to call "the little tyrant" standing in the shadows of the bar, glaring at me. Okay, this made sense: Angelo was Joe's ace in the hole. So that's who Joe called on the phone when we first walked in. They stood at the bar for about twenty minutes, planning strategy, letting me stew in my own juices and gulp down more red wine.

With Angelo, I knew I would have to stay on my toes. Joe didn't know the Benedetto family—he was relying on his buddy Tommy Masotto's word, and crazy Tommy was away doing fed time in Atlanta. But Angelo had grown up around all the Benedettos; they were *paisans* from that same little town on the boot. Also, Angelo was the one guy in town who was so business-savvy about paper and garbage, he could easily trip me up with industry talk. If Angelo ever set his mind to it, he could shred my fragile alibi in minutes.

Ponte came over, dressed in a dark-blue pinstripe suit, maroon Italian silk tie, gold tie clip, cuff links, diamond pinky ring.

"Sit down, Ange," Joe said. "You know Danny, right?"

"How ya doin'?" I said, shaking Ponte's hand.

Angelo put on a perfect amnesia act. "Have we met?"

"Yeah, I met you a long time ago at the Association and at your restaurant."

He sat down, stroking his white goatee, and stared into my eyes for a long time without speaking. "You know, you have a very *dear* friend here," he whispered, "because *nobody* could bring me to the table with you."

It was Ponte's turn now to play detective. He began casually quizzing me about my distant relations. He said he'd known John Benedetto— my supposed father. Then he smiled and asked how well I knew Johnny Tuzzio.

Angelo didn't realize I had my own ace in the hole. Johnny Tuzzio went *way* back with Ponte's dad on the Lower East Side. Early on in the case, Johnny'd told me a funny story that was still quite embarrassing to Angelo, this refined multimillionaire, this elegant Knight of Malta. When Angelo was just a kid, about eighteen years old, he was an organizer with Teamsters Local 27. Johnny was driving a nonunionized truck for Chambers when Local 27 called a strike. Angelo, being union muscle, threatened to kneecap Johnny Tuzzio with a tire iron. He came after Johnny waving the tire iron and Johnny went straight to Angelo's dad, Vincent, to complain. Vincent, who everyone always said was an honest businessman and straight shooter, gave Angelo a real browbeating for it.

"Johnny Tuzzio? I know Johnny very well." I threw back a swig of my red wine and stared right into Angelo's eyes. "I also know about you and Johnny and that day with the tire iron."

His mouth fell open.

"You know about *that*?"

"Yeah, Angelo. I heard that story."

8 | WASTELAND

Somehow, I got the better of that game of nerves. After Angelo left Pierino's Ristorante, Joey Cigars loosened up. "Like Angelo said, I'm the only guy who could get him to the table." He let out a cocky laugh. "Hey, I can bring *anybody* to the table." If Joe had any serious doubts about my loyalty, any suspicion he might be talking to an undercover agent, you couldn't hear it in the tone of his after-dinner conversation. We sipped strong cups of coffee, and Joe spoke his mind. Every incriminating word was picked up by the minuscule microphone hidden inside the Motorola cell phone, broadcast by Kel transmitter, the signal boosted by an unmarked Buick parked out on Reade Street, and recorded on an aid receiver by detectives Harry Bauerle and Camille San Fillipo parked several blocks farther west.

Joe told me that he'd met with his lawyer that morning and they'd worked out a strategy to fight Browning-Ferris Industries. Citywide, Joe said, he was going to assess every club member a $2,000 fee in order to build a war chest to "combat the enemy," go after BFI with everything the cartel could muster. He wanted to expose Browning-Ferris for all its criminal wrongdoing, wanted to educate the public about BFI's history. And then he made a stunning admission to me.

"All right, we're a cartel—we're the *Mafia,* all right? The fuckin' public is tired of hearing it—they read it a hundred times over. But let's tell the story about *you* guys. Let's tell the story about the cocksuckers that you are—"

"All over the country."

"—all over the country."

Joe was blunt in his self-appraisal. "This is what I do, Danny. I'm not a do-gooder. I'm not lily-white. But don't fuck with me, 'cause I'll be the biggest cocksucker in the world. 'Cause I could be your worst enemy or I could be your best friend. Whatever you want me to be. I go after all the outlaws," Joe said, citing the handful of carters still bold enough to go it alone. "Tim Duffy, DeGraw, Tempesta, all of 'em. They all want to make a meeting with me. . . . They're fuckin' outlaws and there's no rhyme or reason for me to sit down with them and discuss anything. Stop what you're doin'. Sell your business. Join the Association or we'll knock you right out of business."

The role of being the industry's new kingpin was sitting heavy on Joe's shoulders, and he confided to me that he'd much prefer to be living the high life in the sun than dealing with these New York headaches. But that's the way things stood. Jimmy Brown was locked up now—Joey Cigars had to step up.

"Rather than having to be here, I got a place in Florida—I have a boat, but I don't use the boat, unfortunately, as much as I'd like to," he said with some sadness. "And I love to be away. I love to relax. I love to have a good time. But my obligation here, now that the other fella's not around, I have more of a burden than before. But duty calls, Danny.

And if I get sandbagged, if I get jabbed, I say, 'Ah, fuck youse all. Throw everything in the air. I don't need the aggravation.'"

When the check arrived, I took out my wallet and offered to pay.

Joe laughed at me. "No, I invited you. Next time. When you invite me, next time, we'll eat in your area. Ah—it was my pleasure."

Ed Tamily wasn't kidding when he told me, "Joe could really help you—if you *know* him." Now we turned a corner in the case. Joe became my two-hundred-fifty-pound fullback, running roughshod over everyone: All I had to do was carry the ball through the hole. Every problem I'd had for two years, Joe straightened them out in two seconds. After work at the Plymouth Street shop, I started coming by the Gambino club in the late afternoon, sipping demitasse and eating pastries with Patty and Joe. Then we'd do walk-and-talks around TriBeCa, smoking cigars, in our double-breasted suits and cashmere overcoats. Joe said he was "schooling me," teaching me the rules. "When I tell you something, pal," he said, "you go to sleep on it."

Joe was an incredibly blunt, plainspoken guy, and he occasionally got careless around me. One day when we were discussing all my beefs and best way to resolve them, Joe smiled, pointed at himself, and mouthed the words, "You go to a *gangster.*" Then he quickly took it back: "I used the wrong word. You go to a *friend* and have a cup of coffee. . . ."

Joe was helping us out with so many beefs—keeping greedy wolves like Dominick Vulpis at bay—that during one of our walk-and-talks he laughed and said maybe I should list him on our Chambers Paper Fibres tax return. "Yeah, should I put down Chambers on my W-2? I'm part of the company." Later, I asked him if he was serious, if there was some tangible way my family could show our appreciation. "No, my primary interest here is to make sure that my membership is respected. And my membership *respects.* It's a two-way street."

Although the cartel, in general, ran the city like a well-oiled machine, there were always strains over territory and control, not surprising when you consider the big-ego Mob figures involved in the various clubs and the three-hundred-odd greedy carting companies constantly gouging their customers for bigger profits.

Joe felt that Angelo Ponte wasn't running his club with respect—Ponte's crew were always scheming and "double-banging" everyone. Angelo's membership would preach one thing and then do the opposite. Angelo himself had a *lot* of beefs to settle with Joe—a lot of the Gambino club guys accused Angelo of robbing their stops. Things got so bad between Joe's club and Angelo's club that Francolino decided to make an example of someone. Mikey Five Brothers was the unlucky example. Five Brothers had taken some stops off Phil Barretti and was refusing to make Phil whole.

We were sitting at one of the card tables in the West Broadway club when Joe told me, abruptly, "Danny, let's go for a walk." We tossed on our overcoats and went on a walk-and-talk, away from any possible surveillance bugs in the club. As we left the club, Joe introduced me to a friend of his named Vito, also sharply dressed, right out of the John Gotti handbook: handpainted tie, double-breasted suit, Italian loafers. Joe's black Mercedes sedan was parked to the left of the club door and he stopped, reached into his glove compartment, and said, "Danny, you want a cigar?"

He had a whole box of Te-Amo Toros, took a couple in his fist, and then Vito, Joe, and I began to walk, three abreast, with Joe in the middle.

Strutting down West Broadway, lighting up our cigars, Joe growled that Five Brothers Carting was out of the Association. Five Brothers was branded an outlaw, and Joe wanted to use me as his personal whip.

"Go after his work," Joe said through clenched teeth and cigar smoke. "Go after 'em. Go get anything you can."

I nodded. "Joe," I said, "they got a big clique down there on Canal Street."

"Yeah, well, we got a *bigger* clique!"

Joe was fearless, willing to take on anyone. But it was a controlled aggression. Joe did not want chaos; if anything, he wanted more *order*. In his own twisted way, he saw himself as a form of law enforcement, the sheriff for the industry. Eventually he was going to sit down and bring peace between the clubs, but only after Mikey Five Brothers was disciplined—after he gave Phil Barretti back his work.

And if Mikey didn't give back the work, then Philly, Patty, me, and the Association at 180 West Broadway—Joe's guys—would underbid him all over the city, lowball all his big stops, and virtually put the Five Brothers operation out of business. We had enough clout to do it, too—in a matter of weeks.

One day Joe called me from his car phone, near my shop on Plymouth Street, and I met him for a walk-and-talk along the Brooklyn waterfront. He was dressed in a beautiful camel-hair overcoat, puffing a cigar and gruffly barking out his rules:

"I mean, if there's a defiance—anybody don't want to comply, I mean, *fuck you*," he said. "I mean, hey, it's a free country. Know what I mean?"

Sure, I knew. Joe, like a lot of gangsters—like Frank Giovinco, in fact—liked to say, *It's a free country*. What he really meant was: *Everyone's free to rob and steal if they do it by our rules.*

I was caught in the middle of this heavy-duty battle of wills between Joe and Angelo, and meanwhile I had my own battle of wills raging at home. My wife was getting fed up with my insane work schedule: Every night she'd ask me when "this thing" was going to end. And I couldn't even tell her what "this thing" was. We had a newborn son and I was never home to spend time with him.

It got even worse after Francolino questioned my identity in Pierino's. That's when I had to become even more of a ghost. Once Joe had inspected my bogus driver's license and knew the address where I supposedly lived on Staten Island, I had to make it look like I was actually in this high-rise apartment we'd rented in the name of Dan Benedetto. I had to leave home when it was still dark, switch vehicles at the highrise, enter the apartment house by a back entrance, make sure I put on the lights, check the mailbox, give the impression to the neighbors that I actually lived there. Who knew when the wiseguys would send some-

one around to ask my neighbors if they'd ever seen Dan Benedetto ordering pizza or taking out his garbage?

My wife and I loved living on Staten Island. We'd been there all the
years I'd been on the job, and a lot of people knew me simply as Rick
the Cop. The thing about Staten Island that most people don't realize is
that it's the parole capital of the United States. There are more people
per capita on parole in Staten Island than anywhere else in the country.
That's not because there's a lot of street criminals, either—it's due to all
the wiseguys who've just come home from the can. For years Staten Island has been home to hundreds of high-level wiseguys. Paul Castellano, Joe Francolino, Jimmy Brown, Allie Shades all had nice houses on
Staten Island.

And it's a small enough place that you couldn't help crossing paths
with these hoods or garbage-company owners. I could never be sure
when I might run into Joe Francolino or Allie Shades while they were
out with their families. In fact, there was one guy who used to own a
carting company living in our very condo complex. Everyone called
him Jimmy Garbage. I used to sit around the pool shooting the breeze
with him. On several other occasions, I noticed a pickup truck in my
condo parking lot, and on the side it said DUFFY WASTE REMOVAL. Joe
Francolino's company.

One day, my wife and I were shopping in an Italian specialty store
when I spotted Alan Longo and his girlfriend one aisle over—Baldie
Longo, whose Lincoln I'd boosted in front of Pastels Disco years back.
By now I'd been around the Brooklyn garbage club in Bensonhurst a
lot, meeting with Frank Allocca, Danny Todisco, and Ray Polidori, and
I couldn't be sure if Baldie had seen me there or not. "Just in case this
guy approaches us," I whispered to Claire, "whatever you do, *don't* call
me Rick. Let me do all the talking."

Then, shortly after my son was born, Claire and I were in the Staten
Island Mall. She was a few steps ahead of me and I was pushing the baby
stroller when I spotted this garbage guy who dumped a lot of paper
tonnage with me at Chambers. He was a prominent member of Jimmy
Brown's club—and his first cousin is a Gambino *capo*.

I didn't want to run into this guy when I was with my family. I hung a stage left into Sears, hopped on the escalator with the baby stroller, and went right up into the little kids' clothing section, where I hid out behind the racks of OshKosh B'Gosh. Claire was still downstairs. When she turned around, she saw that the baby and I were *gone.*

I dodged around upstairs in Sears for about half an hour with my kid laughing up at me like he was on a fair ride. When I finally met up with Claire again, she was so steamed she snatched the stroller away from me.

"Where'd you *go?* Rick, what the hell's the *matter* with you?"

"Well, I saw someone I didn't wanna see, so I had to get lost."

She thought I was having an affair—*goomin'*, as the wiseguys say. I couldn't blame her. Just look at the circumstantial evidence. My whole life, I never smoked or went to work dressed up in fancy Italian clothes. Now I was leaving home before sunrise with two Te-Amo cigars in my shirt pocket, wearing all this jewelry she never saw me in and a waist-length Italian silk jacket just like the hoods wear. I would come home from work maybe in time for a fast bite, take a shower, throw on my nice double-breasted suit and tie and my black cashmere overcoat, and then I'd be out with Joe Francolino and Patty Pecoraro at the club or down at Pierino's drinking until midnight.

My wife never believed me, but the truth was, I didn't have a spare second to think about other women. Every day I was so overwhelmed, I was on the verge of losing my marbles. This is just the point where a lot of guys crack. There was no downtime, not even on the weekends or holidays. If we went to visit Claire's family, I'd go into my father-in-law's garage with my valise and my Walkman, listening to tapes I'd made with my J-Bird body recorder, typing up Fives while everyone else was watching the Giants.

Even the top brass in the department wanted to see how I was holding up. One day Tony Maz told me that Kenny O'Brien wanted to see me. Kenny O'Brien had been bumped up to a full bird now—a full inspector.

Inspector O'Brien was a hugely respected presence in the department. He had years of experience with organized crime; he'd commanded the DEA task force and was as knowledgeable a cop as I've ever known. He arranged for me to meet him on Staten Island, in a parking lot of a restaurant on Victory Boulevard. "I know the pace is just unbearable," he said. "You're meeting all these new people every day—you're in deep with these wiseguys. The commissioner knows that you're in a very involved, complicated, dangerous situation. Do you think you can go much further?"

"Yes, I can go further. I'm with Joe Francolino now—this is just what we've been waiting for. We'll never get another chance like this."

"No one's pressuring you," he said. "Healthwise, are you feeling all right?"

"Physically and mentally, I'm fine. I'm a little tired. But I can go further. I want to see this through."

October 11, 1994, was another big night in TriBeCa. Pierino's looked like a candlelit den of thieves when I walked in. Cigar smoke billowed in clouds over the room as dozens of garbage gangsters drank and mingled at an impromptu party, having strolled down West Broadway together after the weekly meeting at the Gambino club. I found myself perched in the power post—sandwiched between Joe Francolino and Phil Barretti at the far end of the bar. Francolino was instructing Phil and me to start soliciting all our vendors to take out ads in the trade journal that would be published in conjunction with the annual dinner-dance gala—the so-called Garbageman's Ball. The ad revenues from the journal would go into Joe's public-relations war chest for fighting BFI.

The gala affair, Joe told us, was a little-known gold mine. "I used to run the dance and in three weeks I raised a hundred and twenty-five thousand bucks. Three weeks—that's serious money."

"But what if some of our vendors say no?" I wondered.

"Listen to me, once you ask, nobody's gonna turn you down." Joe laughed. "They'd have to be dumb drunk to turn us down—we're their bread and butter."

Patty Pecoraro joined us for a drink, and I asked Pat if he had a second to talk privately in the vestibule. Once we got outside, I handed Patty an envelope filled with $36,000 in extortion for the D'Agostino supermarkets. Patty would have to spread that money around to Jimmy Vigliotti and a few other Bronx guys. I asked Pat if he could get me some breathing room from making these steep monthly payments. "Should I ask Joe about stretching these out? I'm trying to appease everybody here."

"No, after these, the rest of it's gonna be a program. I got a list in my pocket."

I explained that I was going to be traveling out west for a while, visiting some paper mills and customers, and I'd have to start mailing in the checks from the road for Patty to distribute. "Sure," Pat said. "I'll draw up a whole schedule. I'll just fax it over to your office. Then you can send me what you gotta send me and I'll make sure I get it to everybody."

Patty hurried back inside, eager to be dealt into a high-stakes poker game starting momentarily downstairs. I returned to Francolino and Barretti at the bar. Joe was swirling his dry martini and staring hard at me. Suddenly his nose was bent out of joint about something.

"What was that all about?" he demanded.

"I had to see Patty about something."

"About what?"

"About stretching out the D'Ag payments in the Bronx."

Joe's eyes narrowed—he'd turned instantly angry.

"Danny, *never* go around when you can go direct. You call Patty up here. You go down and tell Patty I'd like to see him. Tell him Joey wants to see him. With all due respect to Patty. Patty's a very close friend. I know everything that Patty's doing."

"I didn't want it to look like I was ignoring Patty."

"No, don't you worry about that. But you're supposed to come to me first. I'm in the driver's seat. Don't you understand? *I'm* the guy directing traffic. *I'm* the guy you come to. *I'm* the fuckin' boss!"

Phil Barretti let out a nervous laugh.

"Now I say stupid things," Joe said. "I say things I shouldn't say— because *you* don't listen!"

"Dan's new to this," Phil said. "He doesn't know. He's just learning."

"He don't wanna listen. He don't wanna understand."

"Now he's telling you—now you know," Phil said sternly.

"Say no more, Joe. I'll go get Patty."

Francolino's features softened again. "Hey, want a drink, Dan?"

"Yeah, another red wine."

I opened my wallet to offer Joe my only hundred-dollar bill.

"Whattaya need a loan?" Joe said. "Get outta here—put your fuckin' money away."

Downstairs, I had a little difficulty dragging Patty Pecoraro out of his heavy card game. "I think I just got you in trouble—by accident," I whispered. Patty folded his hand and jumped up like a frightened kid when he heard that Joe wanted to see us both upstairs.

As we rejoined Francolino at the crowded bar, Joe began lecturing Patty, repeating that he was the boss, the guy directing traffic. Then he turned his gaze back on me, his inattentive student.

"Danny, Danny, Danny. No matter who comes to you—whether Pauly Five Brothers comes to you or his sons come to you, whether Frankie the Kid [Giovinco] comes to you or Angelo comes to you—I don't give a fuck *who* it is, you tell them to come to me. Use my name. Tell 'em all to come see *Joey*. Frankie the Kid wants to straighten out, you tell him, 'Sure, straighten out with *Joey*.'"

It was hard to hear in the humming bar, but in the middle of the lecture, my beeper sounded repeatedly. At first I ignored it, tried to keep focused on Francolino's face, but when I glanced down at the pager's green-lit screen, I saw that the crisis code had been entered six times in a row.

"Who is it, Dan?" Patty laughed. "Your goom?"

"Yeah, this crazy broad—she's driving me nuts."

I went back downstairs to use the pay phone. It actually was a distraught woman: Detective Camille San Fillipo of the field team out on Reade Street.

"Dan," she said, when I finally reached her on the pay phone, "somebody's coming into Pierino's right now that you're not gonna wanna see."

"Too late—I already saw." Through the window I caught a glimpse of Allie Shades and Johnny "Geech" Giangrandi, a guy in the Malangone crew. They were on the sidewalk, fast approaching the front entrance of Pierino's Ristorante.

This really was a crisis. For years I'd managed to avoid a face-to-face encounter with Allie Shades. For years I'd carefully dodged him. If I had a meeting at the Kings County Trade Waste Association, I'd have the field team staking out the joint for hours. "Let me know as soon as Allie leaves the building," I'd say, and then I'd go inside to meet Frank Allocca and Danny Todisco and Ray Polidori.

The reason I could not be anywhere near Allie Shades was directly the result of the super-rat—Salvatore "Sammy the Bull" Gravano. In 1991, when we were in the thick of our Pastels Disco surveillance, Sammy flipped. As Gotti's underboss, he was the highest-ranking wiseguy ever to become a government witness, and the FBI wanted to capitalize on the moment by interviewing various prominent captains from all the five families to try to flip them. When I got wind of it, I complained to my boss; at that time it was Sergeant Joe Galligan—he was my boss before Tony Maz replaced him as Headquarters One Supervisor. I said, "I don't want them coming to Allie. Let them go to other captains—we broke our asses getting our bugs into Pastels."

In general, OCID and the FBI share information. But not where our bugs are located. The Feds didn't know what we were up to with Malangone and his crew. They'd also been looking into Allie a long time: He was one of the biggest Mafia catches around, and we were in direct competition to take him down. This FBI agent once said to me about Allie, "Listen, the way I look at it is this: It's a running race. Whoever gets to the finish line first wins."

I couldn't stop the FBI from going to see Allie, but Joe Galligan arranged it so that I could accompany the FBI agent on the interview. I was wearing a full beard at the time and I had on a big trench coat with the collar up. We drove out to Allie's house on Staten Island. He lived on Mob Row—six big houses on the block, and four of them belong to organized-crime figures.

We walked up to his house and we saw this priest standing by the side door. "I'm waiting to see Allie," the father said. "What're you guys here for?"

"We're friends of Allie's," I told him. We rang the doorbell. No answer. For about ten minutes we stood ringing and knocking and finally we decided to pack it in. We were a good hundred yards away from the house, about to get back into my car, when we saw the big guy come running across the lawn, beelining for us. His coat was flapping in the wind and those big catcher's-mitt hands were waving. Of course, he had the dark glasses on.

"Hey, who the fuck are youse guys?" Allie yelled. "Whaddaya want?" His son and the priest were trailing right after him. He turned to glare at them: "Get back in the house!"

We identified ourselves as FBI and NYPD. I let the agent do most of the talking.

"Look, Allie," he said. "Sammy the Bull just flipped. We're coming to talk to all the *capos.*"

"Sammy the *who?* The Bull?" Allie was acting like he'd never heard the name before in his life, like he didn't own a TV or read the papers. "Hmmm . . . I don't know nothin' about no Bull."

While, in fact, I had watched him just a day or two earlier on the video surveillance of the Pastels bug, reading the *Daily News* and commenting angrily about Sammy the Bull turning rat.

"John Gotti?" I asked him.

"No, I don't know nothin' about John Gotti."

I'd personally tailed him for two years to Mob meetings with all the top bosses. Our team surveilled him meeting with John Gotti outside a funeral parlor in Brooklyn; we'd seen him doing walk-and-talks regularly with the Chin's underboss. The Chin, who'd been pulling his crazy act in the ratty bathrobe and slippers for years now, was too smart to meet directly with skippers like Allie in public.

But Allie was one smooth operator—he was not going to admit a thing.

"No, I don't know none of those people," he said, looking me and the FBI agent up and down. "Well, wait a minute now. Well, I did know this *one* guy—*years* ago, in Brooklyn. Mr. Toddo Marino. . . . But he was one of the most *be-you-tee-ful* gentlemen I ever knew."

Sure. Toddo Marino. The only "Man of Honor" Allie ever heard of had been dead and buried for a decade now. I didn't even want to be standing out there in the street anymore, but I had to go through the motions.

"What do you do for a living, Mr. Malangone?"

"I'm the night manager of Pastels Discotheque in Bay Ridge."

And John Gotti was a plumbing salesman in Queens.

It was a worthless session, almost comical, and years later, once I was deep in my Danny role, I'd wake up in the night, cursing myself for even coming out to Staten Island with this FBI agent, offering Allie such a good fifteen-minute look at my face.

"If you come in with us now, we can work something out," the agent said. "But if we come to *you* with a case, we're warning you—there will be no deals."

"Look, you guys, the only thing you can do is lock Allie up for gambling. Allie is a gambler. Allie is a *bad* gambler, but that's all Allie does. . . ." And he kept talking about himself in the third person like that, being civil, jerking our chains.

When I got back in the car, I saw that the FBI agent was sullen.

"What's the matter?"

"I really thought we had a chance of flipping Malangone."

"Come on. I know this guy and how he operates. Allie Shades is old school. He'd sooner go to jail for the rest of his life than talk to us."

Now I was boxed in: There was no way to exit Pierino's without squeezing past Allie Shades. I tried to drift slowly out of Francolino's orbit, slink away to the fringes, get lost among the crowd of barrel-

chested carters and their curtains of cigar smoke. I'd only edged halfway
to the front door when I heard Francolino's booming voice:

"Danny! *Danny!* Come over here!"

Joe and Allie were alone at the far end of the bar with Johnny Geech.
There were no citizens around. Now it was only wiseguys.

"Yeah, Joe?"

"Danny, I want you to meet my friend Allie. Allie, this is Danny. He's
your member, he's my member, he used to be a member of Waste
Paper—but something happened."

"Angelo?" Allie said, nodding gravely.

"See, he knows the name," I said, smiling.

Joe laughed through the smoke. Allie Shades didn't smile. He was
holding the handshake a long time without easing up. I felt the inten-
sity of the Genovese skipper's gaze—*Is he trying to place my face? Does he
remember that windy day on his lawn?*—but, as usual, those dark glasses
gave away nothing. At last Allie Shades released his grip.

"Allie runs Brooklyn," Joe said.

"I'm the *administrator* in Brooklyn," Allie said.

"Oh, yeah, the administrator," Joe said. "I forgot the word."

Allie looked at Joe, then back at me. "He straightening out?"

"Yeah, he's straightening out."

Joe said that he had spoken to Angelo Ponte and he was confident
that Angelo would be willing to sit down and straighten out his long-
standing differences with me.

"Okay, good," Allie said. "Angelo's going to sit down."

"For the record, Allie," I said, preparing for my escape, "I just want
you to know this: Angelo hit me first and I hit him back. I don't want
any more problems with Angelo. I just want to bury the hatchet."

I was so elated when I left Pierino's, I almost got myself locked up. It
was such a relief to get away from Allie and Joe in one piece. It was always a relief to get out of those wiseguy meetings: It was another day
that I wasn't exposed as a cop, that I didn't screw up in my conversations, that I schemed and scammed and gathered good evidence.

I left Joey Cigars and Allie Shades and Johnny Geech at the bar. I was parked right on the corner, and when I got in my Jeep I just sat there for a few minutes, talking to myself. "How good is this now if Allie doesn't recognize me? I'll be able to go to the Brooklyn club anytime I want from now on. No more bobbing and weaving. *Yes!* I'll be right *there.*"

I started driving down the West Side Highway. And when I got caught up in the bumper-to-bumper traffic approaching the Battery Tunnel toll booths, I was still talking to myself. "How good is this? Allie didn't recognize me! It's a *be-you-tee-ful* thing!" I was so happy I even punched the steering wheel a couple of times with the butt of my hand.

As I looked up, I saw a Triborough Bridge and Tunnel Authority officer staring at me. He observed me punching the steering wheel, no doubt thinking I was either three sheets to the wind or a complete psychopath who should never have been issued a license. He made a hand motion, and sure enough, as I pulled up through the booth on the Brooklyn side, two Triborough Bridge and Tunnel Authority cops came up behind me.

"Excuse me, sir, can you pull over, please?"

Truthfully, I don't think I was over the limit, but I did have a couple of red wines in me, and they could probably smell it on my breath. I stepped out of the Jeep and they put me through the DWI test. "Close your eyes, put your fingertip to your nose, walk the line." I could do that fine. "Now, starting from the letter *P,* recite backwards, five letters, no more than that."

"Officers, I'm not sure I could do that if—" I almost said, *if I was sober,* but then I caught myself. "I'm not sure I could do that in the middle of the day—now it's after midnight and I'm just exhausted. . . ."

This whole time I was thinking, *Jesus, I'm down here in Red Hook, I'm getting pinched for DWI, I'm going to jail, I've got a J-Bird device strapped to my groin, and a wire taped to my chest* . . . But I slowed down, took a few deep breaths, recited the alphabet backwards. The cops hemmed and hawed for a few minutes and gave me a warning, then let me drive home.

Just because you're an undercover detective, you can't slip out of character and whisper, "Look, guys, I'm a cop." You have to maintain your identity always. When I took on this role, I took it on *full-time.* If these cops had decided to Breathalyze me and I failed, they'd have booked me, I would've been locked up and fingerprinted; I would've used my jailhouse call to reach Tony Maz, let him know that I got locked up for drunk driving, and I would've had to spend the night in the can until OCID devised some scheme to get me out of there.

Next morning I would've been suspended from the police force and the investigation would've been dead. But that's the kind of adrenaline rush it was at Pierino's. I was so psyched up that Allie Shades didn't recognize me, I almost blew the whole case by getting myself pinched.

In the end, it all came back to the beginning. Alphonso Malangone, the original target of my investigation five years earlier, was now the only piece missing from the jigsaw puzzle.

On Wednesday, October 19, at approximately 2:50 P.M. I arrived at the general meeting of the Kings County Trade Waste Association in Bensonhurst. The Brooklyn association occupied the entire ground floor of 6316 Bay Parkway, a two-story building, with residential apartments on the second floor and a popular pizzeria next door. The club itself held a long, spacious meeting room with octagonal poker tables and coffee machines; there was a small backyard with a few trees, a shaded picnic table, and a crazy rooster that ran around crowing at everyone. A rooster in Brooklyn—can you imagine?

I arrived at the meeting in order to give Frank Allocca nine extortion payments, seven for various Fayva shoe stores and two for D'Agostino supermarkets. When I walked in the club, the meeting was well under way. The vice president of the association, Danny Todisco, sat at the head of the largest poker table, flanked by Frank Allocca. Off to one side, Allie Shades was leaning back in a top-of-the-line black executive's chair. Of course Allie had the only elegant seat in the room. Danny Todisco was addressing the membership about the annual industrywide dance—officially, the Council of Trade Waste Associations Sixth Gala Christmas Celebration, to be held at the Marriott Marquis on December 3—and the overall fund-raising efforts to improve the carters' image in the city. He announced that every carter would be assessed a $2,000 fee for the anti-BFI war chest, and that every carter would be charged $1,000 for tickets to the dance, whether or not he chose to attend.

A Brooklyn carter named John Sindone then stood up and said that he'd met with his own public-relations expert, who had proposed that the Brooklyn club sponsor a "community watch" anti-crime program and toy drive for needy children at Christmastime.

Frank Allocca made a request for members to buy ad space in the dinner-dance journal. I watched as Allie Shades reached into his pants pocket and pulled out a sandwich-sized green wad. Malangone peeled off five crisp hundred-dollar bills as if they were singles. He passed the cash to Frank Allocca. Allocca rose to tell the membership: "Our director is the first one to put in for a silver page in the journal—five hundred dollars." There was a loud cheer.

Then Frank pointed toward the back of the room.

"Danny! Should I put you down for the platinum page?"

"How much is that?" I asked.

"Fifteen hundred."

"Get the fuck outta here! What's below that?"

"Gold. That's a thousand."

"What's the lowest level?"

"Silver."

"Put me down for that, Frank." There was a roar of laughter.

Mingling around at the end of the meeting, Danny Todisco approached me about settling a very old claim that had been made by Waste Paper Association board member Anthony LaCavalla. Todisco told me that Frank Giovinco had assured him that "making LaCavalla whole" would be the key to bringing Angelo Ponte to the table.

"You're gonna have to sit down with LaCavalla in order to sit down with Angelo," Danny Todisco said.

"Huh? For that little *ratty* cardboard stop in the Bronx? No fuckin' way. I'm not gonna sit down with LaCavalla. And I'm *not* chasing Angelo around."

Reverse psychology here. If I was a cop or an FBI agent, of course I

would *leap* at the chance to have a sitdown with a great catch like Angelo Ponte. By saying, "I'm not chasing Angelo around," I was behav-
ing as a more believable Danny Benedetto.

Danny Todisco was taken aback. "Whattaya talkin' about?"

"It's a complicated problem now. We'll have to talk about it with
Frank another time."

"How's it complicated?"

"If a claim is brought up with certain people, I'm supposed to let Joe
Francolino know about it."

Danny whistled for Frank Allocca to come over. "Frank, you hear this?"

Frank Allocca's already gray features turned white when he heard the
mention of Joe Francolino's name. This was Kings County, after all, Allie Malangone's turf, and they did not want to hear any talk about Joey
Cigar's heavy Gambino influence here in the heart of Bensonhurst.

"Danny, walk with me," Frank said, crooking my arm, and we
strolled across the club, straight out the door onto bustling Bay Parkway.
We stood on the sidewalk, out of range of any possible surveillance
bugs in the clubhouse, as a gust of tangy marinara sauce and crusted
mozzarella leapt from the pizzeria next door.

"I wanna be careful throwin' names around," I said, telling Frank the
whole story now. "You know how things got bad for me on Canal
Street—it lasted for months. Frank Giovinco, Anthony Vitale, Michael
D'Ambrosio, all these guys have been breakin' balls. Spreading rumors
around and just causing animosity. I was told in New York—by Joe—he
said, 'If they come up to you with a claim, use my name. I wanna know
about it.'" I shrugged. "Frank, I don't wanna get in the middle of this.
I really don't wanna take sides. There's a lot of behind-the-scenes shit
goin' on."

"I'm working hard on trying to get you and Angelo to sit, okay?" Allocca said.

"Right."

"And if this will be the key to bringing that about, then I will say,
'See, that was a problem—it got straightened out.'"

"I'll tell you, Frank, Joe has been very fair. And Patty too. They know damn well what they're doin'. I'm not gonna be like a little patsy. They're not talkin' to *Sal*—they're talkin' to *me*. And when they do come up to me with this shit, I'm gonna tell 'em straight out."

"All right, just excuse me," Frank said. "Wait right here."

Allie Shades, sharp as usual in a crisp blue double-breasted suit, had now exited the club in the company of a guy in his crew, Fat Gerry Guadagno. Frank Allocca stood whispering close to the ear of his boss. Frank was being precisely what he'd been groomed to be: a buffer. I could see Allie nodding, overheard him say, "No, it's okay—I know him."

The enormous Genovese skipper came over to shake hands.

"Yeah, I met you the other day," he said. "You're Dan. You were with Joe Francolino. I met you the other night."

"That's right. How's it goin'?"

"Good. Is everything all right?"

"I hope so. They're telling me something now I'm not too crazy about. They're breakin' balls."

"What's that?"

I told Allie that those guys at the Waste Paper clique had been starting rumors about me, causing general dissension. I told him that my loyalty was to Joe Francolino, and that Joe had instructed me to tell him if anyone made any claims.

"All right," Allie said. "Joey wants to know. Okay, no problem with that."

"I don't wanna step in the middle of it, 'cause then he'll jump in my face."

"We're the first ones that wanted you here. They don't want you there. Did you join here in Brooklyn?" Malangone asked.

"Oh, way back," I said, nodding.

"Yeah, way back," Frank agreed.

"No problem."

"But I'll answer both of your questions. Yours and Joe's. I'll do what Joe told me. I will sit down with Angelo. I will sit down with him and straighten it out. But Joe's gonna have to know. Because he told me, '*Before* you do something with them, let *me* know about it.'"

"But wait," Malangone said, waving a finger in my face and wrinkling his brow. "I'll straighten it out with Joe. If it's a Brooklyn matter and you belong here, we *don't* have to check with Joe."

Frank and I explained that this was actually a Waste Paper Association beef, falling under Angelo Ponte's jurisdiction, not Joe Francolino's.

"Yeah, well, let Angelo—" Malangone turned angrily at Frank and Danny Todisco. His voice was booming now. "Whatta youse worryin' about *that* for?"

"N-n-n-no," Allocca was stammering.

"I'm losing you," Malangone said.

"There's a problem with LaCavalla, [who] is a Waste Paper man," Frank tried to explain. "I feel that if we could put this to bed, straighten this out, this will bring Angelo into the fold where he would sit down with you."

"Who will?" Allie said.

"I don't understand," I said.

"I don't understand either," Allie said, glancing back at Fat Gerry Guadagno, who was also now visibly irritated. "Whattaya got to do with Waste Paper? I mean, if it's LaCavalla, we've got nothin' to do with them."

"Well, Frankie—" Frank began.

"Let *Frankie* worry about it," Allie snapped.

I explained that it was actually Frankie Giovinco who'd been breaking my balls. "He was down at my shop looking for me and we had a falling out," I said. "That's one of the reasons I don't wanna screw around. And Joe said—Joe told me, 'Don't do it.'"

"Let me tell you something, what you should do here," Malangone said, wagging his index finger again in my face. "Right now my opinion is: Let Joe get together with Angelo and work these things out. That's *their* problem. Let Angelo talk to Joe with him and straighten it out. Whatta we gettin' involved in that? . . . Tell Frankie and tell Angelo to go get Joe Francolino. He'll get them and they'll work it out themselves. . . . What do I give a fuck about anybody else? And, again, and I'll tell Joe, if it's a *Brooklyn* thing, I don't have to check with him."

"I didn't mean that," I said. "I didn't mean that."

"Okay, I'll make him understand that too. If it's Brooklyn and we call you, you *don't* go check with him. New York is New York. What the fuck are youse worried about LaCavalla? *Fuck* LaCavalla! I mean, we're not interested. . . ."

"I don't wanna get in the middle of an argument," I said.

"We don't wanna get in the middle of it—that's all I'm saying too."

We'd stirred up Allie's temper now, but Frank Allocca couldn't let the matter die. For some hardheaded reason the old guy was intent on using this stupid LaCavalla beef to broker a sitdown between Angelo Ponte and me. "Again, in case Angelo agrees to sit—" he said.

"But he's been talking to *Joe,*" Allie snapped. "Let Joe Francolino worry. Joe Francolino will talk to Angelo."

"All right."

"What the fuck are we gettin' into?" Allie barked at Frank Allocca and Danny Todisco. "Youse talk about youse got so much to do! And youse are fuckin' involving yourself in *everything?*"

"All right."

"He'll talk to Angelo!"

"But there's a couple of guys breakin' balls over there," I said. "And he told me to—"

"'Hold off.'" Allie was nodding at me.

"Yeah, he said he'll make a call and that's it."

"Then he's gonna start screaming we went over his head," Allie said.

"Angelo will start yelling?" I said.

"No, *Joe! Joe!* Y'know if we're getting involved with you, then he's gonna say—"

"We actually brought him in," Frank noted, trying to set the chronology straight in Allie's mind.

"All right."

"And *then* Joe stepped in."

"As long as we've got our own thing with him for here, that's fine," Allie ruled. "We have no problem. New York—let Joe talk to Angelo. Don't let us get involved. Tell Frankie [Giovinco]—tell Frankie I said, 'Let 'em, let 'em go see Joe Francolino.' Let 'em straighten it out."

"And Frankie is the one that brought me in it a long time ago. But not as long as you—of course. We've been talking for a long time— way back."

Allie grunted, hovering over me. "Do you belong here? Are you our member?"

"Yeah, for a year now. Right?"

"Yeah," Frank said.

"So I'm not in the middle of nothin'?"

"You're not in the middle of nothin'," Allie said. "Just mind your business, all right?"

"Good—good seein' ya again. . . ." We shook hands, and then the big Genovese captain abruptly turned his back on us, joining Fat Gerry Guadagno, walking to their waiting blue Oldsmobile. I could hear Fat Gerry barking about a strong-arm appointment he had to keep: "I'm goin' there tomorrow—11:30—I got somebody meeting me there to-morrow. I'm gonna go *take* his fuckin' truck. . . ."

I stood there with Frank Allocca and Danny Todisco on the sidewalk, smelling the pizzeria next door and listening to the *cock-a-doodle-doo* of that crazy Brooklyn rooster.

"Frank, d'ya see how I gotta be careful of steppin' in the middle of somethin'?"

"Yeah," Frank nodded. "I sure do."

That conversation clinched it. It spelled out for any jury just who the hidden powers behind the clubs were. The key moment came when I'd captured Allie saying, "If it's a Brooklyn matter and you belong here, we don't have to check with Joe." This clearly showed that Joe was the boss of New York and Allie was the boss of Brooklyn. It also showed that the Gambino clubs and the Genovese clubs had definite lines of territorial control. It was a great moment. I'd been caught in a political triangle between the three most powerful racketeers in the industry: Joe, Allie, and Angelo.

Allie was so annoyed about this ridiculous LaCavalla beef—it was really a rinky-dink cardboard stop on Boston Road in the Bronx that wasn't worth more than a few hundred bucks a month—he started barking at Frank Allocca and Danny Todisco like they were his errand boys. Those guys were successful businessmen in their own right, the president and vice president of the Association—and Frank was a decorated World War II vet, to boot—but our conversation showed that they were nothing more than lackeys and gofers, that Allie Shades made all the decisions in the Brooklyn club.

And then Joe Francolino closed the circle for us. Two days later, I met Joe to tell him what Allie Shades had said. Joe confirmed Allie's view on the power structure of the cartel: "That's right—I don't report to them pertaining to New York and they don't report to me pertaining to Brooklyn." He told me that he would send the president of his club, Michael "Mikey Waldorf" Marone, to deal directly with Allie's president, Frank Allocca. "My president talks to their president." Unless the problem was "a little more tedious, a little more political," at which time, Joe said, "then me and Allie will get together."

Joe made it crystal clear—for me and my J-Bird and the grand jury.

"Me—me and Allie. That's who counts. . . . Me and Allie have a rapport barring none. We have the best rapport. . . . One thing about Allie is, he's a sweetheart. He said, 'Joey, whatever youse want to do is okay with me.' Because he knows I want only to do the right thing. I'm not gonna do anything's that gonna embarrass anybody."

Joe knew that Angelo, on the other hand, was constantly embarrassing people. For example, Joe was steamed that Angelo had tried to send a message to me through Frank Allocca. This was typical of Angelo's political trickery. Joe could see that Angelo was just trying to inject this petty LaCavalla beef, using it as a bargaining chip to get the upper hand and humiliate me. Joe promised to raise the issue with Angelo the next time he saw him.

"What kind of a fuckin' message is that? Now what is it? What've we—what've we got? *Ultimatums* now?"

Those crucial conversations about the power structure of the cartel closed a personal circle for me too. I'd been surveilling Allie Shades for years, following him around New York, New Jersey, even out to Las Vegas. From all those hours of surveillance and wiretapping, I felt I knew Allie pretty well. But now I actually had the big guy yelling at me on the sidewalk in front of his club, waving his king-sized mitt in my face.

After that meeting, when I hooked up for my debriefing with Tony Maz and Bobby O, they were hollering: "We bagged Allie! We got Shades. We got every-fuckin'-body!"

It was true: We had them all now, the whole cartel. We could start taking down the case, start seeking indictments to take down Malangone and Francolino and everyone under them.

Tony Maz was so happy, he started shouting:

"Everybody to the Crop! Pizza and beer on me!"

That was one of the few nights that I didn't worry about transcribing my conversations and typing up my Fives right away. We'd now nailed Allie Shades and Joey Cigars. We had the two top guys—as Ed Tamily would say, the top "banana noses"—guys we'd never *dreamed* we could actually get next to. Now we could celebrate and kick back for an hour or so. We all piled into my little one-bedroom Tony DeMarco apartment on Cropsey Avenue, wolfed down some pepperoni pizza, and cracked open a six-pack of Budweiser.

It was nearly time for me to vanish. But before Danny Benedetto could truly become a phantom, a new high-profile beef erupted. It was a dispute over the property rights to a "14-karat gold" account at 200 Madison Avenue.

Built in 1926, filling the entire block between East Thirty-fifth and

East Thirty-sixth streets, 200 Madison Avenue is a twenty-six-story brick-faced office complex housing the corporate headquarters of textile conglomerate Phillips–Van Heusen, the Insurance Company of Greater New York, fashionable tenants such as Roche-Bobois furniture and the New York Sports Club, and even, at the time, the publisher of this book, G. P. Putnam's Sons. The rubbish and recyclables at 200 Madison Avenue had long been picked up by Vibro Carting, a company controlled by John Vitale. Although Vibro had no fixed contract in place, it charged 200 Madison Avenue a monthly fee fluctuating between $8,000 and $9,500.

In the late summer of '94 the building's manager, Gerard Harris, invited Vibro Carting, Browning-Ferris Industries, V. Ponte & Sons, and Chambers Paper Fibres to submit sealed bids for a three-year contract at a fixed monthly rate. Since all the Vitale brothers were long-established members of the Waste Paper Association, not to mention close friends, Angelo Ponte respectfully declined to bid. Browning-Ferris Industries bid $4,911; Chambers bid $4,450, and Vibro came in at $4,400.

As the lowest bidder, of course, Vibro should have been awarded the contract. But Gerard Harris was angry. This was the cartel's nightmare again: A customer had been "educated." Harris realized that Vibro Carting had been gouging him for years, charging fully twice what it should have, and on November 10 he sent a draft contract to Sal Benedetto at Chambers, hoping that Sal would come down the fifty dollars to match the Vibro offer of $4,400. Sal agreed, signed the contract, and mailed it back to 200 Madison Avenue. Harris promptly sent John Vitale a letter notifying him of the change in service.

John Vitale had repeatedly called to speak to Sal. But Sal would just sit there and not take the calls. Finally, on November 15, Vitale arrived unannounced at the Chambers warehouse on Plymouth Street and demanded to speak to me. John Vitale was suspicious of the Benedetto clan—as were all those paper men from the Old Country, those *paisans* from Basilicata—and, refusing to discuss the matter indoors, he asked me to accompany him outside on a walk-and-talk along cobbled Plymouth Street.

"Whatta you guys intend to do about my stop? Whatta you plan to do about rectifyin' this?"

I had Joe Francolino's direct instructions not to settle up with any of the Canal Street club members and so I decided to stall—and I tried to play surly, venting my annoyance at the entire Vitale family.

"Your brother Anthony's been spreading all kinds of ridiculous bullshit and nonsense about me," I said.

"What?"

"Your brother and Sal Giove said that I was FBI, or CIA, or some bullshit—that I went to school in Langley Field or something like that. It caused me a lot of headaches over the summer. Since then your brother, Frank, and Angelo have been spreading the word around town."

"I don't know nothin' about that."

"How would you like it if people were saying something about you that you're not? Especially in *this* business! John, would you want to be in *my* shoes?"

"No," he said, but then added threateningly, "I was told in New York that you wouldn't take my stop. I want an answer right away."

Both Allie and Joe happened to be friendly with Vitale's old man, the original Tony Vitale, and of course they wanted me to straighten out. "Dan, you were wrong for goin' in," Joe said. "You can't just go out and take from a guy." Everybody wanted me to go back to 200 Madison Avenue with the usual *fugazy* nonsense, resurvey the joint, tell the manager that more yardage was coming out than we thought. That way John Vitale could keep his work. That way we wouldn't "ruin" the stop.

Joe and Allie were slick, double-teaming me on this one. When I went by the Brooklyn club, Allie was sitting there laughing with Frank Allocca.

"Is that Chambers? We were just talkin' about you."

"Uh-oh. Am I in trouble? What'd I do now?"

"No, nothing. Not much. Yeah, I was just talkin' to Joe."

"Oh."

"Come here."

Allie led me to the back of the club, by the filing cabinets. He had me standing in the corner, resting his arm on my shoulder, whispering now. "What happened was, with what's his name, John Vitale, nice guy—Tony is a good guy, John Vitale's father."

"Okay."

I'd never realized how physically imposing Allie Shades really was until he was standing over me like that, with his heavy hand on my shoulder and his lips pressed right to my ear.

"I mean, they wouldn't bother no one—whatever we tell 'em to do, they *do*."

"Okay."

"So I told Joe, 'Joe, you can't—you can't do this to that guy. That guy is a nice guy. Anybody else, I don't give a fuck.'"

I told Allie that I was getting mixed messages, because with all the other Waste Paper Association beefs, Joe had been telling me to hold off.

"No, straighten it out, straighten it out," Allie whispered.

"If Joe and you tell me it's okay, I'll go ahead and do it."

Allie nodded, and his hot breath in my ear was a direct command:

"*Straighten* it out."

It was almost Christmas season and all the gangsters were gearing up for their holiday parties and the formal gala at the Marriott Marquis. None of the Benedettos would ever set foot in the gangsters' black-tie affair, but we supported the cause. It was funny: When you open up their glossy book—*bang*—facing each other on the first two pages, there's Alphonso Malangone's silver ad and my silver ad:

MERRY CHRISTMAS

FROM DANNY & THE BENEDETTOS

I skipped the Christmas gala at the Marriott Marquis—too much of a risk of running into someone who knew me from my neighborhood, half-assed wiseguys or carters like Jimmy Garbage. But I did show up on December 14 at the Christmas party at Allie's club. In fact, I did something I shouldn't have—I got liquored up. I knew I was about to pull out of the undercover role, so I let loose. I was so cockeyed, I had to leave my Jeep at Allie's club and get a lift to the Crop to sleep it off.

Everyone was at that holiday bash. Allie Shades was playing poker with Patty Pecoraro and Johnny Drago. I was standing around moaning with Frank Allocca and Rocky Cimato about our bad backs—every hood I ever met had some kind of slipped-disc trouble. Rocky was moaning about how his back was so fucked up, it was killing him to have sex. But even though it was a time to laugh, smoke, and get liquored up, you think that means the scheming and scamming goes to the back burner? Not with wiseguys. It never stops. All night long I was hearing fat gangsters barking in my ear about beefs. At one point Carl Bivona, the same three-hundred-fifty-pound gorilla who'd blocked my entrance to the Sheraton Hotel meeting a year earlier, grabbed me and started rattling off beefs he was claiming against me: Pork Pack, E&G Foods, A&L Provisions, ABC Bargains . . . I wrote it all down on an envelope in my drunken handwriting, so sloppy I could hardly read it the next day. Bivona was also griping about some $1,100 dumping bill he said we had never paid. I told Carl I'd look into the situation in the morning—which I did, and to my surprise, it turned out, Bivona wasn't bullshitting: We did owe him $1,100.

Frank Allocca came up to me with his own beef. He told me I still had to pay him for the two tickets to the big gala dinner-dance at the Marriott Marquis. I tried to argue that no one from Chambers had even *attended*—and still we'd paid for that silver-page ad in the journal—but Frank said that didn't matter. I knew why he was being so adamant. He had to kick it *upstairs*. That dinner-dance money was going straight to the bosses of the Genovese and Gambino crime families. Fine, I said, and I gave Frank a check for two tickets for the damn dance that had happened two weeks before.

When Allie Shades was finished playing poker, I decided to raise my own beef with him. Allie had already helped me out with that crazy hothead Dominick Vulpis—Allie'd got Vulpis to accept half of what he'd been getting from me for that old Ferdinand Guttman beef. Joe had asked Allie to intercede and get me some "breathing room," and Allie got Vulpis to accept $8,000 a month, down from $16,000.

Now I wanted Allie's help with another beef. A company called Empire Rubbish Removal was going around stealing my cardboard from various stops. Empire was run by a Brooklyn guy named Patty Piccininni—everyone called him Elvis, because he wore a pompadour and '70s-style sideburns down to his jawline. It was an outrage, really. I was paying Elvis extortion every month for one of the D'Agostino supermarkets, and he was still sending his thugs around to steal from me.

The corrugated cardboard market was very volatile: Some months you couldn't get squat for your cardboard; other times the market would be sky-high. And it so happened that the price for cardboard was insane right now—it was a market that only came around once every ten years. You could sell corrugated cardboard on the overseas for $140 to $145 per ton. So of course garbage gangsters were going around on their regular collection routes, tongues hanging out, and my bales of supermarket cardboard looked like unattended bundles of greenbacks.

When I told Allie about my problems with Empire, he shrugged. In his opinion it wasn't Patty Piccininni orchestrating the thefts.

"Drivers are just robbin' without telling the owners," he said.

Theft of recyclables was widespread all over the city. A lot of guys were complaining. I'd also spoken to Joe Francolino and Patty Pecoraro at the Gambino club about the problem. Patty warned me not to try fighting fire with fire, not to take anything back from Elvis: "They'll come back with a truckload of guys and they'll kick the shit out of you—Empire's known for that."

That part I already knew. A couple of my drivers had confronted some Empire drivers about the stolen cardboard, and Elvis's guys had roughed up my guys.

So I appealed to Shades. "Allie, please see what you can do with Empire."

"Yeah, I'll take care of it," Allie tells me. "No problem."

It never was a problem again. Shades saw to that. After the Christmas party, no Empire drivers dared glance at our cardboard. Later on, when we executed the search warrants at the Empire offices on Fifteenth Avenue in Bensonhurst, we found a whole bag of pistols and sawed-off shotguns.

That night at Allie's club, I'd noticed guys like Carl Bivona slipping envelopes to Frank to give to Allie. I knew that you were expected to take care of the big wiseguys at Christmastime. Like Joe Francolino said, on birthdays and Christmas, "I ain't allergic to green." I came by the Gambino club and asked Patty Pecoraro what I should do about Joey's Christmas tip.

"I'm gonna be Danny Claus this year," I said.

"Danny Claus," Patty laughed, nodding, rubbing his thumb and fingers together.

I picked out a nice Christmas card for Joe and slipped five crisp C-notes inside. I also got him a box of his favorite cigars. Just before the holiday, we had dinner at Pierino's. It was a fine night of pasta and red wine and bid-rigging. We were scheming to rig the bid for the Waldbaum's supermarkets chain. At the end of the night we paused in the vestibule to say good-bye.

"Joe," I said, "just wanna thank you for everything you've done for me and my family. We do appreciate it. I wanna wish you and your family a nice holiday." Then I gave him a box of Te-Amo Toros.

"Ah, thanks, Danny," Joe said, then we kissed each other on the cheeks.

Of course, the kiss between two men is fairly common in Italian culture, but among wiseguys it's truly a gesture of respect. Every Wednesday night John Gotti loved to stand outside the Ravenite on Mulberry Street, accepting the kisses of guys like Jimmy Brown and Joey Francolino.

My point man on surveillance that night was Bobby O'Donahue. He was parked close by, operating the Kel booster, keeping a careful eye on me. Bobby was a typical conservative Irish-Catholic from Queens; he often said: "There's only two times in life when you touch another man—that's when you're shakin' his hand and when you're *knockin'* him out."

Bobby was in the unmarked car with the Kel booster, and when he saw Joe and me embracing and kissing, he started broadcasting over the radio to the rest of the field team: "*Jesus!* You won't *believe* what just happened. Danny's in the foyer with Francolino, and Francolino just slipped his *tongue* down Danny's throat! Ah, I'm gettin' sick. . . ."

Everybody in the surveillance van burst out laughing, and Bobby kept going on with this. It became a source of comic relief for months, throughout the grand jury testimony and the trial. Bobby would tell everyone, the brass, the DAs, anyone who would listen: "I've seen these guys Frenchin' each other"—and then make a face like he was going to retch.

When I left Pierino's that night, I circled around, cleaned myself of any possible tails, then drove down to the Old Sailor's Home below Battery Park City, parked, and walked down to the waterfront.

In a few minutes Tony Maz and Bobby O showed up. Bobby jumped out like the car was on fire, hollering: "Dan! You're *lettin'* me down! You're *grossin'* me out—whaddaya doing lettin' Francolino stick his *tongue* in your mouth?" Even Tony Maz was getting in on the act: "You two fuckin' lovebirds."

But Tony and Bobby both knew that this was our best night yet: A great conspiracy captured on tape, ending with a sign that I'd fully become one of the big boys. We're now greeting in the most intimate Mob fashion. Joey Cigars doesn't go around kissing just anybody.

9 | THE CLEAN SWEEP

I couldn't quit my Danny life cold turkey. I knew that I would be required to testify before various grand juries in the months ahead, and I needed to avoid seeing the mobsters without losing touch with them or raising them up.

We decided that the best solution would be for me to disappear from view but maintain regular phone contact. I'd already laid the groundwork for my alibi: For months I'd been complaining loudly of back problems; at the last few meetings with Joe Francolino and Patty Pecoraro at the Gambino club, I moaned that I couldn't even sit down because my lower spine was hurting so much.

I'd also been telling the members of the associations that I was going to visit various paper mills in the Midwest on family business. My plan was to tell them that while traveling, staying with my brother-in-law in Chicago, my back problems had drastically worsened. I settled on a neurological ailment called clonus—severe spasms emanating from the lumbar region were affecting my toes and leaving me unable to walk. I'd say I'd been told to have emergency back surgery, which would require a month's rest and recovery time before I could return to the city. The Tech Services guys in the PD were even able to arrange for a number with a Chicago area code to bounce directly to an answering machine in One Hogan Place, the Manhattan DA's Office, where I could either answer the phone as Danny or Detective Camille San Fillipo's voice would come on an answering machine as my fictitious sister-in-law. Sometimes Camille even answered in person, shouting in the DA's Office, "Danny, there's a call for you!" Then, one by one I started calling guys like Joe and Patty and telling them that I'd just had emergency back surgery.

I only *wish* I had something as straightforward as clonus. What happened defied medical explanation. It started when I was in the heat of the grand-jury testimony. I had too much on my plate. I was on the witness stand for hours and hours, listening to tape recordings that I'd made, reliving all my conversations with these subjects going back three years, being expected to recall their phone numbers and addresses, appearing calm and well prepared during many hours of testimony.

And to top it all off, these *same* guys kept beeping me throughout the grand jury proceedings. My pager was going off nonstop: Joe Francolino, Patty Pecoraro, Frank Allocca, Danny Todisco, Phil Barretti. I couldn't call any of them back right away—and these guys *hated* to be left waiting.

In the middle of my testimony I was colluding with Barretti's son Mark to rig the bids for 90 Washington Street, a lucrative office building that Phil badly wanted to keep. I'm supposedly in Chicago, flat on my back in agony, but I'm really just outside the grand-jury room, bid-rigging with Mark Barretti and Five Brothers. We all did the right thing this time—put in our bogus sealed bids and let Philly keep his stop.

But the funniest thing was what Danny Todisco and Frank Allocca kept beeping me about. Just before my grand-jury testimony started, around Christmastime, they'd asked me to meet them at the Americana Diner in Bensonhurst. I thought it was probably about some garbage routes they wanted to sell me in the Bronx. "No, it's *better* than that," Danny Todisco told me. I couldn't believe what they wanted: When I got to the Americana, Danny said he had a big moneymaking proposition for me.

Turned out that Danny and Frank had decided they wanted to go into business with me. They wanted to start a paper-packing plant in Brooklyn—Todisco even owned a huge empty building on the waterfront, right near Chambers, where we could house our operation. It was just going to be Danny, Frank, me, and two other guys from the Brooklyn club as the owners. And they said they wanted me to be a principal in the company because of my years of paper expertise! That's how badly I had these guys fooled—they actually respected my knowledge of the industry. "Dan, what type of balers should we buy?" And I told Frank and Danny the pros and cons of the various new baling machines on the market. Even I couldn't believe that I'd mastered this stuff.

Of course, I knew that if I went into business with Frank Allocca and Danny Todisco, I would actually be getting Allie Shades as a silent partner. And I also knew that when Joe Francolino got wind of it, his nose would get out of joint and right away he'd put the arm on me, expecting me to cut him in as my silent partner.

It would have been beautiful, from a law enforcement standpoint, to actually operate a business with the two leading wiseguys in the industry. Unprecedented. But as much as I wanted to string them along, I knew it was just a fantasy. We didn't need to gather any more evidence against the cartel, and we didn't need to spend any more taxpayer money.

I had to keep making up excuses for Danny and Frank. As usual, they wouldn't take no for an answer; they kept beeping me while I'm on the stand in my suit and tie, being questioned by assistant district attorneys Ann Ryan and Bruce Berger.

I just couldn't keep all these balls in the air. My whole body started to rebel against me. First, every inch of skin turned swollen and raw. My face ballooned. I had strange hives and rashes everywhere—like I'd been stung by a swarm of bees. When I looked in the mirror it wasn't even me: It was the Wild Man of Borneo.

I called up my family physician in Manhattan—a guy from the old neighborhood in West Orange, New Jersey. Now he had a nice little practice on the East Side. The moment he saw me, he knew I was in bad shape, could see I wasn't getting enough sleep. He said he'd give me a mild sleeping pill and some ointment for the rashes.

"You and that crazy undercover life. Why don't you get some regular detective's work?"

"I kind of like this organized-crime shit."

Then he got up and closed the door to his office. He started to whisper. "The other day, I had a guy in here that was definitely Mafia. He came in unannounced and told my receptionist that he needed to speak to somebody in charge."

My friend is a soft-spoken Jewish guy, and he had three partners in the building, also Jewish doctors. He came out into the reception area and he saw that there was an odd individual waiting up front. Definitely not a patient. Dressed like John Gotti, gray hair blow-dried in place, black mock turtleneck, expensive double-breasted suit, lots of gold jewelry on his fingers and wrists.

"Just need to let youse know we gotta increase your garbage rate. Youse guys are generating more garbage now and we gotta increase your fee."

My friend was a little taken aback. He said to himself, *It's the same business here, nothing's changed over the past few years.* "Hold on. Let me go check with my partners."

He rounded up the other three doctors. "Listen, don't be alarmed, but there's a mobster-looking character up front—a gangster straight from central casting. He says that he wants to raise our garbage rate, and he's talking about a lot more money. It has to be bullshit. We're not pro-ducing any more garbage." They were all nodding. "So what do you want me to do?" All three of these doctors looked at each other, and with-out missing a beat—like three marionettes—they mouthed the words: "*Pay* him!"

This mysterious condition got so bad, I was in such physical pain, that I couldn't leave my bed for weeks. In the end, the Manhattan district at-torney had to postpone all grand jury testimony for a month until I recovered.

My doctor couldn't understand what was wrong. He ordered the whole battery of tests: MRIs, CT scans, EEGs. Nothing conclusive.

Looking back, I realize that I'd been ignoring the warning signs for a long time. During one of my meetings with Ed Tamily, down at his pa-per shop on East Third Street, I got so visibly angry that my face was flushed and my heart was racing. It was so aggravating trying to negoti-ate with these garbage gangsters; they'd constantly try to pull little last-minute shit on you to rip you off. On this particular day Ed was telling me that some of the cash payments I'd been making to him and Joe Virzi, the ones for $2,400, didn't count against the total nut of over $200,000. Only the payments of $8,000 were going toward whittling down that HBO nut. There was no actual reason for this; it was just their crazy criminal logic. We got into a heated argument, trying to cal-culate the tens of thousands I'd already paid, and Eddie was slightly taken aback. He could see how bad-tempered I'd become.

"Dan," he said, "you don't look too good." It so happened that Joe Virzi's son was with Eddie that day. Joe Virzi's son was a doctor—a car-diologist, in fact. I'd met him a few times up at the Waste Paper Associ-ation. He glanced at me once and said, "Dan, you're a setup for a stroke or a heart attack."

"Why don't you just have him check you out?" Ed said, smiling. "His office is right on Thirty-fourth Street."

I had the J-Bird taped to my crotch, the mike taped to my chest, and now Eddie Tamily was telling me take my freakin' shirt off to be checked out by Joe Virzi's son, the big-shot cardiologist?

But I didn't keel over from a massive coronary. And finally the diagnosis came in: I had fibromyalgia, a chronic disorder characterized by acute musculoskeletal pain, fatigue, and tender points in the joints.

"What causes it?" I asked my doctor.

"You've suffered extreme stress over a prolonged period of time and it's affecting your nerve endings."

I was seeing my family doctor and friend in Manhattan, and I felt I could confide in him. Although he didn't know the details of my job, he had a general sense; he knew that for three years I'd been undercover in a top-secret organized-crime investigation, that I'd been living a double life, pretending to be friends with people who weren't really my friends, guys who would've killed me in a second if they knew who I really was. He understood that for three years I'd been living one huge, high-risk lie.

My underlying ailment, he told me, was PTSD: post-traumatic stress disorder. That disease of the Vietnam vets. PTSD had brought on the fibromyalgia.

"What's the cure?"

"There is no cure. We just have to hope it gets better. Eat better. Cut sugars out of your diet. Get rid of the stressors."

Get rid of the stressors? In a few months I was scheduled to be the star witness in the most high-profile organized-crime prosecution Robert Morgenthau's office had ever attempted. Not to mention the fact that I still had to keep in touch with all these garbage gangsters by phone. I'd been lying low for so long that it was starting to look fishy.

One day Patty Pecoraro even said to me: "Where are ya, Moe? Are ya on the *lam*?"

I was recuperating in bed in Staten Island, waiting to get back on the stand to testify against him, and Patty was asking me if I'm on the lam!

After a month or so I figured Francolino might've been raised up. I kept making excuses about being stuck out of town. And like any smart wiseguy, Joe wouldn't say *anything* on the phone. I remember one day—

months earlier—when I was in his Duffy Waste office on West Nine-teenth Street, Joe was mumbling his *yeah*'s and *naw*'s on the phone to somebody and then he held the receiver away, looked at me, and mouthed the words: "It's just an *ornament.*" Now whenever I called Joe, he kept me on hold for a long time, listening to easy-listening music. (Ironically enough, on one of the tapes you can hear me listening to the song "Everybody Plays the Fool.") When he did pick up the receiver, Joe said he wanted to see me at the club so we could talk face-to-face. "What's the matter, Dan?" he said finally. "Two friends can't meet sometime for a cup of coffee? . . . Well, just so long as you're getting the right treatment now—that's the most important thing. . . ."

I took my doctor's advice: I ate better, tried to sleep longer, relaxed more. And it worked. The hives and rashes healed. I got back on my feet. It was a full year before I felt like myself again, but after a month I was ready to get back on the stand in front of the grand jury.

Despite my doctor's warnings about living a healthier life, there was one vice I couldn't give up entirely: cigars. The year I'd spent smoking with Joe and the guys had me hooked. I was buying cigar magazines. I even had my own well-stocked humidor at home.

Testifying in front of the grand jury every day was not only stressful, it was tedious. I had a team of detectives meeting me at my place in Staten Island every morning, taking me back and forth to the district attorney's office. I felt claustrophobic, like I was under house arrest. I needed to break out. One night I called my brother-in-law and told him there was a cigar aficionado's convention at the Marriott Marquis in Manhattan. It was called the Big Smoke. I wasn't sure who might be there, but I had to prepare my brother-in-law in advance. On the drive uptown I told him, "If anyone at all comes up to me, I'm not Rick, okay? My name is *Dan*. Either don't say anything at all to me or just call me *Dan*."

I didn't think we'd run into any hoods at the Big Smoke, but I couldn't be sure. After a few hours in the Marriott sampling the fine se-lection of cigars, I see this strange look crossing my brother-in-law's face. Then I hear a voice yelling: "Danny! Danny!"

When I turned to my left, I saw Mike Cammallare, the same big,

muscular, busted-nose Bronx carter who'd answered the door for me
that first day at Jimmy Brown's club. He looked like a million bucks in
a dark-gray double-breasted suit and black mock turtleneck and shiny
black loafers. I still had some big beefs to settle up with Mike, but he
was being patient because Joe and Patty had told him to wait his turn.

"Hey, Mike! How's it goin'?"

I put on a good act, limping, unable to hug him due to my *incredible*
back pain.

"How you feelin'? I heard you been outta town. I heard you had surgery."

"Yeah, I'm on the mend here, Mike."

I knew that Mike would *immediately* call Joey and Patty to report that
he'd seen me back in New York at the Marriott Marquis. So I had to
make up another lie quick.

"I just got back into town last night—I been cooped up in Chicago,
recuperating from this back shit, and I needed to get outta the house.
Y'know, smoke some cigars and relax. I'll tell ya, I'm coming home to
a shitload of headaches here, Mike."

"Yeah, I heard," he said.

We wished each other well, recommending a couple of Dominicans
to each other, and then shook hands. When I turned back around, I
didn't see my brother-in-law anywhere. I left the Big Smoke and found
him out in the lobby.

"What happened?"

"I don't know who that was, but I heard him calling you Dan and I
said to myself: That guy's a gangster—no doubt about it."

In the midst of my secret grand-jury testimony, the cartel's publicity
blitz against Browning-Ferris Industries hit the newspapers and air-
waves. As BFI's visibility in the city had increased, and Bill Ruckelshaus
was giving more tough-talking anti-Mob interviews to the press, the
trade-waste associations counterattacked with their multimillion-dollar

campaign. Drawing on Joe Francolino's war chest, the associations produced a series of TV commercials that began airing on CNN and local
New York stations.

One ad depicted a cash-stuffed attaché case and an ominous voice-
over narration listing BFI's history of accepting bribes, antitrust convictions, toxic-waste violations, and heavy fines for price-fixing in six
states. A second, more humorous commercial showed a cowboy hat–
wearing Texan wrangling with a New York City street map inside his
BFI garbage truck, unable to find an address on Third Avenue.

Both BFI and the cartel had employed high-profile public-relations
firms: Howard J. Rubenstein Associates was coordinating the BFI campaign, and Edelman Public Relations Worldwide was working for the
local carters. And both sides had raised eyebrows with their mudsling-
ing tactics. Several local stations, including the ABC and CBS affiliates,
refused to air the anti-BFI ads, while Browning-Ferris was accused of
perpetuating unsavory Italian-American stereotypes in a widespread
print campaign that depicted the local carters as fat-faced, slick-haired
mafiosi.

The grand-jury testimony was finished, the indictments had been
handed down, and we were about two weeks away from arresting all the
subjects and executing search warrants in all their companies and clubs.

Now I had to face the music with my wife.

For the last year of the case, our marriage had become extremely
strained. I left the house when she and my son were still asleep and returned home when they were asleep. When I did have a moment to see
Ricky, I was always dashing out the door with him holding on to my
legs. He was just learning to talk, and practically the first words he
learned to say were "Daddy, don't go!"

All my other undercover assignments, in Narcotics, posing as outlaw
biker Gene Mazza, had been short-term stints—one, two, three days
max. But this investigation had now lasted exactly three years and three

months. I hadn't brought home a lot of the buy-and-bust stuff when I did that, either, because I didn't want to scare Claire. My wife's kind of old-fashioned; she's from a traditional Italian-American family, and she doesn't ask me a lot of prying questions.

But as this operation continued, things were getting increasingly bizarre on the home front. Not just me coming home at weird hours, but spending hundreds of dollars on batteries and gauze and surgical tape. We had a spare bedroom that was filled with boxes of surgical tape, gauze, piles of three-ring-binder transcripts and DD5s, and *mountains* of tapes. Thousands of hours of tapes.

There were also the personal things that only a wife notices. In order to wear the wire every day, I was always shaving in the most intimate places, not to mention that first night at Ponte's Steakhouse when I burned my privates with the Kel transmitter. And you have to understand: When she married me in 1980, I was just a kid, just starting out as a patrolman. This is no longer the life of a typical cop.

"When's it going to end?" she kept saying.

I promised her so many times. "Soon, soon. We're almost done."

Finally, in the spring of 1995, we were preparing to take the case down. No one—not Commissioner Bratton, DA Morgenthau, or Mayor Giuliani—had ever imagined the case would mushroom into its current size and scope. It had taken on a life of its own. It was now the biggest organized-crime case in the history of the New York Police Department and the Manhattan district attorney's office. There were very few Mafia cases in any jurisdiction that even approached the scale and complexity of the indictments we were preparing.

Coming out of a long-term undercover role is always the most dangerous moment. Even more so with the Mob. This is when they can strike—when they can retaliate and take vengeance on the people around you. I had to be straight with my wife about everything now. Our whole lives were turning upside down. It was going to be dangerous living on Staten Island. We might have to move to a new home, someplace far from the city, before the trial started.

I knew that Claire was not going to react well to the news. She's not naïve: She knows just how vicious and ugly the Mob can be. I knew that this Mafia stuff wasn't going to fly with her.

I told Tony Maz I was worried. "You gotta talk to her, Rick," he said. "Let's see what her concerns are, then Inspector O'Brien will come talk to you and Claire."

I was dreading it. Every week I kept putting it off, kept telling myself that the time wasn't right. And Bobby O'Donahue was such a hands-on, detail-oriented guy, he wanted to keep abreast of everything, even my conversations with my wife. Every day we were together in the DA's office, preparing for trial, Bobby was bugging me:

"Did you tell her yet? Did you tell her? What'd she say?"

"No, no, last night wasn't the right time. . . ."

I put it off until the last possible moment. Until there really was no more time. The indictments were going to be unsealed any day, and it might be front-page headlines in all the papers.

One day Claire was standing in the dining room of our condo on Staten Island and I just said: *Okay, this is it.*

"Claire, listen. You know the *thing* that's been going on forever and ever and I keep promising you it's gonna end someday? Well, this is it— it's ending right now. In a couple of days the case is coming down and there's a whole lot of people getting locked up."

"Thank God."

"Yeah, but I have to tell you something else too. Don't get mad. I want you to hear me out first, and then let me know what you're feeling. What I've been doing all these years—I've infiltrated the Mafia, I'm dealing with some very heavy Mob guys—"

I was serious as a heart attack as I was telling her this, of course. But my family and friends and everyone I work with know that I can be a practical joker. They all know that I'm capable of putting on a straight face and saying some extremely dumb shit. "I'm dead serious," I said. "For three years I've been thick as thieves with some powerful men in the Mafia."

"Right, Rick."

And she walked away across the kitchen—completely blew me off.

"This is for real. We're taking down the garbage cartel. We're taking down some major, major people here. No bullshit. The case is coming down and a lot of heavy-duty gangsters are gonna get locked up. My boss wants to come out here to talk to you about your concerns—"

"Tony?"

"Inspector O'Brien."

"Inspector O'Brien wants to come *here*?" In about half a second her expression went from disbelieving to concerned to livid. Now she started lashing out at me with everything she's got. "You're not kidding around, are you? What the hell's the matter with you? Everything you ever do, Rick, you can't be a follower, can't be someone in the background. No, you always have to be out front, leading the charge. Balls to the wall! *Everything* you do! You couldn't just buy a motorcycle, you have to get a big Harley chopper! You couldn't just be undercover, you had to go into Narcotics, get into all that weirdo makeup and disguises . . ."

This was another story. When I was doing a lot of buy-and-busts, I became very good at drawing track marks on my skin. If you put them on your arm or hand, the drug dealers will want to inspect them too closely, so I started putting them near my groin. They don't inspect that area up close. When I came on the set with the cash, the dealers would always say, "*You're* bangin' it in? You're shootin' *montéca*?" because I was a big guy and pretty beefy to be shooting heroin. "Lemme see your tracks, man." Then I'd have to open my pants and let them see the needle marks in my groin. But I didn't just draw something on with a felt-tip pen. I went up to Bob Kelly's theatrical makeup store on West Forty-fifth Street, a professional joint where Hollywood makeup artists go. I got so well known in the Narcotics unit for my makeup skills, I was doing it for all the other undercovers, giving them scars, stitches, lumps, bruises. This stuff was good. You could rub the makeup hard and it wouldn't come off.

At least, usually it wouldn't. One time I used a little too much red makeup for my track marks. I was lying there in bed, fast asleep, and my wife starts shouting at me. When I cracked open my eyes I saw her waving my underwear in my face. "What's *this*? What's *this*?" Doing the laundry, she noticed the red smudges from the makeup in my boxer shorts and she thought it was another woman's lipstick.

I'd talked my way out of that jam, but I wasn't sure I could talk my way out of this one.

"You can't just do *regular* undercover work, you're telling me you're involved with *Mob* people? What's the matter with you? You idiot! Don't you know we're surrounded by them here in Staten Island?"

Yes, I did. That very morning, in fact, I had waved hello to our own condo-complex carter, Jimmy Garbage.

"You're a streetwise guy, Rick. You carry a gun, you know how to handle yourself. But what about me? We have an *infant*. You know how long it takes to get an infant in and out of the car? Now, I have to have eyes in the back of my head? How can I *live* here like this? Some of the girls at my job go out with these hoods. They're all *around* us. And they're not like other criminals, they're very resourceful—they can *find* us. Rick, I don't want any of these gangsters coming to our front door!"

I'd never seen her so angry. She was yelling for about fifteen minutes without coming up for air. And I just stood there like a big dummy. Because I knew she was right. When she was done, I snuck into the spare room to call Bobby O'Donahue. I had to whisper the whole time.

"Did you tell her yet?"

"Yes. She screamed at me like a maniac."

"And what'd you say?"

"What could I say?"

"You always say something."

"I didn't say a word for fifteen minutes."

"*You*? Mr. In-Your-Face? I've *never* seen you at a loss for words. You always say something! I wish I was there to see *that*."

On June 5, 1995, a grand jury in New York County returned a sweeping 114-count indictment—Number 561495—detailing charges of arson, assault, bribery, grand larceny, enterprise corruption, coercion, and antitrust crimes against seventeen individuals, four trade associations, and twenty-three companies:

> Frank Allocca, 67; Philip Barretti, Sr., 56; Michael D'Ambrosio, 29; Joseph Francolino, Sr., 57; Frank Giovinco, 28; Alphonso Malangone, 58; Louis P. Mongelli, 60; Paul P. Mongelli, 30; Patrick Pecoraro, 50; Raymond Polidori, 48; Angelo Ponte, 69; Henry Tamily, 68; Daniel F. Todisco, 41; Vincent Vigliotti, Sr., 66; Joseph Virzi, 68; John Vitale, 41; Dominick Vulpis, 54.
>
> The Association of Trade Waste Removers of Greater New York Inc.; the Greater New York Waste Paper Association Inc.; the Kings County Trade Waste Association Inc.; the Queens County Trade Waste Association Inc.
>
> ABC Recycling Co., Inc.; AVA Carting Inc.; All Service Paper; Barretti Carting Corp.; Bay Sanitation Service Inc.; Crest Carting Co., Inc.; Delmar Waste Services Ltd.; Delmar Recycling Corp.; Duffy Waste & Recycling Corp.; Five Brothers Inc.; Litod Paper Stock Corp.; Lyn-Val Association; Mongelli Carting Company Inc.; Nekboh Recycling Inc.; V. Ponte & Sons; Professional Recyclers Inc.; RJP Recycling Inc.; Robros Recycling Corp.; Rockaway Recycling Corp.; Silk Inc.; VA Sanitation; Vaparo Inc.; Vigliotti & Sons Inc.

In the predawn hours of June 22, 1995, an army of nearly five hundred NYPD detectives and cops all along the eastern seaboard simultaneously executed search warrants, seizing masses of financial records and documents in Brooklyn, Manhattan, the Bronx, Queens, Staten Island, Long Island, New Jersey, and various resort communities in Florida. All the principal members of the cartel were arrested, cuffed, and paraded before a mob of newspapermen and television crews. That night, both local and national network news broadcast stories about the unprecedented takedown of Operation Wasteland featuring videotape of the grim-faced "daisy chain": Philip Barretti shackled to Frank Allocca shackled to Allie Malangone, one garbage gangster after another led from the paddy wagon through the indignity of the perp walk.

Joe Francolino was not arrested until the following morning; he turned himself in to the police—in classic wiseguy style—without any of his expensive jewelry or Italian-made clothes.

The news release from District Attorney Morgenthau's office announced that the forfeitures seized in that single day totaled $268 million in assets. Mayor Giuliani and the DA held separate press conferences to crow about the city's success in bringing down the cartel. After Morgenthau spent considerable time acknowledging Bill Ruckelshaus's role—"BFI's cooperation has been enormously valuable to the investigation"—Commissioner Bill Bratton spoke up before the assembled media about the role of an anonymous NYPD detective: "He was at considerable risk throughout these three years. His ability to insert himself through his own creativity into these organizations—and over the last several years become a very important member—really moved this investigation forward. It significantly altered his family life, it altered his professional life, and he really played an incredible role in this. Accordingly, we're promoting him to Detective First-Grade, effective immediately."

It would be two years before my name appeared in any newspaper stories. Shortly after the first wave of arrests, in an official ceremony at One Police Plaza attended by Commissioner Bratton and the top NYPD brass, I was promoted to Detective First-Grade, the highest rank a detective can achieve in the department. (I later received department recognition in the grade of Honorable Mention.) Sergeant Tony Mazziotti and Lieutenant John O'Brien also received immediate pay-grade promotions.

When we took the case down, one of Tony's responsibilities was to go in there and give all the hoods our pitch. It was the standard-issue *If you want to cooperate, now's the time, fellas.* . . . Of course, guys like Francolino and Malangone wouldn't give a cop the time of day. But they were both gentlemen about it. Allie showed his typical charm, even under the circumstances. In fact, when they executed the search warrants on the Kings County Trade Waste Association, Tony tried to strike up a lighter conversation.

"So how'd you get the the nickname Allie Shades anyway?"

"Ah, that *name*—it means nothin'," Allie shrugged. "Some knock-around guy in the street gave it to me 'cause I always wore sunglasses. Look, I'm just a regular guy. . . ."

But some of the other defendants went out of their way to act like hard-ons. When we executed the search warrants in Brooklyn, Frank Allocca stood there ranting at our detectives: "It's a *disgrace* what you're doing to a World War II *veteran*! I served with the *paratroopers* in Europe!" And he kept up that rant in the interview room with Tony—saying he's just a sick old man who served his country proudly and deserves better treatment from the government. Patty Pecoraro was even more of a hard-on. He turned away from Tony with a big huff, wouldn't even give up his name.

For such a young guy, Frank Giovinco handled the takedown with dignity. When we went into the Canal Street club with our warrants to seize all the financial records and computers and everything, Angelo Ponte was going nuts, and some of the other WPA guys were screaming, but it was Frank who took charge and told everybody to cool it. "They're just doing their job—let 'em get what they need!" Then in the interview room with Tony, Frank managed to be both polite and hard-core at the same time.

"I believe you have a pretty good idea of who I am and what I'm all about," Frank said. "Well, then you should *also* know that I don't have another word to say to you."

Jury selection was set to commence on February 18, 1997. But in the weeks before the trial, eight individual defendants chose to plead guilty to the Organized Crime Control Act charge of attempted enterprise corruption: Frank Allocca, Daniel Todisco, Michael D'Ambrosio, Eddie Tamily, Joseph Virzi, Jimmy Vigliotti, Dominick Vulpis, and Angelo Ponte.

In pleading guilty, each of the defendants admitted both the existence of and his own participation in a cartel whose sole purpose was to restrain competition in the city's carting industry. All of them received state prison sentences and waived any possible appeal. Their companies also pleaded guilty, agreed to fines and forfeiture, and waived appeal.

Sobbing uncontrollably in court, Angelo Ponte, Knight of Malta, agreed to pay a personal fine of $7.5 million and begin serving a two-to-six-year prison sentence. The next morning's *Daily News* printed a picture of Angelo in better days, down in sunny Florida.

CARTED OFF TO PRISON

A carting industry kingpin who led a double-life as a civic-minded businessman pleaded guilty to racketeering charges yesterday and agreed to quit the industry. Standing meekly before state Supreme Court Justice Leslie Crocker Snyder yesterday, Angelo Ponte, 72, admitted that he attempted to rig garbage-hauling contracts worth millions of dollars at two Manhattan office buildings.[1]

His $60-million carting company, V. Ponte & Sons—started as a push-cart business by Angelo's father in Little Italy in 1909—came under the control of a court-appointed trustee. By judicial court order, Angelo was permanently barred from playing any future role in the city's carting industry. His son, Vincent, who'd pled guilty in connection to the bid-rigging of 55 Water Street, was given five years' probation but also was barred for life from the industry.

§ix months before the trial, the body was discovered—slumped forward, chin touching chest, inside a Dumpster at the back exit of the Chambers warehouse on Plymouth Street. One of the transfer-station workers found the corpse: opening the Dumpster, releasing the stench of human decomposition, he turned away to retch.

---

[1] New York *Daily News,* the, January 28, 1997

The victim was a heavyset white male of average height, roughly in his thirties, thick dark hair and a dark goatee. He'd been murdered execution-style with a single shot from .380 semiautomatic. There was no wallet or other identification on him. Dried blood had caked, black and gluelike, over the face and neck. The bullet had blown apart the back of his skull, bounced around the brain cavity, creating a tremendous cranial pressure that caused the eyes to bulge out and the entire face to swell like a grotesquely inflated mask.

I had an eighteen-hour-a-day detective detail accompanying me back and forth to my desk in the Manhattan district attorney's office at One Hogan Place. Suddenly, I received multiple beeps with the the crisis code and called Tony Maz from the DA's office.

"What's up, Tone?"

"Just checking to see if you're still breathing. We found a guy murdered on Chambers property. Shoved into a Dumpster."

"Who is it? You can't ID him?"

"Nope. Nobody can ID him. He's a stocky-built male white. About five nine, between two hundred and two twenty. Single gunshot to the back of the head. The face is all puffed up and distorted. I'm calling everybody connected to the case, making sure they're okay."

There were a half-dozen detectives at Chambers with Sal and his family round the clock. I called Sal immediately and talked to him; he and his brother and sister and all the cousins were safe and accounted for. The homicide squad in the Eight Four Precinct did the investigation— regular gumshoe detective work. Took them a few days, but they finally ID'd the victim as a young artist from Manhattan who'd been murdered, probably robbed, and his body dumped on Chambers property. It didn't seem to have any connection to our case. Just a sick coincidence.

Still, it's just the type of message the Mob likes to send you. We can get to you. Here's a body right on your property. You got all those cops around you twenty-four hours a day. Here's a fresh corpse right on your doorstep.

It spooked all the Benedettos, and it showed us that they were too

vulnerable there. After that, we installed the highest-grade video surveillance system throughout the transfer station. For years ahead we
knew we would have to maintain a full-time police presence on Plymouth Street, and up at the Bronx transfer station, and Sal would have
to have detectives with him every minute of the day, taking him to and
from work.

Just before the case came to trial, Tony Maz debriefed a confidential
informant who gave up some very credible information about a hit
being planned. The threat was specific. "The little fat guy under the
bridge" was how they referred to Sal. We even had information that the
assassins would be two women, non-Italians, coming at a time and place
when we'd never expect it. Then the informant said something else,
something clearly directed at me: "The Gambino family won't allow
anyone to testify against them." When Tony told him that the main witness was going to be an NYPD detective, the informant said: "Then the
undercover better watch his ass."

The trial began in New York Supreme Court, Part 88, on May 26,
1997, before the Honorable Judge Leslie Crocker Snyder. The first female justice in New York State history to preside over murder trials,
Judge Snyder, fifty-six, had a reputation for being one of the nation's
toughest judges—dubbed "the Ice Princess," for her steely demeanor
and "Judge 213," because she'd once doled out a sentence of 213 years
to a member of the murderous Wild Cowboys drug gang. Another of
her more infamous nicknames was "Judge Dread."

On May 26, prosecutor Pat Dugan, chief of the district attorney's
Rackets Bureau, set out to establish the organized-crime ties of the top
defendants by playing a videotape for the court. The television placed
before the jury box showed Joseph "Joey Cigars" Francolino and
Alphonso "Allie Shades" Malangone meeting with John Gotti, "the
Dapper Don," then boss of the Gambino crime family, in front of the
Ravenite Social Club on Mulberry Street. After hearing expert testi-

mony from former FBI supervisor Brian F. Taylor about the hierarchi-
cal structure of the Genovese and Gambino crime families, the court
was told that Dugan would be calling his star witness to the stand.

"Let me talk to you a little bit about what the proof will be with respect to Detective Richard Cowan," Dugan told the jury during his
opening statement. "You will see that he is an ordinary human being.
This isn't like any TV show. This isn't like that show *NYPD Blue* or any
other TV show that fascinates you at ten o'clock at night when you're
tired and fatigued. This man is not a Hollywood star. This man, on May
11, 1992, had no idea of what he was getting himself into.

"This isn't a situation where the police department scoured its ranks
to find the best undercover detective to infiltrate the carting industry.
He is an ordinary human being. He was a police officer with the New
York City Police Department for about eight years. At the time that Sal
Benedetto introduced him as 'Cousin Danny' he was assigned to the
Organized Crime Investigation Division for about three years. He is a
high school graduate with a few college credits. For the next two and a
half years, he *became* a carter. He learned the wastepaper business. When
he wasn't doing undercover work, he was at Chambers, fixing trucks,
fielding customer complaints, and learning the business. For the next
two and a half years, he had seventy-five meetings with these defendants and with their accomplices. No gun. No shield. Sometimes
backup police officers were blocks away. [There were] almost four hundred telephone conversations that he was involved in.

"The recordings, you will learn, are not studio quality. It's difficult to
make recordings in this city on the street and in restaurants. . . . There
were several different recording devices: Some worked, some didn't.
One one occasion, you'll find that he went to a meeting with a recording device and—as probably has happened to some of you—he locked
himself out of his car. . . . Sometimes there was no recording device.
Particularly after the assault of the driver of Paper Services up in the
Bronx, after being patted down and having his back felt and his stomach felt, there were occasions when he did not wear a recording device.

"He is an ordinary human being who, you will learn, did his job as a

New York City detective. He will be examined and cross-examined, undoubtedly. But the evidence that he gathered, along with the other evidence in this case, will prove to you that these defendants committed the crime of enterprise corruption. . . ."

After my first day on the stand, one of the court officers came back to my guarded witness room outside Part 88. The CO was smiling about something that had just happened in the courtroom.

An NYPD detective—unconnected to our case—had been watching the testimony from the back of the courtroom and began muttering to the court officers about the witness on the stand.

"Just look at this piece of shit," the detective whispered. "The way he talks with his hands, the way he keeps touching his tie—Jesus, what a fuckin' gangster."

The court officer laughed. "That's the undercover detective. He infiltrated the Mob for three years."

I stayed on the witness stand for the entire summer of 1997. My testimony—direct, redirect, cross, and recross—lasted twenty-nine consecutive days on the court calendar, which worked out to be a period from June through the end of August.

I'll never again face anything as scary as that courtroom the first day I hit the stand. It was the most intimidating collection of people I've ever seen gathered in one place. The whole tone was set from the outset by Francolino. Joe was a hard-liner every single day of trial. He would not allow any attorney for any of the defendants to go across the room and talk to a prosecutor without his expressed okay. Not one. Even there in the Centre Street courthouse, Joe's rule was absolute. From the well forward, Judge Snyder ruled. But from the well backward, Joe Francolino ruled.

When I began my testimony, it was standing room only. The Gambinos came down in force. They stacked the whole defense side of the court, all the way back: thugs, relatives, friends of thugs and relatives. Some of these three-hundred-pound hoods walked in with their ninety-pound grandmothers who hadn't left the stoop in Bensonhurst for thirty years. They all sat there mumbling "liar" under their breath, giving me the *malocchio*—the Italian horns—and mouthing the word *motherfucker.*

It was strictly a Gambino presence. Nobody was there from the Genovese side at all. Ironically, while I was on the witness stand testifying about the Chin's position as boss of the Genovese Family, Gigante himself was being tried that very week on Federal racketeering in the Eastern District in Brooklyn. It was kind of sad, because as deep and powerful a family as those West Side guys were, nobody showed up for Allie Shades. Not even his wife and his kids, not Fat Gerry or Johnny Geech or any of the guys in his crew. Joe had a whole battalion of hoods behind him. The one guy Allie had was old Rocky Cimato, his personal driver, taking him to and from the court every day in his Oldsmobile. And one day after the court proceedings, Rocky Cimato died suddenly of an aneurysm.

Joe sat like an angry statue throughout my testimony, and when our eyes would meet, I'd catch him muttering curses under his breath at me. When some of the humorous stuff came up in the tapes and even the judge herself had to let out a laugh, Joe would not show even a hint of a smile.

Allie Shades, on the other hand, was smooth as a baby's ass. You have to know Allie, I guess. He can be a mean bastard and yell like a real street thug if you cross him. But he can also show a lot of charm and good humor. For most of the trial he sat there unperturbed, like he was back at his poolside cabana at the Mirage in Las Vegas, sunning himself and smoking a Cohiba. Sometimes when Pat Dugan, the prosecutor, would play our audiotapes, the jury couldn't help but burst out in laughter. One conversation we made with Allie in Pastels Disco was soft for a long while, and everyone strained forward trying to hear, and then suddenly there's this deafening thud and Allie's voice is shouting, *"Vaffanculo!"* so loud it's like a gunshot in the courtroom.

The jury cracked up, and when I looked over at Allie, he was doubled over, holding on to the table for support.

But Allie wasn't laughing when I sat there testifying about the Mafia hierarchy, about how Vincent "Chin" Gigante was the boss of the Genovese crime family and Alphonso "Allie Shades" Malangone was a powerful *caporegime*. Allie looked like he'd give anything in the world to get his hands on me just then.

One by one, throughout the weeks of my testimony, I had to stare these guys in the eyes, point my finger, and tell the jury who they were.

"Now, do you see Phil Barretti sitting in this room?" Pat Dugan asked.

"Yes, I do."

And I pointed straight at silver-haired Barretti as he stared daggers across the courtroom.

"Now, do you see Joseph Francolino sitting in this room?"

"Yes, I do."

"Now, do you see Alphonso Malangone sitting in this room?"

And so on—down the line of defendants.

As with most racketeering cases, the majority of my trial testimony was dry and detailed, rehashing the finer evidentiary aspects of the investigation, but in nine weeks there's bound to be some lighter moments. There was that infamous tape that I'd made—that Dugan knew the jury would get a big kick out of—when I was going down to meet Frank Giovinco at the Waste Paper Association and locked myself out of my Jeep with the engine running and my thousands of dollars in extortion payments in plain view on the passenger seat.

The courtroom heard me telling Giovinco, Virzi, and D'Ambrosio about the little Puerto Rican kid who managed to break into my Jeep in seconds. When I said, "He must do it professionally," the whole club erupted in laughter. And so did the jury box.

"During the undercover case," I told the jurors, "I made mistakes just like everyone else does in life. The only difference is I tape-recorded them so you could laugh at me three years later."

Actually, the biggest laugh of the whole trial came at Angelo's expense. It was a clear recording I'd made during my sitdown with Phil Barretti and Joe Francolino at Giando Ristorante when we'd settled up our One Wall Street dispute—the beef that had started it all. At the end of the tape, Phil and I are trying to explain to Joe how the Genovese paper association bills its members. In Joe's club, and in all the other clubs, dues are calculated on a per-truck basis. That was industry standard—a guy with a bigger company pays bigger dues. But in Angelo's club, things were different: They had a flat-flee system. Joe can't believe it, and he keeps telling Phil and me that we're wrong. But we keep repeating that's the way it is with Angelo. Phil explains that Angelo specifically wants it that way because he has a fleet of a hundred trucks, the biggest in the city, and he can get away with paying the same dues as some little guy with just one truck. Joe's just dumbfounded as this sinks in, and he realizes the sneaky trick Angelo's been pulling. "Angelo, Angelo," he says, cursing under his breath. "He's got his own rules on the other side of the fence."

When the courtroom heard that tape, it was bedlam. I don't know if it was the pent-up tension of the moment, but everyone lost control. Allie Shades was slapping the table, and Phil Barretti got up from his chair, walked clear across the courtroom, just laughing his ass off. I looked at Joe and thought I caught him—for a fraction of a second— holding back the slightest curl in his upper lip.

After my eighteenth day of direct testimony, almost all the remaining defendants came running to Pat Dugan begging to plead guilty. Phil Barretti copped a plea. So did Frankie Giovinco, Patty Pecoraro, Lou Mongelli and his son Paul. Before the trial, Lou Mongelli's defense counsel, Murray Richman, had tried to argue that Mongelli was hardly a violent, multimillionaire mobster. In fact, he claimed Lou only had $4,198 in the bank. "He didn't even know what the word *cartel* meant until I told him," Richman said.

But now Richman and all those various high-priced lawyers had heard enough of my tapes and my testimony. They knew that once it was in the jurors' hands, their clients were going to be hit with some serious double-digits: maximums ending in twenty and thirty years. And if you're OCCA'd and you get that kind of time, it's mandatory that you do it in a max joint. But Pat Dugan let them plead guilty to attempted enterprise corruption, a Class C felony, waiving all possibility of appeal.

Barretti and Mongelli handed over their multimillion-dollar companies to trustees appointed by a civil court judge. Patty Pecoraro lost his string of companies, and he lost the Queens Trade Waste Association.[2]

The only guys proceeding with the trial were Allie Shades and Joe Francolino. They proved themselves to be true gangsters, through and through. They both knew they could've shaved off some prison time, but that's not the way it's done, at least not by their own rules. A real wiseguy is never supposed to cop any kind of plea.

The day all the other guys pled, I went out for lunch with Bobby O'Donahue on Mulberry Street, right behind the Supreme Court Building. Every few days Bobby and I would go eat lunch together at this nice Italian restaurant. I was facing the door, and Bobby's back was to it, and our food was just being served when I saw them.

"Aw, man," I said. "Look at this."

First it's Joe Francolino and his wife, then Lou Mongelli and his common-law-wife, coming into the restaurant. Next, only a couple of minutes behind them, it's Morgenthau himself. We're all sitting in the same space of about thirty feet. Joe, Lou, the DA, Bobby, and me. Joe and Lou weren't eating together, so they had me in a kind of crossfire, both glaring at me from different angles. I mean, if looks could kill I would have been chopped up, Glad-bagged, and thrown in the back of one of their ten-wheel packers, bound for the landfill.

Suddenly, near the end of his meal, Joe threw back his martini—and then abruptly stood up and stared at me. Bobby got up very calmly and put his hand on the butt of his gun. Joe stared at Bobby, and then he sat back down. We left the restaurant after that.

On my last day of testimony, Joe let his temper get the best of him. He'd probably had a few too many drinks over lunch, and when I finished up on the stand that afternoon, the judge made it clear they were done with my testimony. Most of the trial, I'd been trading quick glances

---

[2] All received sentences in New York State prison. Philip Barretti received 4½ to 13½ years; Frank Giovinco, 3 to 9 years; Louis Mongelli, 3 to 9 years; Paul Mongelli, 4 to 12 years; Patrick Pecoraro, 1 to 3 years.

with Joe, but now I really returned his killer stare. He was bright red in the face. I could've taken a long, circuitous route down from the stand, but to me that would've been punking out. I walked right in front of Joe, two feet away from him. I looked him right in the eye, and his lips were quivering.

Then, as soon as I left the room there was a major commotion. "I'm gonna *fuck* that guy!" and some other choice words. The court was officially in recess now, and the court officers came over and said, "Rick, you better stay here for a while. We'll take you out back. Francolino just said he was going to *get* you in front of about fifteen people." They told me that they'd heard Joe saying, "Get that motherfucker *back* on the stand!" His lawyer said, "Joe, he's been on the stand the whole summer. We had him on cross and on recross—we can't get him anymore. It's done, Joe. It's over."

Francolino started barking right in the courtroom. He got so loud that Judge Snyder had to come out from her chambers. "Is there a *problem* in here?" she said. Francolino had had conflicts with Judge Snyder from the get-go. In the first place, Joe will not recognize a woman in a position of power. And Judge Snyder isn't just any powerful woman, she's a legendary jurist: She's known for being so tough, she was even the target of an assassination plot hatched by some stock-swindler who was in the Tombs awaiting trial in front of her. Some of her critics say she's too pro-cop, but I say that's bullshit. Judge Snyder is a true legal scholar and she's fair with both sides. If you read the trial minutes, you'll see she gave Allie and Joe's attorneys a good deal of latitude in defense.

When she said, "Is there a problem here?" Joe stood up, started walking right through the well, up to the bench.

"Listen, Judge! I make it to court every day. I'm a fifty-eight-year-old man, I have a bad leg, and the other day I was a few minutes late after lunch and you bawled me out. You will show me some respect!"

The court officers who watched all this told me Judge Snyder's jaw dropped.

"Let me tell *you* something, Mr. Francolino," she said. "You are a defendant in my courtroom. You will show *me* some respect, and you will *back* away right now, or you'll be going in *there.*"

She pointed to the door that leads to the Department of Corrections lockup.

When it came Sal's turn to take the stand, he felt the heat of the wiseguys' wrath. He was trying hard not to even glance in the direction of Francolino and Malangone. He made it through one complete day of testimony, but collapsed in the hallway of the courthouse on his way out. Tony Maz and Bobby O rushed him to Downtown Beekman Hospital. Later, Sal seemed to be on the road to recovery—and was discharged for bed rest—but within forty-eight hours he'd relapsed and was in full respiratory failure.

I had a case of phlebitis in my leg," Sal recalls today.[3] "Actually, the night before I had to testify, I had big sweats and I should've gone to the hospital right then. The first day in court the leg was hurting a little bit, 'cause I was cooped up in the stand for so long. Everyone says I had a heart attack in court, but I didn't have a heart attack. What happened was, the phlebitis moved to my heart. Tony and Bobby got me into a wheelchair and raced me down on a special elevator. The trial was adjourned until Monday morning. But over the weekend out on Long Island, that's when I flat-lined. Sunday night my heart stopped twice in St. Francis Hospital. Twice they brought me back with the paddles."

After his heartbeat and breathing stabilized, he agreed to continue testifying. Since they couldn't bring Sal to the court, they brought the court to Sal. Judge Snyder, Pat Dugan, and the defense attorneys for Francolino and Malangone came to St. Francis Hospital for an unusual videotaped cross-examination to be played later, before the trial jury in Manhattan.

"They asked the Nassau County cops for protection, and Nassau

---

[3] Interview with Douglas Century, July 2001

County came out with machine guns," Sal says. "They had guys posted all around my room and down the hall with machine guns—like Elliot Ness! Judge Leslie Crocker Snyder came out and she presided over the [makeshift] courtroom in the hospital. The defense attorneys cross-examined me as tough as they could. But how tough could they be on a half-dead guy in a wheelchair who's hooked up to tubes and a heart monitor?"

You know from the testimony," Pat Dugan told the members of the jury in his summation, "that Francolino and Malangone were going to the Ravenite in 1989 and 1990—particularly Francolino at that point in time. He's going to see John Gotti with Jimmy Brown Failla. You know from the evidence that Francolino was meeting with Malangone as early as 1991. But the point I'm trying to make, from the evidence, is this: Malangone and Francolino are one and the same in terms of their criminal responsibility. They are the bosses. They are the leaders. They are the supervisors of their respective associations in this cartel. Malangone is not charged with as many crimes as Francolino because he's smart enough to allow Allocca to do his talking for him. . . . As a matter of fact, of all the leaders of the associations, it's Malangone that is the most careful. But there is no question, from the evidence, that he has the power, he has the control, over the Kings County Trade Waste Association and the property rights system. . . .

"They both derive their power from the same source. They derive their power from the Mafia. The only distinction between the two men is that Malangone is not a carter. He's the manager of some discotheque. Now, of course, the evidence begs the question: How do you suppose that the manager of the discotheque became the administrator of the Kings County Trade Waste Association when there's no evidence he has any carting experience? I think the evidence tells you what the answer to that question is. . . .

"Disputes have to be resolved by these associations. But the leaders of the associations, in order to resolve these disputes, have to have a reputation for power, have to have the reputation for fear, in order to enforce the rules. That's where organized crime steps in. Organized crime fills the leadership positions and resolves the disputes because of people's fear of organized crime—the fear of violence, physical and otherwise, that the Mafia has a reputation for. . . .

"It's pretty clear from the evidence, ladies and gentlemen, that the Genovese crime family runs the Waste Paper Association. Tamily told you two things that are substantially corroborated by other evidence in the case. He told you that Vincent Gigante, the Chin, controls Local 958 and that the carters have to pay five thousand dollars a year to Ponte in order to ensure labor peace. Tamily told you in the tapes that it's the Chin that controls the association through Ponte and through Giovinco. Corroboration exists for this based upon surveillance . . . that this person by the name of Palmeri who was the business agent for the Waste Paper Association and another person by the name of Esposito had a close relationship with Vincent Gigante. The surveillances show that Ponte and Giovinco are people who almost daily attend the Waste Paper Association. The surveillances show . . . that when Vincent Gigante moved to 505 LaGuardia Place, it was Palmeri and Esposito that were consistently visiting him every day and then going directly across to Sullivan Street, communicating with members of the Genovese crime family who operate out of that social club.

"The Genovese crime family also runs the Kings County Trade Waste Association through Alphonso Malangone. You heard expert testimony that he is a *capo* in the Genovese crime family. . . .

"It's also pretty clear that the Gambino family runs the Association of Trade Waste Removers of Greater New York. You've heard testimony that Failla is a *capo* in that family and has run that association for decades. From evidence you're able to glean that Francolino was groomed to succeed Failla and that he was observed meeting on numerous occasions with John Gotti and Salvatore Gravano at the Ravenite Social Club.

"This evidence is relevant to show you the reasonableness of fear. The evidence shows you this: That it is a commonly understood fact within the industry, that there is no need for explicit threats, that everyone knows what they are, and the reputation for violence that is behind them and supporting them. The defense effort to kind of laugh it off as some kind of street-corner boys club is pure cynicism in the face of a terrible fact. That organized crime is insidious, that it's well-structured, and that it controls these associations. . . ."

On October 21, 1997, following a grueling eight-month trial, the case against Joseph Francolino, Alphonso Malangone, Duffy Waste & Recycling, and the Association of Trade Waste Removers of Greater New York was in the hands of twelve New York County jurors.

After twelve days of deliberation, Judge Snyder received word that the jury had reached a verdict. The defendants were convicted of so many counts of enterprise corruption, grand larceny, extortion, coercion, and Donnelly Act restraint-of-trade violations that, as the next morning's *Daily News* reported: "It took forty-five minutes for the jury forewoman to say all the 'guiltys.'"[4]

On October 23, Mayor Rudy Giuliani was at the World Trade Center to deliver a speech titled "Freeing the Economy from Organized Crime and Restoring Open, Competitive Markets." His speech dealt with the impact of the unprecedented carting investigation:

> *The day before yesterday, a jury convicted two of the leaders of the Mafia cartel and four corporate defendants for their roles in holding New York City's private carting industry hostage. The organized crime leaders, Joseph Francolino, Sr., and [Alphonso] Malangone, were found guilty of 44 criminal counts between them, including the top charge of enterprise corruption. . . . In the past, cynics looked at similar rulings and said, "That's just the way New York City is." They thought that the carting industry . . . would always be under Mob influence. . . . Today, we can look at this Tuesday's convictions with the confidence that these organized crime leaders will not be replaced by other Mobsters who will keep the basic structure of corruption in place.*

---

[4] New York *Daily News,* the, October 22, 1997. "Two More Fall in Garbage Racket," by Barbara Ross

On November 18, Judge Snyder sentenced Joe Francolino to a prison term of ten to thirty years, to be served in a maximum-security prison, and ordered him to pay a personal fine of $900,000. The Greater New York Trade Waste Association—the "club" Francolino had inherited from Jimmy Brown—was fined more than $9 million. In revoking Francolino's $500,000 bail, Judge Snyder said: "There's overwhelming evidence that you held the entire city in a massive criminal vise."

On January 12, 1998, Judge Snyder sentenced sixty-year-old Alphonso Malangone to a prison term of five to fifteen years and fined him $200,000. She showed Malangone slightly more leniency than she'd shown Francolino: Because he was already scheduled to undergo eye surgery, Allie Shades was released on bail pending appeal.

In the months after the first mass arrest, based on my undercover role and evidence discovered during the search warrants, the Manhattan DA's office brought down a second and third wave of indictments—known as Carting II and Carting III—bringing racketeering and bid-rigging charges against a total of seventy-two individuals and companies.

The two defendants accused in the most violent aspects of the case, Raymond Ramos and Steve Georgison, were separately convicted. In 1996, Ramos pled guilty in New York County Supreme Court in connection to the 1992 arson at Chambers Paper Fibres and received a sentence of three and a half to seven years. Steve Georgison was prosecuted in Bronx County for the near fatal attack on Chambers driver Alex Fernandez on Barretto Street. In 2001, Georgison was convicted of first-degree assault and other felonies and received a sentence of twelve years to life.

In the most complex investigation and prosecution of Robert Morgenthau's twenty-one years as the district attorney of New York County, his conviction rate was 100 percent: Every individual, corporate entity, and trade association indicted in Operation Wasteland either pled guilty or was convicted by trial jury. A total of $43 million in fines was paid by the defendants.

Under the Giuliani administration, the City of New York created the Trade Waste Commission and passed Local Law 42, which states that "it shall be unlawful for any person to operate a business for the purpose of collecting trade waste without having obtained a license from the Trade Waste Commission."

I was called to testify as a witness dozens of times during Trade Waste Commisssion hearings. To date, several hundred individuals and companies with criminal backgrounds or known Mob ties, though not indicted during Operation Wasteland, have been denied licensing by the Commission.

In one clean sweep it was gone: the Mob candy store, the Mafia cartel that had been in place since Jimmy Squillante and Albert Anastasia saw the golden vision of a future heaped in garbage.

Because of that one freak encounter on Plymouth Street, so many people's lives changed forever. Sal Benedetto knows he's got a target on his head for the rest of his life. Sally's in danger every single minute of every single day. And if the Mob does get its hands on him, it's not just going to shoot him in the back of the head with a .22 and stick him in a Dumpster—it's going to make it ugly, real torture.

It's not just that Sal's cooperation with the NYPD and my testimony put guys like Joe Francolino and Allie Shades in prison for decades—that's an occupational hazard of being a wiseguy. Remember what Frank Giovinco once said to me? "I couldn't give a *fuck* if I go away for the next hundred years. That's the way I gotta think."

Much, much worse was the fact that we'd cost the Mob its money-making machine, that we took away the livelihoods of organized-crime figures and Mobbed-up companies. These were family fortunes that had been built up for generations. Angelo Ponte's company went back to 1909. Lou Mongelli and Phil Barretti couldn't stop talking about how their kids were fourth generation coming into the industry. These were dynasties—multimillion-dollar-a-year dynasties—that these guys had always expected their grandsons and great-grandsons would inherit. On June 22, 1995—*poof*—all gone.

Sal's been given the option of Witness Protection, but he's always refused. He refuses to give up his freedom, refuses to give up the paper business. That's the only life he's known, and he's just going to keep being Sally Skates.

In 1998, after all the convictions, there was a *Dateline NBC* story that, typically, exaggerated the whole BFI role in the investigation. They kept referring to "the BFI undercover," never mentioning the fact that Morgenthau's investigator inside BFI never once took the witness stand in the trial. Neither did Bill Ruckelshaus or any other executive from Browning-Ferris.

That's one thing that left a bad taste for me, Tony, Sal, and everyone else in the NYPD who worked their asses off to make this case happen: how this gigantic Texas company whose role was at *best* a minor complement to the NYPD investigation—and, quite frankly, was far more often a hindrance—somehow ended up getting the lion's share of the credit in the press. BFI kept being described in articles as "the fearless heavyweight national company" that dared to take down the Mob cartel. These *Dateline* producers even got hold of our NYPD videotape—tape that Detectives Vito Aleo and Joe Chimienti shot showing me being surrounded and "motherfucked" in the South Bronx by Steve Georgison and Tommy Oddo. But NBC gave you the impression I was assisting BFI in its investigation.

They kept talking about the physical danger to BFI's employees and executives, and the kicker came when they hauled out this writer for *Fortune* magazine, Richard Behar, to sit on camera and actually say that Bill Ruckelshaus "had more guts than most people I've ever seen in the business world." I turned to my wife and said, "That's 'cause this asshole's never met Sal Benedetto."

Ever since the case came down, my wife and I have lived far away from the city. We've taken steps to make it very difficult to find us. My own eight-year-old son doesn't even know that I'm a detective: When he gets older, of course, I'll have to explain everything to him from the beginning.

I'll always feel some guilt about putting my wife and son though all this aggravation. The Mob has a memory like an elephant, and we've both had to come to terms with the fact that because of my role in bringing down the cartel, we'll have to live like this—in the shadows— perhaps for the rest of our lives.

Am I personally afraid? No. Let's just say I'm *careful*. My tapes and testimony put Joe Francolino and Allie Shades in maximum-security prisons—not a real pleasant place to be, especially for guys coming into their mid-sixties and seventies. They certainly still have the power to come after me, but I doubt either of them would make a move now. The real danger is elsewhere. A lot of the young guys coming up in the Mob today are crazy, not disciplined, and the situation is always unpredictable.

As a cop, you always feel you can take care of yourself, but you can't take care of *everyone* around you. One of the scariest things happened right after we took the case down. My parents are fairly visible people in their community, and I'm named after my dad. Just after the indictments, during discovery, some documents were turned over to the defense with a tiny but unfixable mistake: The very first affadavit I'd signed as an undercover was inadvertently turned over unredacted. So the name *Richard Cowan,* which was blacked out in hundreds of other places, was left clearly visible for the defense on one document. The page was a detailed conversation I'd had with Frank Giovinco. It was now obvious to the defense that the undercover, the guy posing for years as Danny Benedetto, was really named Richard Cowan.

Suddenly, in the summer of '95, my parents started to receive strange phone calls—and then a black Cadillac with strange-looking characters would park in front of their house, watching it for days. Sometimes there would be one guy, sometimes two; always large, Italian-looking men, with their hair combed back. My mother would call to let me know they were on her block. "They're back! They're in front of the house again."

My mother is one tough and resourceful Irish lady. She had her hands full raising four rambunctious boys and, once we were out of school, she went back to work full time. She certainly wasn't scared by these mobsters. Once she realized that they were watching her house, she rushed out on the lawn, trying to get the license plate. The first time she was blocked—ironically enough, by a garbage truck—and could only get a partial number. The second time she ran out with a pen and paper to get the plate, but the driver of the Cadillac saw her, took off, screeching its tires.

Just like with my wife, this is something I feel bad about. My mother and father didn't do anything to hurt the Mafia. My parents shouldn't have to deal with Mob guys showing up in their neighborhood.

One weekend, after the case came down, I went down to visit my parents at Seaside Heights on the Jersey Shore. My parents were curious about how I'd infiltrated this Mob-run industry for years. They could see that I was tense, I hadn't been sleeping, and I leveled with them about everything.

"This is gonna be a massive trial," I said. "I feel like it's taking over my life."

We were sitting on this sunporch of a little weekend house. It was around sunset and we were looking out at the bay, drinking cold beer. I was smoking a Dominican Casa Blanca and I had on the diamond pinky ring my wife got me for our wedding anniversary. I could see that my parents were looking at me kind of funny—my dad kept shaking his head, amazed that I'd even been able to insert myself into the role of Danny.

"How'd you ever get inside there in the first place?" he said.

"Well, this guy named Sal had his truck blown up, and when I got down there to interview him, these two thugs suddenly show up and one has a gun and then Sal blurts out, 'Hey, that's just Cousin Danny. . . .'"

I sat there on the porch with a Budweiser, telling him the whole story about this garbage underworld I'd infiltrated, all these crazy characters I'd come across—an ex–World War II paratrooper, an ex-NFL star, a Knight of Malta, the sunglass-wearing night manager of Pastels Discotheque, the Chin's own knockaround kid . . . Mikey Five Brothers, who was always under a sunlamp, and Patty Pecoraro, who looked like Alfred Hitchcock, and Patty Piccininni, who looked like Las Vegas Elvis . . .

I told him about red-in-the-face Dominick Vulpis and Philly Barretti almost coming to blows with me in the Americana Diner, and Mongelli's brigade of thugs with baseball bats and ax handles and lead pipes, ready to open my head up in the Bronx . . .

"How the hell did you make it out of there?"

I told him how I found protection, how I built a relationship with this powerful gangster in the Gambino Family named Joseph "Joey Cigars" Francolino. I told my dad how it was Joe who put an end to all the threats and craziness. "He said, 'Don't you worry, Danny—you send 'em right to me. You tell 'em to come see Joey. There won't be any tough-guy tactics once I talk to 'em.'"

"Really? He said that to you?"

"Yes."

I told him that once I had Joe "schooling me," there wasn't a garbage guy in the city who dared to pull any shit with me. "'If anybody tries to bully you, Danny, it's like they're trying to bully *me,* and you gotta be a hell of a man to get past me. You're gonna need a *steamroller* to get past me.'"

"He told you all that? He really helped you out?"

"In a criminal sense, yeah, he did help me out. He became my friend—in a *criminal* sense. He went to bat for me."

"And you gotta *face* this guy in the courtroom?"

"Yes."

Then I started to think how strange it all was: Here my father is from the same generation as Joey Cigars and Allie Shades, but they couldn't be more opposite. These wiseguys never did a hard day's work in their lives. Their whole lives are one big scheming, scamming, rip-off session, from sunrise to sunset: gambling, shylocking, extorting everyone in sight.

My dad's worked two jobs simultaneously most of his life. Even into his sixties he's putting in six days a week. He's been a proud blue-collar guy, a union card–carrying hard hat. He's still very strong—he was an athlete growing up, played semiprofessional baseball—and he always liked working the most physically challenging jobs: in steel factories, welding, construction. Any job where you get your fingernails dirty and your palms good and callused. He's got a face like the map of Ireland, all red and windburned from being outside on construction sites.

He was sipping his long-necked Budweiser, looking out at the bay with me, mulling over everything I was telling him about Joe Francolino being like my criminal father figure, my wiseguy protector, shielding me from all the sharks out there.

Then he asked me the question that's hardest to answer—the question that *everyone* always asks me.

"Do you feel bad for this guy, Rick? Do you feel guilty? I mean, he was protecting you, like you said. Helping you out?"

"You have to understand—Joe was protecting me and being my friend as long as I followed his rules, Dad. But the minute I broke his rules, the minute I showed any defiance, believe me, I'd see a *different* side of Joe."

"But do you feel, I dunno—like you stabbed him in the back?"

"You know, that's been on my mind a lot. Because, I mean, I'm a cop. And everyone thinks to be a cop you must be heartless and have no conscience. But I'm a human being and I've got the same thoughts as everybody else. Sure, I feel a little bit bad for this guy."

Most of the other guys we locked up—especially guys like Phil Barretti and Lou Mongelli—I feel no qualms about what I did. I'm 100 percent convinced that New York City is a better place without them on the streets. Joe, too, but I have to admit, at least Joe had some likable qualities. I enjoyed his company. He was a criminal, sure, but within his criminal world, he carried himself with dignity. He was a straight shooter, unlike a lot of the other hoods. One of the things I admired about Joe was his directness. He was just the opposite of a politician, saying phony things to please people. "Sometimes you may not like what you hear," Joe said that night in Pierino's. "You're gonna hear it *regardless*. Whether you like it or not."

My dad and me watched the yachts out on the bay, the kind of fifty-

and sixty-footers that most working stiffs never set foot on. But gangsters like Joe Francolino and Allie Shades and Angelo Ponte could live the good life—drinking booze, puffing cigars, barking commands into flip phones—out on the ocean every weekend. All of a sudden it was so real to me again: I could see Joe and me on one of our walk-and-talks outside the club on West Broadway, both in our double-breasted suits and cashmere overcoats, smoking Te-Amo Toros and scheming up a storm.

"Joe Francolino is the most confident person I've ever been around," I said. "He is so proud to be—the word he uses to describe himself—a *gangster*. The guy directing traffic. The fuckin' boss. Joe Francolino is what he is. A made member of the Mafia—a wiseguy in the Gambino crime family. And I am what I am, Dad. A New York City Police detective. Joe wouldn't want his life any other way. Neither would I."

EPILOGUE

DOUGLAS CENTURY

In the the years following the takedown of New York's carting cartel, it often seemed that there wasn't enough credit to be spread among New York's lawmakers. Politicians as diverse as Mayor Rudy Giuliani and Public Advocate Mark Green each championed his own role in the cartel-busting case, referring to it as "the biggest tax break" in recent civic history. In a speech delivered during his 1997 reelection campaign, the mayor recalled:

> Two weeks ago, I was walking along Columbus Avenue—it was after the first mayoral debate. I noticed my signs in the window of a Chinese restaurant, so I stopped in to say hello. The owner of the restaurant and I started talking, and he said to me, "I want to thank you for reducing

*taxes." I said, "You mean the commercial rent tax?"—that was my first
reaction, because we've reduced or eliminated the commercial rent tax all
throughout the city. He said, "No, not that. . . . I'm talking about
the Mob tax. Because you've ended the Mob tax, my carting bill has been
reduced from $1,000 per month to $150 per month."[1]*

During Mark Green's unsuccessful 2001 bid for the mayoralty, campaign literature on the Internet boasted that Green's number-one ac-
complishment as both the city's commissioner of consumer affairs and
public advocate was his role in ending the Mob cartel's reign:

*As Consumer Affairs Commissioner, Green opened the New York mar-
ket to national carting firms, driving down prices through competition. As
Public Advocate, Green introduced the first bill to restructure the carting
industry and worked with the Mayor and City Council to pass the 1996
Giuliani-Green bill that led to a $500 million a year cut in the "garbage
tax" for all city businesses.*

Revisionism crept into the recollections of some; those unfamiliar
with the minutiae of the investigation could easily assume that there'd
been a handful of visionary commanders behind the lines: Rudy Giuliani, Mark Green, Bob Morgenthau, Bill Ruckelshaus. . . . In a 1997
Reader's Digest story, "Undercover Against the Mob," the district attorney recalled giving an ambitious pep talk to the troops after hearing
some of the NYPD's early recordings:

*"We can make a case for simple extortion," Morgenthau had said.
"But we won't do our job right if we don't take down the whole organization. Let's see what kind of fish Detective Cowan can catch."*

---

[1] "Freeing the Economy from Organized Crime and Restoring Open, Competitive
Markets," speech by Mayor Rudolph Giuliani, October 23, 1997

Others, however, remember a slightly different attitude coming from the district attorney's office.

"I wish you could've been there the day, midway through the case, when John O'Brien and me went into Pat Dugan's office for a briefing," recalls retired Lieutenant Tony Mazziotti. "I said, 'Okay, these are our targets: We're gonna get Frank Giovinco, we're gonna get Angelo Ponte, we're gonna get Allie Malangone, we're gonna get Joe Francolino . . .' Everyone from the DA's side scoffed—I mean, looks of sheer contempt on their faces. I could just imagine what they said to each other when we left. 'These dumb cops actually think they can *pull* this off!'

"And to be fair, I'm not sure if *we* really believed we could get to all these guys. Law enforcement had been gunning for the carting cartel since the '50s—why should we succeed when so many excellent federal and state investigations had failed?"

Mazziotti chalks up the success of the investigation to persistence, but also a good deal of luck. "In order for this thing to work, you had to have four things in place," he says. "Number one, you had to have an undercover who knew how to blend in and could learn the jargon, could stand toe-to-toe with guys who'd been in the business fifty years. Number two, you needed a businessman with a white-horse company that had been around for generations and who was brave enough to cooperate with law enforcement. Number three, you needed a police administration in place that understood the scope and perspective of what it meant to crack this case. And number four, you needed divine providence to bring those things together at the exact same moment."

Former New York City Police Commissioner Bill Bratton—whose administration's policies are still credited with spearheading the unprecedented drop in crime in the mid to late 1990s—and who departed his post in 1995 after a well-publicized falling-out with Mayor Giuliani—today sees Operation Wasteland as a case study of the way in which a single detective's intuition and street sense can ignite a sprawling police investigation affecting the lives of millions.

"The scope of the case is so enormous that everybody and his brother, from the mayor on down, *did* get involved on some level," Bratton told me in early 2001. "But some people would have you believe that an investigation against the cartel had been moving forward for years. That's just not the case. I sat in on many briefings when the investigation was in progress and the simple fact is this: Rick was the catalyst, using his own creativity and ingenuity, every step of the way. When those characters came down to Brooklyn that day to intimidate the businessman he was interviewing, if Rick had done *anything* other than he did, this case would never have gone anywhere. And I'm certain that the carting cartel would still be in place today."

According to industry analysts, by ridding the marketplace of grossly inflated Mob fees, New York City's carting costs fell instantly by an average of 40 percent. (Some dramatically more: The Empire Blue Cross–Blue Shield building at 622 Third Avenue had been paying $650,000 a year; its carting costs fell to under $80,000. The World Trade Center had been paying $3 million; its costs fell to $600,000.) Estimates vary, but most place the annual savings to New York's economy at between $500 and $640 million.

But in some respects, the true cost is incalculable. "It was an extraordinary toll," Pat Dugan said during an NBC television interview. "We will never be able to estimate the number of businesses that were unsuccessful because of the thievery, because of the gluttony, because of the greed, of these carting companies."

Today, the commercial waste of the New York metropolitan area is largely collected by a few national companies, and by dozens of smaller New York–based independents with no organized-crime ties—Chambers Paper Fibres, among them.

Ironically, those big blue trucks that arrived in Gotham to such fanfare are no longer seen on its streets. Before the Manhattan district attorney's office had even brought the cartel case to trial, BFI, Morgenthau's much ballyhooed investigative partner, found itself the target of several major federal probes for unlawful monopolistic and environmental crimes. On February 15, 1996, BFI and WMX Technologies, the parent of Waste Management, settled Department of Justice charges of "unfair competition through restrictive contracting" in Georgia, Iowa, Louisiana, and Tennessee. Without admitting wrongdoing, both companies entered into a consent decree with the Department of Justice, paying $1-million penalties each.

On March 7, 1997, after a joint investigation by the Environmental Protection Agency, the FBI, and the Department of Justice, BFI Services Group, Inc., a wholly owned subsidiary of Browning-Ferris Industries, Inc., agreed to pay over $5 million in fines and restitution in West Chester, Pennsylvania, for illegal disposal of wastewater treatment sludge from 1989 to 1992. Previously, BFI had pled guilty to a twenty-three-count federal indictment charging them with conspiracy, mail fraud, and Clean Water Act violations involving the illegal disposal of the sludge at five plants in Pennsylvania and Delaware.

On February 2, 1998, Waste Management and BFI announced their decision to stop competing against one another in twelve major United States markets. In the face of diminished profits, a massive wave of mega-mergers swept the solid-waste industry: The nationals began swallowing one another like cannibalistic whales. Waste Management and USA Waste completed an $18-billion consolidation in 1998, and in March 1999, Browning-Ferris Industries, the trash giant that had started as a one-truck operation in Houston, was bought out by the much smaller, Arizona-based Allied Waste Industries, Inc., for $9.1 billion. In many American markets, municipalities were left with but one choice for their waste-hauling needs.

Meet the new boss, same as the old boss? New York newspaper editorialists began to wonder if a new, more corporate monopoly system had merely replaced the Mob cartel—if the city hadn't chased three hundred foxes from the henhouse, only to let in two or three lions.

Sal Benedetto, one of the few businessmen with firsthand experience competing against both the Mob and the national conglomerates, gave me his succinct and characteristically wry viewpoint: "Look," Sal said, "the only difference between the majors and the boys is that the majors don't actually kill you."

The sweeping arrests and seizures of Operation Wasteland dealt New York's Cosa Nostra families a crippling economic blow; having lost their golden goose, mobsters began scrambling for other sources of illegal revenue. On February 10, 1997, Selwyn Raab reported in an A-1 story in *The New York Times:* "Mafia crime families are switching increasingly to white-collar crimes" with a focus on "small Wall Street brokerage houses." According to the experts cited in Raab's story, "The Mafia's entry into the securities markets was spurred by its reported loss of $500 million a year in profits from the dissolution of its garbage-hauling cartels, as well as its reported loss of $50 million a year in profits following its eviction from the Fulton Fish Market."

In the summer of 1999, Jimmy Brown Failla, the eighty-year-old *caporegime,* died of cancer in a Fort Worth prison hospital. His body was flown home from Texas and his wake was held on his native Staten Island, at Azzara Funeral Home, where, by bizarre coincidence, a relative of an FBI agent was also being waked.[2] For a while the Failla family thought of moving the wake to another location, but they settled on having Azzara's move Jimmy's casket to the back of the funeral home. Throughout the two-day wake, FBI agents and their families were on one end, staring warily at acting Gambino family boss Peter Gotti, *capos* Joseph "Joe Butch" Corrao, George DeCicco, Louis "Big Lou" Vallario and members from the other crime families who came to pay their respects. Even in death, Jimmy Brown had the ability to create a spectacle.

While Angelo Ponte was serving his two-to-six-year sentence in a New York State prison, Ponte's Steakhouse had undergone a $2-million renovation, reopened and rechristened as F. illi Ponte Ristorante ("Home of the Angry Lobster"). In the front lobby today, a framed black-and-white picture shows the family patriarch, Vincent, circa 1947,

_____

[2] As reported by writer Jerry Capeci in his online column, *Gang Land,* August 12, 1999

flanked by his babyfaced sons. In Angelo's absence, F. illi Ponte has remained a meeting place for the well-heeled and the boldfaced. In
October 1999, when the New York Yankees won their unprecedented
twenty-fifth World Series, Joe Torre, Don Zimmer, and the Bronx
Bombers took limos down to TriBeCa for their victory party there. A
replica of that historic World Series trophy is proudly displayed in F. illi
Ponte's bar.

And by now, HBO's saga about the garbage gangsters of North Jersey, *The Sopranos,* had been acclaimed by *The New York Times* as "the
greatest work of American popular culture in the last quarter century," while Eddie Tamily, one of the real-life gangsters who'd "owned"
HBO—or at least been "caretaking it for Matty the Horse"—was away
on an upstate excursion doing one and a half to four. Now nearly seventy, talkative Tamily was upbeat about the turn of events. "Prison, ah,
it's *beautiful,*" he was heard to say. "I shoulda went twenty years ago. I
lost thirty-five pounds. I got my blood pressure down. I got my choles-
terol down. I feel *great.*"

On September 10, 2001, Rick and I were down in TriBeCa ourselves,
putting a little shoe leather and cigar smoke into this book. We passed F.
illi Ponte, walked by 511 Canal Street, former site of the Waste Paper
Association, the first of the Mobbed-up clubs Rick infiltrated. As we
finished our tour, we were drenched by one of the hardest rains of the
season. One of those fierce, cool, almost tropical rains that leaves the
streets of Manhattan looking fresh and pristine.

Twelve hours later we were all living in a different America. The
Twin Towers had been brought down, F-18s were circling the New
York skyline, thousands were dead and missing, and all those clean corners of lower Manhattan—One Wall Street, Trinity churchyard, most
of TriBeCa—were blanketed in dust and debris.

In the days after the September 11 attack, although security issues
have long prevented him from working the streets of New York, Rick
managed to get into that maelstrom. He fought to get time on the

"bucket brigade" of firemen, cops, and construction workers looking for signs of life buried in Ground Zero.

For the past few years Rick has been assigned to the FBI Task Force, and he soon found himself working on Pent-Bomb, the Pentagon and World Trade Center terrorism investigation. After years of being a star witness in various organized-crime trials and hearings in New York, Rick was back in the trenches—a cog in the largest criminal investigation in American history. Another detective chasing leads.

"I've never seen the various branches of law enforcement standing shoulder-to-shoulder in such a focused effort," he says of his work alongside the FBI, INS, and local police. "This is the biggest thing of my lifetime—and this is not running down street criminals or wiseguys. This is the enemy of the United States."

And his alter ego? Is Danny Benedetto dead? No—merely dormant. Every few weeks, when Rick calls up Sal to check on his welfare or arrange a rendezvous in a top-secret location, you can catch a conversation starting with the words: "Hey Cuz—it's Dan here. . . ."

—NEW YORK CITY, 2002

GLOSSARY

administration: the upper-level power structure of an organized-crime family, composed of the boss, underboss, and *consigliere*.

associate: someone who works with wiseguys, but who hasn't been sworn in as a member of the family. Also called "connected guy."

beef: a complaint or disagreement within the organization, usually discussed during a sitdown with higher-ups.

big earner: someone who makes a lot of money for an organized-crime family.

borgata: a crime family.

boss: the head of the crime family; he is the only one who gives permission to "whack" or "make" someone, and he makes money from all family operations; synonyms: don, chairman.

button: a "made" member of the Mafia; a soldier, wiseguy, goodfella.

capo: ranking member of a family who heads a crew (or group) of soldiers; a skipper, short for *capodecina* ("boss of ten") or *caporegime.*

cleaning: taking the necessary steps (driving around, stopping in various locations) to avoid being followed.

clip: to murder; synonym: whack.

comare: a Mafia mistress; *goumare, goumada,* or goom (in slang pronunciation).

Commission, The: the Mafia "ruling body," typically a panel made up of the bosses of the five New York families: Gambino, Genovese, Lucchese, Colombo, and Bonanno and representatives from other American organized-crime families.

compare: crony, close pal, buddy; goombah (in slang pronunciation), literally "godfather" in Italian.

consigliere: the counselor in a crime family; advises boss and handles disputes within the ranks.

contract: a murder assignment.

Cosa Nostra: Italian for "this thing of ours"; a Mob family; the American Mafia.

crew: a group of soldiers that takes orders from a *capo.*

cugine: a young tough guy looking to be made; a wannabe.

earner: someone whose expertise is making a lot of money for the family.

friend of mine: introduction of a third person who is not a member of the family but who can be vouched for by a family member.

friend of ours: introduction of one made member to another.

fugazy: slang for "fake."

goombah, goomba: slang for the Italian *compare;* plural: *goombata.*

goumare, goumadah, goom: girlfriend; see COMARE.

hot place: a location suspected of being the target of law enforcement or surveillance.

joint, the: prison; synonyms: the can, the pen, go away to college.

made: to be sworn into La Cosa Nostra; synonyms: to be "straightened out," to "get your button."

nut, the: Mob slang for "the bottom line"; also, the gross profit figure.

OCCA: the Organized Crime Control Act, New York State's version of the federal RICO statutes.

off the record: an action taken without the knowledge or approval of the family.

omertà: the code of silence and one of the premier vows taken when being sworn in to a family. Violation is punishable by death.

on the record: an action sanctioned by the family.

piece: a gun.

pinched: arrested.

points: interest or percentage that must be paid, often as tribute to organized-crime figures.

rat: a member who violates OMERTÁ; synonyms: snitch, stool pigeon, canary.

shylock: someone who lends Mob money at an exorbitant interest rate.

sitdown: a formal meeting to settle disputes.

skim: tax-free profits, as in the money taken that is not reported to the IRS.

skipper: a CAPO.

stand-up guy: someone who refuses to rat no matter what the pressure, offer, or threat.

vig: the interest payment on a loan from a loan shark (short for "vigorish"); synonym: juice.

walk-and-talk, take a walk: to conduct a sensitive discussion while striding up and down the block to avoid being overheard by eavesdropping devices.

whack: to murder; synonym: clip.

BIBLIOGRAPHY

Capeci, Jerry and Gene Mustain. *Gotti: Rise and Fall*. New York: Onyx Books, 1996.

Fried, Albert. *The Rise and Fall of the Jewish Gangster in America*. New York: Columbia University Press, 1980.

Gotti, John. *The Gotti Tapes*. Foreword by Ralph Blumenthal; afterword by John Miller. New York: Random House, 1992.

Jacobs, James B. with Colleen Friel and Robert Radick. *Gotham Unbound: How New York was Liberated from the Grip of Organized Crime*. New York: New York University Press, 1999.

Kennedy, Robert F. *The Enemy Within: The McClellan Committee's Crusade Against Jimmy Hoffa and Corrupt Labor Unions*. New York: Harper & Brothers, 1960.

Kwitny, Jonathan. *Vicious Circles: The Mafia in the Marketplace*. New York: Norton, 1979.

Lardner, James, and Thomas Repetto. *NYPD: A City and Its Police*. New York: Henry Holt, 2002.

Maas, Peter. *Underboss: Sammy the Bull Gravano's Story of Life in the Mafia*. New York: HarperCollins, 1997.

———. *The Valachi Papers*. New York: Putnam Publication Group, 1968.

McClellan, John L. *Crime Without Punishment*. New York: Duell, Sloan and Pearce, 1962.

Miller, Benjamin. *Fat of the Land: Garbage in New York, The Last Two Hundred Years*. New York: Four Walls Eight Windows, 2000.

Mustain, Gene, and Jerry Capeci. *Murder Machine: A True Story of Murder, Madness and the Mafia*. New York: Onyx Books, 1992.

The People of the State of New York v. Association of Trade Waste Removers of Greater New York, et al. New York Supreme Court. Docket No. 5614/95.

Pileggi, Nicholas. *Wiseguy: Life in a Mafia Family*. New York: Pocket Books, 1985.

Puzo, Mario. *The Godfather*. New York: Signet, 1969.

Sanitation and Recycling Industry, Inc. v. City of New York. United States Court of Appeals for the Second District. Docket No. 96-7788.

Shawcross, Tim. *The War Against the Mafia: The Inside Story of a Deadly Struggle Against the Mob*. New York: HarperCollins, 1995.

Smith, John L. *Running Scared: The Life and Treacherous Times of Las Vegas Casino King Steve Wynn*. New York: Four Walls Eight Windows, 2001.

Volkman, Ernest. *Gangbusters: The Destruction of America's Last Great Mafia Dynasty*. New York: HarperCollins, 1998.

NOTE ON OTHER SOURCES

This book is primarily the reflection of Detective Richard Cowan's extensive consensual tape recordings, notes, and memories. The text has been supplemented with interviews that Douglas Century conducted with Salvatore Benedetto; retired NYPD Lieutenant Anthony Mazziotti; former New York City Police Commissioner William Bratton; and J. Bruce Mouw, former FBI supervisor of the Gambino Squad in New York.

For the historical sections dealing with the rise and fall of Vincent J. Squillante, the origins of the carting cartel, and the hearings of the Senate Select Committee on Improper Activities in the Labor or Management Field, we have drawn on the contemporaneous coverage of *The New York Times* and the New York *Daily News* found in The New York Public Library.

For the coverage of Detective Cowan's role in the Operation Wasteland investigation and trial, we have referred to the reportage in the following newspapers, magazines, and journals: the *New York Times,* the New York *Daily News, The Wall Street Journal,* the *New York Post, Newsday, The Village Voice,* the London *Times, Fortune, Reader's Digest,* and *The New York Law Journal.*

ACKNOWLEDGMENTS

Foremost, Rick would like to thank his wife, parents, and family for being so understanding and supportive over the long, grueling years of this investigation and the writing of the book. Doug would like to thank his wife, parents, and family for their constant encouragement and support.

In addition, we could not have written this book without the unflagging support and keen editorial eyes of our publishing team.

Several individuals who played a role in Rick's police career or provided encouragement during the writing process sadly did not live to see this book's publication. New York County District Attorney's Office Senior Investigator Bobby O'Donahue took an invaluable leading role in the investigation; without Bobby O's diligence, the case could never have proceeded as far as it did. Billy "Crazy Horse" Aronstam, Rick's old partner from the Sixty-Seventh Precinct, was another great cop who died too young. Johnny Tuzzio, lifelong Chambers Paper Fibres, Inc., employee, was a good friend to Rick throughout the years of the investigation. Doug's uncle, Abe Levy—a Brooklyn-born World War II vet, avid reader and lover of true Mob stories—died a few months before the book was completed, eagerly awaiting its publication. And Rick's younger brother, Jim Cowan, died tragically during a car-jacking as the book was being finished; Jimmy had often declined Rick's offer to read a draft of the manuscript as he wanted to wait to enjoy the published book.

All are sorely missed.

Rick would personally like to thank numerous individuals for their support during the investigation, trial, and subsequent years.

From the Organized Crime Investigations Division, special thanks go out to Inspectors Kenny O'Brien and John Regan for their leadership during the case. They understood the unique toll my undercover work might have on my family and they took department action to help out—often unprecedented measures.

Thanks to OCID Lieutenant Tony Mazziotti: a rock-solid friend; a cop with a heart of gold. Tony Maz and Bobby O were my seven-day-a-week, 24-hour-a-day support system throughout this investigation. I could not have done this case without Tony as my boss.

Thanks to OCID Detectives at Headquarters One: John "B.T." Prindle; Joe Lentini; Kevin Dunleavy; Michael Sheahan; Harry Bauerle; Camille San Fillipo; Jimmy "Juice" Argenziano; Wally Huthansel; Billy Sanborn; Pat McLaughlin; Tony Farneti. No undercover can survive without the support system of his team.

Thanks to OCID Detectives in Intelligence and Analysis: Joe Chimienti; Joe Moore; Vito Aleo. I&A surveillance and backup were crucial to so many of the meetings when I was undercover as Dan Benedetto.

Thanks to the other OCID personnel who assisted: Detective Barbara Werbeck and Public Administrative Aid Lisa Gaetani.

Thanks to the NYPD Confidential ID Unit who provided me with my Dan Benedetto background and credentials: Sergeant A. Cardaio; Detectives Jack Moscato; Allen Caplan; Marybeth Meyers; Corey Diaz.

Thanks to the NYPD Tech Services Unit: Detectives Joe Tabeek; Matt Murphy; Joey Vincent; Patrick "Patty" Codd; Carlos Ponce; Frank Ferrara; John Lombardi; Jimmy Allen; Peter Del Dubbio.

Thanks to the NYPD Legal Bureau: Sergeant Tommy Gambino; Lieutenant Kevin McAlister.

Thanks to former Police Commissioner Bill Bratton, who believed in this case and understood its scope. Thanks also to Lieutenant Greg Longworth.

Thanks to my old bosses in Manhattan South Narcotics, who gave me my break to become a detective: Inspector Donald Faherty; Lieutenant Jimmy Wood; and Sergeant Dan MacSweeney. And especially to the undercover who broke me in and taught me all his disguise tricks: Detective Woody Drury.

Thanks to my good friends and former partners: Ron Torromeo; Donnie Cali; Pete Eagan; and my old radio car partner Ray Rosania, for being there when my family really needed them.

Thanks to the New York County District Attorney's Office personnel: assistant district attorneys Marybeth Richroath (without whom we could not have got all the warrants we did during the years of the case); Bruce Berger; Ann Ryan; Ann Prunty; Janet Cohen; Donna Russo; Gerald Conroy; Maryann Wong; Miles Oroszco; Owen Heimer; and Dan McGillicuddy.

Thanks to the New York County District Attorney's support staff: Chris Donohue; George MacMillen; Erin Delorier; Alison Genova; Betty Law; John Frost.

Thanks to the Bronx County District Attorney's office, Assistant District Attorney Larry Hartstein.

Thanks to the New York County District Attorney's Office Senior Investigator Frank DeMarco, who played a crucial role early on in the investigation.

Thanks to Suffolk County Police detectives Frank Morro and Rick Means.

Thanks to Dr. Donald Kaminsky for his help and advice.

Finally, thanks to Sal Benedetto, loyal friend and "cousin."

ABOUT THE AUTHORS

RICK COWAN is a nineteen-year veteran of the New York Police Department, where he remains on active duty as a Detective First-Grade in the Organized Crime Investigations Division. He is a renowned authority on the Cosa Nostra.

DOUGLAS CENTURY is the author of *Street Kingdom: Five Years Inside the Franklin Avenue Posse.* A contributing writer with *The New York Times,* Century's work has appeared in *Details, Newsday, The Guardian, Rolling Stone,* and *Talk* magazine, and *The Village Voice.*